Fighting Organized Crime

≈ ≈ ≈ ≈

Advisor in Criminal Justice to Northeastern University Press
GILBERT GEIS

Fighting Organized Crime

~ ~ ~ ~

POLITICS, JUSTICE,
AND THE LEGACY
OF THOMAS E. DEWEY

Mary M. Stolberg

NORTHEASTERN UNIVERSITY PRESS

BOSTON

ACKNOWLEDGMENTS

MANY PEOPLE played a role in the creation of this book. My grandparents piqued my curiosity in history by their activist lives and their gifted storytelling. Jean Baker of Goucher College provided my first glimpse of the fascinations of professional history; she remains my model of teaching and scholarship.

As a reporter for *The Pittsburgh Press,* I received invaluable lessons in justice from the exemplary judges of the U.S. District Court for Western Pennsylvania—especially Robert Cindrich, Gustave Diamond, and Donald Ziegler. My historical skills received further honing from the faculty at the University of Virginia. Robert Cross, Charles McCurdy, D. Alan Williams, and Calvin Woodard provided helpful critiques of this manuscript in its early stages.

Other scholars read later versions and offered valuable suggestions, including Lynn Doyle of Appalachian State University, Mark Haller of Temple University, and Mary White of Lees-McRae College. The New York State Archives in Albany provided a helpful research grant. Lawrence Friedman of Stanford University Law School, Arthur Evans of Wayne State University Press, and William Frohlich of Northeastern University Press helped my manuscript become this book.

Friends and family too numerous to name provided material and moral support. David Hendin, Christine Lawrence, and Mark and Hannah Kinn assisted me with housing in New York City. Leo and Marilyn Doyle of Houston furnished comfortable accommodations and encouragement while I wrote. My greatest thanks go to my immediate family— Lynn and my parents—who never lost faith.

Contents

Illustrations

Fighting Organized Crime

~ ~ ~ ~

Introduction

$\mathcal{A}$ NY DISCUSSION of crime in the 1920s and 1930s conjures up stereotyped vignettes of gangsters in pin-striped suits, blonde molls, and hulking getaway cars driven by machine-gun-toting thugs. Given such exotic trappings it is easy to think that crime in the 1930s is as remote from today as a gunfighter in the Old West. In reality, the similarities are greater than the differences, and an examination of crime fighting in New York City during the 1930s sheds light on our own era's failed war against crime.

Today police battle drug dealers; in the 1930s, law enforcement's bête noire was the gangster. In both cases, sophisticated criminal enterprises with more money, better organization, and greater efficiency over-whelmed local police and prosecutors. Throughout the 1920s, reformers recognized this growing imbalance and urged changes in New York's legal system. Their efforts, however, were piecemeal and largely ineffec-tual because the reformers had little political acumen, and the public provided no groundswell of support. All that changed in the 1930s when a remarkable constellation of canny politicians—including Franklin Roosevelt, Fiorello La Guardia, and Thomas Dewey—galvanized the public and joined forces in a dramatic fight against crime.

Like modern politicians, they fomented fear of a crime wave to fur-ther their own political ambitions. Yet their overblown rhetoric was also rooted in a genuine concern about the pernicious effects of organized crime and political corruption. By emphasizing the cost of crime in the bleak Depression economy, they convinced the public that gangsters constituted a shadow government that manipulated city government and levied hidden taxes through payoffs. Because of their efforts, New York State's legal machinery was modernized and Manhattan's criminal courts became a laboratory for the nation's fight against organized crime.

Although politicians led the fight against crime, they did not launch it. New York's crusade began with an unusual display of citizen zeal: the last case of successful grand jury independence in the nation's history. Throughout most of American history, prosecutors have dominated grand juries. But the jury impaneled in March 1935 to investigate gambling in Manhattan rebelled against the district attorney, accusing him of blocking its investigation to protect Tammany's links with gangsters. To show their displeasure, the jurors barred him from their deliberations and appealed for help to Governor Herbert Lehman. The grand jury's bold action captured the attention of the New York press and led to the appointment of Thomas E. Dewey as special prosecutor in the summer of 1935.

Before the appointment Dewey was a middling lawyer whose only claims to fame were his low-level attempts to help revitalize Manhattan's lackluster Republican Party and his work as an assistant U.S. attorney. He was struggling to build up a fledgling private practice when he became special prosecutor. Soon, however, with his matinee-idol good looks, booming voice, and cool demeanor, Dewey became an overnight sensation as the nation's leading racket buster. He starred in newsreels and turned down offers to play himself in Hollywood films. Within five years of the appointment he made the first of his three runs for the presidency, demonstrating the degree to which crime and those who battled it had taken center stage in the national consciousness.

To the extent that crime stories are modern versions of medieval morality plays, New York City in the 1930s provided a perfect cast. The era's rhetoric pitted the incorruptible, handsome, young Dewey—product of a small town in the wholesome Midwest—against swarthy, alien, ethnic evildoers who learned their trades in Manhattan's sinister slums. The most famous of his adversaries was Charles "Lucky" Luciano, a Sicilian who has been portrayed falsely in crime annals as the father of the American Mafia. Dewey's other targets included labor racketeers and corrupt politicians, including the last of the great Tammany bosses, Jimmy Hines.

Contemporaries praised Dewey as the nation's premier prosecutor, and historians have accepted the hyperbole. But the reality was far more complex than the myth. The real lessons of the Dewey years demonstrate that successful crime fighting rests more on wide-ranging legal reforms and costly mobilizations of resources than on individual heroes or simplistic solutions. Dewey was an able lawyer and administrator, but he also received massive funding, an office separate from the district attorney, the freedom to choose employees without regard for civil service requirements, and uncritical praise from the media and public.

Dewey also worked without many of the constraints that hinder modern prosecutors. He was able to handpick jurors favorable to his cause in a way that now would be deemed discriminatory to defendants. He arrested witnesses in secret round-ups, kept them sequestered from their families and lawyers for days, and jailed them indefinitely until they agreed to testify. He tried his cases before specially chosen and sympathetic judges. When one jurist dared to question his handling of a case, Dewey went on the attack and won a more amenable forum for the retrial. In many ways, the Dewey trials stand as a testament to the elasticity and fragility of constitutional rights during perceived crime waves.

Dewey pioneered several techniques that have since become standard for state and federal prosecutors who followed. His use of teams of lawyers and investigators working together in complex litigation is now common. Dewey also revitalized the grand jury system, showing how the panels could gather evidence that otherwise would be unavailable to prosecutors. At his suggestion, New York's legislature implemented necessary and long-overdue changes in the state's criminal laws.

New York's anticrime crusade reveals much about the rapid social and political changes occurring in the tumultuous 1930s. This transformation, especially apparent in cities, was amply demonstrated by three of Dewey's most famous cases: his prosecutions of Luciano, restaurant union racketeers, and Tammany Hall leader Hines. The Luciano case planted the seed of the later Mafia myth and became a symbol in the nation's romance with the gangster—a fascination that began as a form of entertainment during the dreary Depression. The restaurant racketeers were a visible example of the complexity of labor relations during the 1930s, when bitter union disputes were so common that the *New*

York Times' index box listed them separately. Finally, Hines's conviction signaled the waning of political machines that had long dominated the nation's urban landscape. Other bosses, such as Carmine DeSapio, would later arise in New York and other cities, but their power bases were different and considerably weaker than those enjoyed by their predecessors.

Events in New York typified, foreshadowed, and helped influence happenings in other parts of the nation. As the country's largest and most important city, New York's problems loomed larger, ran deeper, and received wider publicity than those of other places. Dewey was not the only prosecutor in the country battling organized crime, but he garnered the most attention, largely because he was in New York City. The degree to which New York's "good guy" received attention was largely a reflection of how much the city's criminal element attracted. In the hinterlands, no criminal seemed so bad as a big city gangster. During the 1920s, Chicago had shared center stage by virtue of Al Capone. But by the early 1930s, New York was poised to regain top billing as the nation's gangland capital; it would remain number one for the rest of the century.

~ ~ ~ ~

Prologue

$\mathcal{E}$VERY SOCIETY creates its own archetypal villain. When the Old West was still the romantic frontier of the American imagination outlaws captured the national attention. Later, as once-remote regions were brought into the economic and social mainstream, more people increasingly made cities the focus of their dreams and aspirations. As a result, sophisticated urban gangsters replaced western outlaws as the scoundrels of the nation's fancy. During the teens and twenties the career of New York gambling kingpin Arnold Rothstein offered a preview of how well-heeled gangsters would change the face of crime in the United States. He also served as the common link between the men who would become the major criminals and heroes of New York City's crime-fighting extravaganza in the 1930s.

Today Rothstein's name conjures up only the dimmest recognition. But the fact that two of the Roaring Twenties' best-known writers immortalized him in their works indicates the mythic reputation he enjoyed during his lifetime. In *Guys and Dolls*, Damon Runyon portrayed Rothstein as Armand Rosenthal, a man without a conscience who was "the biggest guy in gambling operations in the East, and a millionaire two or three times over." F. Scott Fitzgerald used Rothstein as the model for Meyer Wolfsheim, the wealthy, street-smart gambler who financed bootlegger Jay Gatsby in *The Great Gatsby*.[1]

Much of Rothstein's notoriety stemmed from the contemporary belief that he had fixed the 1919 World Series. Before football and basketball claimed their share of America's sporting interest, baseball reigned supreme. Writer Eliot Asinof argues that it was the "biggest entertainment business" in the nation. This was especially true in 1919 when "war-weary fans returned in droves, bringing unprecedented profits." The 1919 World Series became a Cinderella story when the underdog Cincinnati Reds defeated the heavily favored Chicago White Sox. Millions of fans wanted to believe that a modern-day version of David and Goliath had been played out on the baseball diamond. But a few skeptics, led by reporter Hugh Fullerton of the Chicago *Herald and Examiner*, believed the victory was too good to be true. With the aid of legendary player–manager-turned-sportswriter Christy Mathewson of the *New York World*, Fullerton mapped out suspicious plays and tracked down rumors. Meanwhile Bancroft Johnson, president of the American League, hired private detectives and in September 1920 accused Rothstein of rigging the series.[2]

Rothstein's actual role in the plot remains murky. Most historians agree that the scheme originated with White Sox players disgusted at the miserly salaries paid by the team's owner, Charles "The Old Roman" Comiskey. They then approached several gamblers, including Rothstein, to finance the fix. At least one historian has adopted contemporary opinion that the New Yorker paid the White Sox to throw the series. Rothstein, however, always maintained his innocence, saying only a fool would become involved in such a harebrained scheme. Chicago's district attorney and grand jurors believed Rothstein and freed him while indicting eight players and five other gamblers. Nothing came of the indictments when the players' confessions and the grand jury minutes disappeared from the prosecutor's office. The players refused to repeat their stories; key witnesses disappeared or recanted, and the defendants were acquitted. Nonetheless, newly appointed baseball commissioner Judge Kenesaw Mountain Landis barred the players from the professional game and they were branded the "Black Sox."[3]

Although it did not deprive him of a livelihood, the scandal haunted Rothstein, who became known ever after as the man who fixed the series. In 1921, in an unsuccessful attempt to get out of the limelight, Rothstein publicly announced he was abandoning gambling. The fact that few people believed him presaged the mystique of gangsters.

His contemporaries claimed that Rothstein transformed crime by organizing it along business principles. Writers such as Herbert Asbury asserted that crime in New York and other cities was parochial before Rothstein and that gang leaders limited their success by choosing ethnically similar compatriots. By contrast, Rothstein chose the best men for the job; his coterie included Jews, Germans, and Italians. As a good businessman, he attempted to control all facets of his operations. In gambling, for example, he owned the banks, hired his own tipsters, and ran his own gaming houses. When he branched out into bootlegging, he contracted with purchasing agents in Europe, bought boats to ferry the liquor to shore, and controlled the trucks that transported it to warehouses and speakeasies. Even when he did not control a racket, Rothstein "provided money and manpower and protection. He arranged corruption—for a price. And, if things went wrong, Rothstein was ready to provide bail and attorneys."[4]

In fact, the most successful criminals always have been good businessmen. There is little doubt that Rothstein was better suited in that regard than many of his would-be rivals. Whereas most New York City criminals of his time came from the city's teeming slums, Rothstein hailed from a prosperous Jewish mercantile family. His father, Abraham, had made a fortune as a cloak merchant and "was considered by everyone who knew him a man of rare integrity and generosity of nature." In 1919, after earning the respect of workers and management in settling a labor dispute, he was honored at a testimonial dinner by guests such as Supreme Court Justice Louis Brandeis and Governor Al Smith, who called him "Abe the Just." The fact that Rothstein came from a good family—and then went bad—added greatly to his mystique. His biographers, such as newspaperman Donald Henderson Clarke, always pointed up his good manners, fine dress, and educated mien.[5]

Rothstein's power rested on his wealth. He began his career as a teenager at the turn of the century by using his gambling winnings to finance other gamblers. His growing profits and willingness to fund illegal activity attracted other wrongdoers, who found Rothstein to be a willing mentor. One of Rothstein's more prominent young associates was Irving Wechsler, better known in crime sagas as "Waxey" Gordon. Before 1920 Gordon was a mere drug peddler, pickpocket, and sneak thief. Recognizing the profits to be made with the passage of the Volstead Act in 1920, Gordon asked Rothstein to finance a bootlegging operation.

Rothstein was intrigued with the idea, and not only agreed to back the operation, but also helped organize it.[6] By the time Rothstein quit bootlegging because it was too risky and tied up his money for long periods of time, Gordon had made his fortune. Like Rothstein, Gordon left an unintended but powerful legacy with his downfall. His 1933 conviction on tax-evasion charges catapulted little-known federal prosecutor Thomas Dewey into the limelight.

Rothstein's protégés in labor racketeering, Louis "Lepke" Buchalter and Jacob "Gurrah" Shapiro, became household names in the 1930s. Beginning in the 1880s, some employers hired thugs to attack strikers and the unions fought back by hiring their own henchmen. Rothstein put his businesslike mark on these arrangements by supplying gangsters to both sides. This became apparent during a bitter twenty-eight-week garment strike that began in 1926, when Rothstein reputedly made hundreds of thousands of dollars by supplying strong men to both sides. His goal was to gain a permanent foothold in the garment industry, but he did not live long enough to carry out his plan. Lepke and Gurrah did, however, and "built up an industrial empire in New York City which by the mid-1930s yielded them an annual income of some $2,000,000."[7]

Through Rothstein, Lepke and Gurrah met Charles "Lucky" Luciano, who became the most notorious gangster of the 1930s. Although later known as a gambler, Luciano began his career as a drug peddler on the Lower East Side. In the first decades of this century an estimated one person in 400 to 460 was addicted to opium, which was available in cough syrup and patent medicines. After 1921, when the federal government began enforcing narcotics regulation, users were forced to seek their drugs on the black market.[8] Luciano persuaded Rothstein that there was money to be made in illicit drug dealing, and Rothstein rewarded Luciano by taking him under his wing. Later Rothstein also provided capital for Luciano's gambling and bootlegging ventures.

By the mid-1920s bootleggers Gordon and "Dutch" Schultz had made more money than Rothstein, but the older man remained New York's best-known criminal because of his wide-ranging connections, especially his links with Tammany Hall. Ever since the early nineteenth century politics and crime had been bedfellows in New York. In exchange for intimidating voters and stuffing ballot boxes, gang members

enjoyed "extralegal privileges, like the right to shake down bordello operators, operators of shady hotels, and small gambling places. If arrested,
they could depend upon the district leader to get a word to a magistrate,
who would then mete out mercy with a soup ladle." Early in his career
Rothstein recognized the need for political friends; when he was sixteen
years old he ran errands for Timothy Sullivan, the Tammany district
leader in the Bowery. Sullivan became ill in 1911, but his influence was
transferred to several protégés, including James J. Hines, whom Dewey
convicted in the 1930s.[9]

To contemporary observers, nothing confirmed Rothstein's link with
the politically powerful more than his shooting death on Election Day,
1928. The events that led to the gangster's unsolved murder began on
September 8, 1928, during a two-day poker game. Rothstein and a well-
known bookmaker, George McManus, each lost more than $50,000. Mc-
Manus redeemed his markers promptly, but Rothstein procrastinated.
Rothstein had bet heavily against Al Smith in the 1928 presidential election and hoped to use his $200,000 in winnings to pay his poker and
other debts. Meanwhile, McManus brooded about Rothstein's failure to
pay quickly. He holed up in a suite at the Park Central Hotel in mid-
Manhattan and drank heavily. On the night of November 2, 1928, he
invited Rothstein to his room. Rothstein, hoping to avoid trouble, left
his pistol with a friend. When McManus pulled his gun, Rothstein was
defenseless. After McManus shot him and fled, Rothstein staggered out
of the hotel and collapsed in the employees' entrance. He was taken to a
nearby hospital and died two days later without identifying his attacker.[10]

Contemporary and retrospective versions of the subsequent police
investigation and trial provide further evidence of Rothstein's mystique.
Newspapermen and politicians accused police of pursuing the case in a
lackadaisical fashion by failing to interview Rothstein or follow up other
leads. Mayor Jimmy Walker publicly criticized the investigation and replaced Police Commissioner Joseph Warren with Grover Whalen. District Attorney Joab Banton also came under attack, and critics scoffed
when he said he could not pursue the case without more evidence from
the police. The wisdom of the time, and the writers who have followed,
claim: "It was not lassitude, but fear and the instinct of self-preservation
that marked the investigation of Rothstein's killing. . . . Too many politi-

cians, too many gangsters, too much money, too many reputations joined in covering up the facts."[11]

The truth was far more prosaic. Police quickly pieced together what had happened through interviews and physical evidence. McManus had rented the hotel suite several days before the shooting and fled the murder scene wearing Rothstein's coat. Rothstein left a clear trail of blood from McManus's room. Even though both men had political links, the district attorney's office pursued the case with diligence. Nonetheless, the prosecution's efforts in court were doomed from the outset. Perhaps because of public pressure in the high-profile case, Manhattan District Attorney Banton charged McManus with first-degree murder, even though the numerous empty whiskey bottles in the room indicated that McManus had shot Rothstein in a drunken rage without premeditation. Moreover, Rothstein's own failure to identify his attacker forced prosecutors to rely on witnesses, none of whom came forward during the trial. Rothstein always had charged high interest rates for his loans, and he was slow to pay his gambling debts. He was feared and respected but never liked by the other denizens of New York's "white light district." By contrast, McManus was generous and popular, and his fellow gamblers were reluctant to testify against him. The case ended in an acquittal because there was not enough evidence to sustain a capital conviction.[12]

Subsequently, reality became secondary as Rothstein's murder took on the trappings of a political cause célèbre. Critics viewed Banton's resignation as an admission of corruption. In fact, Banton left his high-pressure job because of poor health, not the Rothstein case. Banton's successor, Thomas C. T. Crain, ran on the vain claim that he would put Rothstein's murderer behind bars.[13] But it was Fiorello La Guardia who made the most of the cover-up theory. During his mayoral campaign in 1929, the fiery half-Jewish, half-Italian congressman from East Harlem waved a promissory note that indicated New York magistrate Albert H. Vitale had accepted a $19,600 loan from Rothstein. La Guardia, an untiring speaker, addressed as many as ten meetings a night, hammering home his assertion that Vitale's debt to Rothstein was just one indication of politicians' close ties to New York City gangsters.

In 1929, however, La Guardia's gloomy message gained him few adherents from New Yorkers still enthralled with the flamboyant activities of their charming Tammany Mayor James J. Walker, who treated the city "like a pretty girl he took out." The debonair Walker, as a youthful habitué of Tin Pan Alley, had written such popular songs as "Will You Love Me in December as You Do in May?" and "There's Music in the Rustle of a Skirt." His father, a popular Tammany Hall boss, had trouble getting his son to settle down to law school and politics. When the younger Walker took over as mayor, he reverted to his youthful ways. As New York City Councilman Reuben Lazarus remembered, Walker's administration "took on the color of a day-to-day celebration by Walker's myriad friends in the theatrical and sporting worlds. . . . Jimmy Walker was surrounded by as questionable a group of characters as ever afflicted a public official. . . . Every 'con' man on Broadway who had a proposition to make brought it to City Hall." Although these friends "who swarmed around the mayor like bees" would later be his downfall, they added to his popular aura during the Roaring Twenties.[14]

Walker threw lavish parties for foreign dignitaries and won widespread support for refusing to enforce Prohibition. His good humor and quick wit fit in well with a decade during which, as Frances Perkins recalled, "All the people suddenly stopped being puritanical Baptists or Methodists and started out having a good time." In contrast to the debonair Walker, Perkins added, the five-foot two-inch, swarthy, often-disheveled La Guardia "looked like a lump." His aide, Ernest Cuneo, later characterized La Guardia as a Jeremiah who forecast doom whenever the stock market seemed to indicate more prosperity.[15]

Even Tammany foes not entranced by Walker's flamboyance did not cotton to the feisty Italian immigrant. La Guardia had taken the "Republican" label because he detested Tammany's dishonesty, but his affinity for immigrants and labor and his hatred of the rich and powerful made him an irregular party member. Reformers viewed La Guardia as a radical and an impetuous demagogue. His 1929 mayoral campaign became especially difficult when he criticized the city's real estate assessments, antagonizing business leaders such as John D. Rockefeller, Jr. According to Paul Windels, who handled the campaign, most people did not know what to make of the candidate, whom he described as "a very unusual type—short, and not stout as he became later on, very energetic, full of enthusiasm, a mercurial temperament which went off in every direction from extreme optimism to profound pessimism." Windels also attributed La Guardia's defeat to strong-arming by Tammany henchmen at the polls and the poor packaging of his anticorruption message. La Guardia was resoundingly defeated; he failed to carry even one assembly district and received only 26 percent of the popular vote.[16]

The loss temporarily removed him from city politics, and he returned to Congress, where he gained national prominence as a leading Progressive and champion of labor. Meanwhile, his charges of corruption took on a life of their own, and Rothstein's memory was revived repeatedly throughout the next decade. Leo Katcher, a New York newspaperman during the 1930s, remembered that "He was as newsworthy in 1935 as he had been in 1925. The election of Fiorello La Guardia, who ran almost as much against Rothstein as against Tammany Hall, the Seabury Investigation, the Dewey onslaught on organized crime, all concerned themselves with this long-dead man. It came to me that the world in which I lived was partially shaped by him."[17]

~ ≈ ≈

CHAPTER ONE

Setting the Stage

$\mathcal{E}$FFORTS TO clean up New York
City's corruption might well have
failed had La Guardia's 1929 charges not struck responsive chords with
three extraordinary men who shared his disdain for Tammany Hall. It
would be hard to imagine four people more temperamentally different
from the charming, brilliant politician Franklin D. Roosevelt; the self-
righteous, politically naive Samuel Seabury; the able, self-effacing Herbert Lehman; and La Guardia. Fueled by their individual ambitions and
a hatred for old-time corruption, the quartet overcame their differences
and rivalries to become architects of reform throughout the 1930s.

Their complementary efforts were set in motion when the staid New
York Bar Association eagerly picked up La Guardia's charges and pushed
for an investigation of Magistrate Vitale's links to the underworld. A
bastion of conservatism, the association's largely Republican membership seized any opportunity to criticize the Democrats who held most of
the minor judiciary posts in New York County. Reformers found much
to criticize. Court conditions in the city were deplorable. Political hacks
usually made lazy judges, and their inability to keep up with caseloads
created a four-and-a-half-year backlog in the city's trial courts. The situation was even worse in the magistrates' courts, where politicking was
more blatant and corruption was rampant. Gangsters lavished payoffs
on the lower judiciary rather than the higher courts because it was easier
to get cases killed by magistrates, who labored in relative obscurity. One
New York City parole officer remembered how clerks used code words
to inform magistrates when "protected" defendants came before them.[1]

New York's antiquated magisterial system fostered the corruption and kept reformers busy campaigning for modernization throughout the 1920s. The Greater New York Charter enacted in 1898 had merged five counties into what became New York City. Although the counties or boroughs retained their own district attorneys and trial courts, they shared one police department and, theoretically, one municipal court. In reality, a commission appointed by Governor Al Smith reported in 1923 that "the court remains a loose association of forty-eight justices of the peace" laboring in twenty-five often-ramshackle buildings across the city. Poor record keeping made it impossible to know how many "cases out of 267,061 reported as pending on the General Calendars" were still open or which justices were doing the most work. Public disaffection with justices who ruled according to their political affiliations was widespread. Magistrates needed political favors to get their jobs. Republicans and Democrats had drawn district lines to ensure their parties of office. In Manhattan, for example, Democrats controlled three districts, while Republicans controlled two wards.[2]

Smith's commissioners argued that the easiest way of removing political partisanship was by centralizing the magistrates' offices in one location. The city's improved transportation system made this a more feasible solution in the 1920s than it had been at the turn of the century. Even after this was accomplished, the commission predicted correctly, successful reorganization would be slow because of New York City's complexity and the parochial outlooks of some of its citizens. Older arrangements simply no longer worked in a city of six million people belonging to seventeen ethnic groups. The commissioners drew a parallel between the courts and commerce: "The country store is the precursor of the modern department store but the modern department store is not merely the assembling of many country stores in one building." Even though a number of small judicial districts had been combined in New York City, they said, "no organic whole has been created."[3]

The commissioners' prediction that legal change would come slowly in New York proved accurate. Legal reform is sluggish under the best of conditions, and New York City—with its large population, complex demographics, and antiquated institutions—did not provide an ideal setting. Although the reforms might have worked in normal times, Prohibition proved to be a formidable barrier to good and honest government.

Bootlegging was a headache, not only for the federal government, which had jurisdiction over violations of the Eighteenth Amendment under the Volstead Act, but also for New York, which made whiskey a state matter in April 1921 by passing the Mullen-Gage bill banning liquor sales in New York. The result was what one prosecutor called "a rapidly growing cancer of public corruption. [Prohibition] was organizing the underworld as it had never been organized before, and it was endowing the underworld with immense sums of money for corruption." Rumors of crooked police prompted one member of the New York State Assembly in 1923 to oppose a pension for retiring New York City Police Commissioner Richard Enright because of his alleged ties to bootleggers. Assemblyman Louis A. Cuvillier of New York County called the Mullen-Gage bill "the greatest graft the police department ever had . . . it was no wonder Enright could go to Palm Beach and fan himself with the palms while we up here are freezing to death." Cuvillier urged repeal of the state law in hopes that the police would concentrate on solving murders and robberies.[4]

The law also put a tremendous burden on New York County's court system. A grand jury presentment filed on December 21, 1922, estimated the county was paying $800 daily to fight liquor. Grand Jury Foreman Wyllys E. Dowd, Jr., argued that Prohibition should be left to the federal government because "the time and efforts of the grand jury should be devoted to the consideration of matters of a more practical and serious character." This was especially true, he said, because most of the cases were so poorly investigated by police that they ended up being dismissed for lack of evidence.[5]

Prohibition and the corruption that went with it was a ticklish political issue that cut two ways in New York City, where alcohol control was never popular with Catholic voters—the mainstay of Tammany Hall. Even after the Mullen-Gage law was repealed on June 1, 1923, politicians tried to appease high-minded citizens by supporting the federal law. Mayor Jimmy Walker became adept at this and made a joke of dumping thousands of cases a year on the already-overwhelmed U.S. attorney's office. La Guardia won national headlines by ridiculing Prohibition during 1926, when he staged a beer-making exhibition in his congressional office. Arguing that Prohibition hurt the poor who could not spend money to get quality bootleg, he vowed to help "the little guy" by show-ing how to mix .5 percent beer, which was legal, with malt extract con-taining 4 percent alcohol, sold for medicinal purposes. He won the affection of the fifty photographers at the scene by promising them sam-ples.[6]

La Guardia's public beer production, Walker's purposely ineffectual attempts to curb liquor, and the New York Police Department's lack of enforcement were popular with most New Yorkers. Among those who backed Prohibition, however, such laxness only fueled hostility toward Tammany. That, combined with continuing skepticism about the effec-tiveness and honesty of the police and magistrates, created a cauldron of dissatisfaction. Some Democrats recognized a pending political disaster and advocated reforms. Chief among them was Jeremiah T. Mahoney, who sat on the board of judges for the Supreme Court in New York County in 1927. Mahoney enlisted the aid of Governor Smith to convince Tammany boss George Olvany and Mayor Jimmy Walker to clean house, but neither had the foresight to see the danger or the need for change.[7] In fact, the two men epitomized the growing weakness of Tammany lead-ership that began with the death of Charles Murphy in April 1924.

Murphy, a figure similar in many respects to his Irish counterparts across the nation, began his career as a saloon keeper. He hosted political meetings in his taverns and eventually was rewarded with the Demo-cratic leadership in 1902. Murphy adjusted adeptly to the increasing in-tolerance of political corruption during the Progressive Era. In New York City this intolerance was manifested in the election of reform mayor John Purroy Mitchel in 1913. Mitchel's stiff-necked behavior and Tam-many's dirty tricks led to his defeat at the polls in 1917. Ironically, in the same election women won the vote in New York state. Frances Perkins, one of many activists galvanized by Mitchel's election, claimed that well-born, well-educated suffragists "were bringing into politics an element of the population that never before publicly had been in it. That didn't just mean ladylike women, but their husbands, brothers and fathers. That is, they brought in the kind of man who held aloof from politics as being dirty business for the muckers."[8]

Unlike the leaders who followed him, Murphy "had sort of an innate judgment that seemed to sense what the people wanted." After Mitchel's defeat he recognized that voters were less tolerant of Tammany corruption and shifted the party's reliance on payoffs from criminals to "honest graft"—bribes from companies and businessmen seeking city contracts. As journalist Arthur Krock said, Murphy "was terribly against the . . . kind of political organization, which got its supporting funds out of prostitution and crime. He believed it was perfectly all right to get it out of concessions on taxation, on contractors' fees, and things of that kind, but he would never have anything to do with what he considered immoral." Adapting to changing voter sensibilities, Murphy cultivated promising, honest, intelligent young men. The most famous of these, Al Smith, served four terms as governor of New York and in 1928 became the first Catholic presidential candidate when he unsuccessfully ran against Herbert Hoover. Smith's success was in some measure attributable to the fact that Murphy went to great lengths to insulate him from Tammany's dirty deals.[9]

Tammany fell on hard times after Murphy's death. Smith successfully lobbied to replace him with fire commissioner George W. Olvany, a college graduate he hoped would represent a "new" Tammany. But Olvany remained at heart a typical Irish boss, opining on one occasion that "the Irish are natural leaders. The strain of Limerick keeps them at the top. They have the ability to handle men. Even the Jewish districts have Irish leaders. The Jews want to be ruled by them." Even those who had forged working relationships with other Tammany types found Olvany hard to stomach. Frances Perkins described him as "one of those large men with . . . a little bit of a mouth in a great big face, a long nose and very, very shifty eyes." Although Olvany was a lawyer, Perkins said, "there was nothing about him to warrant anyone asking him for advice. He didn't have a good mind. He didn't have any great legal knowledge. . . . He practically never practiced, except on shyster stuff. He was a 'fix-it' lawyer."[10]

By 1929 the split between Smith and Walker had further weakened Tammany Hall. Smith disliked the night-clubbing mayor's high life, and Walker wanted more control over city politics. One indication that the popular mayor prevailed was the replacement of Olvany with Walker's handpicked choice, John F. Curry. Curry looked like the party's answer to calls for modernization. Unlike some of the old "sachems . . . who just fairly rolled around, murdered the King's English and that sort of thing," he was well spoken, dressed elegantly in gray striped pants and cutaway coats, and had the mien of "an English colonel." In keeping with its new image, in January 1929 Tammany moved its headquarters to a new building on the north corner of Union Square at East 17th Street and Fourth Avenue. There Curry presided in "a beautifully furnished office—magnificent with good taste."[11]

Even in its new home, however, Tammany was unable to shake off its old ways. Amid the black marble floor, curved stairway, and wrought-iron railings moved from its previous headquarters, old rituals continued. Perkins recalled visiting Curry in the new building. "Here was this very beautiful room with a shallow dome over it. . . . There was a strange barricade at one end with a mahogany rail. There was beautiful white painted paneling. There were very handsome chairs. They were Empire in type and very lovely in their curves. There were beautiful hangings and a great gold eagle with a flag in its mouth draped over some sort of rostrum. It wasn't really a rostrum. It almost looked like a chancel and altar." Curry told Perkins how the Tammany sachems dressed up in Native American headdresses to perform rites based on their interpretation of tribal religion. He insisted that members still took the ceremonies seriously. "This is what binds us together. We're all one band of brothers. . . . When you become a sachem of Tammany Hall, by George you are committed to something. You cannot let your brothers down. You've got to help each other." When the meetings ended, Curry said, the bosses went downstairs to drink and conduct their political business.[12]

As Perkins recognized, the new Tammany differed in veneer only; in substance little had changed. Curry and his cronies dismissed the role of idealism and reform and failed to recognize that their cynical view of politics was outmoded. Without political machines, he believed, "we'd be like the French—always turning governments in and out and always having no stability. We'd have lots of trouble . . . you've got to keep your people with you between elections. That's what the party's about and that's why it's so useful to have them feel that their district leader . . . can say a word to somebody and it will open the door to getting a job and a promotion."[13]

Curry discounted the growth of a new generation of politicians—

women with the vote and men nurtured in Progressive ideals—who shared a larger vision. Reform Democrats like Perkins and Herbert Lehman always had existed in New York, but they usually had been isolated and "kept in line" by the party. That changed with the advent of Smith and Franklin Roosevelt—who used their charisma and keen political acumen to bring idealists together with pragmatic politicians such as James A. Farley and Edward J. Flynn. Whereas Perkins and Lehman focused on Curry's lack of ideals, Farley and Flynn criticized his parochial interest in New York City politics to the exclusion of events in Albany. They argued that, unlike Murphy, who had helped Al Smith gain the New York governor's chair, Curry was too territorial; instead of building a statewide coalition, he mistakenly believed his personal domination of New York City would translate into control of the entire state. As Roosevelt advisor Samuel Rosenman put it, Curry had "been a successful district leader. He had no conception of policy. He figured that Tammany Hall could exist on patronage, on tribute, on contributions."[14]

Early in Roosevelt's first term, Curry assumed, correctly, that he had little to fear from the patrician governor from Hyde Park. Roosevelt, like his ambitious predecessors, recognized the need to appease Tammany. Criticizing the city's corrupt political party always had played well with voters in the hinterlands of the state and the nation. Attaining and staying in the governor's chair long enough to attract national attention, however, meant winning elections in New York City. Roosevelt understood the delicate game and played it masterfully, while Curry seriously miscalculated, overestimating his own power and underestimating Roosevelt's canniness and the formidable coalition he was building. Roosevelt's supremacy became apparent late in his first term.[15]

In 1929 voters had ignored La Guardia's charges that Magistrate Vitale took loans from gangster Arnold Rothstein. But the magistrate, who had organized Italian voters for Walker in the Bronx, showed a penchant for getting into trouble. A month after Walker defeated La Guardia, masked gunmen crashed a local Democratic Club dinner honoring Vitale. Vitale hid his diamond ring in his pants, but his guests were robbed of their valuables. After leaving the dinner, Vitale went to his party clubhouse, collected the stolen items, and returned them to his friends. His "useful connections" and the fact that his guest list included the well-known racketeer Ciro Terranova, the so-called Artichoke King, and a number of other unsavory characters drew the attention of the New York Bar Association, which called for an investigation.[16]

News of Vitale's antics came as no surprise to observers, who realized that the lower courts were as corrupt and political in 1929 as they had been in 1923, when Smith's commission had recommended consolidation and reform. Piecemeal changes had not addressed the underlying problems, which went to the heart of Tammany's organizational structure. Tammany had carved New York City into eighty-five districts, each headed by a leader who received more than $7,000 a year for holding jobs such as county clerk, deputy sheriff, and record keeper. As writer Herbert Mitgang said, "Those beneath the rank of leader had to content themselves with what they could get by extortion from fixing traffic tickets, on the lowest level, to arranging for judicial 'contracts' and departmental licenses, on the highest."[17]

Despite the Vitale revelations, Curry and Walker saw no reason to change the system. Joseph Clark Baldwin, the only Republican among New York City's sixty-four aldermen, warned Walker he would instigate a legislative investigation if Walker did not clean house. The mayor laughed and dared him to try. When Baldwin wrote to Roosevelt seeking support for the probe, Walker responded: "If he can't cook up something better, then he ought to get himself out." Roosevelt, however, took the threat more seriously—especially when Vitale's resignation was followed by revelations, in early 1930, that his successor, George F. Ewald, had bought his job from a Tammany leader for $10,000. Roosevelt, facing reelection, played to both camps, seeming to encourage reform while checking what could have been an embarrassing Republican investigation. He forestalled the inquisition by first threatening a similar probe of Republican counties; when that failed he vetoed a bill calling for a legislative probe. To offset charges leveled by his Republican opponent, former U.S. attorney Charles Tuttle, that he was protecting Tammany, Roosevelt met with Acting Presiding Justice Finch of the appellate division and urged him to appoint Samuel Seabury to investigate the magistrates.[18]

As members of the reform wing of the Democratic Party, Seabury and Roosevelt had worked together on several occasions. At the 1916 Democratic state convention, Tammany had tried to block Seabury's gubernatorial nomination by unsuccessfully trying to persuade Roosevelt to run instead. Later, the two men joined hands to help Al Smith's campaign for governor. In 1920 they worked together to reform the rules at the Democratic National Convention in San Francisco. Seabury's good reputation at the bar and his well-known hatred for Tammany Hall made him the logical choice to head the magistrate's investigation, and his appointment met with universal approval from civic leaders.[19]

Raised in genteel but economically modest circumstances, Seabury traced his ancestry to the *Mayflower* and the first American bishop of the Episcopal church, his great-great grandfather Samuel Seabury. A lawyer and supporter of Henry George's single-tax ideas, Seabury combined his love of law and politics by becoming the state's youngest judge in 1901. He was elected to the New York City Court in the Fusion landslide, which led to Seth Low's election as mayor. Recognizing that long-term political success in New York required alignment with one of the major parties, Seabury became an independent Democrat. The Democratic label did not, however, fool Tammany, which fought his candidacy for governor in 1916. Seabury blamed the Hall for his defeat and publicly nursed his grudge throughout the 1920s. As his biographer Herbert Mitgang notes, "His anti-Tammany stand was not merely a cause; it was a mania that prevented him from reaching any accommodation with the New York County leaders." Effectively excluded from politics, Seabury focused on his law practice and channeled his reform impulses into lobbying for court improvements. His efforts earned him respect and, eventually, the presidency of the New York County Lawyers Association. Even so, his stern and self-righteous demeanor kept would-be allies at a distance and earned him the nicknames "the Bishop" and "the Saint."[20]

Frances Perkins's reminiscences provide a classic description of the famous reformer:

Mr. Seabury was always dressed in a dark suit. In the wintertime he wore a black Chesterfield overcoat, with a velvet collar—very elegant and very correct. He wore a black hat, which was not the sombrero type, but smallish and elegant looking. It was very correct, never banged-up, always carefully brushed. He was a very handsome man with white hair and a very ruddy face. He wore eyeglasses and had, I think, the most arrogant face I ever saw. . . . At any rate, he looked very disdainful. . . . I remember in my own mind having a picture once of him with flowing robes and ermine capes on, with some kind of a headdress indicating authority upon his head. It was possible to think of him in almost cartoon form as a man assuming the purple. A Roman emperor could have looked like that when he strutted into the Circus Maximus.[21]

Seabury's aloof demeanor and his hatred of Tammany served him well in his new task. After receiving word of his appointment in August 1930, he eagerly returned home from his English vacation. The opening of the Seabury investigation the following month finally awakened complacent Tammany leaders. Walker tried an old Tammany trick by putting on a show of trying to out-reform the reformers. He publicly appealed to citizens to report incidents of graft and appointed Jonah Goldstein to conduct an internal investigation of the magistrates' courts. Goldstein, a Tammany faithful who had made headlines years earlier by defending birth control advocate Margaret Sanger, later said that Walker wanted to make him a magistrate so he could inform on the judges cooperating with Seabury. Goldstein said he told Walker he was willing to go in, "provided I get the privilege of cleaning it, because I don't want to lose my sense of smell." Goldstein began by literally cleaning up the filthy courthouse, then organized a citywide committee of lawyers and judges to reorganize the magistracy. The commission recommended a host of changes ranging from allowing payment of fines by mail to transferring jurisdiction of some matters—especially domestic relations, adolescent cases, and traffic violations—to other courts, centralizing the magistrates' courts, setting salary schedules, and requiring magistrates to apply uniform procedures from higher courts for setting bonds, sentences, and probation.[22] The proposals fit the pattern of those made in the twenties that largely had been ignored by the public. If conducted earlier, Goldstein's report might have forestalled a large-scale probe; now it proved to be too little too late given the groundswell of public criticism. The city never made the report public, and the startling revelations of the Seabury investigation easily overshadowed Goldstein's recommendations.

Seabury began what turned out to be eight months of public and twelve months of closed hearings on the magistrates' courts in late September 1930. He chose able assistants and taught them what Frances Perkins called "that investigator's technique of not revealing what they know, but giving the impression that they know a good deal, which alarms a man into the position of telling all." Seabury interviewed his witnesses in private, then cross-examined them again at public hearings. Perkins contended that the press did not complain about Seabury's reliance on closed-door proceedings because it gave the newspapers wider latitude to speculate and print innuendo. After interviewing 1,059 witnesses and compiling 15,356 pages of minutes, Seabury concluded that conditions in the magistrates' courts "were scandalous." In addition to job buying, he found many instances of fixes and other favors performed for political bosses. The most infamous scandal centered on the collusion of magistrates, police, bailbondsmen, and lawyers to bring bogus prostitution cases. In those instances, vice police arrested innocent women, then offered to drop the charges against them for a price. Women who refused were railroaded when police testified falsely against them.[23]

Seabury's disclosures, or the fear of them, resulted in a spate of resignations. A magistrate who held stock in a Cuban gambling casino and another whose stock market and real estate speculations amounted to $7 million stepped down in a hurry. Yet another magistrate, Henry M. R. Goodman, quit for health reasons—arthritis in one finger—rather than have his business dealings exposed. Perhaps the most noteworthy of Seabury's targets was Jean H. Norris, who had received national attention in 1919 when she was appointed the first woman judge in New York City. Seabury's investigation showed she had taken part in the prostitution scam, then tried to cover up her involvement by deleting incriminating information from the hearing minutes. She was removed after a hearing before the Supreme Court's appellate division.[24]

To ensure permanent change, Seabury recommended reforms reminiscent of those put forward in the 1920s. He urged merging the magistrates' and children's courts with the court of special sessions. He recommended curbing politics by letting the appellate courts, rather than the mayor, appoint members of the lower judiciary. Lastly, he suggested that clerkships and lower-court positions be made civil service so that political bosses could no longer fill these slots.[25]

Seabury's report was not filed until March 1932. In the interim, reformers reasoned that the widespread corruption his public hearings had brought to light could exist only with the tacit approval of the Tammany district attorney. The suspicions seemed to be confirmed when it was learned that an assistant district attorney who had overseen more than six hundred vice cases between 1921 and 1929 had taken bribes. About the same time, a woman who agreed to tell Seabury how she was framed for prostitution was found strangled in a Bronx park. Her murder prompted outrage from civic leaders, and most of the complaints came from political opponents of Tammany. Norman Thomas, the unsuccessful Socialist candidate for mayor and later for president, accused District Attorney Thomas C. T. Crain of undermining New Yorkers' faith in government. On March 7, 1931, Richard S. Childs and Joseph M. Price, leaders of the City Club of New York, petitioned Roosevelt for a second investigation. Among other things, they charged that Crain "has initiated many investigations but has conducted them inadequately and ineffectively." Specifically they cited his failure to adequately pursue cases involving the magistrates' courts, Rothstein's murder, graft in city government, and racketeering. Moreover, they asserted, he had tried to divert attention from his failures by creating useless committees and conducting "fruitless inquiries." Roosevelt saw a chance to answer the reformers while winning glory for himself and appointed Seabury to investigate Crain on March 10, 1931. The move drew criticism from Al Smith, who called him a "Democrat without any heart." In words that would haunt Roosevelt two years later, Smith correctly predicted that Seabury would "promote himself out of this."[26]

Other party members endorsed Roosevelt's actions against Tammany. New York City attorney James C. Cleary said, "it is far better for our party to clean its own house than to face the certainty that others will do it to our greater disadvantage. There is no mistaking the fact that the city government is practically in a state of demoralization from the mayor's office down. Your recent action is unquestionably a step in the right direction." Roosevelt apparently hoped to find a middle ground between Tammany and reformers. He gave the reformers the investigation and Seabury to conduct it but tried to appease Tammany by telling Seabury he expected the investigation to be geared more toward uncovering inefficiency than corruption.[27] Still, by targeting Crain, Roosevelt, Seabury, and the reformers had miscalculated. Many people who supported political housecleaning in New York did not support the drive against the aging district attorney who had held office only since New Year's Day 1930.

Crain, a wealthy Episcopalian with twenty-five years of experience as a general sessions and Supreme Court judge, enjoyed a good reputation despite his long-standing Tammany affiliation. The more logical choice for the district attorney's job would have been Ferdinand Pecora, a twelve-year veteran of the office with a reputation for independent vigor. But Curry and Walker, disdaining reform, backed the weaker candidate. Crain was seventy years old when he won the election, and he hoped to parlay his visibility as district attorney into the governor's chair. Instead, he became an example of Tammany's weak underbelly. Predictably, party members rallied around him. The wife of one Tammany judge wrote Roosevelt decrying the attempts to "sacrifice [Crain] to the Republican hue and cry." Labor leaders also offered support. John F. Dalton, business representative of the International Association of Machinists District Lodge No. 15, said that as a judge Crain always had handed down "just and conspicuously fair decisions wherever they involved labor"; he attributed the furor to the ravings of "alleged reformers, alarmists or political opportunists." William R. Chisling, business manager of the United Neckwear Cutters Union, said the "investigations are becoming more emotional than judicial." He feared the political hysteria would "result in the sacrifice to public clamor of an honest, faithful, and efficient district attorney."[28]

More surprising was the support Crain received from such groups as the Rutgers Club, whose president described it as a nonpartisan association concerned about the city's welfare. The club passed a resolution registering "alarm" over attacks on Crain and "the present wave of hysteria involving indiscriminate, slanderous attacks upon [the city's] fair name." Even some faithful Republicans were upset at the allegations. Herbert A. Hughes, vice president of a New York real estate company, said he was surprised at how many businessmen hoped Crain would be exonerated. Hughes added that "there seems to be a unanimous feeling and suspicion that someone is trying to make Judge Crain the goat. . . .

I am compelled to repeat what I have heard many others say—that they would much rather have a slow-moving, honest district attorney than a fast-moving, dishonest district attorney."[29]

When Crain hired Samuel Untermyer to represent him, the defense attorney tried his case in the newspapers, to offset what he believed was the frenzied crusade against his client. Untermyer's scenario depicted Crain as a "courtly and cultured gentleman who is being unjustly submitted to this cruel humiliation at the close of his distinguished career." He railed against the City Club, which had called for the investigation, and at Seabury, who, he said, was acting unfairly as both investigator and judge. The result, Untermyer said, was "a hostile, intensive, hypercritical delving into every nook and corner of the vast records of the greatest law office in the world, this scraping with a barbed-wire, fine-tooth comb in search of a weak spot." Untermyer's constant charges that both the probe and Seabury's tactics were unfair irritated Roosevelt, who publicly chastised the lawyer for unprofessionalism. Untermyer responded that he had a duty to protest "the doubtless inadvertent unwisdom of [Seabury's] appointment and his manifest bias."[30]

Seabury's report on the district attorney, which came out August 31, 1931, alleged no serious wrongdoing by Crain. In spite of an exhaustive probe, Seabury questioned the handling of only "about one-tenth of one percent" of the 18,000 cases that annually poured through the New York County district attorney's office, including the magistrate cases. Noting that Crain had sought indictments against seven crooked bailbondsmen, Seabury conceded that he had failed to uncover any evidence of political corruption. He did, however, reject Crain's claim that he had conducted his own grand jury investigation in hopes of making recommendations for legislation that would provide long-term reforms in the magistrate courts. Crain's overriding motive, Seabury said, was to paint his office in the best light.[31]

Seabury also found no serious wrongdoing, but much inefficiency, with Crain's handling of racketeering cases. Seabury wrote that racketeering was a national problem, and that Crain "clearly appreciated the character of the abuse, the nature of the challenge that it presented to government and the fact that it was incumbent upon the local authorities to meet this challenge." To that end, Crain had declared war on racketeering, set up a seventy-member citizens' committee, issued radio requests for help, and sent out questionnaires to businesses. But Seabury scoffed at these efforts, saying that the citizens' committee accomplished nothing and the help from industry and the citizenry never materialized. Although Crain targeted thirty areas of racketeering and won a few indictments, Seabury found several cases that "manifest not only ineffectiveness but . . . incompetency." He concluded that Crain, "confronted by . . . the aggressive tactics of the racketeer, has thrown up his hands and recognizes that, even with the co-operation of the Police Department, he has not been able to do anything of substantial value toward . . . bringing these dangerous criminals to justice."[32]

Realizing the weakness of his case against Crain, Seabury concluded that while Crain showed "personal diligence" and worked long hours at his job, "in many instances he busied himself ineffectively, and . . . did not grasp or act upon opportunities for high public service. . . . I am satisfied that wherever he failed, and I think he did fail in many cases to do all that should have been done, his failure was not due to any lack of personal effort or any ignoble motive." Seabury said the only question before him was whether Crain was too incompetent to hold office: "The fact that the people of the country do not elect the best man to the position, or one who acts in the most efficient manner, is not ground for his removal. In such cases, the people must suffer the consequences of their own conduct."[33]

Seabury's derision of the people's judgment about Crain and the unrealistic standards by which he measured the aging district attorney were good indicators of "the Saint's" faults of arrogance, disdain, impractical idealism, and ambition. He held Crain to an impossibly high standard, and his criticism was a product of hindsight and second-guessing. Seabury had adopted the growing belief of legal reformers that a district attorney had to be more aggressive and better organized to meet the challenges posed by more sophisticated criminals. In this respect, Seabury's investigations were precursors of the modern task force in which a staff of lawyers works closely with investigators to untangle complex webs of illegality. It is not surprising that Seabury's report is infused with his belief that he would have been a better prosecutor than Crain. Some observers, looking at the amount of evidence he uncovered during his two investigations, might have agreed. That conclusion, however, would have ignored one key point: Seabury worked with a select staff and had the freedom to probe deeply into a few carefully chosen matters. Crain's office, by contrast, had to handle every criminal case in Manhattan. Seabury's report conceded this fact, noting that racketeering cases created "extraordinary difficulties" because "they were not a regular or customary part of the routine of the office of the District Attorney."[34] It would take another wave of crime hysteria later in the decade to convince New Yorkers to fund a new, more expensive kind of district attorney's office. Such fine points were lost on Seabury, and his eighty-five-page report stands as a classic example of an unsavory tactic well known by zealous and political prosecutors: ruining a man's reputation through innuendo and public criticism when there is insufficient evidence to put the matter before a legal forum in which the target could clear his name.

In the end, Crain's good reputation, ambiguity about Seabury's allegations, and concerns about the necessity for modern law enforcement machinery proved too complex in 1931. Digging up more dirt on Tammany was still business as usual in the rough-and-tumble world of New York politics, and Seabury apparently recognized this fact. Years later, a Seabury aide claimed there had been enough information to seek Crain's removal but Seabury decided against it for political reasons. "We had advance information that, regardless of what the report said, Tammany's leadership was going to nominate Crain anyway. And that meant he would win in controlled Manhattan. We knew we would be left looking silly—that it would look like a repudiation of our efforts. So we decided to do the practical thing, set out all the damaging evidence that we uncovered but not recommend removal. We knew that there was much more to be gained by continuing the investigation into the whole city's affairs."[35]

Seabury found willing allies among New York City's good-government reformers, who disdained Walker and Tammany Hall. League of Women Voters members were appalled by the mayor's carefree attitudes. At one league dinner featuring a discussion of the virtues of a city manager form of government, Walker "made a lot of wisecracks, shot his cuffs, and rolled his eyes. There wasn't a laugh in the audience. They didn't come to be entertained. They wanted the Mayor of New York to explore the possibility of the City Manager Plan as applied to New York City." For his part, Walker was angry at his cold reception and vowed he would never attend another league meeting. On the left, Rabbi Stephen Wise and the Reverend John Haynes Holmes, who represented the Citizens' Civic Committee, filed charges against Walker for allowing mismanagement and corruption. On the right, Herbert Brownell, a young Republican Club member and future Eisenhower advisor who was getting his feet wet in the campaign to oust Walker, supported Seabury's efforts. However, it was one of New York's oldest and best-known civic watchdog groups, the Citizens' Union, that created the broad-based demand for a legislative investigation of Walker. It complained that Walker was often late to Board of Estimate meetings and it contended that his slipshod management meant the financially strapped city was paying illegally appointed city employees.[36]

Revelations of the Seabury probes peopled these traditional groups with a host of new critics—disenchanted Democrats and businessmen concerned that the worsening Depression and fiscal mismanagement would combine to bankrupt the city. The Union's president, William Jay Schieffelin, recognizing the groundswell of outrage at Walker, spearheaded efforts to create demand for an investigation by organizing the "Committee of One Thousand."[37] In 1931, only a year after the clamor began, the Republican-controlled state legislature initiated a joint legislative investigation of New York City. Labeled the Hofstadter Committee after its chairman, Republican Samuel H. Hofstadter, the panel chose Seabury as its chief counsel. Roosevelt, whose upcoming reelection campaign enhanced his willingness to go along with the probe, approved a $250,000 bill funding the committee's work. He also was beginning to eye the Democratic presidential nomination, for which a reputation as a Tammany foe would be a decided asset.

When Tammany attempted to block the investigation, Roosevelt countered with a special session of the legislature to pass a bill allowing the committee to give witnesses immunity, thereby forcing them to testify. He later authorized another half million dollars for the investigation, which began on April 8, 1931, and lasted until December 1932. Seabury displayed his usual knack for drawing publicity while exposing the corrupt underbelly of Tammany politics. One of the most important of his revelations concerned New York Sheriff Thomas M. Farley. Roosevelt removed him from office in early 1932, after he failed to explain how he had accumulated $400,000 while in his job, or why former associates of gambler Arnold Rothstein were found shooting craps in his party clubhouse. Still, Seabury's efforts would have constituted just another hohum probe had he not amassed devastating evidence against Jimmy Walker. Exhaustive subpoenaing of New York bank records finally turned up a letter-of-credit to Walker from a consortium of businessmen and politicians trying to take over the city's bus lines. Evidence showed that Walker had supported the group in exchange for money he used for a 1927 trip to Europe. As Seabury pointed out, "This is a fatal blow to Tammany Hall. It is the first time in the history of New York that a mayor is caught taking money with his actual receipts for the bribe."[38]

Seabury uncovered several more examples of Walker's corruption and aired them at a series of public hearings that ended just before the June 1932 Democratic National Convention. The timing posed a clear dilemma for Roosevelt's president aspirations. As the *New York Times* noted, "Failure to act decisively . . . might be interpreted as bowing to Tammany Hall, while precipitate action would alienate the local organization and cast doubt on Mr. Roosevelt's ability to carry his own state." Seabury clearly enjoyed the governor's discomfort. It is not clear at what point Seabury's hatred of Tammany and his success at grabbing headlines rekindled his own political ambitions; but by February 1932 he saw himself as a possible Democratic presidential nominee. That month, in a speech to a good-government group in Cincinnati, Seabury made thinly veiled attacks on Roosevelt as a politician who catered to Tammany Hall.[39]

The speech infuriated Roosevelt supporters but came as no surprise to Tammany stalwarts, who always had suspected Seabury of harboring political ambitions. Jonah Goldstein, whose own investigation of the magistrates' courts had been overshadowed by Seabury's dramatic revelations, said the judge never wanted to promote long-lasting reform: "The Seabury report . . . was there to turn up dirt to bring charges against a couple of magistrates." If Seabury's real goal had been reform, Goldstein reasoned, he would have consulted with city magistrates, the Society for Cruelty to Children, the bar association's lawyer committee, the League of Women Voters, and other groups that conducted business in the magistrates' courts. As it was, he made recommendations without consulting those directly involved. Also typical, he said, was Seabury's recommendation that the children's courts be abolished even though "he had never stepped into the children's court in all the years of its existence."[40]

A few civic leaders recognized the questionable aspects of Seabury's probe. Dr. William H. Allen, director of the Institute for Public Service, said Seabury did not act on information his group provided and on one occasion lost the notes they had given him. "The fiasco was characteristic of the inefficiency of the way Seabury did his part of the job. He'd ask a question and preen himself, look at the bench or the newspapermen to see if they appreciated his skill. My explanation is that he knew too little of actual government administration, could visualize too little of this tremendous machinery the city had, the only thing he could see was a headline-making scandal. He spent hundreds of thousands of dollars trying to pin scandal on Walker—where, if he had only pinned extreme inefficiency and waste, he could have made headway and caught much more scandal too." Allen's institute issued a report criticizing Seabury for making "what Governor Roosevelt is going to do to Mayor Walker seem more important than what Mayor Walker has been doing to 7,000,000 citizens."[41]

Goldstein's and Allen's interpretations contained elements of truth, but they misunderstood the depth of Seabury's reformist zeal. Seabury's desire for the 1932 presidential nomination stemmed from his belief that he was the best man for the job, not from naked ambition. He was an idealist and a moralist whose black-and-white vision left no room for compromise. It would have been inconceivable for him to have consulted Tammany or those he perceived as its allies. Seabury's major flaw was not his ambition but his self-righteousness. Like certain other 1930s reformers, his smugness about his own purpose translated into a belief that he was justified in stretching ethical boundaries to achieve his goals. Most New Yorkers ignored his arrogance and applauded his effectiveness. Even liberal Democrat Jeremiah T. Mahoney believed Seabury "did get pretty good results."[42]

Seabury behaved toward Walker and Roosevelt as arrogantly as he had toward all the other politicians he had targeted during the previous two years. When his hearings against Walker ended on the eve of the Democratic National Convention, he put both men on the hot seat by not filing charges against the mayor. Roosevelt now faced a dilemma: should he offend Tammany by taking the initiative against Walker or offend everyone else by not standing up to the machine? Roosevelt finally called Seabury's bluff by issuing a curt statement pointing out that the legislative committee had not given him a specific charge. Until he had something more to work with than newspaper reports, he said, he could not move against Walker. He urged Seabury and the Hofstadter Committee "to stop talking and do something. It is not the time for political sniping or buck passing." Seabury filed his report, without the backing of the committee, on June 8. Roosevelt delayed forwarding the complaint to Walker for two weeks, so he would not have to take action before the convention. When Walker received it on June 21, he did not have time to respond. With the charges thus hanging in the air, all three men set off for the convention in Chicago.[43]

Seabury's staff members preceded him to Chicago to line up support while the judge arranged speeches in other parts of the country to show his lack of interest in the nomination. Meanwhile he hoped that Smith and Roosevelt would clash and that he could prevail as a dark horse candidate. Seabury mistakenly believed that he would be swept into the nomination by a national groundswell of support for his honest and fearless investigation of Tammany Hall. His efforts had received attention in the national press and in some unexpected quarters. Raymond Moley, a Columbia University law professor who assisted Seabury and later joined Roosevelt's Brain Trust, described how a *Yale Review* editor wanted him to replace references to Plato with compliments about Seabury in an article he had written. Moley rejected the suggestion, saying it showed "the tendency of the average Democratic high-brow to look upon Seabury as a savior of the State."[44]

Seabury's efforts attracted the attention of the nation's most high-minded reformers but did not translate into more than one or two delegates at the national convention. As Tammany sage Mahoney pointed out, the probe had not made Seabury any more of a sympathetic character than he had been when he ran unsuccessfully for governor of New

York. Reformers, Mahoney aptly noted, have a limited popularity because the traits of arrogant determination that make them successful are not endearing. Frances Perkins, then serving as Roosevelt's industrial commissioner, recognized Seabury's unappealing side. Never a target of the investigation and never a friend of Tammany, Perkins nonetheless said that "one couldn't help observing that there was a stiff upper lip, hard-boiled, exact, rigid rule of conduct being applied." During the investigations she wondered whether Seabury could "actually understand the shortcomings of human beings who find themselves in positions of temptation, or positions of trust? I wonder if he understands what ignorance, stupidity and frustration do to a man? . . . Does he understand that a man can be both crooked and kind?" Seabury's naive understanding of politics showed when he predicted that "lightning would strike him" and that "the convention would have to somehow or other choose him."[45] His belief that personalities rather than political organization were the key to success at the polls hampered and would continue to hamper his efforts in years to come.

For Roosevelt the more crucial test at the 1932 convention came from Tammany Hall. Curry and other Tammany bosses believed Roosevelt had mistreated Walker, and they attempted to block his nomination by joining hands with other big city bosses to support Al Smith. Their efforts kept Roosevelt from winning on the convention's first three ballots. But when Roosevelt agreed to accept Texan John Nance Garner, speaker of the U.S. House, as his vice president and to provide a cabinet post for William McAdoo, the votes from Texas and California delegates broke the deadlock.[46]

With the presidential nomination in his pocket, Roosevelt returned to New York free to tackle Tammany. Although he had been irritated by Curry's action, he felt less animosity toward Walker. Frances Perkins said Roosevelt appointed Seabury to appease the critics but never believed the mayor was stupid enough to get personally involved in the corruption of his associates. Edward Flynn, the Bronx's Democratic boss and a member of Roosevelt's Brain Trust, said Roosevelt liked Walker and would have saved him if he could. Both Flynn and Roosevelt believed that Walker "never did a deliberately dishonest thing. The situations developed and he allowed them to drift rather than to do something about them. He accepted what he thought were presents and things of that sort, not with any viciousness behind them. He loved people and he didn't question their motives much. I think he was honest in that respect."[47] Once the charges were filed and the convention was over, Roosevelt realized he would have to preside over the mayor's removal trial in Albany.

The proceedings against Walker began August 11 and lasted until September 1, 1932. Seabury, no longer acting in an official capacity because he had brought the charges as a private citizen, still commanded awe from the Albany crowds massed for the hearings. Seabury put out the word when he was leaving the Executive Office Building so he would have a clear path. When Seabury got off the elevator, Perkins recalled, everybody stopped "whether they were the baker's boy come to get an order, or whether they were a window cleaner seeking to get a permit to insure his employees, or whether they were a man on crutches looking for the Compensation Bureau to see when he could get his compensation, or whether they'd come about the parkways, or whether they were public officers. They all stopped short. Utter silence would reign while Seabury went out to lunch."[48]

Still, Seabury was now a bit player in the main drama between Roosevelt, who had postponed his presidential campaign, and Walker, who was fighting for his political life. Their struggle was played out "before an audience of millions, which followed the events . . . every day and evening on the radio and in the newspapers." Even hardened politicians were amazed at the proceedings. Reuben Lazarus, who helped handle Walker's defense, recalled that Walker gave "the most dramatic speech of his whole career" during the hearings. "In that speech he characterized the trial as a hanging; he charged that he was there to be removed not tried, and he would look up with his hair shaking down in his eyes, saying 'Gone character, gone reputation, gone life itself.' " Despite his eloquence, Walker's charges of unfairness did not play as well against Roosevelt as they had against Seabury. Accepting the inevitable, Walker resigned as mayor and left for Europe with his girlfriend, actress Betty Compton.[49]

Two months later, Roosevelt was elected president. Before he left for Washington, he helped seal Tammany's demise by ensuring that his lieutenant governor, Herbert Lehman, would replace him in Albany.

Lehman never had hidden his enmity for Tammany Hall. As scion of a wealthy, liberal, Jewish family, he had been tapped by the machine in 1910 as a party delegate. He soon became disgusted with the rough-and-tumble atmosphere of the Democratic State Convention and eschewed involvement for more than twenty years, until he was pulled back into politics by his admiration for Al Smith's liberalism. In 1926 Smith garnered much independent and Republican backing, and he asked Lehman to serve on the Independent Citizens' Committee that was supporting his gubernatorial campaign. Smith rewarded Lehman for his efforts by naming him finance chairman of the Democratic National Committee in 1928. Although he was close to Smith, Lehman confounded both Tammany leaders, who referred to him as "a little tin God," and Republicans, who were puzzled by his self-effacing modesty, superscrupulousness, and gracious politeness to his enemies. In an era of colorful politicians such as Walker, Smith, and Roosevelt, Lehman appeared lackluster. George Harrison Combs, Jr., described him as "a curious guy [who] never appealed to politicians" because of his straightforward and shy manner. Unlike most of the politicians with whom he dealt, Lehman had spent most of his life increasing his family's considerable banking and textile fortune rather than scheming for public office. He was one of the few politicians of his era who even skeptics believed had sacrificed personal gain to accept public office out of a sense of service and idealism.[50]

Raised in a brownstone on Manhattan's prosperous East Side, Lehman received from his parents a sense of social responsibility. Decades later, Lehman said: "I remember that at an early age my father took me on a tour of the slums of New York City. I saw the squalor, the congestion, the disease, the misery of people forced to live under conditions which seemed to me at the time subhuman, in quarters that seemed utterly uninhabitable. . . . I was deeply impressed by the conditions in these slums. The sight of them seared my soul." After graduating from Williams College in 1899, Lehman went into business but also volunteered at the Henry Street Settlement, a New York settlement house. He said later that his work there with Lillian Wald made him realize "the utter hopelessness of attempting this entire job [caring for the sick, feeble, aged, and unemployed] on a voluntary, purely philanthropic basis."[51]

Lehman's idealistic view of public service left no room for corruption. Whereas Roosevelt had been willing to help Tammany to achieve his political ambitions, Lehman would not engage in any activity he considered compromising. Curry, recognizing Lehman's independence, tried drafting him for the U.S. Senate when his name came up as a gubernatorial candidate. But neither Roosevelt, who still was nursing his grudges against Tammany, nor Lehman would accept the idea. Al Smith also threw his support to Lehman by threatening to run for mayor of New York against Tammany if the Hall refused to back the nomination. When Curry asked Smith on which party ticket he would run, Smith replied: "On a Chinese laundry ticket, I can beat you and your crowd." Curry backed down.[52] Thus, the mild-mannered candidate was poised to kill the Tammany dragon—a task that had eluded New York's most flamboyant reformers for nearly a century.

~ ~ ~ ~

CHAPTER TWO

The Runaway Grand Jury

*F*RANKLIN ROOSEVELT continued to play a hand in New York City politics, but his distant Washington perch and national problems posed by the worsening Depression necessarily limited his role. Likewise, Herbert Lehman was settling into the governor's chair in Albany. That left the impetus for reform in the nation's largest city to Seabury. Still nursing his dashed presidential ambitions, Seabury threw himself into the job of consolidating his stature as the patriarch of New York's good government forces. By lending his prestige, advice, and support, he galvanized disparate groups of reformers into what would be the city's most successful Fusion movement. As the alternative political party, Fusion was able to draw on a broad base of support from civic leaders, disaffected Republicans, and Democrats, all alarmed by the disclosures of Seabury's investigations. Earlier Fusion movements led by mayors Seth Low and John Purroy Mitchel—elected, respectively, in 1901 and 1913—had been flawed by the parties' haphazard organization, the candidates' own shortcomings, and the strong opposition of Tammany Hall. In 1933 the situation was different because the Tammany Tiger never had been so weak, and the Fusion candidate, Fiorello La Guardia, never had been so appealing.

Even so, it was not a foregone conclusion that good-government forces would triumph. Several factors came together to foster change. Providing a backdrop to all the political machinations of the 1930s was a concern about crime that stretched back to the mid-1920s. Accompanying this concern was a sense that law enforcement increasingly was unable to cope with organized criminals. Canny politicians, recognizing the value of crime fighting, adopted legal reform rhetoric to persuade the public that crime and corruption had reached menacing proportions. The 1933 battle for the mayor's seat, pitting Tammany against reform Democratics and Fusionists, made good use of this rhetoric. After La Guardia's election, Fusionists, reformers, and Republicans focused their attention on the Tammany-controlled New York County prosecutor's office. Their goal was to oust or circumvent District Attorney William Copeland Dodge. Their anti-Tammany, anticrime efforts dovetailed with attempts to save the grand jury system and prompted the famous 1935 runaway grand jury that led to Thomas E. Dewey's appointment as special prosecutor.

Beginning in the mid-1920s, many judges, legal reformers, and concerned citizens became convinced that a growing crime wave gripped New York. But then, as now, the public and experts had trouble defining crime, determining its causes, and suggesting its cures. They complained that New York increasingly resembled the "Wild West" because of the rising number of such vague offenses as "banditry," "gangsterism," "thuggery," and "armed insurrection." New Yorkers failed to distinguish among organized crime, street crime, and changing social mores. Not surprisingly, they had just as much trouble defining crime's causes. Most cited the well-worn complaints that seem to characterize all crime waves—breakdowns in moral values, Godless youths, laziness, more sympathy for the crooks than their victims, dishonest lawyers, and the general laxness of the legal system. Others blamed conditions specific to the era. One author thought that World War I "with its awful sacrifice of human life may have given some ignorant and thoughtless boys the impression that what the state or nation could do in time of war they could likewise do with impunity in time of peace." Many claimed that Prohibition had convinced police that "it is more glamorous to catch a man selling whiskey than to catch a highway robber and bandit." Others said the prosperity and social atmosphere of the 1920s had encouraged boys to attend prize fights and girls to run wild.[1]

Perhaps the only point on which those concerned about crime could agree was that the existing legal system could not meet the challenge. As one judge said, police were "as helpless in facing an army of thugs as a

THE RUNAWAY GRAND JURY

citizen would be if he tried to sweep the Atlantic back with a broom."
Predictably, solutions ran the gamut of possibilities, depending upon
which cause of crime the speaker favored. Some advocated better moral
education. Others suggested fingerprinting immigrants because they
seemed to make up a disproportionately large percentage of criminals.
Gun control and an end to the "indiscriminate manufacture of firearms"
were seen as a solution by some, while others fell back on the tried and
true methods advocated by jurists of previous eras: quicker detection of
crime, immediate trial, and swift and certain punishment. Only a few
people seemed to realize that certain kinds of crime had changed because
they were becoming better organized. Improved transportation—
especially the car—and the profits of Prohibition had speeded up a process that began earlier when Arnold Rothstein created a crime empire
along modern business lines. District attorneys and police were hamstrung by parochial laws designed to fight street criminals that were
largely ineffectual against more organized bandits who crossed state lines
with impunity.[2]

Events in New York typified national trends. In 1925, concern about
crime and its causes prompted the formation of the National Crime
Commission, which received financial backing from the U.S. Steel Corporation and moral support from prominent politicians, including Al
Smith and Franklin Roosevelt. At its first meeting in Washington, the
commission announced its purpose "to apprise the public of all available
information regarding the cause of crime in America, its growth in
America and its current status." Although the organization never accomplished these goals, its agenda already had been taken up in New York
by state Senator Caleb Baumes of Newburgh. The legislative hearings
held by what became known as the Baumes Commission resulted in
several criminal law reforms in New York, the most famous of which was
the mandatory life-sentencing of fourth-time-convicted felons. In 1928
the Baumes Commission estimated that crime cost the nation $13 billion
annually; in 1935 J. Edgar Hoover set the costs at $15 billion annually.
Cost, like cause and cure, became a matter of dispute and ambiguity. As
one author said, "Sufficient data on the many items of cost and expense
of crime simply do not exist. . . . What is more, assembling specific

information on the cost of crime to the average business organization or to the individual is practically impossible. One thing is generally admitted and that is that the total cost is appalling."[3]

It is impossible to evaluate how much or in what form the anxiety about crime felt by the experts translated into public concern. Then as now newspapers and movies put a heavy emphasis on crime, especially organized crime; and the fact that people subscribed and bought tickets shows some level of interest. Most probably viewed crime as something fascinating but far removed from their everyday lives. In 1929, when La Guardia railed against Arnold Rothstein, it did not make much of an impression. Making crime and corruption seem relevant to the public was a key achievement of the 1930s politicians who capitalized on the startling revelations of the Seabury investigations.

When Gentleman Jimmy Walker left for Europe, the city's charter called for his temporary replacement by the president of the Board of Aldermen, Joseph McKee, a handsome former schoolteacher. Because McKee had filled in for Walker, who was habitually late and missed many board meetings, he felt entitled to serve out Walker's term, not just the two months until a special election could be held in November. His plans ran afoul of Tammany leaders still nursing grudges against Roosevelt for his handling of the Walker case. McKee, as a friend of Roosevelt's trusted ally, Bronx machine boss Edward J. Flynn, was viewed as an enemy of Tammany. He sued to block the special election scheduled by Tammany and won a favorable judgment from fellow Bronx resident Judge John E. McGeehan, whose decision was overturned on appeal. In November 1932, John O'Brien was elected on the Tammany ticket. By pushing for a man like O'Brien, Tammany Boss Curry insulted Roosevelt and the voters of New York. As even O'Brien's campaign manager, George Harrison Combs, Jr., admitted, "We realized that we were battling almost a lost cause right from the outset. The Mayor continually got into laughable troubles whenever he made speeches. He departed from carefully written script and always managed to utter some either stultifying or bathetic word and was a source of great embarrassment to everyone concerned." In one speech at the Yale Club, O'Brien prompted guffaws from listeners when he departed from the text to say, "Gentlemen, you have no idea how hard it is to be Mayor of New York. The problems are many and pressing. Sometimes I retire to my sanctum-sanctorum and just sit and think. And sometimes I go there and just sit!"[4]

O'Brien's obvious flaws fanned reformers' hopes of triumph, but forging the disparate Fusionists behind one candidate proved a lengthy and difficult task. Fusion was a broad movement whose membership included Republicans and Democrats along with reformers, journalists, artists, businessmen, and others who had been angered by the revelations of the Seabury investigations and continued to be disenchanted with both of the major parties. Others, who once had been inspired by John Purroy Mitchel and had been waiting for a renewed Fusion opportunity since 1915, were essentially nonpartisan. Moreover, each strand in the Fusion movement hoped to push its own agenda. Republican Newbold Morris saw Fusion as a way of getting Democrats "who couldn't congenitally pull down the Republican lever" to vote for a Republican. Fusion Democrats, on the other hand, wanted a genuine third party as a vehicle for McKee. After his rejection by party regulars, McKee spoke out against the corruption of Tammany, won endorsements from newspapers, and "overnight . . . became the idol of Fusion forces." Their hopes were bolstered by his success as a write-in candidate in the special election, in which he received more than 241,000 votes. But McKee hedged about his candidacy and in early May 1933 dropped out, declaring he was disgusted with politics. The next logical candidate was Seabury, whose stature as New York's leading reformer was unquestioned. Seabury too declined offers to run, saying he could be more effective fighting the Tiger from the sidelines. He agreed, however, to become honorary chairman of the Fusion campaign committee. During the spring and summer, Fusion was still "a very poor thing," according to Charles C. Burlingham, a civic leader and president of the New York Bar Association. Burlingham, a Wilson Democrat, had played an important role in putting together Fusion backing for John Purroy Mitchel and played a similar role in 1933. At a series of breakfast meetings he plotted strategy with Roy Howard, an independent Democrat and publisher of the *New York World-Telegram*; Adolph Berle, a Columbia University law professor and New Dealer; Richard S. Childs, chair of the National Municipal League; and Republican Paul Windels. They met at the apartment of William M. Chad-bourne, a former Republican who had left the party to become a Bull Moose follower of Teddy Roosevelt.[5]

The committee considered several candidates, including Nathan Straus, Jr., a merchant, former state senator, and brother-in-law of Governor Herbert Lehman. Straus declined the nomination after consulting with Jewish leaders who feared a rise in anti-Semitism if the governor of the state and the mayor of New York were both Jews. Meanwhile, La Guardia, who had lost his congressional seat in the Democratic landslide that swept Roosevelt into the White House, pushed his own candidacy. He received help from Berle, who had worked with him to pass New Deal legislation in Congress. Berle admired La Guardia's grasp of economic problems and his "unbounded energy" and "unquestioned honesty."[6] Eventually the field narrowed to La Guardia and two others: General John F. O'Ryan, a World War I veteran and conservative Democrat who had the support of most Fusion leaders; and Robert Moses, who had served in Al Smith's cabinet despite his Republican party affiliation.

Fusion's top nominees ran afoul of Seabury. Seabury thought Moses was tainted by his association with Smith and Tammany. He disliked O'Ryan because he had backed former Republican Governor Charles S. Whitman, who had defeated Seabury in the 1916 gubernatorial race. By contrast, Seabury was impressed with La Guardia's zeal, independence, and Progressive voting record on social legislation in Congress. When La Guardia's candidacy was announced in early August 1933, conservative Republicans recognized the inevitable and halfheartedly backed La Guardia, who ran technically as a Republican with Fusion endorsement. Seabury kicked off the campaign by announcing that a vote for La Guardia meant a repudiation of Tammany and would lead to "the election of an honest, fearless and capable anti-Tammany mayor, a sincere and militant opponent of graft, corruption and waste, who will put an end to the squandering and wasting of the people's money by Tammany Hall for the enrichment of the politicians and their friends and restore it to unemployment relief, schools, hospitals and the other purposes for which it was intended."[7]

La Guardia proved an excellent choice. As usual, he was a tireless and brilliant campaigner. Because the Seabury investigations had borne out his 1929 accusations against Tammany, he appeared less demagogic than he had four years earlier. Newbold Morris recalled that La Guardia so captivated the conservative members of his club during one speech that "by the time he was through there wasn't anybody there who didn't think he was a powerful moral force." Fusion was tailor-made for La Guardia's egocentrism, idiosyncrasies, and political acumen. Without pressure from Fusion, conservative Republicans would have rebuffed him as a self-proclaimed Progressive who had turned his back on party policy to support labor legislation in Congress. Although La Guardia was too independent to have fit easily into either party, he was adept at performing a balancing act between different factions. Reuben Lazarus, once one of Walker's attorneys, described him as "the most resourceful of all politicians I've known. . . . You have to be . . . better in your ability than the old-line leaders to succeed as a Fusion candidate for mayor. He had to beat them at their own game."[8]

La Guardia still would have lost had he not benefited from a split in Democratic ranks. Faced with Curry's rebuff and upset with Tammany's poor choice for mayor, Roosevelt and Flynn continued the dismemberment of Tammany Hall by making a bold move. Reasoning that it would be better if the Democrats rather than the opposition cleaned up New York, in late September they persuaded McKee to run as the "Recovery Party" candidate for mayor. Thus, while the old-liners stood behind O'Brien, the more progressive wing of the party, typified by Frances Perkins, Henry Morgenthau, and James Farley, endorsed McKee. Initially the division took the city by surprise. As Republican Paul Windels remembered, "for the first time in my recollection in politics, official Democratic party leaders publicly participated in an opposition ticket after the choice of the party had been officially designated in the primaries. This meant teaching Democratic voters to vote other than a Democratic ticket in a general election. It was an astonishing development." Fusion forces and Republicans responded by trying to convince voters that the new party was nothing more than "a shifting of the Tammany gang from one false front to another without any essential change in the real parties . . . who remained the same whether marching behind O'Brien or McKee."[9]

As the election of 1933 came down to the wire, Tammany leaders unwisely discounted the threat posed by La Guardia. Because he had been defeated for mayor in 1922 and 1929, Tammany leaders calculated that he would lose again. Believing that La Guardia would take only the Italian wards, the machine saved its wrath for McKee. As one former Tammany politician George Combs put it, "In any three-sided war, the hostility is always greatest toward the renegade than toward the outsider of the third party. Things were said about McKee which were very much more abrasive and vituperative than were ever said about La Guardia." La Guardia exploited the split by quoting each Democrat against the other. O'Brien made a particularly easy target because he was obviously little more than a Tammany pawn. When asked whom he would appoint as police commissioner, O'Brien said: "I don't know. I haven't got the word yet." As the campaign wore on, the Recovery Party became even more of an orphan. Two of Roosevelt's key advisors—Farley and Louis Howe—were convinced that La Guardia would win and that the President should stay out of a local party squabble. As a result the Recovery party never received promised support from Washington. Lacking sage political advice, the McKee campaign made a mistake that ensured McKee's loss. Ironically, the blunder came about because of Seabury's pettiness. He had thrown himself into La Guardia's campaign and used the forum "to take a swipe at everybody he didn't like," which included most Democrats. One of his targets was the Jewish Lehman. "Instead of speaking for La Guardia and against Tammany, he began to pan Governor Lehman." When McKee seized the opportunity to accuse Seabury of anti-Semitism, the Republican campaign responded by releasing an anti-Semitic article McKee had written years earlier for *Catholic World*.[10]

Looking back, Flynn conceded that McKee was a poor choice. "He is an intellectual and I don't think he could take what you have to take in order to be in public life." But even if McKee had been a stellar candidate, New York voters probably would have continued a historic trend by turning to a Fusion candidate after a scandal in city government. The city's deepening fiscal crisis also undermined Tammany. Even civil service employees—a group long taken for granted in machine politics—began deserting the Hall as declining tax revenues threatened their jobs. Throughout the campaign, Fusion candidates appealed to the taxpayers' pocketbooks. Citing the revelations of the Seabury investigations, Fusion argued persuasively that inefficiency and corruption were draining city coffers.[11] Against this backdrop, La Guardia brilliantly raised Arnold Rothstein's ominous specter in the public mind, linking the city's economic troubles to racketeering and gangsterism. In so doing, he was able to give simplistic clarity to a long-standing but vague concern about crime.

On November 7, 1933, voters gave La Guardia approximately 860,000 votes and only about 600,000 votes to each of the other candidates. "In Harlem, the Bronx, the Lower East Side, and Greenwich Village, the Little Flower's triumph was celebrated with bonfires, torch light parades, horn-tooting motorcades, and dancing in the streets. Thousands joined in a jubilant procession behind a hearse and six men who bore a coffin surrounded by signs reading, 'Here Lies Tammany—The Big Stiff.'" La Guardia eschewed such hoopla and planned a simple inauguration, saying, "I never heard of a receiver taking possession of a business with a brass band." Instead, he opted for a quiet ceremony held a few minutes after midnight on January 1, 1934, in the polished oak and leather library of Seabury's townhouse on East 63rd Street. He promised New York residents nonpartisan good management and honesty in government, vowing to make his administration an example for the nation.[12]

La Guardia immediately began to dramatize his crusade against crime. On his first morning as mayor he stopped off at Police Headquarters to swear in Major General John F. O'Ryan as his police commissioner. He told the 200 officers at the ceremony that merit would replace political favor as the means for advancement in the department and ordered them to go after racketeers or resign. Early in his administration he excitedly told a group of parole officers how he would solve crime in the nation's largest city. As one remembered, "His little foot would tap and as he talked, his arm would go up higher and higher and higher, along with his voice, as he got more and more passionate . . . he cried, in a high falsetto, 'What I'm going to do is, I'm going to grab every tinhorn gambler in the city of New York by the scruff of the neck and throw him over into New Jersey!' The last words were practically shrieks."[13]

For the time being, however, crime fighting took a backseat to New York's fiscal and unemployment crises. The city's finances were precarious, and its credit was so poor it could not get loans or grants from the federal government. It needed an infusion of $30 million to stave off bankruptcy. Following the example set by Roosevelt during his first hundred days in office, La Guardia used the fiscal problems as an excuse to increase his executive control. In a plan presented to the Board of Aldermen on January 2, La Guardia sought power to sever the city's dependency on Albany, reorganize the city bureaucracy, and override the city charter by cutting back on the powers of the city's elected councils. Tammany's opposition to a bill that would eliminate jobs and patronage posts was expected, but even Governor Lehman objected to the sweeping proposal. He told La Guardia that "No man in this country has ever asked for or received the dictatorial powers which would be yours through the enactment of this bill. Frankly I am deeply disturbed and apprehensive of the thought of a fiscal and political dictatorship, which I regard not only as entirely unnecessary but as un-American." La Guardia responded in kind: "Your charge of dictatorship comes as a hollow mockery to overburdened homeowners, taxpayers, rent payers and wage earners, who for more than a decade have suffered under as cruel and vicious a secret political dictatorship as has ever existed in an American community."[14]

The public fight was embarrassing to both La Guardia and Lehman, and the two men quickly worked out a compromise. Rather than lodging all power with the mayor, La Guardia agreed to share control with the Board of Estimate, where the Fusionists had a clear majority. Roosevelt gave his tacit approval to the deal by offering $23 million in federal aid. Even with the compromise and federal aid, a bitter fight with Tammany Hall dragged on through early April in the state legislature. The result was a much weaker arrangement that saved many of the city jobs La Guardia wanted to abolish. Still, the mayor used the bill to fire personnel, offer employees furloughs, and slash salaries for a savings of $30 million. Next, he turned his attention to unemployment. New York City had been particularly hard hit by the Depression, and an estimated one-sixth of its population needed relief.[15]

When these two problems were under some semblance of control, La Guardia threw his attention back to "the tinhorn gamblers and racketeers" he had railed against during his campaign. As the author August Heckscher notes, it was a war for which La Guardia was well suited: "His combative nature, his sympathy for the poor and for the consumers who were so often victims of the rackets, and not least his love of the dramatic gesture, disposed him to energetic sallies against criminal elements. His lively imagination peopled the urban world with 'racketeers,' 'chiselers,' and 'punks'—characters that loomed sinister and more than life-size upon the public stage; and he viewed himself as their foreordained enemy." Before La Guardia took over, nothing had been done to stop the corruption uncovered by the Seabury investigations, and little was done during his first months in office. Much of the failure was attributable to Police Commissioner O'Ryan. As part of a deal to get Fusion backing, La Guardia had appointed his opponent for the mayoral nomination to head the police. Unfortunately, the two men never got along. O'Ryan believed that keeping order on New York's streets required the same disciplinary tactics he had used to keep his troops in line during World War I, and his preoccupation with civil disobedience distracted him from the fight against racketeers and gangsters. He held strikers in particular disdain, and his strong-arm tactics against them infuriated the labor-loving mayor. As their rift deepened, La Guardia increasingly bypassed O'Ryan and sought advice from the number two man in the department, Lewis J. Valentine, "who had risen in the Police Department and then been sent to the sticks because he had fought the system." Valentine had gained headlines during the Seabury investigation by testifying against fellow police officers and magistrates. By constantly circumventing O'Ryan in seeking Valentine's advice, La Guardia finally drove the police commissioner out of office and appointed Valentine to replace him in September 1934.[16]

Valentine and La Guardia shared a ruthlessness about crime fighting that shocked some Fusion supporters. An early indication of their attitude came in November 1934, when Valentine was angered by the flashy attire of a man accused of shooting a policeman. The chief told his men, "When you meet men like that, don't be afraid to muss 'em up. Blood should be smeared all over that man's velvet collar." La Guardia ignored advice from supporters such as Burlingham and Felix Frankfurter to rein in his police commissioner. His support became even more outspoken the following January after a series of shootings of police, when the mayor railed against "coddling crooks" and talked about the ongoing "war." His words were followed by the massive arrests of more than three hundred undesirables, all later released by the courts.[17]

Even with the tough police stance, however, La Guardia and his fellow reformers faced the reality that the district attorney's office, the key to the prosecutorial system, remained in Tammany hands. This was especially galling in Manhattan, where Tammany stalwart William Copeland Dodge reigned. During the 1933 campaign, Dodge had adopted Fusion's anticrime message and out-campaigned the Recovery and Fusion candidates. For example, in October he told Kiwanis Club members he would be the first "militant" district attorney in New York County in twenty years. In a December 10, 1933, radio broadcast, Dodge promised protection to merchants and other people who provided tips on racketeers. After being sworn in on December 27, 1933, Dodge declared, "I am going to make a definite drive right off the bat against the racketeers." The centerpiece of his plan was a new method of eliminating the leaks from the district attorney's office that routinely tipped off racketeers about investigations and pending charges. Dodge said presenting only a "skeleton of the necessary evidence" to the grand jury would stop leaks and witness intimidation. As a further warning to potential tipsters, the day after taking office, Dodge dismissed ten assistant district attorneys affiliated with Tammany and ordered all but one detective on his staff transferred.[18]

In retrospect Dodge's program was doomed from the outset. Good-government forces lined up against him, despite his vow to work with La Guardia. Within two weeks of the 1933 election, Seabury was lecturing a crowd at Yale University about the "impotence of the district attorney's office in New York County." Discounting any possibility that Dodge could change the situation, Seabury rehashed the faults he found in Crain's office. His investigation, he reminded listeners, "showed how our industries were in the hands of racketeers who were in league with politicians and how this combination of crime and politics inflicted not only a tragic toll upon our industries but kept the workers and employers in a state of subjection to gangsters and other underworld forces." Dodge, recognizing the degree to which he was scorned by reformers, told a good-government group a month after the election that "At the present time I am probably the most unpopular man elected to office during the recent campaign because the opposition had control of the newspapers and not one made a favorable comment on me during the entire campaign." He added: "already the newspapers are advising me whom to select for my staff and crying out that the governor has the power to remove me if he sees fit to; and I have no redress. In spite of all that, I promise that you will not have any cause to regret my election."[19]

Dewey and his biographers mistakenly adopted the Fusion view of Dodge as a corrupt Tammany hack, despite evidence indicating that he was probably the wrong man in the wrong place at the wrong time. Even though Dodge was a Tammany candidate, he represented the better element of the machine. Early in his career he had bucked the party by resigning his Democratic seat in the state Senate and becoming a Republican to protest demagogic appeals from fellow party members. Dodge later switched back to the Democrats and served as an assistant in the district attorney's office from December 1924 until 1927, when he became a magistrate. Judging by his own comments, Dodge saw himself as being in the mold of Al Smith, who remained honest despite his Tammany connection. His biggest problem was not crookedness but his naive belief that "racketeering is no serious crime to combat."[20] Like his predecessor Crain, Dodge failed to comprehend the complexity of racketeering and the drastic changes that New York's prosecutorial institutions needed to meet the challenge.

Within three months, Dodge realized that his optimism was unfounded. In late February 1934, the district attorney complained to the *New York Times* that businessmen refused to testify before the grand jury he impaneled January 1 to investigate racketeering in the trucking industry. He estimated that millions of dollars were extorted yearly by gangsters who took three cents for every hundred pounds of merchandise arriving at the city's docks. He complained that "reputable business men who have been victimized say they would rather pay tribute than injure their businesses." Dodge's impotence fueled continual criticism by reformers who believed his ineffectiveness reflected corruption rather than incompetence. For example, in August 1934 a grand jury faulted Dodge for his office's lax presentation of evidence in a mortgage scandal.[21] Not until December 1934, however, did reformers and grand jurors find the issue they successfully could use against Dodge.

Early in 1934 Dodge impaneled a grand jury to hear evidence about gambling rackets, but after eleven months of questioning lawyers, citizens, and policemen, the jurors gave up with no visible results. They blamed their failure on reluctant witnesses and the fact that they were overburdened with routine cases. They urged Dodge to impanel a new grand jury which could devote all its time to investigating gamblers, the crooked lawyers who represented them, and gambling-related homicides. Specifically, the grand jury suggested that Dodge follow up the testimony of one attorney, who admitted he had a contract to fix cases with a gambler but refused to name the gambler.[22] The link between gambling and politicians was an old issue in New York, as shown by the fact that Arnold Rothstein's affiliation with Tammany was still a subject for public comment five years after his death. Despite the Depression, gambling's popularity soared, and by the early 1930s there were an estimated 15,000 numbers runners in the city.

The grand jurors' gambling investigation caught the attention of George Drew Egbert, a Congregational minister who headed the Society for the Prevention of Crime. On January 30, 1935, Egbert put the long-dormant society—which had been founded in 1878 as a temperance group—back in the headlines when he delivered a sermon entitled "For Every Man Shall Bear His Own Burden." Egbert galvanized his flock at the First Congregational Church in Flushing with these words. "Once in a while the city of New York is rotten with evil. Once in a while a dirty band of plunderers fasten their filthy claws on the vitals of the city and exploit the poor. Once in a while the police and the courts and the prosecutors stand helpless before robber gangs that are bloated with wealth filched from the meager funds of the hungry and the cold. Such a time is now! Somebody who loves his city must tell the black story or lose his own soul." Insisting that rackets needed political protection to survive, Egbert asked why authorities never had disclosed Tammany links with well-known gambling kingpins such as Dixie Davis, Dutch Schultz, and Bo Weinberg. Egbert contended that the big bosses went free while the judicial system put on a show for the public by collaring "small fry." He blamed the situation on corruption, lack of will, and "buck passing" by police, grand juries, judges, lawyers, and the mayor, who kept blaming each other rather than joining hands for useful action.[23]

Egbert's sermon received wide press coverage and set off a flurry of activity and even more name calling. La Guardia held a series of meetings about crime control with leaders of the bar such as Charles Burlingham and George Medalie, the former U.S. attorney who recently had called for stepped-up activity against racketeers. In late February, Egbert released the addresses of fifty-one supposed gambling dens, which he claimed was just a partial list of those his society had uncovered. Valentine defended the police, saying the list included repetitions and addresses that police had had under surveillance without success. He said one location was a Baptist Church "where no arrests have ever been made or complaints lodged as far as police records show." Egbert was unimpressed, accused the police chief and district attorney of stonewalling, and called for the appointment of a special prosecutor. On March 11, 1935, La Guardia released a memo from Valentine blaming the city's continued problem with gambling on the magistrates rather than the police. Valentine's memo showed that 91 percent of the cases brought by police between February 1 and September 30, 1934, never came to trial in the city's Court of Special Sessions. Of the 9 percent that did make it to court, only one-third ended in fines—mostly under fifty dollars. The maximum fine of five hundred dollars was levied only once. The report also showed only 3.6 percent of those arrested were given jail sentences; only one went to the penitentiary while most received ten days in jail.[24]

Valentine's report prompted calls for an investigation of numbers racketeers and their influence in the courts. In late February and early March of 1935, in response to the rising concern, Prosecutor Dodge announced to the press that he would indict Dutch Schultz, the Bronx-born gangster who had consolidated control of Manhattan's numbers business in the early 1930s. Dodge met with Samuel Marcus, counsel for the Society for the Prevention of Crime, to map strategy for an investigation. On March 4, he impaneled a grand jury to focus on bail bondsmen, numbers rackets, and prostitution and confidently told the *New York Times*, "There is no doubt that these rackets are run by rings, and we are going after the higher-ups who head these rings. The main drive will be against the chiefs, not the small fry. These rackets are vicious and they will be prosecuted by my office to the very limit."[25]

Dodge's efforts meant little to his critics, especially the Society for the

Prevention of Crime, whose board members included such prominent Fusionists as George W. Kirchwey, J. Edward Lumbard, and William Jay Schieffelin. The committee claimed Dodge's actions were a smoke screen for relative inaction. Committee members dismissed the grand jury investigation when it did not yield immediate results, notwithstanding the fact that former Republican U.S. Attorney George Medalie and his chief assistant Thomas Dewey had spent several years vainly trying to get enough evidence to indict Schultz and his political allies. Under almost daily questioning by the New York press—especially the pro–La Guardia *New York World-Telegram*—Dodge went on the defensive. On March 12 he told *The New York American* that gambling and prostitution would never be stamped out; the same day he admitted to the *World-Telegram* that he had been unable to provide the grand jury with the names of numbers bosses. Three days later he told the same paper that he was no closer to finding the "higher-ups" and wished Marcus and Egbert would give him some names.[26]

Egbert later admitted he had not told Dodge all he knew about Tammany's links to crime, presumably because he did not trust the district attorney. He apparently hoped to force Dodge into appointing Marcus as a special assistant, but the district attorney, laboring under the budget cuts forced on city departments by La Guardia's fiscal policy, refused to spend the extra money. Both Egbert and Marcus chafed under the perceived slight. Egbert claimed that Dodge "kept Marcus from conducting a proper investigation," and Marcus told a law society meeting at New York University on April 6, 1935, that Dodge's probe was "just a lot of hooey." Unlike Egbert and Marcus, however, many witnesses wanted to cooperate. La Guardia, Valentine, and other prominent city officials and reformers who contended there was a link between gambling and politicians were called before the grand jury to provide details. Under sharp questioning, it turned out that most of what they knew was more rumor and innuendo than hard fact. Although he had scant evidence with which to work, his critics believed Dodge was hiding information to protect his Tammany backers.[27]

He provided his critics with ammunition by mishandling the grand jurors. The jurors quickly concluded he was giving the gambling probe short shrift when he failed to impanel a second regular grand jury to hear routine cases. As a result, the special grand jury spent thirty days during March, April and May hearing ordinary matters instead of gambling evidence. Jurors also were frustrated by the district attorney's failure to maintain secrecy. Names of witnesses routinely leaked out; one hapless man simultaneously received a subpoena and a letter threatening him if he testified. Another witness received a menacing phone call advising him that the subpoena was on its way. Finally, the grand jury complained, Dodge had chosen the two youngest and least experienced members of his staff to handle the investigation. He had hoped to appease the grand jury by assigning one of two Republican assistants, Lyon Boston, whose father was president of the American Bar Association. This concession was lost on the jurors. Admitting that Boston and his colleague were honest and industrious, the jurors said that the investigation was beyond their capabilities: "Any one of the things that we had been asked to investigate was a major problem in itself and to throw it into the laps of these young men and expect them to produce anything worthwhile was asking the impossible."[28]

Under ordinary circumstances the grand jury's dissatisfaction with Dodge would have found no outlet; instances of successful runaway grand juries were rare. Disagreements between grand juries and Tammany district attorneys in New York County were nothing new, but they rarely broke out of narrowly confined legal channels. For example, Tammany district attorneys were much more likely to overlook corruption than the well-heeled, conservative Republicans who generally served as grand jurors. Occasionally grand juries that were particularly miffed issued reports criticizing the handling of problems like the city's widespread prostitution. Such reports made splashes but rarely resulted in long-lasting reform. Tammany controlled the legal machinery, and most grand jury foremen lacked the outside support to take on the machine. Only when this balance of power was upset could disputes become public.

Although the runaway grand jury of 1935 became the most famous, it was not the only one in New York County history. The last publicized attempt at grand jury independence in Manhattan had occurred in 1919 when a grand jury led by New York City architect Raymond F. Almirall challenged District Attorney Edward Swann. That case provides useful insights into what would happen sixteen years later. In the aftermath of World War I, the country was gripped by the Red Scare. New York joined the hysteria by impaneling a jury in August 1919 to investigate the city's anarchists. That vague mission quickly was channeled into a more politically lucrative area by Swann. The district attorney launched an inquiry into allegations that the wealthy, mostly Republican, backers of the Interborough Rapid Transit (IRT) had conspired with its workers to launch a strike and finagle a 3-cent hike in the subway fare. After Swann called his witnesses, the grand jurors independently summoned Mayor James Hylan, the city editor of the *New York American*, and the president of the Public Service Commission. Almirall maintained the jury's action was necessary because Swann had thwarted the grand jury's questioning of Democratic city officials, and he asked Governor Al Smith to appoint a special prosecutor who would be "absolutely free from bias and sinister newspaper and political influence." Swann countered by accusing the grand jury of blocking his probe and misusing its position to promote the interests of the transit system. He noted that Almirall had worked for the Interborough Construction Co., which was 98 percent owned by the IRT.[29]

A stalemate ensued as the grand jury tried to bolster its position by shifting its investigation to Arnold Rothstein's supposed links to politicians. Rumors swirled that the "Almirall grand jury" would indict Charles Murphy, Mayor Hylan, and other leading Democrats but nothing came of the investigation. In June 1920 it began to look even more like a fishing expedition when the jurors set out for the jail to ask prisoners if they knew of any wrongdoing. By tossing out such a wide net, the grand jury prompted some to call for a new grand jury to investigate the first panel's actions. As one critic wrote to Smith, the jurors' tour of the jail "shows . . . that they are working for the Republican Party and their game is to discredit the Democrats."[30] By appeasing the grand jury while keeping a firm grasp on the situation, Governor Al Smith forestalled a damaging probe.

In 1935, by contrast, Governor Lehman lost control of events. Several factors converged to create an atmosphere conducive to a successful grand jury revolt. First, the public outrage was fueled by anti-Tammany politicians, several of whom—notably La Guardia and Lehman—had the power to fight Tammany. More crucial perhaps was the grand jurors' changing sense of their own role and importance and their belief that they finally had found the case with which to pursue their agenda—the salvaging of the grand jury as an independent institution.

By 1935 the grand jury system in the United States was nearly moribund. Most legal scholars considered the panels little more than relics of English common law that had outlived any real usefulness. The drafters of the Fifth Amendment to the Constitution envisioned grand juries as bulwarks to protect innocent citizens from harassment by zealous prosecutors. In theory, the juries did this by screening charges and refusing to file baseless indictments. In frontier communities where professional lawyers were rare, grand juries served as necessary tools of legal machinery and also took over such governmental chores as setting tax rates. But the increasing complexity of government and the proliferation of lawyers had usurped the grand jury's traditional role. Even in cases where the panels still heard charges, they exhibited little independence and usually acted strictly in accordance with prosecutorial or judicial instructions. States began eliminating the use of grand juries in the mid-nineteenth century, and this trend accelerated by the early 1930s as law review articles routinely advocated their abolition. American opponents of the juries had even more ammunition against them after 1933, when tradition-bound England abolished its panels as a costly and unnecessary burden.[31]

Grand juries in New York had enjoyed a long and esteemed history, but even there the outcry against them was increasing. Critics, including judges and the New York County Lawyers Association, argued that grand juries were costly, inefficient, and easily manipulated, and that they should be replaced by more "modern and scientific" investigative tools. Nonetheless, would-be abolitionists faced an uphill battle, because of tradition and, more importantly, because of the wealth and power of grand jurors. Serving on a grand jury was considered such a badge of honor that some citizens schemed to get on the panels to further their social contacts. Like their peers on trial juries, grand jurors had to meet educational, age, and property requirements. To serve as a grand juror a citizen also had to have trial experience, make a special application, and meet the approval of a commission comprising the mayor and four judges. In practice, men who met these requirements tended to be wealthy or prominent businessmen who could take time off from work, had the connections to be recommended to the commission, and took great pride in serving the community. John D. Rockefeller, Jr., was so impressed with the system when he served as a grand juror that he provided money to help found the Association of Grand Jurors of New York County in 1913.[32]

The association survived into the 1920s and found renewed purpose in defending the grand jury system against its critics. To further its goals it began publishing *The Panel*, a journal devoted to criminal justice issues, in 1924. Throughout the mid-1920s, the association's elitist overtones were apparent. Arguing that the best way to silence critics was to improve the quality of jurors, it urged its members to behave in a more gentlemanly manner by not smoking and reading newspapers during sessions. *Panel* articles also suggested a number of procedural changes, including allowing fewer jury exemptions, eliminating petit jury service requirements, prohibiting defense lawyers from reading grand jury minutes, relieving juries of insignificant cases, improving acoustics in the jury rooms, and increasing panel sizes to ease case overloads. Finally, the association opposed allowing women to serve, explaining that details of "atrocious" crimes "would be revolting to their delicate sensibilities." Citing the Supreme Court, an editorial in *The Panel* said, "the future of the race" was more important than women's legal rights and that "the maintenance of healthy women and the need for healthy offspring" outweighed considerations of women's "earning capacity or ambitions." Arguments that a woman was entitled to a jury of her peers were as ludicrous as saying that a "man over seventy who cannot read or write was entitled to a jury of senile illiterates."[33]

The association largely was ignored as long as its message focused only on the grand jury, but as it branched out into larger reform efforts it gained a wider audience. Criminal reform was a hot issue in the late 1920s. The growth of sociology and criminology provided faith that if crime could be studied and its causes isolated, it could be brought under control. *The Panel* played a large role in this new movement, advocating improved statistics gathering, more "modern and scientific" crime detection, standardization of laws, and centralization of criminal justice institutions. The association also lent its support to improvements sought by other groups, including better extradition laws, handgun control, tougher perjury and anti-fencing statutes, bail bond reforms, improved prison conditions, and better self-policing by the bar.[34] Through its support of state legislative committees and its willingness to provide a forum to prominent jurists, *The Panel* gained credibility and willing listeners to its grandiose plans for a revamped grand jury system.

In addition to widening its perspective, the grand jury association refined its agenda. In 1925 it advocated the alarming idea of deputizing the county's twelve hundred grand jurors as a "secret police" force, asserting that other citizens would not mind being spied on by men "of high standing, but more importantly of good judgment."[35] By 1935 the association had adopted the more sophisticated arguments of leading criminal lawyers who believed that existing local law enforcement agencies were incapable of combating organized crime. Grand jurors, and some attorneys, believed the grand jury was the perfect institution to help fight the syndicates that flourished after Rothstein's death. As one law professor argued, the grand jury historically had enjoyed two functions—passing on indictments presented by prosecutors and instituting broad investigations. The first was the most common assignment, but it relegated jurors to the status of little more than tools of prosecutors. The second function, if reinstituted on a regular basis, would provide a long-term method of keeping track of organized crime while arousing public attention. Commentators pointed out that while corrupt politicians could manipulate other parts of the legal system, the grand jury system remained inviolate. Most lawyers and law professors who argued for enhanced grand jury powers undoubtedly envisioned that panels would continue to work under the leadership of prosecutors. They emphasized the broad subpoena powers enjoyed by grand juries and their abilities to get evidence by threatening reluctant witnesses with jail sentences for contempt—a power denied police and prosecutors. Grand jury leaders, on the other hand, took this debate as an invitation to show their independence—to instigate their own investigations and then demand that special lawyers be assigned to help them, rather than vice versa.[36]

The idea of grand jury independence found its voice when the grand jurors impaneled in March 1935 to hear numbers cases joined hands with District Attorney Dodge's political opponents. The precipitating factor was a series of newspaper articles carried in late March by the *New York American*, detailing the continued existence of gambling rackets despite the special grand jury investigation. Reporter Martin Mooney quoted smug gamblers who bragged that they had little to fear from Dodge because their activities were protected by prominent Manhattan politicians. When Mooney appeared before the grand jury, he refused to name his sources—not because it violated his journalistic ethics but because he was afraid of angering racketeers. He was sentenced to thirty days in jail and fined $250 for contempt; the grand jury said the fact that he feared racketeers more than the law was "a sad commentary on our city." The grand jurors aired their frustrations about Mooney and other uncooperative witnesses to Judge Morris Koenig in open court on May 7: "This panel has no desire to be classified as reformers, nor did we hope to change human nature, or legislate morals. We did hope, however, to break up the rings or systems that we have been told prevail."[37]

Word of the grand jury's dissatisfaction prompted the Fusionist *World-Telegram* to hint that Dodge himself could be indicted for his attempts to protect gamblers and crooked politicians. Egbert, railing from his pulpit on May 13, commented on the grand jury's frustration and the fact that it had launched its own investigation by calling both La Guardia and Valentine to testify, despite Dodge's opposition. The minister called for the appointment of a special prosecutor. His suggestion was followed up several days later by the City Affairs Committee, which sent a telegram to Governor Lehman asking him to take action because Dodge had been discredited and "proved himself inefficient or worse. In spite of able and courageous grand juries and an aroused public opinion, there can be little done so long as this man occupies an office which he uses only to cheer himself and jeer his critics."[38]

To forestall action by the governor, Dodge met with grand jurors on May 22 and agreed to appoint a special prosecutor from a list of names they compiled after consulting with leaders of the city bar association and the New York County Lawyers Association. During a meeting with the grand jurors several days later, Dodge balked at the Republican names on the list and what he called "a political plot on the part of the bar association to place him on the spot." He told the jurors they were being manipulated and suggested they compromise on a lawyer pro-

posed by former Republican Governor Nathan Miller. Jurors were unprepared for this, but agreed to check out the proposed candidate, H. H.
Corbin. Dodge then offended the jurors by going ahead and naming
Corbin without their consent on June 4. The district attorney defended
his action by finding fault with all of the other men on the list. He said
several refused the job, others did not live in the city, and Dewey "was
too young and too ambitious and might make political capital of his
appointment." The jury balked at what they considered Dodge's high-
handedness and refused to go along with Corbin's appointment. Dodge
was ill prepared for the row that ensued. Corbin refused the appointment
on June 7 because of negative publicity, and Dodge made a last-ditch
effort to appease the jury. After presenting his last witness on June 10,
1935, Dodge offered to provide any member of his sixty-four-person staff
to help if the grand jurors wanted to call witnesses on their own. Citing
the newspaper criticism, Dodge pleaded with the grand jurors to provide
him with more evidence or instances in which he had been uncooperative. He said, "If you men are fair—as I presume you are—you will tell
me whether you have any evidence, so that I may present that evidence
and so that we will not continue to be coming here perpetually, wasting
our time." But they were not appeased and refused to answer him. Instead, they scheduled an executive session to plan their next move.[39]

The following day the grand jurors agreed to disband, but they issued
a scathing report: "The evidence, while incomplete and inconclusive, has
convinced us that these types of crimes (commercial prostitution, bail
bond abuses, numbers operations, and other so-called rackets) are rampant and have reached such proportions as to constitute a public menace
with potentialities for the corruption of the agencies of law enforcement." The jurors said it was clear that organized crime could not be
attacked by regular law enforcement machinery, and they requested a
meeting with Governor Lehman to explain the need for a special prosecutor and special grand jury to continue the investigation. Lehman met
with them on June 18 at his Park Avenue apartment and called Dodge to
Albany three days later. After reading the grand jury transcript, Lehman
met with La Guardia, Valentine, and two police inspectors, all of whom
favored the investigation.

Only a few skeptical voices spoke out. One Brooklyn newspaper editorialized that "the alleged vice rackets are largely the product of sensational newspapers" and defended Dodge as a "gentleman and a scholar" who had "been crucified by the gutter press and the Fusion and Republican politicians." Two of the jurors on the runaway grand jury wrote to Lehman complaining about what had happened. Abraham Tolleris said he had served on many panels without incident and was surprised by the unwarranted hostility jury foreman Lee Thompson Smith showed towards Dodge. Tolleris speculated that many jurors went along with Smith, hoping they could compromise with the district attorney. When Corbin's name was suggested, everyone thought the compromise had been reached. Tolleris was surprised to read in the next day's newspapers that Smith had rejected Corbin without consulting him or other panel members. The other dissenting grand juror, C. A. Rogers, also believed that Dodge sincerely wanted to help the jury uncover vice. But, he said, when the newspapers began daily criticism of the grand jury investigation, many of the jurors claimed to be "afraid of being held up to ridicule by the press unless we actually were able to obtain evidence to indict the so-called higher-ups in the various rackets." Despite the fact that Smith bucked the district attorney and called his own witnesses, Rogers said, "not one iota of evidence was presented before our body to show that either Judge Dodge or any of his assistants were negligent in their duties." Although several witnesses, including Valentine and Commissioner of Markets William Fellowes Morgan, said they had much information about rackets, the juror declared, all they testified to was gossip and rumors. In his letter to the governor Rogers pointed out that "the particular crime activities which are alleged to exist at the present time have been existing for many years back and in the past years our present foreman, Mr. Lee Thompson Smith, has been foreman of many grand juries and at no time did he ever bring up the question of having the district attorney of New York County who was in office at that time superseded by a special prosecutor." Rogers speculated that if New York City's newspapers "had been as passive during the time the March Grand Jury was in session as they were in the many years past there would have been no necessity of having this matter brought before you."[40]

Lehman shared some of the skepticism. Although he believed the call for an investigation was largely an attempt to discredit the Democratic

Party, he also thought the grand jury's report "outlined a situation that was sufficiently forceful, of sufficient public interest, to justify further careful study." His retrospective account points out that "there were other groups seeking this too, and the newspapers of the time played it up very considerably. . . . Public opinion built up around this issue, and it became very much a cause célèbre." The governor felt compelled "to satisfy the public interest in this matter, either by disclosing the thing or by proving that it wasn't so." Lehman realized that Dodge was ill equipped to mount such an investigation. He did not think the district attorney was dishonest but saw him as a weak administrator who let lackluster assistants run his office.[41]

On June 24, Lehman announced the need for a nonpartisan investigation. He hoped to appease Dodge by saying no one had given him any evidence to discredit the district attorney, adding that such a massive investigation needed the services of a special prosecutor who could devote all his time "in a manner that is not possible for any district attorney who is burdened with the tremendous mass of regular law enforcement functions." He ordered Dodge to appoint one of New York's four most prominent Republican lawyers as a special prosecutor. His list included former U.S. Attorney George Medalie, Charles Evans Hughes, Jr., former bar association president Thomas Thacher, and former U.S. attorney and 1930 gubernatorial candidate Charles Tuttle.[42]

Dodge contacted all four men to no avail. Hughes and Tuttle claimed to have previous commitments; Thacher said he did not want to resign from the commission revising New York City's charter. Medalie, who did not want to neglect his clients, said he would think it over. When Medalie called Dodge the following afternoon, he explained that he had met with Tuttle, Thacher, and Hughes and the four had issued a press release urging that Dewey be appointed. Lehman reacted promptly to the rebuff, publicly stating that he had chosen the four men because they would inspire public confidence. In light of the public furor, he said, he felt he was "entitled to demand cooperation of all good citizens" and asked the four to meet with him privately. After a meeting on June 29, the men refused to reconsider and Lehman agreed to appoint Dewey.[43]

The Republicans clearly had outmaneuvered Lehman. By not acting more quickly, the governor had given Medalie time to rally support for

Dewey from newspapers and such Republican-leaning groups as the Association of Grand Jurors and the executive committee of the bar association. Years later Lehman concluded that there was definitely a pro-Dewey conspiracy. Although each of his four candidates for special prosecutor had told him they intended to devote themselves to private matters, Hughes went on to become solicitor general of the United States, Thacher joined the New York Court of Appeals, Tuttle remained active in politics, and Medalie served as Dewey's political mentor and was rewarded by an appointment to the state's appellate court. Yet in 1935, it was not clear why Republicans had gone to such lengths for Dewey. Most special prosecutors appointed to uncover scandals in New York had been senior members of the bar like Seabury. Lehman had never met Dewey. As far as he could discern, Dewey was a thirty-three-year-old lawyer who never had held elected office, had gained a good reputation working for Medalie, and had but one claim to fame—his successful prosecution of Dutch Schultz while acting U.S. Attorney.[44]

Lehman let his view of Dewey's youth and inexperience cloud his otherwise acute political judgment. Had he known the extent of Dewey's ambitions and the reasons why the Republican establishment had gone to such efforts on his behalf, Lehman might have appointed someone else. As it was, he set in motion one of the most interesting examples of political manipulation of the legal system in American history. The governor's naïveté about Dewey stands in stark contrast to the prescient view of his chief advisor, Charles Poletti. Unlike Lehman, Poletti knew Dewey personally, perceived him as ruthless, and correctly predicted that he was as interested in making headlines as in promoting serious reform. Poletti urged the governor to appoint a prominent and honest lawyer before the Republican leaders had time to marshal their forces. He was vacationing in Montana when he learned of Dewey's appointment: he said, "I was sick for two days, because I just had a feeling that it was such a serious mistake to put in Dewey. I knew Dewey . . . and he was unscrupulously ambitious."[45]

≈ ≈ ≈

CHAPTER THREE

Thomas E. Dewey's Rise from Obscurity

*D*EWEY AND HIS political handlers concocted a legend about how he became New York County's special prosecutor. According to the mythmakers, Dewey was the only lawyer skilled enough, experienced enough, and self-sacrificing enough to tackle Manhattan's racketeers. In reality, Dewey's ascendancy had more to do with politicking than with his prosecutorial abilities. Dewey cultivated ties with Republicans, leading members of the bar, and such civic groups as the grand jury association. They, in turn, recognized his political potential, masterminded his rise, and engineered his appointment. From the outset, Dewey and his allies saw the prosecutor's post as a stepping-stone to the governorship and the White House. Those political plums, however, would be attainable only if Dewey succeeded, and his job was formidable. He faced the awesome task of revamping New York's antiquated legal machinery to fight modern, organized crime. His previous experience as a federal prosecutor served him well. During the late 1920s and early 1930s, federal agents and prosecutors pioneered new techniques to battle gangsters like Al Capone. Among the most innovative federal prosecutors was Dewey's mentor, George Medalie, who mapped out a comprehensive strategy for battling organized crime. Medalie, a leading member of the bar and the Republican party, had recognized Dewey's talents at their first meeting in 1930. More than anyone else he was responsible for the younger man's success.

Writers looking at Dewey's later career have argued, illogically, that his genius was apparent from the outset. In reality, Medalie showed great perception in discerning talent in the undistinguished young lawyer. Little in Dewey's early life presaged his later fame. He was born in 1902 in Owosso, Michigan, where his father edited the newspaper. During his youth, the town in central Michigan's farming belt had a population of about 12,000. In 1966 Dewey told an interviewer that "the beautiful thing . . . about it was that there was total freedom, within hours and within parental limitations. . . . The most dangerous thing that could happen would be a runaway horse, which didn't happen often." He recalled that Owosso "was such a Republican community that it wasn't quite respectable to be a Democrat." Young Dewey grew up hearing that his grandfather had attended the first Republican state convention in 1854 and had accompanied President McKinley on speaking tours. His uncle ran for Congress, and his father held several political posts, including that of postmaster.[1]

As a boy Dewey held odd jobs and gained a reputation among his schoolmates for arrogance, ambition, and contentiousness. In 1919 he entered the University of Michigan to study music, and in 1923 he entered the law school while still completing his bachelor's degree. Dewey maintained only a B— average, in part because he was pursuing simultaneously careers in law and opera. In the summer of 1923 he went to Chicago to study voice and met his future wife, Frances Hutt, a fellow vocal student from Sherman, Texas. When Hutt left for New York, Dewey followed her, transferring to Columbia University's law school and continuing to pursue his musical career. After a disastrous performance in 1924 he abandoned his singing aspirations. Even Dewey's teacher criticized him for performing with too much technique and too little feeling.[2]

After giving up singing, Dewey improved his law grades but was still, according to one friend, only "a fair-to-middlin' student" overshadowed by such brilliant classmates as William O. Douglas. Upon graduation, Dewey received only three job offers; and after passing the bar in 1925, he accepted an offer from the firm of Larkin, Rathbone, and Perry. Frustrated by how slowly his ambition was being met in the large law firm, Dewey argued with a partner and was fired early in 1927. He found another job with a small firm, McNamara and Seymour, despite McNamara's concerns that Dewey might prove to be "a little too bumptious." Dewey overcame all doubts with his hard work. He handled two or three small cases before getting his first big assignment, defending the Empire Trust Company against a suit by one of its investors. The shareholder, Nancy Glover Kaufmann, traded her preferred stock for common stock, and during the transaction, the stock's value plummeted. She sued for the difference in value, a matter of less than $35,000. Although in monetary terms this was a small suit, it gave Dewey the biggest boost of his career when he was told to retain the help of an outside trial lawyer. On the advice of a friend, Dewey sought out Medalie, who was generally regarded as one of New York City's best barristers.[3]

By any measure Medalie was a remarkable man who combined a love of scholarship with practical legal skills. Like many first-generation Americans of his era, Medalie succeeded despite hardship. He was born in 1883 to poor immigrants on New York's Lower East Side. Only seven when his father died, he was forced to work after school to support his mother and two sisters. He studied Greek literature and worked as a schoolteacher before receiving a scholarship to Columbia University Law School, where he was a classmate of Franklin Roosevelt. Between 1910 and 1916, Medalie was an assistant in the New York County district attorney's office. Part of his tenure overlapped with that of Charles S. Whitman, the famous district attorney who parlayed his crusades against Tammany Hall into the governorship of New York between 1914 and 1918.[4]

After leaving the district attorney's office, Medalie, instead of joining a large law firm, set up a small practice based largely on referrals for trial and appellate work. This arrangement allowed him independence from dull retainer jobs and provided the opportunity to select only challenging or lucrative cases. William Herlands, who went to work for Medalie in 1928, said his mentor "was at heart a scholar" who read the history of common law as well as Talmudic, Canon, and Roman law. Medalie surrounded himself with young lawyers, saying they "brought with them the latest ideas, good, bad, or indifferent, but at least they were stimulating, if not irritating." He enjoyed the give-and-take of the relationships and also believed that "senior members of the bar had a moral and professional responsibility to the younger members of the bar."[5]

Medalie recognized Dewey's talents at once. When Dewey showed up at his office in the morning to discuss the stock case, the pair ended up talking until midnight. Medalie, a perfectionist, recognized the same trait in Dewey. Undoubtedly, he also was impressed with Dewey's Republican credentials. While working at Larkin, Rathbone, and Perry, Dewey had met another young lawyer—Sewell Tappan Tyng—a grandson of New York's Episcopal bishop. Tyng was a captain of the Tenth Assembly District, which stretched from Washington Square to 56th Street and from Third to Eighth avenues. Tyng took Dewey to see the district leader, Francis R. Stoddard, who promised Dewey he could become a captain if he rang enough doorbells during the October election. Dewey succeeded and in the following years he canvassed voters and helped guard the polls against the floaters and thugs who plagued the city during these notoriously corrupt years.[6]

It is doubtful that Dewey—or any of the younger Republican organizers—would have attracted much attention if they had stuck to such mundane party activities. But in 1926 Dewey and others, displeased with politics as usual, reorganized the Young Republican Club, which had fallen into lethargy after its incorporation in 1912. The club's new leaders, young professionals who were not native New Yorkers, had been steeped in the anti-Tammany rhetoric of the American hinterlands. They could not stomach the kinds of deals that Republican leaders routinely made with the corrupt Democratic machine. During the late 1920s and early 1930s the Republican party in New York County was troubled by the same weaknesses in political leadership as Tammany. The conservative old guard seemed ill equipped to handle the demands of the changing times. The party had fallen into an uneasy accommodation with Tammany, receiving a few judgeships and other minor patronage jobs as a reward for not making trouble. The Young Republicans' self-proclaimed purpose was to support the party while cleansing it of corruption and undue partisanship. The club grew quickly in both membership and influence. By 1928 it had several committees and 2,100 members, most of whom were bankers and lawyers between twenty-six and forty years of age.[7]

Dewey served on several Young Republican committees. In early 1927, he became a member of the city affairs and law committees, which considered, among other matters, an amendment establishing a preferred jury list made up of citizens who voted. The committees also supported noise-reduction campaigns and lowering the fares of ferries running to the Statue of Liberty. Perhaps Dewey's most important assignment in the organization was as chairman of the city affairs subcommittee investigating Tammany's fiscal mismanagement. Practicing the sarcastic rhetoric he honed in later years, Dewey wrote that "ever since Isaac Newton discovered the law of gravitation, it has been generally accepted dogma that 'what goes up must come down.' So year after year, the taxpayers of the city of New York appear to have placidly watched the Budget of the City rise like a free balloon, sure of its eventual descent. But the Budget of the City of New York vigorously denies the existence of all natural laws, and condemns sane finance as the idle amusement of the feeble-minded. In the absence of a miracle, this Budget will exceed 500 million dollars for the year 1928."[8]

The Young Republicans' activities attracted the attention of the party's old guard, which increasingly enlisted their aid as foot soldiers. In the 1930 gubernatorial campaign, the Young Republicans dug up dirt on dishonest Tammany magistrates, dirt that—thanks to La Guardia's mayoral election the previous year—had become a political cause célèbre. The Young Republicans sent out approximately eight speakers each night in the two weeks before the election. Dewey, who headed the speakers' bureau, already showed political acumen by recognizing the limited appeal of the one issue, anti-Tammany rhetoric used by Republican gubernatorial candidate and former U.S. attorney Charles Tuttle. As Dewey noted, Tuttle and "other Republican speakers have laid great stress on the Tammany issue; they have sounded the keynote of graft, corruption and incompetence and the people are certainly aware of the situation. If these issues interest the people, they are already convinced. On the other hand, if they are not now convinced they never will be." Dewey argued that it would be better if speakers addressed more constructive themes, such as the need for a city charter, water power, and the president's unemployment commission. "I think people will respect our speakers more and listen more closely if we have something affirmative to say." After Tuttle lost the election to Roosevelt, the Young Republicans joined the party's push for a Seabury-led legislative investigation of New York City government.[9]

The party's old guard was willing to enlist the aid of Young Republicans but unwilling to share power. Samuel Koenig, who had been New York's boss since 1911, began meeting with the Young Republican leadership in 1927. His grudging recognition of their efforts was not enough to appease them, however, and by 1929 they wrote to the state chairman seeking "unification" of the party in the city. They decried the splintered leadership among the five boroughs and the appearance of back room decision making, which, they argued, undermined public confidence in the selection of candidates. Dewey endorsed a plan to modernize the party by, among other things, replacing the five borough committees with one city chairman.[10] Enlightened party elders, although they knew it would take several years to reform the party's leadership structure, recognized the merit of the Young Republican efforts and began courting their support. Many of these men, including George Medalie, had cultural, ethical, and philosophical differences with the party's leaders. La Guardia, Medalie, and other liberal Republicans had matured during the Progressive Era; they believed the party had to change its message of wealth and privilege to attract younger, more appealing candidates.

One established proving ground for gathering and molding young Republicans in New York was the U.S. attorney's office. This became particularly true in the mid-1920s with the appointment of Emery Buckner, who wanted to create a high-quality office despite limited funds. To meet his standards, he hired recent law school graduates rather than older party hacks demanding high salaries. He appeased party leaders by telling them, "I will make this office a recruiting ground, not a dumping ground for politicians." True to his word, in 1926 Buckner summoned his assistants and told them he was reviving the Young Republican Club and expected them to join. Medalie kept up the tradition when he became U.S. attorney for the Southern District of New York in 1930. Propitiously, Medalie learned of his appointment while trying the stock case with Dewey in January 1931. Medalie won the appointment after a stalemate developed over the two leading contenders and so became the first Jewish U.S. attorney of the nation's largest federal court district. When he accepted the appointment, he asked Dewey for a list of young Republican lawyers who might be interested in working for him. Dewey supplied the names, including information about himself.[11]

Characteristically, in later years, Dewey embellished the events that led to his appointment as Medalie's chief assistant. Looking back, he told interviewers that he initially had turned down an offer to head the criminal division and only reluctantly accepted the more important job of Medalie's chief assistant. He debated taking the job, he said, because it entailed a $1,000-per-year pay cut but finally accepted "because it was like being offered the governorship at forty. I was then twenty-eight." In reality, Dewey solicited the job with "anything but blushing reticence," according to biographer Richard Norton Smith. Dewey's tax return for 1929 and the recollection of friends that he had lost heavily in the stock market crash suggest he did not suffer financially by accepting the $7,500-per-year federal job.[12]

Dewey painted a similarly exaggerated role of his early days in public office. Because Medalie "picked men he trusted and gave them too much to do and full authority," Dewey maintained, he pretty much had a free hand. In his new job, he picked men fresh from law school, others from downtown law offices, and many from the Young Republicans. At the same time, Dewey said, he took over the income tax division of the office. However taken with Dewey he may have been, Medalie undoubtedly recognized that his young assistant had neither trial nor administrative experience. Medalie, ever the schoolteacher, impressed Dewey and his other young assistants with his demanding requirements. At the outset, he called all his assistants into his office to tell them that although politics had gotten them their jobs, it would not be enough to keep them there. He set extremely high ethical standards for the office, standards Dewey described in later years: "No assistant could have any outside employment, or any outside practice. You had to live on your salary and give your all to the government." Medalie, unlike his protégé, eschewed trying defendants in the press. As Dewey recalled, "No photographs were ever allowed of any assistant and any defendant. That's a cheap way of seeking publicity and very common. No announcements about cases were permitted, the giving away of evidence in advance, except to the extent necessary in the court room upon the handing up of an indictment, or an arraignment." Medalie also held his staff to exacting legal expectations. A perfectionist who "preached the dogma of detail," he told his assistants to operate with the "premise that the truth is usually hidden in, behind and underneath the apparently innocuous, small, innocent-looking circumstance."[13]

It was an exciting time to be a federal prosecutor. Prohibition enforcement, although largely unsuccessful, had fostered an expansion of the federal government's role in crime fighting. The degree to which federal agents had honed their tools against organized crime was demonstrated by the prosecution of Al Capone, whose case was coming to trial in Chicago as Medalie took office. The Internal Revenue Service, emboldened by its success against Capone, was extending its war against gangsters to New York, and Medalie and his staff were willing allies. Medalie recognized that the grand jury, if its powers could be expanded, would be a valuable tool in complex investigations. He assigned William Herlands to research the history of the system to unearth support for a stronger role. Herlands came up with "John Doe" investigatory powers, which the grand jury could use to probe general conditions without having a specific target. While the idea of a broad-based grand jury investigation was not new, by the 1930s it was rarely used; prosecutors mostly used grand juries to approve indictments. By contrast, Medalie impaneled many grand juries for long periods of time and was thus able to collect evidence from smaller cases to amass information about a larger problem. He instructed his staff "to regard each case that came into the office . . . not as an end unto itself, but as a possible symptom of a deeper malady. . . . The theory was not just to prosecute the little fellow, or the small fry, but to use each case as a possible spring board for driving a wedge into a larger criminal activity of which this particular case might have been merely a symptom."[14]

Another practical consequence of lengthy grand jury investigations was what Medalie called "freezing the defense witnesses." Medalie taught his staff to anticipate which evidence defense attorneys would present at trial. By extending the grand jury's investigation, prosecutors could call potential witnesses before the panel to get their sworn statements. Then, when the case came to trial, none of them could change their stories; if they did so, they could be challenged. Extending the grand jury probe also bought time to locate people and to pressure reluctant witnesses until they could be "made to sing." In addition, longer investigations gave victims a sense that serious efforts were being made to address their complaints.[15]

Medalie adopted an equally creative attitude toward other parts of the legal system. Like the prosecutors who convicted Capone on tax evasion rather than bootlegging charges, he recognized "that the armory of the law had many powerful weapons that had not been used." He assigned assistants to sift through federal statutes "to find out what laws, obscure or otherwise, were there that could be reactivated and recruited into the service of the prosecutor." For example, Medalie invoked a law passed during Reconstruction to investigate election fraud in Harlem. To legal sticklers squeamish about using any means to reach an end who found something immoral about convicting a bootlegger on an unrelated charge such as tax fraud, Medalie replied that "from the point of view of the community it makes no difference what statute you use so long as the positive affirmative result of convicting the criminal for a crime which he committed is accomplished."[16]

The aggressiveness and creativity of federal prosecutors provided a stark contrast to the ineffectual efforts of Tammany district attorneys. While Medalie's office was functioning essentially as a legal laboratory, the New York County district attorneys "were ineffective because they were the supine heirs of an archaic way of looking at the criminal law." Whereas federal prosecutors worked with investigators to develop evidence and make their own cases, the local district attorney went into "action only after a case was brought to him on a silver platter" by the police. While federal prosecutors were convinced they could beat organized crime, the district attorney's office saw itself as helpless. In fact, in many ways, Tammany district attorneys were hamstrung. With much broader jurisdiction under state law, they had to prosecute more cases and could not be so selective as their federal counterparts. Nor did the New York City Police have the resources enjoyed by federal agencies. In putting together his largest cases against gambler Henry Miro and bootlegger Waxey Gordon, Dewey worked with accountants who pored over bank records, experts who traced telephone calls, and handwriting specialists.[17]

To some extent, of course, federal law enforcement benefited from the end of Prohibition. During the 1920s, federal agents had been criticized from all sides. Those who favored Prohibition claimed the agents were incompetent and corrupt, while to "wets" federal bootleg agents were viewed as meddlers. Once the public recognized that controlling liquor was a lost cause, however, federal agencies branched out and began to be held in higher esteem. This was particularly true in the early 1930s as J. Edgar Hoover—and to a lesser extent other federal law enforcement officials—switched efforts to more spectacular and successful enterprises such as arresting kidnappers. This trend toward federalism became more pronounced in the late 1920s and early 1930s as legal reformers, disgusted with their inability to remake machine-controlled local law enforcement, began calling for a wider federal role. This national trend was manifest in New York City, where Medalie and his assistants benefited from and were able to exploit the growing hostility to Tammany.[18]

As Dewey remembered, the Seabury investigations were turning up "colorful cases" the Internal Revenue Service was eager to pursue. Dewey organized a tax division in the U.S. attorney's office and "started this long dreary process of building up the cases and trying to break the little people to get them to testify against the big ones." The complex investigations bore fruit in Dewey's two most famous prosecutions as a federal lawyer: his convictions of Harlem numbers boss Henry Miro and bootlegger Waxey Gordon. Dewey had tried other significant cases, but it was Gordon's trial that captured the public attention. Gordon was New York's Al Capone, and his trial became a sensation as Dewey outlined the extent of Gordon's empire. After hearing several weeks of testimony, the jury deliberated only fifty-one minutes before convicting Gordon. He was slapped with a ten-year sentence and an $80,000 fine.[19]

As federal agents bore down on Gordon, Dutch Schultz, one of his biggest rivals for New York's beer empire, conducted business as usual. For him and the other gangsters in New York that meant buying and selling elections. In the summer of 1932, while he was campaigning for a state senate seat, Republican Walter S. Mack, Jr., was taken to a poolroom in Manhattan to visit Schultz. As Mack recalled, "I was the only one seated at the table who didn't have a shoulder holster, so I felt a little lonely. . . . After two or three beers, he said he was very much interested in the upper end of my district and that if I wanted to get elected, he could see to it that I got the votes I needed." Schultz told Mack he would not have to bother campaigning if he paid $5,000. Mack declined the deal, and chaos reigned on election day. Schultz's henchmen intimidated Mack's would-be supporters, while poll watchers "were hit on the head and thrown out." Mack appealed to the police, who did nothing but stand and watch the mêlée. After losing the election, Mack hired a private detective to protect him while he gathered affidavits from voters about the violence. Both the district attorney and state Attorney General John J. Bennett, Jr., refused to take action. Mack then appealed to J. Edgar Hoover, who referred the problem to Medalie, who assigned it to Dewey. Within ten days, Dewey presented the case to the grand jury and won indictments against all election board members. Only a few of them went to jail, however, because most fled to such sunny havens as Miami and the Bahamas.[20]

Mack's experience pointed up several currents at work. First, it showed the degree to which corruption had infected New York politics and state law enforcement. Second, it demonstrated the ability of federal authorities to go where state officials feared to tread. Third, it indicated the degree to which a Republican U.S. attorney was able to use his office for political gain—with an unusual twist. Federal prosecutors, who are often Republican, have always shown a willingness to go after city machines, which tend to be Democratic. In this case, however, Medalie and Dewey also found a way to exploit the rift in their own party. Mack initially took his complaint to Republican leader Samuel Koenig. When Koenig did nothing, Mack threatened to expose him for cooperating with Democratic corruption at the polls.[21] Both Republican and Democratic election judges were indicted by Dewey. The Young Republicans in the U.S. Attorney's Office, spurred by Mack's case and the larger picture of political corruption and compliance painted by the Seabury probe, were quick to exploit the situation.

This was particularly true of Dewey, who had become steeped in party affairs while still an assistant U.S. attorney. Dewey's first stint as a political handler came in 1931 when he worked to elect Herbert Brownell to the state assembly. Brownell, who later became U.S. attorney general, recalled how the Seabury investigation spurred the Young Republicans to concentrate their efforts on electing Brownell as the only anti-Tammany state assemblyman from the city. The Republican old guard gave the go-ahead for Brownell to run from the Tenth Assembly District in mid-Manhattan. Brownell claimed that party leaders acquiesced because they needed the extra manpower in other districts and believed the Tenth was unwinnable anyway. The 1931 campaign Dewey managed focused on only one issue: Tammany corruption and the need for continued funding for Seabury's investigation. Brownell lost, however, when Democratic opponent Langdon Post broke with his own party and promptly won endorsements from Seabury and the *New York Times*. The following year, however, Tammany fought Post with a vengeance, thereby splitting the Democratic vote and handing Brownell a victory.[22]

Lack of party support for Brownell, combined with growing mistrust of Koenig, galvanized the Young Republicans' push for a stronger voice in the party hierarchy. Dewey said later that although he was fond of Koenig, the older man "became a symbol of defeat, and so I went out and punched doorbells to unseat him, and we succeeded." Simultaneously, he ran George Medalie's campaign for the U.S. Senate. Medalie's platform relied heavily on the fact that he had raised the U.S. attorney's office to "new high records of efficiency" with convictions of men such as racketeer Jack "Legs" Diamond; crooked vice cop James J. Quinlivan, who had framed innocent women on prostitution charges; and gamblers Henry Miro and Wilfred Brunder. Republicans also argued that Medalie's many legal reform activities for the New York Bar Association and New York County Lawyer's Association had paved the way "for better handling of the legal problems of the average citizen."[23] But appeals to legal reform proved unpersuasive to a voting public more concerned with the Depression, and Medalie's political hopes were buried in the Democratic landslide of 1932.

After the loss, Medalie, like Seabury, turned away from seeking office to promoting other candidates. While Seabury pushed for La Guardia, Medalie groomed Dewey. Medalie's efforts began soon after his defeat; on November 21, his fiftieth birthday, he resigned his office in order to let Dewey serve as the U.S. attorney for one month. During this period, Dewey garnered headlines and his first newsreel exposure by prosecuting bootlegger Waxey Gordon. Roosevelt's appointee as the next federal prosecutor, Martin Conboy, offered Dewey the chance to stay on as chief assistant, but Dewey chose instead to take over the lease and furniture at Medalie's old law offices at 120 Broadway. In large part thanks to Medalie, Dewey's return to private practice was not a return to obscurity. By managing Medalie's campaign and taking an active role in the Young Republicans, Dewey had gained the attention of party leaders and was invited to join the Republican County Committee in January 1933. Perhaps at Medalie's urging, ex-Governor Charles Whitman also invited Dewey to serve on the party's mayoral committee in 1933. When the Republicans joined ranks in nominating La Guardia as a Fusion candidate, Dewey helped the cause by providing information about racketeering for La Guardia's speeches.[24]

Many of the contacts Dewey made through politics overlapped with ties he was cultivating with leading members of the bar. Medalie had long recognized the advantages of working with the bar association and encouraged his young protégé to become active. Part of the reason for Medalie's appointment as U.S. attorney in 1931 stemmed from his successful investigation of Tammany magistrate Albert H. Vitale. Although La Guardia first raised the question of Vitale's links to gambler Arnold Rothstein during his 1929 mayoral campaign, it was Medalie who proved the charges that led to Vitale's disbarment and removal from the bench in 1930. Following Medalie's lead, Dewey applied for and was elected to the bar association membership in May 1931. He asked at least eleven people for recommendations, most of them lawyers he had met through the Republican Party. A typical letter of recommendation, from attorney William Gilligan, lauded Dewey's work for the Young Republicans and described him as "a well educated and cultured young man with professional ideals of a high order."[25]

During the early 1930s the bar association was undergoing the same kind of transformation as other New York institutions. When Dewey applied in 1931, membership still was tightly controlled. Wall Street law firms and patrician lawyers were represented more heavily than immigrants, and the association was known for its stodginess. But after La Guardia took office in 1933, he received a letter from Kenneth Dayton, chairman of a bar committee offering advice on judicial appointments. "I don't know how you feel about the Association," Dayton said, "but we all know that it has had a reputation of being ultra conservative and snobbish. Whether the reputation was deserved or not, I believe you will find a marked change has taken place in the last few years, and particularly with such committees as mine." Dayton noted that his committee now included men such as Osmond K. Fraenkel, a defense lawyer in the celebrated Scottsboro racial case. The inclusion of such men, he suggested, indicated the association's willingness to "to climb down off the pedestal and do some practical work."[26]

One sign of how much the bar was changing was the elevation of Thomas Thacher to its presidency. Thacher had served as a director of the Young Republican Club and, along with Medalie, believed one way of accomplishing change was to elevate younger, more active men to leadership positions. Both believed the association could play a role in political as well as legal reform. The bar association and Republicans in general traditionally had abhorred Tammany; the rise of La Guardia and Fusion gave them hope that politics could provide meaningful long-term change rather than just a series of fights against the machine. During La Guardia's first successful campaign for mayor in 1933, Medalie spoke about the nexus between crime and politics and the breakdown in law enforcement it signified. As the campaign wore on, Medalie turned up his rhetoric. In late July he criticized the connections between vice and politics, and in mid-August he testified before a grand jury about links between racketeers and Tammany leader James J. Hines, aldermen William Solomon, David Mahoney, and Albert Marinelli, and ex-state Senator Edward J. Ahearn. To make his attack appear less partisan, Medalie also denounced Republican leader William S. Reynolds. When the investigation was dropped, Medalie castigated local law enforcement and claimed that in New York, "People have got out of the habit of looking to the local authorities for law enforcement. This is most unfortunate."[27]

After La Guardia took office, Medalie continued his reform activities. He wrote to the mayor, urging him not to carry through on his threat to dismantle the Crime Prevention Bureau—a special division of the New York Police Department that worked with delinquents. He persuaded La Guardia to hire several of his own former assistants as city lawyers. La Guardia's calendars indicate that Medalie was a frequent visitor to the mayor's office, along with other lawyers concerned about crime. In addition to serving the bar association as chairman of a committee on state law enforcement, Medalie was active in many legal reform groups. He continued to contribute articles to the New York County Grand Jurors' *Panel* and served on such national organizations as the Committee on Public Education for Crime Control.[28] Medalie also continued to promote Dewey's rise to prominence.

In 1934 Dewey conducted a bar-sponsored investigation of magistrate Harold J. Kunstler. Kunstler, who had been appointed by former Mayor Jimmy Walker to fill an unexpired term in 1928, had been re-elected to a nine-year term. Dewey accepted the independent assignment before leaving the U.S. attorney's office in December 1933. Newspaper investigations had raised questions about Kunstler's fitness for the bench, and a preliminary investigation by the bar association's Committee on Courts of Limited Jurisdiction led to a report against him on May 8, 1933. Among other findings, the committee reported that Kunstler owed money to a man who floated around the courts fixing cases for fees. The magistrate also was financially irresponsible, having amassed judgments against himself totaling $32,241. Kunstler resigned after Dewey issued his own final report in 1934. Dewey's handling of the matter won him plaudits from Thacher, who wrote that the difficult case would have been lost had it not been for Dewey's "insistence upon the most careful and detailed preparation."[29]

Thacher rewarded Dewey by appointing him chairman of the association's Criminal Courts Committee. With characteristic arrogance, Dewey fired off a letter to Thacher criticizing various committee members—most of whom had served before he was appointed. Dewey said five members should be dropped for their "lack of willingness to join the constructive efforts to strengthen and improve the Criminal Law." He attacked some members for their conservatism, and provided specific indictments against others. One man was "generally weak"; another's value was "limited by the fact that he does little work"; another's liberalism made him too cautious with regard to criminal legislation "for fear of possible invasion of the rights of individuals by the police"; and a fourth had been in the city district attorney's office "so long as to become a disappointed seeker of higher public office." Dewey then suggested ten lawyers—several of them associates of Medalie or the Young Republicans—to be appointed to his committee. Thacher responded by keeping seven of the eight original members on the committee and appointing five of the ten men suggested by Dewey.[30]

Thacher suffered Dewey's brashness because of his affiliation with Medalie and his success at getting the committee moving. Dewey believed that the bar association, which traditionally had offered its opinion only on pending legislation, should take a more active role in shaping state legislation and lobbying for its passage. To that end, he tried to bring some order to the disparate suggestions for reform. By February, Dewey forged a consensus among the county lawyers' association, the grand jurors' association, and his own bar committee in favor of seventeen bills. State Attorney General John J. Bennett, working through a Democratic senator, already had introduced his own program. Dewey resented the rivalry and reported to Thacher that his coalition approved of only eight of Bennett's bills. He then met with Bennett in order to write a compromise package. Decrying a lack of adequate media coverage about the legislation, Dewey issued a press release saying the bills were designed to prevent jury fixing, close statutory loopholes, and allow jury trials to be waived in all but capital cases.[31]

These reform efforts indicated both a widespread frustration with the legal system and politicians' growing perception that the alleged breakdown in law enforcement was a hot political issue. In a letter to Thacher, Bennett advocated the reforms because "there is a feeling abroad in the land as to the inadequacy of the administration of justice, especially in criminal cases, and there is a tendency to blame not only the law but members of the Bar for this failure." Concern about ineffectual law enforcement in New York was mirrored in other parts of the nation in 1934. The American Bar Association put criminal law enforcement at the top of its agenda for its annual meeting in August. Among other solutions, the ABA advocated drafting new state codes of criminal procedure following guidelines set by a national legal think tank. It recommended that each state establish a department of justice modeled after the federal one. The ABA also suggested allowing the defendant the options of being charged by information or indictment and being tried by either judge or jury. Finally, along more daring lines, the association urged that less-than-unanimous jury verdicts be accepted in criminal cases and suggested weakening Fifth Amendment safeguards by allowing judges and lawyers to comment on a defendant's failure to testify.[32]

These and other ideas received an airing at a national conference on crime convened in Washington, D.C., in December. The leading speakers included Medalie, who argued that crime had become well organized while "our county and local controls are but relics of our ox-cart days." To Medalie, modern, scientific crime enforcement required special investigating agencies outside regular police channels, detective bureaus manned by skilled prosecutors and investigators working exclusively on complex crime. Although existing police departments were adequate for fighting routine crime, to deter racketeers, prosecutors had to "strike at the case not easily solved . . . get at the evidence not easily gathered . . . compel testimony not readily given." Medalie urged using grand juries—which were mandatory in federal cases but optional for the states—to force reluctant witnesses to testify. In other words, he recommended recreating local law enforcement in the image of the federal government.[33]

Medalie had provided a vision for New York's criminal justice machinery; now he needed a "laboratory" to test his ideas. Medalie's success as a reformer resulted from his uniquely paired idealism and pragmatism. He was politically astute enough to see that political events unfolding in New York offered an opportunity to test his ideas if he could put his own man in charge. Approaching Dewey to serve as special prosecutor, he obtained the younger man's agreement to take the job if it was offered. Medalie then worked to rally support from Fusion leaders and other groups, including the bar association and the New York County Grand Jury Association. Both of the latter groups were already disposed kindly towards Dewey. His work on the bar's criminal courts committee netted him an even more influential post in April 1935, when he was appointed to the association's nominating committee, where he served with such eminent lawyers as Charles Burlingham, John W. Davis, Elihu Root, Jr., and Charles Evans Hughes, Jr.[34]

Dewey adopted Medalie's belief that grand juries were the key to complex investigations and became an outspoken supporter of the Manhattan grand jury association. The month before his appointment as special prosecutor, Dewey wrote to a Chicago group at the grand jury association's request. His letter praised the ancient institution as "the most powerful weapon available to a prosecutor for the proper investigation of crime" and the only effective means to stop organized crime and the rackets, which he estimated cost the nation more than $1 billion a year. "Without a grand jury," he pointed out, "a prosecutor would be powerless to command the presence and preliminary testimony of witnesses possessing evidence concerning crime. Without the power of grand jury subpoena, a prosecutor would be relegated to handling the petty cases of the type where one person complains against another and voluntarily gives testimony. Major criminal enterprises could and would thrive undisturbed because testimony in such situations is rarely volunteered and must be compelled." Clearly referring to events unfolding in New York City, Dewey noted that the grand jury also served as a watchdog against lazy or incompetent prosecutors. As Dewey saw it, "a prosecutor who does not wish to prosecute certain types of crime, or wishes to do nothing, might well seek to remove from his daily presence, those representatives of the public conscience who might expose his corruption or ineptness." Finally, he pointed out, grand juries traditionally had protected the innocent from unfair prosecution.[35]

Once it became apparent that a special prosecutor would be appointed, it was not surprising that Dewey's name surfaced repeatedly. In fact, Lehman virtually assured his appointment when he named Republicans Charles Tuttle, Charles Evans Hughes, Jr., Thomas Thacher, and Medalie as prospective special prosecutors. Dewey knew Tuttle in the Young Republicans and through work on his 1930 gubernatorial campaign; he knew Thacher as a sponsor of the Young Republican Club and president of the bar association and Charles Evans Hughes, Jr., through the bar nominating committee.[36] Given these associations, Medalie evidently had little difficulty persuading the three other men to step aside and make way for Dewey.

The fact that Medalie was the moving force behind Dewey's appointment was well known at the time. One anonymous detractor implied that Medalie was pushing Dewey in order to wreck Lehman's political career. He wrote the governor that Medalie "attempts to discredit you whenever he has an opportunity to do so. . . . He has spoken of you . . .

as weak-willed, subservient to the local Democratic organization . . . and as a banker without social vision." The writer speculated that Medalie was promoting Dewey in order to gain control of the Republican Party. Many of Dewey's friends also recognized the political aspects of the appointment; several congratulatory letters predicted that Dewey would parlay his job as special prosecutor into greater fame. One writer assured him his appointment was "certain to make you broadly known far beyond this city and state." Another Dewey fan wrote: "My only desire at this time is for a weekend in the White House when the Investigator-Albany-Washington triple play is completed."[37]

Although politics was never far from Dewey's thinking, he characteristically downplayed such suggestions about his decision to accept the appointment as special prosecutor on July 1, 1935. As he recalled years later: "Organized crime really was so powerful that people in the highest places—judges and leaders in industry—had reached the conclusion that we could never eliminate underworld control of our lives by legal process. When people of such stature reach that conclusion, then our form of government is no good. I thought that it was the most challenging situation the country had ever faced internally. . . . This was just the chance to do the biggest job that any lawyer could do."[38]

~ ~ ~ ~

CHAPTER FOUR

Putting Theory into Practice

*D*EWEY ENJOYED huge advantages over ordinary prosecutors. The aroused public, or at least politicians' perception of that condition, translated into a carte blanche. Governor Lehman, who did not want to be accused of covering up his party's political corruption, ensured that Dewey received a huge budget, his own office space, freedom from civil service hiring requirements, and the ability to choose his own cases. The governor also authorized the impaneling of a special grand jury and assignment of a sympathetic presiding judge.[1] Nonetheless, Dewey's success was not preordained. Both District Attorney Dodge and La Guardia's commissioner of markets, William Fellowes Morgan, had grappled unsuccessfully with racketeering. A major reason for their lack of progress was the hazy nature of New York's underworld; everyone agreed it existed, but tracking its tentacles would prove laborious. Complicating Dewey's efforts was the fact that the announcement of his appointment had been a lightning rod for all kinds of public grievances, few of which concerned organized crime. His office was inundated by complaints from crackpots who wanted him to mediate their disputes with landlords or imagined ill treatment from all manner of crooks and goblins. Their willingness to come forward stood in a stark contrast to the reluctance of the witnesses Dewey actually sought. The real victims of racketeering, skeptical of Dewey's ability to protect them against retaliation, stayed away. When he found them, witnesses often chose perjury over cooperation.

Dewey began laying the groundwork for his investigation in early July 1935. He sought help in Washington, D.C., visiting with Secretary of the Treasury Henry Morgenthau, U.S. Attorney General Homer Cummings, and FBI Director J. Edgar Hoover, an acquaintance from his days in the U.S. attorney's office. Closer to home, he met with Lehman, La Guardia, Valentine, and representatives of the organizations that had pushed for his appointment, including George Drew Egbert, head of the Society for the Prevention of Crime, John Haynes Holmes of the City Affairs Committee, and Lee Thompson Smith of the grand jurors' association. Like Dodge, Dewey found much of the information from these groups uselessly vague, but astutely recognized their political value. As he said later about his meeting with the grand jurors, "We didn't get much evidence from them, but we did want to extend courtesy to them. . . . They . . . were very zealous, and we wanted them to have a chance to give us anything that they had—not just evidence but any opinions or suspicions so that they would feel that we were really going to carry on the work." Public enthusiasm for Dewey's investigation showed that he succeeded in making good-government groups, the press, and New York citizens feel part of his efforts.[2]

Dewey's relationship with the specially appointed judge, Philip J. McCook, proved more valuable. McCook, known affectionately to his friends as "Fergie" and "Puddinhead," was an enormous asset to Dewey during the investigation. The judge was a long-time political ally of La Guardia, whom he had met in 1910 when they shared office space as young lawyers. McCook even taught La Guardia how to clog dance and performed in an Elks Club minstrel show with him. In 1919 they ran together on the Republican ticket; McCook, an Episcopal minister's son from Connecticut who worked as a Legal Aid Society lawyer, was elected to the state Supreme Court while La Guardia became president of the city's Board of Aldermen. When La Guardia went to Congress and, later, became mayor, McCook stayed on the state bench, swearing in his friend as mayor in 1933. McCook wrote La Guardia about job seekers and encouraged him when he became disheartened about the city's financial problems. The judge also served as a sponsor of the Young Republicans. Dewey first met with McCook on July 4, 1935. After their four-hour conference, Dewey came away impressed with the jurist's "high character, great sincerity," and good intentions. McCook was equally taken with Dewey's sense of mission. Over the years, the two forged a unique relationship in which the judge rarely questioned the prosecutor's methods or motives.[3]

In later years, Dewey claimed he had been hampered by his budget—forced to economize on used office furniture and put into the difficult position of trying to attract first-rate people with low public salaries. In reality, Dewey received generous funding. Although Governor Lehman had ordered the investigation, the city of New York paid for it. Because much of La Guardia's popular success was attributable to his own anti-crime rhetoric, the mayor was eager to cooperate with Dewey. He ordered Chief Valentine to give Dewey his pick of the New York police department and to establish a special squad of sixty-three officers to help the investigation. While District Attorney Dodge's budget was being slashed, La Guardia made sure Dewey received everything he sought. In October 1934, Dodge wrote La Guardia pointing out that the work of his office had grown dramatically yet he was forced to reduce salaries, eliminate jobs, and hire less-experienced lawyers. Although he knew La Guardia would fight him, Dodge announced his intention to ask the Board of Aldermen for a budget increase of $9,670 to hire more-experienced assistants. In contrast to Dodge's meager demands, Dewey requested more than $121,000 for six months, a gargantuan sum, considering that Dodge's entire annual budget was $752,000. Dewey's demands included $16,695 for his own salary—the same as Dodge was receiving, even though Dewey was nominally a deputy district attorney—$90,400 for his assistants, $32,000 for investigators, $26,000 for accountants, and $26,000 for rent, telephone, postage, and miscellaneous expenses. The balance covered auxiliary employees. Dewey's staff included twenty assistants, ten investigators, four process servers, four clerks, two grand jury reporters, nineteen stenographers, two telephone operators, and four messengers.[4]

Dewey spared no expense in his office space, renting 10,500 square feet, about three-quarters of the fourteenth floor, in the magnificent Woolworth Building. Built in 1913, the Woolworth Building was the world's tallest structure until completion of the Empire State Building in 1931. Architect Cass Gilbert designed the building in the Gothic style that dime store magnate Frank Woolworth fell in love with during his many trips to England. Its spires, gargoyles, flying buttresses, vaulted ceilings inlaid with brilliantly colored mosaics, and subdued lighting in the lobby created a church-like effect that earned the building its nickname, "the Cathedral of Commerce." In addition to its imposing character, the Woolworth Building offered more practical advantages. Located across the street from the U.S. Attorney's offices, it was one block from City Hall and a short distance from the Supreme Court Building, where grand juries met. Its many entrances also provided witnesses a better chance to come and go without being seen.[5]

Predictably, most Democrats saw Dewey's expenditures as needless extravagance during the Depression. Nevertheless on Lehman and La Guardia's orders, the New York City Board of Aldermen had no choice but to approve Dewey's budget at a July 25 meeting, although they protested bitterly. Recovery Democratic Alderman Walter R. Hart accused Lehman of thwarting the popular will by, essentially, replacing a Democratic district attorney with a Republican authorized to conduct a "fishing expedition." Tammany leader Edward J. Sullivan denied that New York was crime ridden, but added sarcastically, "if the governor wants to replace the police with G-men or X-men, it's all right with me." Democratic politicians, powerless to overturn Dewey's appointment, persuaded Henry H. Klein to file a legal challenge. Nominally acting on behalf of the B.C.L. Company, Inc., Klein said Dewey's budget requests were outrageous and declared, "It is evident that Mr. Dewey intends to set up a separate district attorney's office in New York County and that his power will supersede that of the district attorney himself." Klein argued that nothing in the city charter empowered the board of estimate to create new jobs out of thin air and observed that Dodge would have had a difficult time if *he* had requested seventy-seven new jobs. The suit was dismissed; the judge ruled that the city had a right to appropriate its own funds. Historians have claimed that only Tammany opposed Dewey's budget, but in fact even La Guardia found it excessive.[6]

With his large budget and freedom from civil service requirements, Dewey assembled a stellar staff. His chief assistants included Barent Ten Eyck, a classmate from Columbia, and Jack Rosenblum, William Herlands and Murray Gurfein, all of whom had served with him as assistant U.S. attorneys in Medalie's office. Dewey also chose A. J. Gutreich as his chief accountant. The two had worked together in Dewey's bar association investigation of Magistrate Kunstler. Taking his cue from Medalie, Dewey surrounded himself with a staff of young people "who were impressionable, who were full of zeal, and who were anxious to do well." Shrinking job prospects during the Depression provided Dewey with an opportunity to be very selective. He received 1,200 applications for the thirty jobs for accountants, secretaries, and stenographers and approximately three thousand job requests from lawyers. Some applied when Dewey's name was first mentioned, a month before he actually was appointed. Five years earlier Seabury, by contrast, had had to scrounge for applicants.[7]

Traditionally, prosecutors have been able to draw from the ranks of young, ambitious lawyers who postpone joining large law firms in order to gain trial experience. Dewey was no exception, and the Depression greatly expanded his pool of potential lawyers. Like other professionals, lawyers had difficulty finding work, particularly Jews and Catholics who were still shut out of Wall Street's and the nation's more prestigious law firms. These factors were clearly at work in New York City where, by 1934, fifteen hundred lawyers "were prepared to take a pauper's oath to qualify for work relief." Many Jewish lawyers, who represented an estimated 50 percent of the New York bar, felt the practice of law had become "a dignified road to starvation." As historian Jerold Auerbach points out, the Depression wrought a subtle change by sparking a renewed idealism among law school graduates, who began questioning the accepted wisdom that the best lawyers represented corporations and banks. The anti-Semitism and idealism that led many young lawyers to Washington to work for New Deal agencies prompted others to apply to Dewey.[8]

Dewey showed remarkable open-mindedness in choosing his assistants. His selection of Eunice Hunton Carter, a black woman who had served on Dodge's staff, would result in his famous prosecution of Lucky Luciano. Even more noteworthy, by the standards of the day, was the fact that 90 percent of his staff members were Jewish, some of them attracted by the glamour of the investigation. Emmanuel Robbins, one of several lawyers who agreed to a one-dollar annual salary, recalled that "We were all young enough to be very ardent crusaders. . . . We were battling the whole organized underworld in New York City and we were the forces of decent living." Most applicants, however, shared the outlook of Harris Steinberg, a recent Harvard Law School graduate who was not particularly interested in criminal law; he joined Dewey's office because as a Jew he was excluded from New York's better law firms. Looking back, Steinberg pointed out that a modern prosecutor would be unlikely to have a choice of such men as Charles Breitel, Stanley Fuld, and William Herlands, who became distinguished New York State judges, and Jack Rosenblum and Stanley Gelb, who became leading New York trial attorneys.[9]

Dewey winnowed down the applicant pool through careful screening and a hard-nosed interviewing technique that became legendary among his staffers. As Robbins recalled, "Dewey terrified me the minute I saw him. . . . I was completely unprepared for his interview. His questions were immediate, direct and searching. . . . I was quite taken aback. Whenever I appeared reluctant or evasive on any question, he pressed." Dewey told William Herwitz, who attended the Brooklyn School of Law when financial problems forced him out of Dartmouth, "You're the only one I'm interviewing from a lousy law school." Herwitz, unabashed, said that was because he was a better investigator than anyone else. Dewey later said he hired Herwitz because he was a "snotty son of a bitch."[10]

Dewey would continue to fill staff positions into August, but the investigation formally began on July 29 when McCook swore in Dewey and his staff. The next day Dewey signaled that he was ready for business by delivering a dramatic radio address over the city's three largest stations. In appealing for help from the public, Dewey said he was limiting his investigation to organized crime, governmental corruption, and racketeering, which he defined as "the business of successful intimidation for the purpose of regularly extorting money . . . by organized gangs of low-grade outlaws who lack either the courage or the intelligence to earn an honest living." Dewey insisted he was not conducting a vice investigation, saying, "If this were merely an attempt to suppress ordinary prostitution, gambling and lottery games, I think I am safe in saying the governor would not have ordered it and I know I would not have undertaken it."[11]

Dewey asserted that organized crime differed from ordinary crime because its huge profits were used to "finance its depredations against legitimate business and the lives of the people of New York." Every family in New York, he explained, unknowingly was paying a tribute to racketeers through higher prices for bread, chicken, fish, vegetables, and other consumer items. The crudest form of racketeering at work in New York was simple extortion—threatening a businessman with harm if he did not pay tribute. In industries with low profit margins, however, crooked businessmen had invited racketeers in to organize "trade associations" to help set high prices by driving out competition. Still other racketeers had taken over unions with violence, then used the unions to intimidate legitimate business into paying tributes.[12]

As a result of its control of vice and some legitimate businesses, Dewey said, organized crime accumulated a huge "war chest" that provided the "means of corrupting public officials and buying immunity from punishment. This flow of revenue to the criminal underworld must be stopped and that is one of the objects of this investigation." Racketeers could "succeed only so long as they can prey upon the fear or weakness of disorganized or timid victims. They fail and run to cover when business and the public, awakened to their own strength, stand up and fight." To that end, Dewey invited labor union members, wholesale food merchants, and other victims to provide information: "It is not only your privilege but your duty to bring that information to my office." Dewey denied his investigation was political and promised politics would play no role in decisions about which cases to pursue. "To what extent this investigation succeeds," he concluded, "and how promptly it succeeds, is largely in your hands. Your cooperation is essential. Your confidence will be respected. Your help will be kept secret and your persons protected. If you have evidence of organized crime of whatever kind and however large or small, bring it to us. The rest is our job. We will do our best."[13]

Dewey was well aware of the problems that would result if his investigation were viewed as a failure, and he took steps to insulate himself from the kind of exaggerated expectations and constant criticism that had plagued Dodge. In his radio address, Dewey, reminding the public that federal agents and lawyers had spent three years putting together the tax case against Al Capone, asked for public patience while conducting his investigation: "Crime cannot be investigated under a spotlight. Publicity does not stamp out crime. It is my sincere hope that the work we are doing will vanish from the newspapers until it produces criminal cases to be tried in court. . . . Sensational raids and arrests without months of quiet and painstaking preparation in advance result in nothing but acquittals in court. This only encourages the already over-confident underworld."[14]

Taking advantage of the media's good will, Dewey asked for and received assurances that he would be able to conduct his work without daily scrutiny. Newspapers largely accepted Dewey's explanation that his investigation would be long and painstakingly thorough; in the early months they devoted most of their attention to such routine matters as staff appointments. As one Dewey assistant remembered, "One of the basic troubles when you start an investigation in white heat with a lot of public indignation and publicity is that you have to produce quickly because the public is impatient. . . . You don't want to get completely out of the public eye because then you lose the impetus of the public indignation which is helping you." Realizing that he still needed quick results, Dewey pushed his staff to work Herculean hours. "There was never a time when we considered ourselves a nine-to-five office. There was no limit as to the amount of work, day or night, we might have to do at any particular time," Dewey assistant Emmanuel Robbins recalled.[15]

In the early days, the office's frenetic pace produced few clear results and much confusion. Dewey's first task was to map out the major fields of investigation, hoping that his public appeal and promises to protect witnesses would bring in the evidence. Unfortunately, the hundreds of people who showed up had little useful to offer. Robbins, who handled complaints, said he was unprepared for the onslaught of information about brothers stealing from each other, adultery, tenant-landlord disputes, and repossessions. He estimated that 90 percent of his job consisted of turning people away. The office attracted so many crackpots that the receptionist kept a "nut file." Such nettlesome tipsters would continue to plague Dewey in spite of repeated disclaimers that he was investigating only racketeering and organized vice. In December 1935, Dewey still was complaining to Charles Poletti, Lehman's legal aide: "We have a large number of complaints who come into the office daily, many of whom are obviously demented, and others of whom merely seek redress on civil matters."[16]

In stark contrast to these eager witnesses, few of the people who could have been helpful stepped forward. Despite his reassurances, racketeering victims remained unconvinced that he could protect them. With little help from witnesses and only vague clues from groups such as the Society for the Prevention of Crime and the Association of Grand Jurors of New York County, Dewey faced an awesome task. Although he did not have a blueprint when he began, his experience in the U.S. Attorney's office had provided him with his primary adversaries. From the outset, his main target was Tammany Hall leader James J. Hines. As an assistant U.S. attorney, Dewey had offered numbers boss Henry Miro a deal if he would testify about Hines' links with gangsters. But Miro preferred a prison sentence, reportedly telling his lawyer, "Christ, my life wouldn't be worth a nickel." Dewey also was eager to get evidence on Albert Marinelli, another Tammany boss who was clerk of New York County. Dewey hoped to prove that Marinelli was closely associated with New York and Chicago gangsters. Rumors about both men were widespread; Medalie had discussed their alleged links with organized crime while campaigning for La Guardia in August of 1933.[17]

Gathering evidence against Marinelli and Hines would take years and would require proving their links to criminals who also had to be investigated. To that end, Dewey created "a roving commission to get what we could to break down rackets, to develop what kind of rackets there might be." It was, as assistant Stanley Fuld recalled, "very general talk." Dewey's staff chased down many blind alleys seeking evidence against New York's two best-known labor racketeers, Louis "Lepke" Buchalter and Jacob "Gurrah" Shapiro. Dewey reacted to the dead ends and resulting confusion by delivering pep talks filled with braggadocio about his goals. In the process, he convinced Charles Breitel and some other assistants that the glorious probe "was quite the genuine form of bunkum." Breitel began by investigating the painters' unions; when it did not appear Lepke and Gurrah were deeply involved, Dewey scrapped that angle and assigned Breitel to check out the plate-glass industry. When that fizzled too, Dewey assigned him to a fruitless investigation of funeral directors. Finally, Breitel investigated two productive areas—loan sharking and restaurant racketeering.[18]

Stanley Fuld, who later became the chief judge of New York state, realized within several months that everyone was digging for facts without knowing the applicable laws. He recalled that "the Special Prosecution was growing somewhat like Topsy, and I remember talking to [Dewey] and suggesting that there ought to be some correlation . . . so that there would be a greater sense of what facts ought to be looked for." Dewey recognized the wisdom of Fuld's suggestion and dispatched several younger members of the staff to the county bar association library. Such research was especially important in New York, where all violations are spelled out by statute and common law crimes are not recognized.[19]

Dewey followed the prosecutorial techniques he had learned under Medalie: wide-ranging grand jury probes, "freezing" witnesses, using tax laws, and working closely with investigators to develop evidence. In many respects, it was as easy to apply these tools in the state courts as it had been in the federal system. New York allowed prosecutors wide latitude in using grand juries, and nothing in the state law barred the extensive use of police investigators. Dewey recognized that the majority of policemen were honest but traditionally had been patronized by prosecutors. He rectified this by insisting "that the police at all times must be treated with the utmost respect"; in the process, he eventually won support from the department. In some respects, New York laws were even more favorable than the federal law. For example, it was easier to grant immunity to state witnesses, a privilege that was limited under federal law to a few violations such as interstate commerce. In other respects the state law lagged behind. The law of contempt—a key instrument for forcing witnesses to testify or face jail time—had not yet been developed in New York State. Similarly, the federal government's main weapon against gangsters—income tax evasion laws—had not been used in New York. Thus, Dewey's early days in office were devoted to experimenting with and testing the full capabilities of the law.[20]

Given these tentative beginnings and the high expectations raised by publicity, it was not surprising that the special prosecutor's first case proved disappointing. Having vowed in his initial radio address to move vigorously against any instance of racketeering, Dewey was forced to prosecute the unappealing case of Dominic Tossone, a nineteen-year-old small-time street punk. Tossone was arrested in early August after attempting to extort thirty dollars from a shopkeeper by threatening to blow up his building. So-called protection rackets were common in New York, and had Tossone been part of a gang his arrest would have been significant. Instead, he turned out to be acting alone, and his indictment and conviction in September prompted some critics to proclaim, "Dewey's investigation lays an egg."[21]

Dewey's first case looked even more foolish when Judge McCook gave Tossone an indeterminate sentence at a reformatory rather than a prison term. Wisely, assistant Murray Gurfein told McCook during the sentencing hearing on September 25 that other Dewey cases would take much longer to investigate. If nothing else, the Tossone case taught Dewey never again to prosecute insignificant wrongdoing. The following year when La Guardia passed on information about alleged racketeering in the ice cream workers' union, Dewey told the mayor: "As a general principle, I may say that I have not regarded a single isolated extortion of $5,000 by labor union delegates as a matter which is properly within my jurisdiction. If I should investigate properly and prosecute all such extortions, I would make little progress on the major aspects of this job."[22]

Throughout the fall, Dewey continued to seek a case that would bring glory to his investigation. His attention turned to Arthur Flegenheimer, an old adversary from his days as a federal prosecutor. Better known as "Dutch" Schultz or the "Dutchman," Flegenheimer made his fortune in bootlegging and numbers racketeering. In 1934, J. Edgar Hoover had labeled him "Public Enemy Number One." As an assistant U.S. attorney, Dewey prepared the tax evasion case that led to Schultz's indictment in 1933. After the charges were filed, Schultz evaded capture and lived openly in New York City for nearly a year under the protection of Tammany Hall boss James J. Hines and the police. When La Guardia became mayor in 1934, he ordered police to find Schultz. As the pressure mounted, Schultz turned himself in to Albany authorities in November 1934. Because of extensive pretrial publicity in New York City, Schultz's trial was moved upstate. His first trial in Syracuse in April 1935 ended with a hung jury, while the second, held during July in the small town of Malone, ended with an acquittal. Outraged law enforcement officials included the trial judge, Frederick H. Bryant, who told jurors: "You will have to go home with the satisfaction, if it is a satisfaction, that you have rendered a blow against law enforcement and given aid and encouragement to the people who would flout the law." U.S. Attorney General Homer Cummings called the verdict "a terrible miscarriage of justice."[23]

La Guardia reacted with typical flamboyance to the verdict, vowing to ban Schultz from the city. Schultz responded to that unenforceable threat by declaring that nothing would keep him out of New York. Dewey too saw the Dutchman as a worthy target and signaled his intentions to move against him by hiring Jack Rosenblum, an assistant U.S. attorney who had worked with Dewey in the Schultz tax case. Rosenblum joined Dewey's staff in mid-August as the last of his four chief assistants but was robbed of his target in late October when Schultz was assassinated. Gangland folklore attributes his murder to other mobsters worried about Schultz's increasingly impulsive threats. According to this scenario, Schultz bragged that he was going to arrange for Dewey's death, and other underworld denizens, such as Lucky Luciano, decided to kill Schultz before he could carry out an action that would have brought more attention to their activities. The truth remains elusive: the dying Schultz refused to identify the assassin who gunned him down at the Palace Chop House and Tavern in Newark.[24]

Deprived of his main target, Dewey faced a public relations problem. Although he had managed to buy time for his investigation initially, the public's patience was wearing thin. Aside from the Tossone case, most of the publicity surrounding Dewey's efforts in late September and early October centered on contempt proceedings brought against reluctant witnesses. To skeptics, such mundane activities hardly justified Dewey's salary or the expense of his investigation. Then, at the end of October, the special prosecutor seized headlines with raids against twenty-seven loan sharks. The cases had grown out of an investigation of loan sharking conducted by the Russell Sage Foundation. In early July the foundation's report provided Dewey's office with sufficient leads to begin an investigation. Luckily for Dewey, the usury cases proved easy to prosecute. Unlike other racketeers, New York's loan sharks were disorganized, and victims were more willing to testify against individual sharks than they would have been had they been organized by the mob. The ready pool of witnesses undoubtedly was increased by victims who ordinarily would not have crossed social barriers to conduct business with usurers but were forced to do so by the Depression. In any case, witnesses came forward voluntarily, and Dewey had reason to be grateful for both the ease of the cases and their timing.

The cases were easy in part because Dewey was able to expedite them by taking advantage of the complex organization of New York's court system. New York City had two courts for misdemeanor cases. In the magistrates' courts, which conformed to New York state law, one magistrate heard minor cases on indictments handed up by the grand jury. By contrast, in the special sessions courts, three-judge panels used less stringent rules of procedure and heard cases based only on "informations," that is, evidence from a city prosecutor. Normally, such informations, with the names of witnesses written on the back, were presented to a magistrate, who then filed them. This procedure made it easy for suspects to identify and intimidate witnesses before trial. Dewey, however, came up with a way to avoid making the names public; he presented his information before the grand jury, with McCook sitting as a magistrate. In that way, he was able to invoke grand jury rules of secrecy to protect his witnesses' identities while obtaining McCook's signature on the charges. When the loan shark cases came to trial before the sympathetic three-judge panels, only one was thrown out on a technicality. Thus, Dewey avoided many of the delays and problems he might have encountered had he presented his information to regular, mostly Democratic magistrates. As assistant Harris Steinberg remembered, Dewey's handling of the usury cases demonstrated a key aspect of his success: "One thing about Dewey was that if it was a powerful weapon, he wanted to use it. He didn't want to become a law breaker, but if he could bend the law a little bit with a new interpretation in order to get a good result, he would."[25]

In addition to the validity of willing witnesses, the usury cases were fairly straightforward. A victim could testify against a loan shark directly, eliminating the need for the elaborate record searches that marked most of Dewey's cases, in which criminal and victim were separated by layers of middlemen. Finally, because the cases were decided by judges, Dewey's assistants did not have to "develop the cases with the same infinite care" entailed by jury trials.[26] As would become characteristic, the press failed to notice that Dewey's success rested largely on the red carpet treatment he received in the courts—a benefit elected prosecutors did not enjoy. It made better copy to publicize Dewey as the boy wonder and his efforts as heroic. The *New York Mirror* said: "Dewey . . . doesn't go fishing with a brass band; nor does he come back with a string of minnows and talk about how the big ones got away. Those who have felt that the law was designed only for men with money enough to hire lawyers will be encouraged by the nature of Mr. Dewey's first catch—the loan shark." Even the normally restrained *New York Times* lauded Dewey as a "savior and hero to thousands" and reported that "thousands of poverty-ridden clerks, taxi chauffeurs, office boys and men and women on home relief hailed the stroke with fervent joy. Shabby, broken-spirited men approached the shylocks' rat holes with money scraped up at great sacrifice of pride and honor on the day of the raids and could not believe their ears when detectives met them and told them, 'Stick the money in your pocket; your Shylock's in jail.' "27

Dewey recognized that his public relations coup had hit a receptive nerve with a Depression era populace even more upset than usual about the "dirty business" of loan sharking. He admitted the usury probe "was scarcely a major investigation" but noted that it was "useful to put the glare of publicity on one of the slimiest criminal practices and to demonstrate how comparatively easy it was to stop it if anybody would take the trouble." The investigation was even more important because it bought time. As Dewey told an interviewer years later, "you can't keep public opinion, or public support for an investigation that doesn't announce what it is going to do; if it doesn't make wide sweeping statements about its evidence in advance; if it waits until it has a case. You just can't keep public support for an investigation unless you produce a case once in a while." Dewey conceded it was a good thing the usury cases were ready in October because "we had to keep public support."28

The loan shark trials and sentencing continued into January and gave more public credence to Dewey's proclamations that he was making headway against rackets. His efforts received a further boost when the grand jurors issued their report on December 26, praising Dewey, describing their own hard work, and outlining the deplorable conditions that needed further investigation. It is not clear whether Dewey's staff or the grand jury actually wrote the report. In either case, it bore Dewey's imprint: it bragged about success in the usury cases, described the complexity of racketeering in New York, and decried the reluctance of witnesses to cooperate in other cases. Grand jurors described the loan sharks as "professional criminals of a dangerous type" and said their convictions constituted a telling blow against usury in the city. With continuous investigation and vigilant prosecution, the grand jury optimistically predicted, loan sharks could "be wiped out, at least as far as New York County is concerned." The jurors were impressed that the "poor and obscure" witnesses in the usury cases "displayed a courage which has been lamentably absent in many substantial businessmen who have appeared before us." Considering Dewey's ability to protect witnesses, the jurors said it was disgraceful that the city's more prosperous citizens were reluctant to cooperate with the investigation of industrial rackets. Finally, the exhausted jurors asked to be disbanded. They pointed out that while normal grand juries sat for two hours each day for a month, they had been in session continually since early September, some days sitting for five or six hours; on one day they heard evidence from 2 P.M. to 3 A.M. The report suggested that two juries be convened concurrently to sit for three-month terms during the next two years. The day after the grand jury report, Lehman ordered McCook to impanel two grand juries. The governor told the media, "I am determined that the investigation and prosecution of racketeering progress as energetically as possible and I shall continue to do everything within my power to effectuate this."[29] By then Lehman already had embarked on his own crusade against crime. In the process, the governor would provide Dewey with the new and powerful tools he would need to battle the more entrenched forces of organized crime in New York.

A rare early portrait of Thomas E. Dewey taken in November 1933, less than two years before he became Manhattan's special prosecutor and gained fame as the nation's premier racket buster. Department of Rare Books and Special Collections, Rush Rhees Library, University of Rochester.

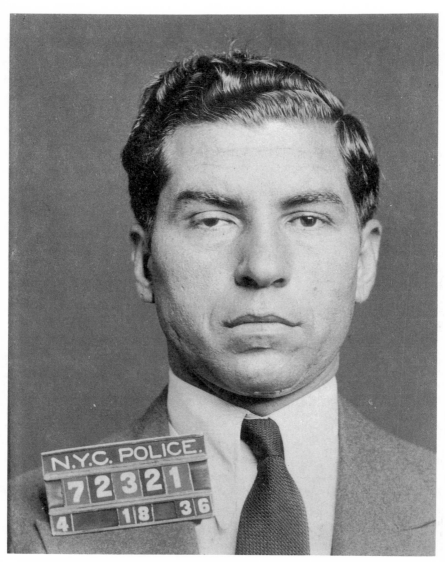

Charles "Lucky" Luciano drew little attention before Thomas E. Dewey plucked him from obscurity and portrayed him as New York's most powerful gangster. This mug shot was taken April 18, 1936, after Luciano was brought back from Arkansas, where he had fled to escape prosecution. The extradition proceedings stirred the city's press to sensationalist heights and set the stage for one of the nation's most famous organized-crime trials. Municipal Archives, Department of Records and Information Services, City of New York.

On April 27, 1938, Thomas E. Dewey approved a collective bargaining agreement between the Cafeteria Employees Union and the Affiliated Restaurateurs. Dewey's 1937
prosecution of Dutch Schultz's allies, who had taken over the union, constituted the
opening salvo in his war against labor racketeers. His victory paved the way for the
union's success; its membership grew from 6,000 to more than 15,000 six months after
the trial. William Herlands, who did the legwork for the case, sits to Dewey's left. On
his right is the Reverend John P. Boland, a member of the state labor board. Department
of Rare Books and Special Collections, Rush Rhees Library, University of Rochester.

Judge Charles C. Nott, Jr., who presided over the Jimmy Hines retrial, administers the
oath of office to newly elected New York County district attorney Thomas E. Dewey
on January 1, 1938. To Nott's left is Justice Philip J. McCook, the special judge appointed to hear most of Dewey's cases. Behind Dewey are his mother, Annie, and his
wife, Frances. Department of Rare Books and Special Collections, Rush Rhees Library,
University of Rochester.

Dewey's ambition propelled him into an aborted attempt to win the Republican nomination for president in 1940. Even though he had held only one political office, for two years as New York County's district attorney, some commentators thought he had a chance. This photo was taken December 29, 1939, in an Augusta, Georgia, hotel, while Dewey worked on a campaign speech. Department of Rare Books and Special Collections, Rush Rhees Library, University of Rochester.

It was not unusual for news photographers to capture thrill-loving Mayor Fiorello La Guardia racing to the scene of a crime or, as in this case, a three-alarm fire. His antics drew criticism from opponents and sometimes from supporters who resented his grandstanding, but most citizens appreciated his displays as signs of committed action in the war against gangsters. Municipal Archives, Department of Records and Information Services, City of New York.

Mayor La Guardia used his flair for publicity to draw New Yorkers' attention to the dangers of organized crime. Soon after taking office La Guardia instructed police to seize thousands of revolvers, machine guns, other weapons, and slot machines, which police then dumped into the waters surrounding New York City. Municipal Archives, Department of Records and Information Services, City of New York.

Three of New York's top politicians gathered for the dedication of the Triborough Bridge in October 1936. Governor Herbert Lehman, left, and President Franklin Roosevelt, center, undercut Tammany Hall's traditional patronage strength by funneling federal and state moneys away from the machine to Mayor La Guardia, right. Herbert H. Lehman Papers, Rare Book and Manuscript Library, Columbia University.

Cartoons aptly captured some aspects of New York's crusade against crime. Republicans seized on the 1935 runaway grand jury's rebellion against Tammany Hall District Attorney William Copeland Dodge and cornered Governor Lehman into appointing Thomas E. Dewey as special prosecutor. Herbert H. Lehman Papers, Rare Book and Manuscript Library, Columbia University.

Historically, critics focused on Tammany Hall's alliance with criminals. That changed, however, when Governor Lehman introduced his sweeping crime package to the state legislature in 1936, where it ran into heavy opposition from Republicans, caricatured here. Herbert H. Lehman Papers, Rare Book and Manuscript Library, Columbia University.

≈ ≈ ≈ ≈

CHAPTER FIVE

The Politics of Crime Fighting

*T*HROUGHOUT Dewey's investigation, he would jockey with
other New York politicians for crime-fighting headlines. Mayor La
Guardia and Governor Lehman, jealous at the special prosecutor's success in gaining publicity, stood by eager to capitalize on his failure or
claim much of the glory for his success. Their efforts to make crime and
criminal law reform fodder for their political ambitions point up the
recurring similarities of all crime waves. When fear of crime takes the
center stage of American public comment, politicians typically engage in
rhetorical bombast about declining morals and propose dangerous pleas
to undermine civil liberties, shortsighted quick fixes, and a handful of
meaningful reforms. New York politicians during the 1930s were no exception.

Lehman, La Guardia, Dewey, and others learned that it is easier to
talk about crime than it is to solve it. The mayor and governor eventually
realized what Dewey had discovered early in his investigation: crime is
an amorphous problem with multifarious causes and no easy solutions.
Still, the 1930s was a decade of undue optimism about crime fighting.
The rise of sociology and criminology during the 1920s and 1930s lent
credence to the simplistic belief that crime could be eradicated once social scientists diagnosed its causes, studied its development, and offered
its cures. Crime conferences became the showcases of scientific criminology know-how. In September 1935 Lehman convened the largest such
conference ever held at the state level. The meeting gave civic reformers
a sense of participating in a good cause, experts the chance to pontificate,
and citizens the opportunity to air their grievances. In retrospect, much

of what happened was mere rhetoric and foolishness, but the conference did result in several legal changes that helped Dewey's prosecutions.

In tackling the crime issue, Lehman drew on the experiences of his immediate predecessors in Albany, Al Smith and Franklin Roosevelt, both of whom had deep roots in the criminal justice reform movement of the 1920s. Smith, arguably New York's finest governor, cultivated a national and state reputation as a crime fighter. He began the push for change in 1919, when he appointed a committee to survey deplorable prison conditions. The resulting report, which called for better organization, more sophisticated classification of prisoners, and improved education and working conditions, led to the creation of a state Bureau of Corrections. Seven years later, Smith became one of the nation's first prominent politicians to argue that the country was experiencing an unprecedented crime wave. Citing figures showing a steady increase in U.S. homicide rates—from 9,500 in 1922 to 11,000 in 1924—he pointed out that only 151 people met violent deaths in England and Wales during 1923.[1]

Smith's charges hit a raw, if ill-defined, public nerve. He received letters from across the country agreeing that crime threatened public well-being, even though his admirers held widely disparate views of what constituted crime and criminals. One writer opined, "The biggest crooks—and meanest—in the United States are in big business. The combined sum of all the burglaries, robberies, forgeries, and other illegal forms of thievery is a mere trifle in comparison with the amounts eased out of the pockets of the common herd by the local forms of thievery practiced by some of the big business interests." Another writer said the most serious crimes involved bootlegging "devils" who stayed out of jail "by bribing officials, district attorneys, judges, clerks, lawyers, go-betweens, and hangers-on." Still others blamed the foreign-born and labor activists.[2]

Smith's correspondence reveals similar disagreements about the causes and solutions of crime. One attorney attributed most violent crime to drug addicts and alcoholics who "become slaves of habit [and] rob to buy booze or dope." This claim fit in well with the beliefs of Prohibition critics who claimed that the unpopular law had created a new class of criminals. Some blamed the laxity of the legal system and the coddling of juvenile delinquents; one writer spoke for many when he said permissiveness had "turned many a child, who might have been saved if promptly taken in hand, into an habitual criminal." A school administrator believed most crimes were caused by the perpetrator's emotional and intellectual instability, while others blamed guns, poor family life, and declining morals.[3]

To get a clearer picture of the problem, Smith and other politicians proposed sweeping studies. During the 1920s, the most common vehicles for these studies were crime commissions; in 1925 both Smith and Roosevelt helped found the National Crime Commission, a private group largely funded with money from U.S. Steel Corporation. Roosevelt used his connection with the association to gain both national attention for himself and as a means of financial support for his chief political advisor, Louis Howe, who was hired as an assistant to its chairman.[4] Smith, who was eyeing the presidential nomination, also viewed the commission as a vehicle for gaining national recognition.

Encouraged by the many letters he received praising his commitment to the national crime-fighting group, Smith decided to adopt the crime commission idea for New York. In mid-May 1926, the legislature approved the state commission and provided $50,000 in funding. Smith appointed two newspapermen, a surgeon, a volunteer with boys' groups, a social worker, two state senators, and two assemblymen to the commission. Notable for their absence were legal experts—perhaps a reflection of Smith's desire for publicity as well as the failure of a committee that Smith had appointed three years earlier to modernize New York's laws. The committee, comprising only lawyers, labored in relative obscurity.[5]

Smith's new crime panel took on the name of its chairman, state Republican Senator Caleb Baumes of Newburgh. Under his direction, the Baumes Commission showed both the strengths and weaknesses of commissions. At its best, the Baumes Commission provided political capital for its members and Governor Smith while offering a clearinghouse and sounding board for citizen complaints and do-gooders' suggestions. To its detriment, however, it followed in the footsteps of the National Crime Commission, confusing crime with Prohibition and fostering simplistic notions of crime's causes, including xenophobia.[6]

At its worst, the Baumes Commission's hardline positions demonstrated the potential dangers of anticrime measures adopted in the heat of public fury and the absence of a clearly defined agenda. With the advice of other law-and-order groups, notably the Association of Grand Jurors of New York County, the committee persuaded the legislature to adopt the Baumes Law—a harsh mandatory sentencing act that evoked opprobrium from enlightened critics nationwide and ultimately threw New York's sentencing and parole system into chaos. The Baumes Law, passed in 1926, mandated that all fourth offenders receive life imprisonment. Get-tough proponents from around the nation hailed the measure; one Texan praised Smith for the "wonderful effect the Baumes Law is having on crime suppression in the Empire State" and asked for more information so he could urge its adoption in Texas.[7]

The Baumes Law served as a prototype for similar legislation in other states, including West Virginia, Michigan, and California. Two years after its passage Julius Hallheimer, writing in *The Century Magazine*, said a case in which a man was sentenced to life for having a pint of liquor "demonstrates . . . the lack of a thoughtful discrimination in dealing with the complex problem of the enforcement of the criminal law." He added:

> In 1926, it was loudly proclaimed that a gigantic crime wave was engulfing the nation, and the daily press began carrying columns devoted to the increase in crime. We fulminated against judges, juries, lawyers and the administration of the criminal law in general. The agitation for law revision became relentless, and in customary American fashion, it was decided to legislate the crime wave out of existence. The rest is a matter of common knowledge—the product of the revolt, as was to be expected was one more Draconian law. . . . Throughout the country the legal machinery was geared up, and virtually the entire tempo of our judicial system was altered. . . . [The Baumes Law] . . . was heralded far and wide "as the most progressive criminal legislation of the century." The "Babbits" heaved a sign of relief; crime assuredly was banished.[8]

Meanwhile, in New York the Baumes Law quickly gained critics. One citizen wrote to Smith claiming to be "one of the few voices crying in the wilderness against the barbaric absurdity of an arbitrary life sentence after a fourth felony conviction without regard to the character of the felony, the capacity and condition of the prisoner or the circumstances of the crime." He wasn't alone; a December 1926 article in the *New York Daily News* reported that some New Yorkers believed there had been a rise in the number of police shootings because criminals would do anything to avoid capture and life in prison. Even New York County District Attorney Joab Banton said the law was often too harsh, explaining that it was sometimes difficult to define a habitual criminal: "We may recognize him in the street and in the theater, or as he is depicted in fiction, but before the bar of justice he becomes a most elusive character." In 1930 even Baumes repudiated his law by supporting a parole system recommended by a Roosevelt-appointed commission.[9]

The most famous crime commission of the era was appointed by President Hoover, in 1929, to investigate why Prohibition was failing. Known officially as the National Commission of Law Observance and Enforcement, it was more popularly recognized by the name of its chairman, former Attorney General George W. Wickersham. After a two-year investigation, the Wickersham Commission issued a report decrying lax enforcement of the liquor laws but arguing against repeal of the Eighteenth Amendment. The disparity between the Wickersham Report's findings and its conclusions, and the questionable results of crime commissions in general, led to their abandonment in favor of crime conferences in the 1930s. Manned by experts, meeting for shorter periods of time, and conducting business with less expense, these conferences served the same purposes as commissions by offering do-gooders a forum and politicians a chance for recognition. George Medalie, for example, presented his blueprint for Dewey's special investigation at a national conference called by U.S. Attorney General Homer Cummings in 1934.[10]

Lehman announced plans for his own conference, which he titled "Crime, the Criminal and Society," in July 1935, several weeks after Dewey launched his investigation. To ensure that the meeting garnered sufficient publicity, the governor invited such nationally known speakers as J. Edgar Hoover and U.S. Chief Justice Charles Evans Hughes. When neither could attend, Lehman settled for a virtual "who's who" roster of legal experts in New York. Among the best-known speakers was Dewey, who considered the conference little more than a publicity stunt and later told an interviewer, "It was a dull summer, crime was big news, and he decided to hold a crime conference to indicate that he was on top of what was bothering the people."[11]

Dewey tried to duck the conference, but Lehman insisted he attend. His vague speech—basically a rehash of what he had told the public in his first radio broadcast—outlined again the complexity of rackets, the need for "modern," intensive investigations, and the usefulness of public cooperation. Another skeptic was New York City magistrate Anna Kross. After reviewing the proposed agenda, she warned that it was "far too academic, and as a result, the conference is in danger of deteriorating into a seminar, which will be merely talky and ineffectual." Dewey's reluctance and Kross' dubiety were the exceptions; most of the state's criminal justice experts were eager to attend. For example, attorney Robert Daru wrote to Lehman aide Charles Poletti, expressing surprise that he had not been asked to the conference in light of his "extensive" experience in anticrime activities. Robert Appleton, head of the Association of Grand Jurors of New York County, registered similar pique that his organization was not asked to send a representative.[12]

Even those with prior commitments wrote to Lehman suggesting items for the agenda. Radio commentator Phelps Phelps told Lehman he should remodel the state Department of Justice after Hoover's FBI. Charles Burdick, a member of the state's law-revision commission, said the conference should spread information rather than come up with more legislation, much of it needless. Another would-be guest suggested the conference be aimed at using the machinery of the law against "real crooks, instead of flooding the prisons and cluttering up the courts with fools, bums and simpletons." Others recommended that the conference deal with proposals to fight juvenile delinquency, expedite trials, and curb recidivism by doing a better job of making punishment fit the crime.[13]

To some extent Lehman addressed all these concerns; his crime conference agenda covered practically every issue of New York law enforcement. In his widely broadcast opening speech on September 30, Lehman cited the increasing boldness of racketeers whose "arrogance and cynicism" posed a "constant challenge not only to law enforcement officials

but to the very fundamentals of our democratic form of government."
He attributed the alleged increase in organized crime to public indiffer-
ence and impotent law enforcement and set five goals for the conference:
better integration of law enforcement machinery, improved cooperation
between states and between states and the federal government, new laws,
an improved public consciousness prompting citizens to help police, and
an "aroused public opinion which will constantly demand efficient, honest, and courageous action on the part of public officials."[14]

Given the broad generality of most of these goals, it is not surprising
that the conference degenerated into a cacophony of differing agendas
and vague rhetoric. For example, New York City's commissioner of cor-
rection told one session: "The criminal of today is the product not only
of the society of today but of human society since man began." Former
U.S. Attorney Charles Tuttle said: "Much of our crime is merely the
symptom of profound maladjustments and injustices. Much of our criminal law is ineffective because [it is] not in harmony with sound sociolog-
ical principles." State Attorney General John J. Bennett, Jr., observed that
the home is the best place to teach moral behavior, but added "the home
that America once knew has almost disappeared."[15]

More substantive ideas were raised when the conference split into
smaller groups to discuss such subjects as detection and apprehension of
criminals, prosecution and the courts, juvenile delinquency, and prisons
and parole. Many of the reforms suggested were unconstitutional. For
example, Tuttle proposed, among other things, weakening the Fifth
Amendment to allow prosecutors to comment on a defendant's failure
to take the stand and accepting majority rather than unanimous verdicts
in capital cases. Attorney General Bennett wanted thirty minutes of every
school day to be devoted to religion or ethics; and one panel envisioned
a new relationship between church and state that would require all children to read the Ten Commandments. Others proposed fingerprinting
all citizens or requiring everyone to carry an identification card. One
grand jury association member angered newspaper editors by suggesting
that journalists be licensed, while other participants favored driving
shady lawyers out of business by replacing private criminal practice with
a public defender system. Not all the suggestions sound unfamiliar to
modern ears. Gun control was a popular issue but, then as now, the

National Rifle Association fought it bitterly and successfully. George Medalie recommended that judges be appointed by the governor rather than elected. Several lawyers suggested useful changes to New York State law—including a proposal to permit conspirators to testify against each other without the necessity for corroborating evidence.[16]

When the four-day conference ended on October 4, it was unclear whether Lehman had achieved any of his stated goals. The public had been bombarded by radio speeches and newspaper coverage; but citizen concern about crime was already high before the conference, as shown by the outcry that led to Dewey's appointment. The conference seemed to have no better effect on encouraging reluctant witnesses to come forward; Dewey still had to pry out testimony by threatening witnesses with contempt proceedings. Nor was there any noticeable increase in cooperation between law enforcement agencies in New York and other states or the federal government. Yet, whatever its stated goals, the conference clearly boosted Lehman's image as a crime fighter. The governor received many letters praising his efforts. One newspaper editorial called the anticrime crusade "the greatest peacetime movement ever taken by any governor of the State of New York." Because his opening address was broadcast nationally, letters flowed in to Lehman from around the country.[17]

As had been true during other wars on crime, Lehman's conference provoked numerous suggestions and offers of help. One woman from Salamanca, New York, offered to accept a mere $500 a week plus expenses to fight organized crime: "I would like to help you all in your crime racket drive and I know that I can help and fine out a lot for I had some experience in Fla., about five years under cover I worked in secrete there and I all ways got what they wanted me to get for them." Another man suggested that Lehman create a force of detectives to stamp out concealed weapons by asking everyone on the street, "Are you carrying a pistol or a weapon?" Innocent citizens, the writer predicted, would not be upset by the question and police could easily identify guilty suspects because they would flee. He added: "I am willing to be stopped and asked fifty times a day, if I can be of any assistance to the anti-crime movement and I am sure every good citizen feels the same."[18]

Other correspondents used the crime conference as an excuse to air

grievances against perceived social ills. One wrote that crime would decrease if married women were thrown off the public payroll—a move he
claimed would cut down on the number of idle young men. A Rochester
citizen opined that movies like *Little Caesar* encouraged boys to admire
criminals instead of cheering for "sports idols." A Williamsburg resident
complained that American Federation of Labor President William Green
had refused to take action against the unethical activities of a union
representative. Not all letters offered frivolous complaints; Lehman received suggestions on juvenile delinquency, extradition, and grand jury
selection. On October 22, he appointed a thirty-member commission of
law professors, politicians, and legal experts to sort through the correspondence and the ideas raised at the conference and then draft a legislative package.[19]

The governor, always cautious by nature, hoped to avoid the pitfalls
described by Raymond Moley in his conference speech. Moley, a Columbia professor who helped draft New Deal anticrime policy, had warned
of the dangers of politicians' overreacting to "the goad of sharp public
opinion." He recited some of the Draconian measures advocated by the
Baumes Commission, likening the legislator who voted for them to "a
man or a horse, or a dog, [who] if whipped, will violently seek the short-
est line between the place where he stands and the place where the whip
will no longer reach him. When looked upon in retrospect, sometimes
his movements are entirely irrational."[20]

Lehman's crime conference and Dewey's success against usurers
eclipsed La Guardia's own efforts to get headlines as a crime fighter.
Behind the scenes, however, the mayor continued to meet with anticrime
groups and officials—the grand jury association, the police chief, and
Dewey. But there were few headlines in such activities. As Dewey aptly
pointed out, the mayor "tried to regard himself as a racket buster as
well as a mayor. He'd keep on making these speeches about 'punks and
tinhorns' wherever he could to get in the act . . . [but] he had no tools
at hand, except publicity."[21]

On December 20, 1935, the mayor made one of his most famous
grandstand plays. Its target was Ciro Terranova, better known to New
York newspaper readers as the "Artichoke King" because of his alleged
control of the city's market in miniature artichokes—a delicacy of the

Italian diet. La Guardia arranged an elaborate attack but kept the details from Commissioner of Markets William Fellowes Morgan until the last minute. When the two men arrived at the Bronx Terminal Market, La Guardia was carrying several large proclamations under his arm. He had arranged for bugles, but the instruments froze in the frigid weather. "Undaunted the mayor climbed to the platform of a truck where, unrolling one of the large proclamations, he read it to the astonished crowd. Under an ancient law permitting the mayor in an emergency to ban the distribution of food, the sale of artichokes was now prohibited in the public markets."[22]

La Guardia's performance drew negative reviews. The *New York Herald Tribune* said the mayor's efforts on behalf of the artichoke led it to wonder if "the world today is a bit mad." The *New York Post* asked: "Where does La Guardia get the idea that he had the right to keep merchants from selling artichokes. . . . What induces him to believe that New York City can be ruled by proclamation." Typically, the morning of his performance La Guardia covered his legal bases by dispatching an aide to Washington to persuade the U.S. Department of Agriculture to revoke Terranova's license to sell artichokes. When the license was canceled, the mayor quietly rescinded his proclamation.[23]

La Guardia seized another opportunity to gain headlines in early January, when the New York Court of Appeals struck down a vaguely worded public enemy law, which prohibited "persons of bad reputation from associating with criminals." The mayor's displeasure with the ruling was clear: "Our criminal jurisprudence was not developed under conditions with which we are confronted today. Law must keep ahead of organized crime. The number of known criminals at large and their present activities is the living example that the present system is ineffective. . . . I cannot get sentimental for the crooks, the pimps and the punks. Every executive knows how difficult it is to protect life and property today. Without the aid of the courts it becomes an almost impossible task." La Guardia said city police would follow the law, but, he warned, "That does not mean we will pamper, pet or parley with criminals."[24]

La Guardia's dispute with the appellate courts pointed up the difficulties of balancing concerns about constitutional safeguards with stronger anticrime measures. Propelled by public outrage, many politicians and lobbying groups, such as the grand jury association, felt they had a mandate to push harsh measures that violated the spirit of the U.S. Constitution. Their efforts were rebuffed by labor unions and the American Civil Liberties Union, which had long-standing concerns about the conservative way in which the courts already interpreted the law. Moderates attempted to steer a middle course. Many civic leaders, including La Guardia and Lehman, largely were motivated by ideals, although other politicians of various stripes hoped to gain headlines by fighting bills offered by opponents. The grand jury association and like-minded groups sought measures that would increase their own power while other organizations, including the National Rifle Association, fought to protect their turf. All of these crosscurrents surfaced when Governor Lehman unveiled the legislative package he claimed was the first attempt to attack all aspects of New York's crime problems in a unified manner. Lehman's sixty proposals covered virtually every aspect of New York law enforcement.[25]

Many of his bills were aimed at unifying New York's scattered efforts and bringing smaller communities up to the same professional level as cities. To that end, he advocated improved police training, consolidation of jails and police departments in rural areas, stricter bans on prosecutors' private practices, the establishment of probation departments in the fourteen counties without them, and the unification of all of the state's disparate parole systems under the state Department of Corrections. Other bills were relatively uncontroversial attempts to modernize New York law enforcement. They included measures to permit women jurors, set up different security levels of prisons, improve record keeping on juvenile delinquency, create a state department of justice modeled after the federal one, ease maximum sentencing requirements to allow judges greater discretion, and ease crowding in local jails by establishing a farm colony or work camp for vagrants, alcoholics, and drug addicts.[26]

Had his proposals been limited to such noncontroversial actions, they might have produced only the usual flak from Republicans concerned about increased costs. Many of Lehman's suggestions, however, were get-tough measures directed at conditions in New York City. These bills and suggested amendments to curb civil rights guaranteed by the state constitution rankled civil libertarians, labor groups, and defense attorneys. Lehman knew many of these bills faced an uphill battle, but he had come to believe that the serious social menace posed by crime justified them. The public enemy statute was struck down as unconstitutional on the same day he proposed it. In advocating the fingerprinting of every New York resident, Lehman conceded that the measure could succeed only with a massive public education campaign.[27]

Some of Lehman's proposals had been promoted unsuccessfully in the past, many by the grand jury association. These included reducing the number of peremptory challenges in criminal cases, permitting waiver of a jury trial, allowing less-than-unanimous verdicts, and giving attorneys the right to impeach their own witnesses. The grand jury association also had advocated creating a state department of justice, tightening bail bond requirements, and allowing judges and prosecutors to comment to the jury about a defendant's failure to testify. In 1934, the association's laundry list of reforms had been ignored by the legislature. At the time, association president Robert Appleton sourly noted: "Not one bill was passed, or even seriously considered that would have tended to modernize a system of criminal procedure that is essentially the same now as it was when the Constitution of the U.S. went into effect on the first Wednesday of March 1789 in the days of the ox cart and weekly stage coach." Appleton attributed the failure to the fact that "every loophole, every bar to justice and incentive to crime," in New York "was sturdily and successfully defended" by legislators, many of whom were lawyers. After Dewey's appointment, however, the grand jury association became a power to be courted. The change was symbolized by the retirement of the association's long-time president, Robert Appleton, and his replacement by Lee Thompson Smith, the foreman of the runaway grand jury. In March 1936, the association held its first banquet. Lehman, Dewey, La Guardia, and several judges spoke, and numerous law professors, reporters, and senators unable to attend sent their regrets.[28]

To his credit, Lehman parted company when it came to the association's more extreme and questionable proposals, such as instituting regular grand juries to investigate government in New York City and abolishing Fifth Amendment privileges against self-incrimination. In the first proposal, the association argued, city corruption could be curbed if grand juries served for six months every year to investigate government.

To ensure their independence, the grand juries would have legal counsel appointed by the state instead of being advised by members of the district attorney's staff. It wasn't only Tammany Democrats who objected to giving grand juries such sweeping power. Under New York law, grand juries had the power to investigate specific allegations of public corruption; but, one lawyer noted, under the proposed change grand juries would be able to act out of "malice, speculation, curiosity or politics." In a memo to the mayor he wrote: "The bad feature of the bill is that eventually persons moved by considerations of self-interest would maneuver for places on the grand jury list and it might easily become an adjunct of party politics and be used as an engine of oppression."[29]

Other politicians were not so solicitous of civil liberties, and many judges and lawyers agreed with the association that the Fifth Amendment should be abolished. One judge, writing in *The Panel*, asserted that innocent people rushed to defend themselves so the right of silence was invoked only by the guilty. He added, "Whatever the necessity may have been to protect the liberty of the individual in the past, such a rule today is productive only of injustice. It no longer protects the innocent, but has become the strongest shield for the guilty." New York Attorney General Bennett also held this view, as did Dewey. In a speech on January 25, Dewey said: "we are living an age of ox cart criminal law enforcement. It has not yet risen even to the efficiency of the much publicized horse and buggy days. We are still submitting, in criminal law enforcement, to strait-jackets imposed centuries ago upon royal tyrants by revolt of an oppressed people. The privilege against self-incrimination now embedded in our Constitution is an appropriate example." Dewey claimed that most citizens opposed this provision of the Fifth Amendment but that it had not been abolished because it "is enshrined only in the hearts of the bar [and] is of value to the professional criminal." Dewey supported several other elements of the governor's program, including Lehman's proposals that witnesses' names not be made public before trial, that lawyers and judges be able to comment on a defendant's failure to testify, and the use of majority rather than unanimous jury verdicts. Dewey argued that the public was increasingly aware of the problems of inefficient, outdated law enforcement and warned lawyers and politicians that if they did not "join wholeheartedly in the movement initiated by the governor to overhaul the entire structure of the criminal law and its enforcement . . . there will be a reaction of incalculable force."[30]

Lehman's crime package ignited a firestorm in the legislature. One cynical journalist, who incorrectly speculated that Lehman had launched his crusade against crime only because the Democrats had no other serious issues, said the Republicans fell right into the trap. Noting that a war on crime "hardly seems an issue at first glance," Powell Hickman said, "the Republicans played true to form and made it one. Enough of them opposed the anti-crime bills to stir up a real, lively fight." No doubt politics did create hardships for Lehman's crime package in the legislature; 1936 was an election year, and Republicans assumed that Lehman would run for reelection.[31]

Not all the opponents were politically motivated Republicans. Lehman's package had inspired other groups, including the grand jury association, to sponsor their own bills. The result was a confusing mass of legislation—some of it mild and some of it so farfetched that critics went on the attack. In its February 1936 bulletin, the American Civil Liberties Union condemned six of the bills: "The gain in increased efficiency does not compensate for the serious threat of harm to law-abiding citizens who because of their political, religious or labor views are feared or disliked by administrative officials or the police." The ACLU objected to three fingerprinting bills: one calling for universal fingerprinting, another calling for fingerprinting in misdemeanor cases, and a third forbidding the return of fingerprints to the defendant after an acquittal. The organization also criticized a bill allowing New York City magistrates to hold lawyers in contempt, another that permitted judges and juries to be informed about a concealed weapon, and a third giving lawyers and judges the right to comment on a defendant's failure to take the stand.[32]

Unions added their objections. To the West Bronx Workers' Club, several of the proposals "are not only Un-American but also they are unnecessary encroachments upon the rights of individuals." The secretary of Local 1102 of the Retail Dry Goods Clerks' Union had even more specific objections to several bills he said were directed specifically at trade unions. He complained that fingerprinting would have an unfair impact on strikers arrested for misdemeanors. He also objected to a proposal eliminating the need for corroborating testimony, arguing it would benefit "unscrupulous labor spies and strikebreakers, who will be able to claim that they were hired by a union leader for the purpose of committing a depredation." Finally, he said, attempts to limit voir dire would give prejudiced judges more freedom to pick hostile juries in labor disputes.[33]

The National Rifle Association also organized a letter-writing campaign to Lehman opposing any new requirements for licensing, including a proposed bill to standardize the licensing process statewide. Many criminals in New York City who were unable to obtain city permits for guns simply applied upstate, where requirements were laxer. Typical of the many letters Lehman received was one from New York City whose author said the proposed gun restrictions would "decrease the number of honest citizens possessing guns but will considerably increase the number of crimes in this state." If it becomes tougher to get guns, he reasoned, honest citizens will not get them; then, "after the public is particularly disarmed, the criminals will naturally become more cocky." Like other NRA members, this correspondent urged that policemen be given greater latitude to shoot gangsters and other criminals.[34]

Lehman glossed over all these concerns as he campaigned for his package. He maintained that "in our desire to protect the innocent we have made the conviction of the criminal frequently impossible." Arrogant racketeers, he said, were taking advantage of legal loopholes to menace decent citizens and ridicule honest government. If the governor could sidestep the pitfalls, the legislature could not and the bills had heavy going from the outset. Although the Senate passed many of Lehman's proposals, most of his anticrime package was scuttled in the Assembly. Problems began when the Assembly's Republican-controlled Codes Committee took the unusual action of reporting out the bills without recommendation. Chairman James R. Robinson said the action was taken to overcome the objection of some members who bitterly opposed the measures. The committee as a whole decided it was better to give the full Assembly "an opportunity to vote on the anti-crime measures than to strangle them in committee and permit them to die a slow and painless death." Robinson's prediction was accurate; both Republicans and Democrats attacked the bills when they arrived on the Assembly floor. Republican Speaker of the House Irving Ives said some of the bills would "throw back the administration of justice by trial into the system prevailing in the Middle Ages." Horace Stone, a lawyer who headed the Judiciary Committee, called the crime package "ninety percent rot." Even Democratic Assemblyman John A. Byrnes of Manhattan dismissed the bills as "crack-brain" and "a hodge-podge of ill-considered legislation."[35]

Because members of both parties derided the bills it was difficult to blame partisanship for their defeat. Both the newspapers and Lehman attributed the loss to the fact that most New York legislators were lawyers. There was nothing new to this argument, but the complaint gained a wider public resonance when Lehman seized on it. As the *New York Herald Tribune* reported, "Republicans vied with Democrats in their opposition. But one perceived in them an even more sinister conspiracy than that of politics—the conspiracy of lawyer-legislators to perpetuate for their profession the obstructions to justice by which it prospers." This argument had widespread public appeal. One New York City businessman suggested that Lehman introduce a bill barring lawyers from holding any public offices except legal ones, such as prosecutor or attorney general. He admitted such a proposal "might stir up more of an uproar, but if you did make this suggestion you would get a tremendous response from those in favor of it, as I have heard a great many men comment on the fact that our nation is run by lawyers, and the sorry mess they have made of it." Another correspondent wrote Lehman that, in light of what was happening to the crime bills, he would make it a point in the future to vote against all lawyers running for the state assembly.[36]

New Yorkers accustomed to Lehman's calm approach to the state's problems were taken aback by the governor's heated campaigning for his anticrime package. After the bills seemed destined for failure in February, he publicly criticized legislators, accusing the Codes Committee of sabotaging his program "without publicly bearing the responsibility of their slaughter." He complained that as soon as his package hit the floor of the Assembly, it became the target of "a flood of criticism, far-fetched argument, hypothetical calculation, bitter opposition and vituperation." He asked legislators to consider what their "strangling" of the crime bill meant "to the mother in her home with her children, to the father who is doing his best to lead an honest, law-abiding life, to the small merchant, retailer or tradesman who is trying to earn a living to support himself and family by honestly running a small business but who is harassed by gangsters and racketeers." He described one critic, Horace M. Stone, as "a great reactionary force" and noted that other legislators "took almost a delight in killing bills, instead of in passing bills to prevent killing." Throughout the spring, Lehman appealed to the public for help. The Association of Grand Jurors of New York County responded with a letter-writing campaign, and other groups, such as the New York Federation of Churches and the League of Women Voters, also supported him.[37]

From the outset, it was clear that Lehman was scoring a political victory with his anticrime crusade. His efforts won plaudits from newspapers and voters across the state. Even though Lehman always looked back with pride on his anticrime accomplishments, most of his major proposals never were passed. The most famous law resulting from the 1936 legislative session was suggested by Dewey and was widely known as the "Dewey Law." It was modeled after a seventy-year-old federal statute permitting the offenses of different people to be combined into one indictment (joinder). Dewey argued that the change was necessary because it was difficult to connect a mob boss to crimes he had delegated to subordinates. In fact, the only way to prove such a link was to charge all ring members with conspiracy, which in New York was still a misdemeanor. Charging many crimes in one indictment made it possible to prosecute an entire criminal organization. Lehman endorsed Dewey's proposal to the legislature on March 4, and it passed the following month. Looking back years later, Dewey said the joinder bill was his "most signal success in the amendment of the criminal law." That fact became apparent almost as soon as the bill was passed. Dewey used the new law immediately in what would become his most famous case—the prosecution of Lucky Luciano.[38]

≈ ≈ ≈ ≈

CHAPTER SIX

Luciano: The Preliminaries

OF ALL HIS CASES, Dewey's prosecution of Lucky Luciano for heading a prostitution ring created the most indelible public impression. More than his other efforts, the Luciano case epitomized the battle between good and evil. Dewey had tangled with other crooks—for example, bootlegger Waxey Gordon and the loan sharks—but none of them could match Luciano's sinister aura. Luciano was the archetypal gangster. Sicilian-born and bred in the rough streets of Manhattan's Lower East Side, his lavish lifestyle and arrogance seemed to reflect a complete disdain for decency. By linking him to the degradation of women, Dewey tore away all the potential glamour that perversely might have flowed from Luciano's gambling and bootlegging activities. The public and the courts, already predisposed for a Dewey success story, lapped up the high drama of a morality play that pitted the dashing midwestern prosecutor against the swarthy gangster.

The hyperbole overshadowed several bizarre aspects of the case. First of all, Dewey had to recast Luciano as the nation's worst racketeer. Before he ran afoul of Dewey, Luciano was little known outside New York's underworld, and even in that environment he was just an average bad guy. Turning him into the nation's arch gangster and convicting that phantom creation required extraordinary, and high-handed, measures. These began when Dewey's men and the New York police rounded up more than a hundred witnesses and kept them isolated from outside contacts until they agreed to testify. The result was the shaky evidence that became the basis of Luciano's conviction. In the hysterical atmosphere surrounding the trial, it became impossible to determine whether, in fact, Dewey had convicted Luciano for the one crime he had never committed. A handful of contemporary critics raised the question, but their voices were drowned out by those who cared little about legal niceties and recognized that Dewey had scored a stunning victory against organized crime. Perhaps the most surprising aspect of the case was that Dewey himself did not realize its importance until he was persuaded by his only black, female assistant. Ironically, the Luciano conviction, which cemented Dewey's national reputation as the era's greatest racket buster, cast a shadow over his later political career. Instead of ending his time as governor of New York in peace, Dewey saw his career forever shrouded in suspicion because he had granted the nation's Public Enemy Number One a commutation and safe passage back to Italy.

Separating the fact from the fiction of Luciano's life is nearly impossible. Even the alteration of his name from Salvatore Lucania to Charles "Lucky" Luciano is shrouded in legend. Journalists claim that he dropped "Salvatore" because the nickname "Sallie" sounded feminine and adopted the moniker Lucky after surviving a brutal beating by rival gangsters. The changed spelling of his last name reportedly occurred after an encounter with police.[1] What is clear is that while Thomas Dewey was growing up in the bucolic security of rural Michigan, Luciano was learning life's harder lessons in the impoverished Sicilian village of Lercara Friddi. Enticed by tales of riches in America, Luciano's parents and their five children emigrated to New York in 1906.

The Lucanias soon learned they had traded the security and poverty of Sicily for the insecurity and poverty of New York's teeming slums. The horrid conditions made a particularly deep impression on Luciano, who recognized the disparity between his father's dreams and the reality of life on the "gold-paved" streets of America. Alienated from school, he spent more time on the streets than his brothers. From his perspective, there were but two career paths in America. The first was the plodding, honest route taken by his father and brothers. The second was the fast route taken by the well-heeled dons who preyed on their newly arrived fellow countrymen. Luciano ran afoul of the law at a young age. In 1911 he was sent to the Brooklyn Truant School. Five years later he was arrested for peddling heroin outside a poolroom frequented by addicts and pushers; he was freed after leading police to more important drug dealers. During the next decade he formed friendships and alliances with other neighborhood toughs and became involved in a variety of illegal activities, including gambling and petty thievery.[2]

As young hoodlums on the make, Luciano and his friends Meyer Lansky and Benjamin "Bugsy" Siegel were initially indistinguishable from thousands of gang members who had risen from New York's immigrant slums during the previous century. By 1855 New York already had an estimated thirty thousand people who were either gang members or owed their allegiance to the mostly Irish toughs. Before the Civil War most gangs operated in the congested slums of Lower Manhattan, but after the war, as the city grew, the gangs diversified and extended their power and reach. The trend continued with the late-nineteenth-century wave of immigrants, and soon Italian and Jewish gangsters were threatening Irish supremacy. By 1920, the Irish gangsters controlled Manhattan's West Side, while the Jews and Italians held sway over the East Side.[3] Like the Roach Guards, Plug Uglies, Shirt Tails, Dead Rabbits, and Whyos of the previous century, Luciano and his compatriots wore distinguishing clothes, carried weapons, and prowled the streets looking for profit and purveying violence.

Although there was nothing new in the circumstances of their birth or their early careers, Luciano and his friends lived in an era that ensured them a notoriety denied to their predecessors. In Luciano's Lower East Side neighborhood, many of the richest men were dons of the Unione Siciliano—a secret society that arrived with the Italian immigrants and was modeled on the Sicilian Mafia. Members were initiated into the society in a blood rite that involved scratching their wrists and rubbing them with the bleeding wrists of older members. At first the Unione also included some respectable members, but by Luciano's time, the gangsters had taken control.[4] With their Sicilian clannishness and Old World outlook, the Unione was feared in the Italian slums but not beyond them.

The Unione's mode of operation contrasted sharply with the outward-looking enterprises of such homegrown criminals as Arnold Rothstein, who applied the genius of American business principles to illegal enterprise. Rothstein, best known for the popular but unfounded accusation that he had fixed the 1919 World Series, amassed a fortune in gambling and reinvested his profits in the varied activities of younger protégés like Luciano and Lansky. Unlike the Italian dons, American criminals made deals across ethnic boundaries and eschewed hierarchy and tight organization.[5]

Luciano's genius rested in his bridging of these disparate worlds, but he learned his early lessons from Rothstein. Although it is not clear when the two first met, Rothstein did provide the capital and advice that transformed Luciano from a small-time hood into a well-heeled bootlegger. Running illegal liquor required capital and organization, and Rothstein initially provided both. Lending money to a host of aspiring bootleggers, including Gordon and Luciano, he then organized supplies and arranged transportation from Scottish distilleries. Prohibition fostered a competitive environment in which only the best financed and best organized survived. By the end of the 1920s a few gangs had replaced the many independent operators and the resulting turf wars had become the stuff of Prohibition legend. In New York, the most famous rivalry pitted two Sicilians, Salvatore Maranzano and Giuseppe "Joe the Boss" Masseria, against each other in the Castellammarese War for control of the Italian underworld. The bloody confrontation, a throwback to Sicilian feuds, sparked headlines during 1931 and worried nonaligned racketeers like Luciano, who feared the publicity would provoke intensified attention from law enforcement. As a Sicilian, Luciano was well placed to end the feud. He met with Maranzano and offered to kill Masseria. After that was accomplished, Luciano feared Maranzano would turn on him; so he struck first, arranging Maranzano's assassination in September 1931.[6]

Legend maintains that when Luciano took over the Unione, he created the modern Mafia and became the chieftain of the American underworld. This assertion is based on Dewey's characterizations of Luciano, subsequent biographical hype, and the belief that "organized crime is a monolithic alien conspiracy" controlled by secretive Sicilians who dominate crime in America and exert their corrupt influence over politics and honest business.[7]

In reality, then as now, the Mafia was only one part of a complex, constantly shifting underworld. A subtle and complicated process was at work in the vilification of Luciano and his spectacular rise to notoriety. There is no doubt Luciano was a powerful force among New York's criminals. The Unione Siciliano had enjoyed power before he took it over, and Prohibition and Luciano's business acumen certainly increased its influence and profits. But Italian gangsters were still just one element of New York's underworld. Irish mobsters continued to hold sway on the West Side of Manhattan, and other groups controlled their own bailiwicks. As historian Alan Block points out, it is more useful to look at organized criminals in terms of their organizing efforts than at the actual structures they create. By engaging in a series of deals, rather than creating a static organization, they could adapt to changing situations. Block notes that "the most efficient organized criminals were the most individualistic, the least committed to particular structures."[8]

Seen in this context, Luciano was not the head of New York's underworld, although he was a likely candidate when an emperor had to be found. With his scarred face, arrest record, garish and expensive lifestyle, Italian ancestry, and Lower East Side background, he epitomized lawlessness. Still, it would take a major publicity campaign to turn the obscure Luciano into the nation's most notorious gangster. On the eve of the Dewey investigation, Luciano was known only by the criminal community, his former bootleg customers, politicians, and members of New York's Italian community. Neither Luciano nor his name had the public recognition of Rothstein, Schultz, or Gordon. According to Dewey assistant Sol Gelb, "Luciano had never gotten any publicity to speak of before." Tellingly, Gelb said he had not recognized Luciano's prominence until after his conviction, when "the newspapers began to write about his position in the underworld."[9]

Although Luciano had a low profile with average citizens, he was well known to New York City's reform mayor, Fiorello La Guardia. The Little Flower hated all gangsters, but he nursed a special wrath for the Italian underworld that fostered negative stereotypes of Italian-Americans. As La Guardia aide Ernest Cuneo said, most publicity about Italian immigration centered "around tabloid headlines about the Capones, Fiaschettis, Costellos and similar scum of gangland. These lice were as typical of the Italian immigrant as John Dillinger was typical of the American Midwesterner. People knew John Dillinger was not representative, but they tended to think of Capone as a prototype of the Italian-American." One of La Guardia's first actions as mayor was launching a crusade against Frank Costello's slot machine racket. He made the newsreels by smashing the one-armed bandits and dumping them in the East River. Later (as described in Chapter 5 above), he challenged Ciro Terranova's hold over the artichoke market.[10]

Although La Guardia nursed a vendetta against Italian gangsters, his main focus in 1935 was Dutch Schultz. He shared a desire to get Schultz with Dewey and J. Edgar Hoover, who had labeled Schultz Public Enemy Number One. Once Schultz was killed, the crime busters sought a new target. It was not clear in the beginning how much Dewey knew or even cared about Luciano. He was far more interested in nabbing Tammany bosses and industrial racketeers, particularly Lepke and Gurrah. He had undoubtedly heard about Luciano's reputation as a bootlegger and gambler but preferred to steer clear of morals crimes. Left to his initial pursuits, Dewey might never have targeted Luciano; even when he learned of a probable path to convicting him, he needed much persuading to follow the leads. Eventually Dewey realized that going after Luciano "might provide, if nothing else, another dazzling headline grabber to satisfy the public while work on industrial rackets proceeded quietly."[11] He never looked back to consider whether his initial misgivings might have been warranted.

The Luciano case originated in New York's lower courts where, despite reformers' efforts, cases were still more likely to be settled by bribes than by law. This was particularly true in prostitution cases. Many of the women charged showed up with the same lawyers and had been coached to tell the same hard-luck stories. The prostitutes invariably claimed to have been innocently visiting friends or playing bridge when they were arrested. In spite of the similarity and implausibility of their stories, magistrates usually dismissed the charges. This pattern was particularly disturbing to Eunice Hunton Carter, the prosecutor in District Attorney Dodge's office responsible for handling the cases.

Carter was a rarity in New York City during the 1930s. In addition to being a female prosecutor, she was prominent in politics and community affairs and the first black awarded an honorary LL.D. degree from Smith College. A native of Atlanta, her parents had moved to New York City when she was six. After attending schools in Brooklyn, she earned bachelor's and master's degrees from Smith. She was a social worker for ten years and, later, a supervisor for the Emergency Home Relief Bureau. In

1932 she received her law degree from Fordham University and accepted a post as assistant district attorney in Dodge's office. In 1935 she served as secretary of the mayor's commission on conditions in Harlem. Carter was also a member of the housing committee of the Welfare Council of New York City and an active promoter of legislation to improve slum housing conditions. Under political pressure to hire blacks with a knowledge of Harlem, Dewey hired Carter away from Dodge's office.[12]

A "street-smart" lawyer, Carter was the first law enforcement official to discern new patterns in the fixing of prostitution cases and to recognize that the business was being better organized during the early 1930s. Corruption in vice cases was nothing new. The Seabury investigation's most scandalous revelations had centered on dishonest handling of women in the magistrates' courts. By focusing on corrupt law enforcement machinery instead of the pimps, madams, and whores, Seabury's investigation had the unintended consequence of relaxing police pressure on the business. Polly Adler, who ran a high-class call girl operation from a townhouse off Fifth Avenue, described the change. After the Seabury investigation, she said, "The police no longer were a headache; there was no more kowtowing to double-crossing vice squad men, no more hundred-dollar handshakes, no more phony raids to raise the month's quota. In fact, thanks to Judge Seabury and his not-very-merry men, I was able to operate for three years without breaking a lease." Ironically, by driving police out of the whorehouses, Seabury's probe had left the door open for hoodlums. When Prohibition ended in 1933, some gangs branched out into prostitution, attempting to organize it with the methods they had used to sell illegal liquor.[13]

Although Carter saw evidence of an organized racket, she had difficulties convincing others of its existence. Dodge ridiculed the idea. Dewey too was skeptical about setting out on what might be perceived as a moral crusade. He relented only when assistant Murray Gurfein argued that if Carter was right prostitution "had been turned into an assembly-line operation with justice corrupted and laws flouted." So Dewey told Carter, who had been pursuing leads on Dutch Schultz's empire in Harlem, to follow up her hunch. In September 1935 she began the arduous task of uncovering a syndicate amid the city's thousands of independent pimps and prostitutes.[14]

Dewey's initial skepticism was prescient; the public had a difficult time recognizing the distinction between a moral crusade and a rackets investigation. Probably no other Dewey probe evoked a public response as enthusiastic as the mistaken impression that he was moving against the world's oldest profession. Immediately after his appointment, Dewey began receiving letters complaining about the prevalence of prostitution. One urged a crackdown on the blackmailing activities of male prostitutes who frequented Times Square, Greenwich Village, and the park behind the New York Public Library on East 42nd Street. The complainant suggested passing a law requiring every citizen to carry a passport and added, "Tolerating those dangerous criminals is an error which can easily make the population believe that the police does not like to fight vice." Another writer complained of being cheated by prostitutes working out of an apartment on 46th Street. Giving the address of the apartment, the author, who signed himself "A Sucker," wrote: "Do your work, get them. Jip me for $3 and how." Not all the correspondents had obvious axes to grind; Dewey also received letters from neighbors, priests, and concerned relatives, naming names and locations.[15]

In addition to these leads, Carter had to sift through the voluminous records gathered by a Rockefeller Foundation study of New York prostitution conducted several years earlier. This report, covering the years 1927 to 1932, consisted largely of cards bearing names and addresses of brothels. In late October Carter spent hours combing through these records at the New York Public Library, despite the misgivings of George Worthington, general counsel for the Rockefeller study, who correctly predicted she would find the information outdated and useless.[16]

It is not clear how much, if any, information Carter gleaned from citizen complaints or the Rockefeller Foundation records. Had her information been limited to those well-worked fields, she would have made little progress. In this investigation, as in all Dewey probes, the key to success would lie in examining old problems through new lenses. Instead of attacking prostitution through the whores and working up, the Dewey investigators began with the fixers and worked down. Detectives watched the courts, then tailed the suspects. Dozens of whorehouses were wiretapped, with the permission of Judge McCook. As the evidence began to come in, Dewey recognized its significance and assigned other assistants to help Carter. By December they had charted the prostitution racket and by late January 1936 had compiled a list of the gunmen, narcotics peddlers, and pimps associated with the syndicate, as well as a partial list of whorehouses.[17]

Up to that point, Carter and other Dewey staff members had followed standard procedures for complex investigations. They sifted through thousands of documents, interviewed witnesses, and pounded much pavement. Then, at the end of January, the investigation took a spectacular twist that dazzled even jaded New Yorkers. Dewey reasoned that arresting one or two suspects would tip off the others; so, he set up an elaborate dragnet to ensure that none of the witnesses or suspects could escape. Imaginatively invoking a 1915 statute allowing prosecutors to jail witnesses who might flee, Dewey used it to imprison more than a hundred women and their associates until he obtained the evidence he needed for an indictment.

The first phase of Dewey's plan began during the early hours of January 31, 1936, when a squad of detectives assigned to his office rounded up twenty-nine major suspects—gunmen, narcotics peddlers, men who booked women into brothels, and their assistants. Detectives even went to Philadelphia to arrest Peter Balitzer, a key organizer. The second phase began the following night with the help of the city's plainclothes detectives except those assigned to the vice squad. To ensure secrecy, Dewey delayed telling his aides about the raids until the day they took place. To keep the regular police from tipping off suspects, he "created teams of men who hadn't worked together before, and sent them to unfamiliar neighborhoods where, at precisely five minutes before [the raids were to start], they would open envelopes with detailed instructions." The memos, which listed the madams' names and other information about the houses, advised police to "make every proper effort to make a complete case which will stand up in court" by catching girls in the act, searching the houses for records, and interviewing everyone present. Before being released, customers were asked their names, addresses, the prices they paid, and how they learned about the house. The prostitutes, madams, managers, maids, and doorkeepers were asked their names and excuses for being there before they were booked. Most of the prostitutes and their customers claimed to be playing bridge, an alibi usually belied by circumstance. When officers burst into a bedroom at one location on East 12th Street, they found a naked woman hurriedly putting on her coat while her customer, clad only in shorts, tried to pull up his pants. In the next room, another woman, clad only in a white evening gown, donned underwear in front of police.[18]

Rather than alert other suspects by dispatching patrol wagons, Dewey used taxis to bring the arresting officers and approximately one hundred prostitutes to the delivery entrance of the Woolworth Building. There they rode freight elevators to the special prosecutor's office, where, one lawyer recalled, "I've never seen so many prostitutes before or since. The rooms were crawling with them." For the next two days twenty assistants interrogated the witnesses. For younger staff members the marathon questioning provided valuable training; Charles Breitel said, "in the course of just one night I learned more about questioning people than I did in my entire life." In most cases, Dewey's assistants used what Breitel called a "soft, confidential approach," cajoling the men into admissions by saying they already had the goods on them and reassuring the women that they were not targets but witnesses.[19]

Still, the going was hard. Breitel said questioning the women was "like opening oysters." By Sunday evening only five women had admitted they were prostitutes; the rest claimed to be seamstresses, beauty operators, and other innocents wrongly arrested. By then Dewey's staff had sorted through the explanations and, releasing women believed to have been wrongfully caught up in the dragnet, continued to question the rest. Dewey said later that one key to a successful interrogation was convincing the woman she would be protected from the ring's vicious leaders.[20]

In all likelihood, it was neither brilliant questioning nor offers of protection that persuaded most witnesses to talk. Accustomed to being arrested and then summarily freed, the women undoubtedly decided to keep their mouths shut until a lawyer arrived to fix their cases. Instead, they were greeted by Judge McCook, who began holding bond hearings at five o'clock in the morning. Instead of releasing them on a nominal $300 bond for prostitution charges, McCook set exorbitantly high

$10,000 bonds and sent the women and their male associates to jail as material witnesses.[21] Most of the women, unable to pay the fee, landed in jail, where they underwent tests for drug addiction and venereal disease.

Not surprisingly, many confessed. Others held out, an act Breitel attributed to their female courage: "You could scare the men but you could not scare the women for their own fate. You could threaten a woman with imprisonment for life and nonsense like that, and it wouldn't frighten her." A more plausible explanation is that many of the women were confused about the type of cooperation expected from them. This was apparent in many letters they wrote to friends and family from jail. Initially, the women were not allowed any outside contact, but after several days they were permitted to write and receive letters, all of which were read by Dewey's office. One perplexed woman claimed Dewey's assistants had told her she could be held for a month or as long as it took to interview all the women. Other women, who already had been questioned, complained that they were being held even though they had no information. One asked a friend in Atlantic City to check on her children, saying she had no idea what was going on or when she might be released. Still another wrote to her husband saying she wished she could give Dewey's men "some information that they want" but claimed she did not "even know the people they are talking about." Her attempts to speak to Dewey personally were unsuccessful, and she urged her husband to try to see him. Other women expressed ignorance and fear. Their efforts to get information were hampered by Dewey's unwillingness to meet family members and his and Judge McCook's orders barring lawyers from seeing their clients.[22]

The men appeared more eager to talk than the women. They knew more about the operations and more quickly realized the seriousness of their situation when they learned their cases could not be "fixed." It was not surprising, therefore, that the first link between the prostitution ring and Luciano came from a man, not a woman. One of the pimps, David Marcus, described how independent operators were threatened by the racketeers. In exchange for his cooperation, Dewey's office took care of his wife and family. Marcus's story was bolstered by prostitute Mildred Balitzer, who was married to one of the defendants.

Just why Marcus pinpointed Luciano as head of the prostitution ring remains unclear. Dewey's detractors claimed Marcus was a two-bit hustler trying to puff up his own importance and get a better deal from prosecutors hungry for headlines. Dewey and his assistants insisted that Marcus pointed to Luciano without any prompting simply because Luciano did head the ring. According to his version, Dewey initially disbelieved Marcus's story because it seemed unlikely that Luciano would make himself vulnerable by becoming personally involved in running prostitutes. Slowly Dewey came around, but then had a hard task convincing his skeptical colleagues, including Sol Gelb who "dismissed Lucky's involvement out of hand" and concluded that his boss had gone crazy.[23] Dewey went to great lengths, then and later, to convince the public that Luciano was not his initial target for at least two reasons. First was his desire to overcome the appearance that he had gone into the case intending to get Luciano by any means possible. Second, he realized critics would suspect any story obtained by holding witnesses in jail for several months with no likelihood of release until they told him something.

Dewey always rejected speculation that Luciano was his main target as "sheer nonsense." Even though his office knew that the ring's active leaders, Thomas "Tommy Bull" Pennochio and David "Little Davie" Betillo, were Luciano henchmen, they claimed to have no firm link until Marcus "flatly stated that Luciano controlled the prostitution syndicate, though he claimed he knew it by hearsay only." Even after Marcus's admission, Dewey found it difficult to gather evidence against Luciano because witnesses were afraid of him. That difficulty broke down "by the middle of March, when a majority of the witnesses were talking quite freely, [and] it became apparent that Luciano was the head of the prostitution syndicate, and there was sufficient evidence to warrant his indictment." This statement was an exaggeration; in fact, only a handful of witnesses ever linked Luciano to the prostitution racket. Moreover, it was never clear at what point Dewey's men began suggesting to witnesses that Luciano was their main target. Dewey always maintained the witnesses came forward without helpful hints during interrogation.[24]

Dewey's comments about the early stages of the Luciano investigation were always ambiguous. He usually glossed over the prostitution angle by enumerating Luciano's other failings. For example, Dewey stated that, at first, he did not know about Luciano's links to whoring, but that "it was also known or generally believed that Luciano's subordinates had control of the largest illegal narcotic business in the United States, a substantial interest in the operation of policy rackets in New York City, that they were widely interested in the operation of illegal bookmaking houses throughout the country, and that Luciano controlled certain industrial rackets." Dewey often described the difficulties in getting direct evidence about Luciano. Luciano's "rapid rise to power and almost complete dominance of the underworld in New York City had allowed him . . . to conceal his participation in the actual operation of any of his criminal enterprises so sufficiently that specific evidence of such connection was not available." Dewey's argument seemed to be that Luciano was a prostitution overlord but even if he was not, he still was a menace to society.[25]

Dewey's attempts to convince the courts and the public that Luciano was the worst criminal in America since Al Capone were enhanced by his commanding control over publicity surrounding the case. Dewey's efforts to keep the raids and arrests secret worked surprisingly well in a city known for its leaks. His round-up received no immediate coverage in the press. By the time Dewey was ready to indict Luciano, he had had ample opportunity to paint him in the worst possible light. In a matter of weeks the theretofore little-known gangster became the nation's best-known public enemy, as newspapers embellished his career while reporting on the long, drawn-out Arkansas extradition proceedings.

In late March, Luciano, probably tipped off by a Waldorf Hotel employee that detectives had come to arrest him, fled to Arkansas. On April 1 Dewey announced his indictment and declared Luciano Public Enemy Number One in New York. The pronouncement captured widespread attention and prompted a nationwide manhunt that ended two days later when a New York City detective on another assignment spotted the gangster in the resort town of Hot Springs.[26] Finding Luciano, however, proved easier than returning him to New York.

Arkansas, a poor state severely ravaged by the Dust Bowl, greedily lapped up money poured into its economy by organized crime during the Depression. Officials of both Hot Springs and the state government had been well paid to provide a haven for gambling. Luciano felt particularly safe there and, initially at least, he was right. When town officials received New York's extradition request, Luciano was held for only a few hours before being released on a mere $5,000 bond. Recalcitrance in Arkansas raised Dewey's ire. He lambasted the state's brand of justice and turned up his rhetoric against the gangster. To force Arkansas officials to respond to his requests, Dewey called in New York reporters and told them: "I can't understand how any judge could release this man on such bail. Luciano is regarded as the most important racketeer in New York if not the country. And the case involves one of the largest rackets and one of the most loathsome types of crimes." Luciano's lawyers drafted a response calling Dewey's case political and denying their client's involvement in prostitution. But Dewey and the public criticism he incited drowned out Luciano's protestations. Finally, Arkansas Attorney General Carl Bailey sent twenty Arkansas Rangers to bring Luciano to Little Rock, where Governor Futtrell held the hearing that led to his extradition.[27]

On April 18 Luciano, manacled to two detectives, arrived in New York City, where the press had been stirred to sensationalist heights. His bond was set at an extraordinary $350,000. The indictment Luciano and his colleagues faced set a new standard for complexity. The charges incorporated two new features of New York law passed as part of Lehman's crime package. The first, enacted on February 24, repealed a state law requiring the listing of witness names on the indictment. In theory, the change provided safety for grand jury witnesses while making it more difficult for the defense to prepare its case. More significant, however, was the April 9 passage of the so-called conspiracy or Dewey Law. This legislation paved the way for charging Luciano with ninety counts of compulsory prostitution, even though he had not served directly as a pimp. It also saved Dewey the burden of having to try a multitude of cases. Many versions of the indictment—with various combinations of defendants—were drafted before the final one was handed up on April 23. The case would be known as the *People of the State of New York* v. *Charles Lucania*, but the rest of the defendants represented a fine roster of New York hoodlums.[28]

The indictment described a pyramid-like organization, with Luciano at the top far removed from the day-to-day dealings by layers of middle managers. According to Dewey, the prostitution ring actually was over-seen by Luciano lieutenant David Betillo. His financial aides were Thomas "Tommy the Bull" Pennochio, Abraham Wahrman, who col-lected money, and Benny Spiller, whose main job "was to invest money in the corporate enterprise." Jimmy Fredericks acted as general manager, directing the "bookers" and terrorizing uncooperative madams. Ralph Liguori acted as "hold-up man" for houses that would not join the syn-dicate, while Jesse Jacobs and Meyer Berkman "ran the machine by which these women, when arrested by the police, were immediately bailed out, advised, coached how to testify. They provided the lawyer to try the case." Lastly, David Marcus, Peter Balitzer, Al Weiner, and Jack Eller oversaw the operation by taking calls from prostitutes and telling them where to work. One of the defendants, Pennochio, was believed to have "murdered a narcotic peddler who had turned state's evidence." Betillo too was "widely reputed to be a desperate killer," and Wahrman and Liguori were "widely known for various acts of violence."[29]

After filing the indictment, Dewey's office had the arduous task of preparing what probably was the most complex criminal case ever tried in the state court system. After the arrests, ten Dewey assistants labored around the clock seven days a week to process "new information that was coming into the office from the various witnesses who were confess-ing almost daily." In addition to getting evidence from those still held in jail, Dewey's office tracked down witnesses in New York, New Jersey, and Pennsylvania. By the time the case was ready for trial, his staff had jailed more than a hundred and twenty witnesses and questioned another three hundred people.[30]

It was not always clear why witnesses confessed. Dewey's staff claimed they were reassured by repeated promises of safety. Others prob-ably decided to testify after being threatened with three-year prison sen-tences for prostitution and narcotics use. When prostitutes agreed to cooperate, their treatment in jail improved dramatically. As Dewey would explain later, "With each of these witnesses when they have told the truth, we have done our best to make life in a prison where they are kept as comfortable as possible." That included buying them new clothes, letting them visit with relatives, even taking some to movies and restaurants and providing liquor to help drug addicts cope with withdrawal.[31] Given the public latitude for Dewey's efforts and the low social status of the witnesses, only the defense attorneys and a few skeptics ever questioned the propriety or expense of jailing witnesses until they were forced into or rewarded for telling virtually the same story.

Even Dewey's critics had to admit his tactics had resulted in an impressive mountain of evidence. His staff's excellent preparation of the case fueled Dewey's optimism, and several favorable pretrial rulings handed down by Judge McCook helped the prosecution. The most beneficial was McCook's decision to allow use of the new Dewey conspiracy law, even though the crimes charged had taken place before the law went into effect. McCook also allowed the pool of potential jurors to watch as three defendants pleaded guilty and agreed to testify for the prosecution. The first two men to plead were Peter Balitzer, a thirty-three-year-old Brooklyn native, and Al Weiner, a twenty-seven-year-old furniture weaver. Neither man had prior convictions. The state's third witness was forty-five-year-old David Marcus, who had first linked Luciano to the prostitution ring. Like Balitzer and Weiner, he was a first generation Jewish American and had been in jail since February 1, 1936.[32]

Dewey also benefited from McCook's decision to try the case with a blue ribbon jury. Like the grand jury that first heard the charges, the special trial jury was comprised of middle-class New Yorkers likely to be offended by prostitution and suspicious of immigrant defendants. A condition of serving on the special trial panels was previous jury service, which entailed a time commitment that could be made only by the self-employed or by those in management positions. The jury pool was thus weighted heavily with professional men, stockbrokers, writers, and men who owned their own companies. As added insurance that the panels would be "unbiased," Dewey's staff investigated potential jurors to screen out any who had caused a hung jury or had questionable political connections.[33]

Jury selection got off to an unusual start when McCook allowed Dewey to present a summary of the case that sounded more like an argument for conviction than a dispassionate outline of the major issues. He began by asserting that the syndication of whorehouses, not prostitution, would be the key issue. He described how, by enlisting the aid of crooked lawyers and bail bondsmen, the syndicate ensured that no women would ever go to jail. If arrested, a woman would be shuffled to work in another location. Dewey described Luciano in an especially sinister light as the one who "sat way up at the top of his apartment at the Waldorf as the czar of organized crime in this city where his word, and his word alone, was sufficient to terminate all competitive enterprises of this kind." Finally even McCook agreed that Dewey's comments were too heated, although he disagreed with one defense attorney who labeled them "inflammatory."[34]

Dewey's cockiness and McCook's predisposition to the prosecution angered defense attorneys and set an acrimonious tone that characterized both jury selection and the trial itself. During one sarcastic exchange between Dewey and Luciano's lead attorney, George Morton Levy, McCook stepped in and warned both men to avoid "broadsides" because the jurors were anxious to get on with the proceedings. The jury pool included more than fifty men; winnowing it to twelve trial jurors and two alternates proved a time-consuming task. Defense attorneys and Dewey agreed not to bar jurors without good reason. Many, however, asked to be excused because of pressing work obligations or sick relatives. One man was let go after saying he had been summoned three times earlier in the year. A handful of others said they had read the newspapers and already made up their minds. One man, who had watched the three government witnesses plead guilty, said he would not believe their testimony.[35]

It is often hard to discern the strategy trial lawyers use in picking and excluding jurors. But the selection for the Dewey case was unusual in several respects. Because the case had received such widespread publicity, most jurors had followed the pretrial proceedings in the newspapers. That might have prompted a change of venue, but McCook never contemplated such a move, principally because of his great faith in blue ribbon juries. In theory, better-educated, more experienced jurors were less swayed by emotion. Whether that was true or not, defense attorneys tried to discern which prospective jurors were telling the truth when they vowed to keep an open mind. The questions they asked raised several interesting points about men who served repeatedly as blue ribbon jurors. One said he would judge a defendant guilty if he declined to testify; another admitted that he would not be able to consider each defendant individually; he conceded that he would probably cave in if the vote came to eleven to one and he was outnumbered. Not surprisingly, defense attorneys attempted to avoid jurors who had a long history of serving in criminal cases. Under cross-examination, a few prospective jurors admitted they believed the lengthy indictment, combined with Luciano's high bail and his fight against extradition, indicated probable guilt. Because so much of the defense case rested on discrediting government witnesses, defense attorneys tried to pinpoint the men's views on prostitution and struck jurors who saw the prostitutes as victims.[36]

Defense attorneys complained that they were hampered by McCook's decision to allow them only twenty peremptory challenges while Dewey had ten. Jury questioning left little doubt that Dewey had less need of strikes; his detectives had investigated potential jurors, and the pool was already heavily weighted with men favorable to the prosecution. His ten strikes were sufficient to get rid of any who had eluded his elaborate screening process. For example, Dewey barred one man who said he would "hold out until hell froze over" if the evidence warranted it. He struck another juror who admitted talking to the detective sent to investigate him. Dewey also dismissed one man who said it was "always a shame to find that somebody is guilty," another who found the bail set for Luciano excessive, and several others who thought pimps and prostitutes were not credible witnesses.[37]

After two days of questioning prospective jurors from early morning until late at night, the lawyers chose a panel of twelve jurors and two alternates. By today's standards it was a rare jury, including as it did no women or minorities. It was made up of fourteen white, successful businessmen with prior jury experience, all of whom had read about the case in the newspapers and several of whom had discussed its details with their families. Because of publicity, McCook sequestered the jurors when selection ended at 8:18 P.M. on May 12 and set the opening of trial for the following day. To speed the case along, he scheduled trial sessions from 9:30 A.M. to 7 P.M., over the objection of one defense attorney who said the long regimen gave him little time to confer with his client. This was a distinct handicap because Dewey had provided no indication of what testimony he planned to present.[38]

≈ ≈ ≈ ≈

CHAPTER SEVEN

Luciano: The Trial

W HAT WOULD turn out to be Dewey's most celebrated trial opened on May 13, 1936. Luciano's attorneys, Moses Polakoff and George Morton Levy, realized they faced an uphill battle because of the complexity of the case and Dewey's numerous witnesses. Other defense attorneys feared that being codefendants with Luciano would sink their clients regardless of the evidence. Dewey, if he was at all nervous, never showed it as he opened his case before the jury. Even though all ninety counts in the indictment concerned placing women in whorehouses and collecting money for it, Dewey insisted the case was not about prostitution but about its syndication. He called prostitution "an age-old institution, which I certainly should be insane if I thought I were going to interfere with or stop." Before the racket organized it, Dewey said, prostitution in New York City was highly individualistic. Some women worked alone, or madams ran houses with from one to four girls. "They were separate, isolated, they kept the money they earned; they were not blackjacked, nor was the money stolen from them by anybody else." But in 1933, he said, all that changed, when several men took over the houses at gunpoint with the goal of organizing a large-scale monopoly. Even the city's most strong-minded madams quickly learned there was no point in resisting.[1]

Dewey described the mechanics of the business as simple. The women normally lived in hotels with their pimps, who then "booked" them into whorehouses for about a week at a time. Because his evidence was fragmentary, Dewey never pinned down how many houses existed in the territory that spanned Manhattan, the Bronx, Queens, and Brooklyn. It was clear the women worked under conditions of virtual slavery, laboring from ten to fourteen hours daily and receiving less than 40 percent of their earnings, out of which they had to pay board. In addition to scheduling the women, the gang schooled them in lying to magistrates. Dewey said the defendants had set up such a finely honed system that their bail bondsmen sometimes got to court before the women were brought in. If a case could not be fixed, the "girl" was sent away until conditions cooled. The ring's methods worked well; in 1935 none of its prostitutes went to jail, even though there had been 170 arrests. The women were so smug about their legal immunity, Dewey said, that it took great efforts by his staff to convince them to stop lying.[2]

Dewey warned jurors that the evidence would present an incomplete portrait. "All we can give you is a fragmentary picture of any great criminal enterprise. We can give you a fairly full picture of what happens at the bottom, a smaller picture of what happens at the next stratum . . . and very little up at the top. After all, great criminal enterprises do not run under arc lights in Madison Square Garden." As a result, Dewey said there was little evidence linking Luciano directly to the scheme. Most prostitutes laboring at the bottom of the pyramid did not know him or his lieutenants. "We have in other words glimpses, and that is all you could ever get out of the man at the very top." While the women worked long hours, the leaders who reaped the profits devoted little time to the organization. It did not "appear that this business took anything more than a few minutes in a day of Luciano's time. It probably took only an hour or two a day of the time of Tommy Bull [Pennochio] and Little Davie [Betillo], maybe not that much."[3]

In their opening statements, defense attorneys took several different tacks to plant doubt in the jurors' minds. Several argued that the facts simply did not support the cases against their clients. James D. C. Murray, who represented bail bondsmen Jesse Jacobs and Meyer Berkman, said that his clients did nothing more than offer bail to prostitutes, who were entitled to it under the law. Other lawyers made similar claims of insufficient evidence, although the argument was difficult to sustain, given the ninety-count indictment and the large number of witnesses. Therefore, they also relied on two other tactics. The first was to seize on Dewey's remarks that there were few links tying the major defendants to the ring. The second was the well-worn strategy of attacking the prosecutor while avoiding the evidence. Not surprisingly, lawyers for the ring's middlemen, realizing that their clients' names would be mentioned most often, took the latter approach. Lorenzo C. Carlino, who represented Ralph Liguori, asserted that Dewey's assistants had threatened his client with a twenty-five-year jail term when he refused to implicate Luciano. When Liguori continued his silence, Carlino said, Dewey indicted him out of spite and told him he was sure to be convicted because he was Italian.[4]

Other lawyers called the government's witnesses unreliable. David Siegel, who represented Abraham Wahrman, put the witnesses into three categories. The first, he said, were the "prostitutes, who have trafficked not only in their bodies but in their souls. They would sell anything on earth for money, and we will show from the lives that they live that they have abandoned any principles that are worth while, that they would say anything about anybody, and that no man is safe in their power, including even Mr. Dewey the prosecutor." The next group was made of up of pimps and madams, "who have lived on vice, who have lived on the commercialization and trafficking in souls, who will take this stand in order to whitewash themselves." The third class was comprised of defendants who became government witnesses and would "blame anybody on earth if they can free themselves."[5]

Luciano's lawyer, George Morton Levy, did perhaps the best job of melding two lines of defense by decrying the government's tactics while stressing the meager links to his client. Levy was an experienced trial lawyer who had assisted Samuel Seabury during the investigation of the Walker administration. Bowing to the sinister buildup his client had received, Levy admitted to the jury that Luciano was no saint. But, he insisted, his client was a gambler, not a whoremonger. "There is not one witness in this case who can truthfully say that Luciano either visited these houses [or] discussed any matters with pimps, whores, madams or bookers." Levy said there were only two ways Luciano's name could have been mentioned. He conceded it was possible that the ring's leaders may have invoked Luciano's name without his permission to enhance their own positions. But it was more likely, he said, that several witnesses had been induced by Dewey to testify against Luciano. According to Levy,

there was nothing initially sinister about the prosecutor's office's handling of the case. What happened, he reasoned, was that someone took
a rumor linking Luciano to the ring too seriously, and a self-fulfilling
logic ensued. When witnesses named Luciano, prosecutors believed
them; when they denied his involvement, prosecutors sent them back to
jail for lying.[6]

Even the defense attorneys' best arguments were drowned in a sea
of testimony. One prosecutorial advantage of the Dewey Law became
immediately apparent. In addition to linking together key defendants,
the conspiracy indictment necessitated a mountain of evidence. Although Dewey eventually dropped twenty-eight counts of the indictment, more than fifty charges remained for the jury to consider. Even in
the fairest circumstances a jury would have had a hard time maintaining
objectivity in the face of such an onslaught. Today, when juries are more
jaded, occasionally one will balk, accuse the government of overtrying a
case, and acquit the defendants. But in 1936 the Dewey indictment was
seen as a testament to the modernization of justice, and the experienced
trial jurors recognized it as something new. Moreover, Dewey's skillful
portrayal of his witnesses as victims, not immoral women and pimps,
evoked the jury's sympathy.

Dewey began his case by calling a New York State bureaucrat who
testified that neither Jesse Jacobs nor Meyer Berkman were licensed
bondsmen, undercutting the claim that they were merely doing their
jobs. This prosaic beginning was quickly offset by a parade of prostitutes;
nearly thirty women told similar stories of degradation and exploitation.
Most were in their twenties and had become prostitutes after running
away from home, coming to New York City from small towns, or getting
caught in bad marriages with children to support. Many were poorly
educated or drug addicts. The majority had turned to prostitution because they were unemployed or could earn more on the streets than by
working in factories, restaurants, or stores. Most of the women used
aliases—some even while testifying. As one prostitute declared, "I can
use any name I like in case of trouble." The women generally charged
between two and three dollars a trick, and the more popular ones often
entertained fifteen clients a night. Some claimed that they had tried to
maintain their independence but had been forced into houses by the

racketeers, who threatened to drive them out of business if they did not cooperate. When arrested, they were coached by the ring's attorney, Abe Karp, who provided them with a variety of stories to tell magistrates. Some claimed to be out-of-town visitors; others said they were hairdressers, department store clerks, or were playing bridge when the police arrived.[7]

A typical witness was Rose Cohen, a twenty-five-year-old woman who said she had been a streetwalker until Pete Balitzer picked her up and began booking her into houses. She testified that out of one week's earnings of $260, she took home about $78. Some of her earnings went for room and board; the rest was divided among the madam, Balitzer, and a doctor. As the syndicate's grip tightened, Cohen said, the cost of her board went up to cover bond money, so she kept even less than before. Cohen had been arrested only once. Berkman bailed her out quickly and Karp coached her on telling lies that would get the case dismissed.[8] Other prostitutes testified about the low pay, harsh working conditions, and their arrest experiences.

Madams told the same hard-luck tales. A handful said they had never worked as prostitutes but only went into the business to support their families. Most, however, had begun as prostitutes. Joan Martin, a Romanian émigré first convicted of prostitution in 1913, said she used the money to support her family and eventually worked her way up to running whorehouses in tenements. When Wahrman first approached her about the ring, he told her it would cost ten dollars per girl and five dollars for herself. When she refused to join, she said Wahrman "told the fellows to take the joint apart. . . . They took the furniture and smashed it all to pieces." She screamed and the building superintendent came to check out the ruckus, but one of the toughs told him, "Get out of here; it is the police; don't interfere." When they finished, she said, only the kitchen chairs were left intact. As the Depression worsened, she had cut her prices from three dollars to a dollar and a half, which left her less money to pay the ring. She secretly moved, to avoid payments, but Jimmy Fredericks discovered her new location and knocked her unconscious with a lead pipe. After recuperating, Martin moved back to Manhattan and returned to business. Again the ring's strongmen visited her, held her up for thirty-six dollars, took her watch, and dumped coffee and cereal cans looking for valuables. She resumed her payoffs.[9]

Defense lawyers tried to show that Dewey's staff had threatened, then cajoled the women into telling stories that bolstered the prosecution's case. Only one woman had come forward voluntarily. Helen Kelly, a nineteen-year-old Kentucky native, was not caught in the February 1 dragnet but turned herself in after reading newspaper accounts of the arrests. Kelly claimed she wanted to clear up a two-year-old bail-jumping charge and also "get back some of the self-respect I lost when I got into prostitution." Her forthrightness was the exception. Cross-examination showed most of the women to be hardened streetwalkers who had to be questioned several times before agreeing to testify. Many said they had been threatened with one to three years in jail if they refused to talk.[10]

Until they accepted grants of immunity for cooperating with Dewey, the women were allowed out of jail only to go to the Woolworth Building for questioning. Once they cooperated, they could go out for two movies a month and a "decent" meal every week. Many also went shopping, using the witness fees they collected while in jail. Muriel Ryan testified that until she agreed to talk she had to wear a jail uniform because the only clothes she had were the evening gown, coat, and gloves she wore when arrested. After she cooperated, Ryan was taken on eight shopping trips and went to see three movies, including *Mr. Deeds Goes to Town* at Radio City Music Hall. After one movie, Dewey's staff took her and three other women to a Chinese restaurant on Broadway, where they did not dance but "did enjoy the music." Another prostitute told of being taken to the Paramount Theater followed by dinner and martinis at the Oyster Bar restaurant.[11]

Dewey's witnesses included a number of pimps and their assistants, who described how they had been forced into doing business with the ring. Like the hookers, these men had been held in jail without privileges until they agreed to cooperate. Sam "Spike" Green said it took ten weeks in jail and threat of a twenty-five-year prison term to get him talking. He testified that the hard times of the Depression had turned him to the prostitution racket. Before the Depression he belonged to the painters' union. In late 1932 he could not find legitimate employment and began working for a pimp, driving his car and taking telephone messages. When the pimp left New York in January 1935, Fredericks assigned Green to take over his former boss's five houses, which he eventually sold to David Marcus. After he confessed, Green was allowed to go out to the movies but still lived in jail. Peter Tach, another pimp, testified that Fredericks beat him when he balked at paying fees to the ring. He had been living at a hotel since his arrest and was allowed to go to the theater and out to eat but could talk only to the three detectives assigned to protect him.[12]

The roster of pimps also included two defendants who had been indicted with Luciano. Although they never named him as the boss, they did describe how they were forced to pay for the ring's bonding services. In May 1935, Al Weiner's father started a prostitution business for which he was soon sent to Sing Sing. When the son took over the business he paid Abraham Wahrman $100 a week by leaving cash in a bag at a candy store on Delancey Street. Marcus also had been booking women, including his wife, since 1927 but said arrests and violent gangsters had so disrupted his business that he left New York temporarily. When he returned, he sought help getting a job from Benny Spiller, Fredericks, and David Betillo. Under cross-examination, Marcus, who also used the name Miller, admitted he had struck a deal with Dewey to help his wife and three children. His testimony lost credibility when he conceded that he would lie to help himself.[13]

Only one madam and a few pimps offered testimony linking Luciano to the prostitution racket—and then only through rumor. Molly Leonard, who ran a house in Brooklyn and had a prior conviction for opium possession, said Pete Balitzer booked girls into her house and advised her that she would have to pay the organization. When she asked where her money was going, Balitzer told her, "There is good people behind the combination." When she pressed for details, he said, "Lucky is behind it." Her story was collaborated by Daniel Caputo, a former bootlegger, drug dealer, and whoremonger with a lengthy prison record. He had been brought from Dannemora Prison to testify, agreeing to talk only after seven weeks and twenty interviews with Dewey's staff. He said Fredericks and several associates visited him in the fall of 1933 and told him "they were going to bond all these cathouses." A few weeks later, Fredericks returned and said Lucky had ordered Fredericks to turn over his books to Betillo and Wahrman. Defense attorneys asked that the hearsay testimony against Luciano be stricken, and Dewey agreed, saying he had only introduced the statement as evidence against Fredericks. Caputo testified that Fredericks told Marcus in his presence that the ring was run by Betillo, Wahrman, and "Charlie Luck." Joseph "Jo Jo" Weintraub, another pimp, also declared that Fredericks had told him Lucky had ordered him to turn over his books to Betillo and Wahrman. During cross-examination, Weintraub said that a Dewey assistant threatened him with prison but that he did not confess until angered by Fredericks's failure to provide him with a lawyer during his six weeks in jail.[14]

With hearsay references to Luciano technically barred, Dewey called on another raft of witnesses. The last defendant who pleaded guilty was Peter Balitzer. He said he agreed to join the prostitution ring after being guaranteed that his women would not be jailed when arrested because Charlie Lucky backed the group. Balitzer, a former bootlegger once suspected of murder, said when Luciano was mentioned Fredericks told him not to use the gangster's name. On one occasion a whorehouse bonded to the group was held up by mistake. Fredericks found out who did it, and he and Balitzer tracked down the man. As Balitzer watched, Fredericks "smacked him in the face" and said: "Didn't I tell you to stay away from these joints that are bonded, that they belonged to Charlie Lucky."[15]

Balitzer's testimony did not indicate whether Luciano knew Fredericks was using his name. Balitzer's wife supplied more concrete evidence. Mildred Balitzer testified that her husband began booking women in August of 1932 to pay his gambling debts. Through him, Mrs. Balitzer said, she had met Betillo, who told her he was working for Luciano. A short time later, Betillo introduced her to Luciano, whom she saw five or six more times. Before she and Peter were married in 1934, she asked Betillo to release him from the racket because of their pending wedding; Betillo refused, alleging that Balitzer owed him too much money. She said she then took up the matter with Luciano, who refused to intervene. During a cross-examination Dewey called "nauseating," Mrs. Balitzer described the seamier side of her life. She denied being a lesbian, provided details of her drug habits, was sketchy about her first, fifteen-minute meeting with Luciano, and denied that she had "unnatural sex love" with a male homosexual performer.[16]

Another direct link to Luciano was supplied by "Cokie Flo" Brown, a prostitute who recently had contacted Dewey's office from jail, where she was awaiting sentencing on a soliciting charge. Brown began her checkered life in Chicago as the mistress of various underworld figures, then moved to New York by way of Cleveland and Duluth. In New York, she became an opium and heroin addict and ran whorehouses on the Upper East and Upper West sides. Brown said she met Luciano through Jimmy Fredericks, with whom she lived for two years until arrest. In the spring of 1934, Brown said, she accompanied Fredericks to a 4 A.M. meeting with Luciano, Pennochio, and Betillo at a Chinese restaurant. She said she did not follow much of the conversation because it was in Italian, but she did hear Luciano say he did not like the prostitution racket because it paid poorly and too many women were reluctant to join. During another meeting at a Lower East Side restaurant in October 1935, Brown said Luciano complained that "his name was getting mentioned quite a bit, and he didn't like it." When Betillo urged him to keep the operation alive a little longer, Luciano replied: "Well I don't know; this Dewey investigation is coming on, and it may get tough, and I think we ought to fold up for a while." He finally agreed to continue for a few months after Betillo predicted that Dewey would never be able to connect Luciano to the ring. Under cross-examination, Brown admitted that Dewey's office had arranged to delay her sentencing on the soliciting convictions until after her testimony. She also acknowledged using several aliases when arrested for drugs and prostitution. Soon after Fredericks was arrested, she offered to help defense lawyer Samuel Siegel prove that some of the women were lying but switched sides to help Dewey after falling out of love with Fredericks. She claimed she wanted "to go straight" and denied that her desire for reform was linked to a pending case against her. She had been arrested for offering sex to a policeman for five dollars but maintained that he had lied.[17]

The other prostitute linking Luciano directly to the scheme was Nancy Presser, who claimed she had known Luciano for eight or nine years through her friendship with Liguori. During an evening of drinking at a tavern, Presser said, she heard Betillo tell Luciano that a lot of houses did not want to join, including one run by a madam called "Dago Jean." When he heard that, Presser said, "Lucky turned around and told him to go ahead and wreck the joint." Presser also testified that she had gone to Luciano's suite at the Barbizon Plaza four or five times in the fall of 1934. When she told him she was not earning enough as a call girl and would have to go into a house, Luciano told her he would give her enough money to stay independent. On another occasion, she said, Luciano told her that he could not depend on Betillo.

Under cross-examination, Presser admitted that her real name was Genevieve Fletcher, that she had previous arrests for prostitution, suffered from syphilis, smoked opium, and had been addicted to morphine and heroin. She said Dewey's men questioned her so many times she had a hard time keeping track of what she had told them. Initially she had denied knowing Liguori, even though she lived with him, admitting it only when a Dewey assistant threatened her with six months in jail. Of the six times she claimed to be in Luciano's room, Presser said, they had had sex only twice; on the other occasions he just gave her fifty or seventy-five dollars because she needed money. Presser never fully explained why Luciano was so generous or how a whore who worked in the streets and tenement houses had gained the favor of a mobster who frequented the most expensive prostitutes in the city.[18]

The last witness linking Luciano to prostitution was Joe Bendix, an artist who admitted supporting himself by robbing hotel rooms; at the time of the trial he was serving a fifteen-year-to-life sentence at Sing Sing. In the summer of 1934, during one of his brief stints of freedom, Bendix said he had asked Fredericks to persuade Luciano to give him a job as a bagman for whorehouses. Luciano supposedly met Bendix at a restaurant and asked him why he wanted a job that paid only $35–$40 a week. Bendix claimed he told Luciano, "It is better than going back to stealing." If he was caught committing another crime, he faced a long sentence as a fourth offender. Luciano accepted his logic and said he would tell Betillo to hire him.[19]

Under cross-examination, Bendix said he had begun stealing when he was eighteen years old and had rarely been out of trouble since. At one point, he became confused about his record and said, "If you had as many convictions as I have you would probably forget the date." He claimed to have first met Luciano at a club in 1927 or 1928 but could not remember the details except that they had been introduced by a state trooper. He saw Luciano six times in 1929 and another half dozen times in 1931 but not at all during 1930, 1932, or 1933 because he was in prison. After the 1934 conversation about a job, Bendix said, he never spoke with Luciano again, because he had gone back to stealing and was arrested again. He wrote Dewey offering to testify against Luciano in exchange for help with his sentencing. Bendix was perhaps the most unreliable witness Dewey called. His story was full of holes, and it was hard to imagine Luciano dealing with such an unsuccessful thug.[20]

Judge McCook instructed the jury that hearsay evidence naming Luciano had been introduced only to implicate others, including Betillo and Liguori. Luciano's attorney, George Morton Levy, worried that jurors would not be able to ignore the incriminating testimony. He objected whenever Dewey found ways to allow witnesses to repeat hearsay evidence against Luciano. Levy also found fault with Dewey's tone of voice, characterizing "the cryptic utterance, the sarcasm of the learned Special Prosecutor in this case, as extremely prejudicial." Dewey countered that no one on his staff had forced the witnesses to name Luciano. The altercation was just one of many bitter squabbles between defense attorneys and Dewey. At another point, David Siegel accused Dewey of sitting in the witnesses' line of vision in an attempt to influence their testimony. When Dewey said Siegel had no right to tell him where to sit, the defense lawyer retorted, "There are no wings off your shoulders, even though you have got a title." Dewey answered, "And since when does the prosecutor have to submit to such personal vilification by counsel for criminal defendants?"[21]

Dewey concluded his case by presenting a number of hotel employees who testified about Luciano and his visitors at the Barbizon Plaza Hotel and the Waldorf Towers apartments. The manager of the Waldorf said he knew Luciano as Charles Ross. In October 1935, after the manager learned his true identity, Luciano moved out. Marjorie Brown, a maid at the Waldorf, said she had seen Wahrman visiting Luciano about twenty times, and a bellboy at the Barbizon identified Betillo and Pennochio as frequent visitors. Yet another maid identified Jacobs and Betillo. However, an assistant manager of the Barbizon, where Luciano lived between

April 1934 and February 1935, said he could identify none of the defendants but Luciano, who had registered as Charles Lane. The manager had changed his testimony, provoking Dewey to call him a liar and intimate that he could be sent to jail. Levy objected that Dewey was badgering the witness, but McCook took it in stride: "Mr. Dewey started to argue, which he is a little prone to do." A bellboy at the Barbizon testified he had seen Jack Eller visiting Luciano in September 1935. During cross-examination, he admitted he had originally picked out Fredericks's picture, even though the two men looked nothing alike. In court, he changed his mind again, saying it was Fredericks he had seen, not Eller.[22]

Dewey ended by cutting twenty-six counts from the indictment because he had promised to present his case in two weeks and already had gone on for more than two and one-half weeks. He rested before lunch on May 29, 1936. The defense began that afternoon, pinning its hopes on three types of testimony. The first strategy, as it had been throughout cross-examination, was to attack the credibility of the main witnesses. Levy took a second tack by arguing that Luciano was a gambler, not a whoremonger, trying to prove his contention by calling a long stream of bookies, horse owners, and track habitués. Finally, Liguori and Luciano testified disastrously on their own behalf.

The only direct testimony linking Luciano to the scheme had come from Mildred Balitzer, Brown, Presser, and Bendix. The defense called two witnesses to discredit Balitzer. The first, a former boyfriend, Gus Franco, was a twenty-nine-year-old convicted dope dealer and numbers runner. He testified that he had dropped Balitzer because she would not give up prostitution but that they remained friends. When she was arrested, she had called him for help, and he had sent a lawyer to see her. She had called again two weeks later, he testified, saying Dewey's office was pressuring her to link Luciano to the ring even though she did not know him. Balitzer told Franco she was planning to cooperate with the prosecutors to help her husband and family. Under cross-examination, Franco denied he knew Luciano or that he had threatened Balitzer if she testified against Luciano; he also denied that he had a history of violence, that his uncle was a Tammany captain, and that his father was a member of the Unione Siciliano. The defense next called George Heidy, the policeman in charge of the witnesses. He testified that he had gone out with

Balitzer to clubs on several occasions, and that she sometimes drank between twelve and fourteen brandies and became very drunk. On one occasion, Heidy said, he heard Balitzer ask other girls how tall Luciano was and whether he had a bad eye.[23]

Defense attorney Samuel Siegel testified for Luciano in an attempt to discredit Cokie Flo Brown. Siegel said that while he was preparing his defense of Fredericks, Brown had called him three times and visited his office. During one interview he asked her how Luciano fit into the picture, and she said she did not know him.[24]

Evidence discrediting Nancy Presser came from Anna Liguori, the defendant's sister, who told the following tale: Presser had become alarmed when a Dewey assistant told her Liguori would get twenty-five years unless he pinpointed Luciano. If, on the other hand, he cooperated, Dewey would ensure his freedom. When Presser grew tired of being jailed as a material witness, she reportedly said, "They are killing me up there . . . [to] get out of this darned place, I will do anything." Defense attorneys noted that Ralph Liguori originally was held as a witness and was indicted later than the other defendants—a fact they believed showed Dewey had unsuccessfully pressured him.[25]

The defense called two witnesses against Bendix. A New York state trooper said Bendix lied when he claimed the trooper had introduced Bendix to Luciano; the policeman claimed he did not even know Luciano and had never met Bendix. Moreover, Morris Panger, the assistant district attorney who handled Bendix's burglary case, said both he and District Attorney Dodge had told Bendix there was no way a man with his record could plea bargain; even so, Panger said, Bendix tried several times to convince him he had useful information. In February he offered to inform on his fellow prisoners; later he provided what proved to be worthless information about a Manhattan bank robber. In March, Panger said, he received a plaintive letter from Bendix claiming that word of his cooperation had leaked out and his wife was being threatened. Panger answered that there was nothing he could do; on April 8 he informed Bendix he either had to plead guilty or go to trial on felony charges.[26]

Luciano's counsel called many witnesses who testified that his vice activities centered on gambling rather than prostitution. Max Kalik, a longtime Brooklyn bookmaker, and his assistant, Henry Goldstone, said they had seen Luciano at the racetrack nearly every day during the previous decade. Thomas Francis, who owned stables, said he often drove to the track with Luciano, who was there almost every day. Robert Crawford, a music publisher, said he had gone to Saratoga with Luciano and also played in a dice game Luciano hosted. Others testified they had met Luciano at crap games.[27]

Only two defendants took the stand in their own defense—Liguori and Luciano. Neither helped his own cause. Liguori denied having been part of the prostitution ring and claimed to have a clean record. He admitted to living with Nancy Presser for about eight months and said he had visited her at Dewey's office soon after her arrest. Liguori was arrested for the third time as a material witness in early April; at that time a Dewey assistant informed him that the only way to keep Presser from going to jail for three years was to testify with her. Otherwise, she would go away and they would indict him. During one nine-hour questioning session Presser was sent in to see him and told him Dewey's men wanted him to testify that he had introduced her to Charlie Lucky in 1934. She further advised him that Dewey's office would finance a trip to Europe if he cooperated; even so, Liguori testified, he refused to lie. Under cross-examination, Liguori admitted he could not marry Presser because he was already married and had taken up with yet another woman while involved with her.[28]

Luciano was thirty-eight years old when he took the stand to testify that he was a gambler and convicted drug dealer but not a prostitution ring operator. Before his arrest, Luciano said, the only other defendant he knew was Betillo; he had never seen Fredericks until they were jailed together, and the only witnesses he recognized were the hotel employees. When asked if he had put women in houses, Luciano emphatically replied, "I didn't have to do that"—a claim he would make the rest of his life. Luciano said he had fought extradition from Arkansas not because he was guilty but in order to give his lawyers time to study Dewey's case. He held up well during direct testimony, but his self-confidence disintegrated under Dewey's withering cross-examination. Dewey demonstrated that Luciano had a long history of lying to law enforcement officials about gun charges, drug peddling, bootlegging, and income tax evasion. In what would today be considered highly improper questioning, Dewey asked Luciano many rhetorical questions about his relationships with other gangsters, including Joe Masseria, Lepke, Gurrah—whom Dewey characterized as "the biggest clothing racketeer in the city"—and Ciro Terranova, "the Artichoke King." He even dragged in Al Capone's name by asking if Luciano knew that Betillo had spent five years working for the Chicago mobster. Levy objected to much of Dewey's cross-examination as improper attempts to prejudice the jury by introducing evidence of unrelated crimes. McCook barred Dewey's comments about Gurrah but let the rest of his remarks stand.[29]

In their closing statements to the jury, defense attorneys expended as much effort lambasting Dewey as they did defending their clients. Caesar B. F. Barra, who represented Pennochio and Betillo, accused Dewey of using the case to launch his political career. He told the jury, "Mr. Dewey expects to be the Governor of the State of New York"—an assertion Dewey called "perfectly preposterous and ridiculous." Barra also told jurors to keep an open mind and not be swayed by the fact that Dewey and his men "have got to justify the spending of large sums of money." Even under normal circumstances, Barra argued, prostitution "arouses a prejudice in the breast of normal men." In this case he said it would be particularly hard to maintain objectivity in light of the extended press coverage and the daily interviews about Public Enemy Number One. David Paley, who represented Benny Spiller, emphasized the unreliability of the prosecution's witnesses and the thinness of the evidence against his client. He pointed out that only one witness had linked Spiller to the scheme. Paley alleged that the sole reason Dewey had indicted his client was to get witness Thelma Jordan to link Luciano to the ring, even though Jordan's evidence was hearsay and should have been ignored by the jury. He maintained that Dewey introduced it as a form of trickery to bolster the case against Luciano.[30]

Liguori's attorney, Lorenzo C. Carlino, viciously attacked Dewey by belittling him "as a boy . . . invested with tremendous power [and] unlimited resources" who lavishly spent taxpayers' money. He called Dewey the "greatest actor" he had ever seen and said he particularly enjoyed Dewey's performance of "slinking smoothness" and his "sallies, and his thrusts, his mirth, his laughter, his anger, his disappointments." Referring sarcastically to "our distinguished special prosecutor," Carlino added: "When things didn't go quite his way you could see that anger of the striking python; when things were going his way he springs right up with the strike of the kill." Carlino said Dewey's "smug self-satisfaction, supreme ego and vanity" explained why he had indicted Liguori when his client "refused to become part and parcel of a frame-up against these other defendants." Carlino feigned amazement at Dewey's portrayal of professional whores as meek women who had gone into prostitution because of sick relatives or other "maudlin" reasons but never by choice. "Why, sometimes to hear Mr. Dewey qualify his witnesses, you would think they were virgins as they took the witness stand."[31]

Samuel Siegel, who represented Fredericks, also emphasized the un-reliability of the witnesses: "If I put mud and filth on this floor, it is going to remain mud and filth; and if I pile it up and pile it up and pile it up until it gets as high as this ceiling, it still remains mud and filth. Numbers do not change the character of the testimony that was pre-sented in this case." Siegel said in his thirty-four years as a lawyer he had "never heard of a prosecutor supplying witnesses with liquor, or permitting them to have it, and go around in the various cabarets and get drunk. It is a novelty to me." He also asked jurors to put themselves in the witnesses' places "sitting in jail, sitting in jail as a result of the prosecutor, thinking, thinking, thinking, how can they get out, like the famous convict who wrote the letter to his wife, 'Think up some story that I can tell Mr. Dewey.'" Siegel also asked the jury to consider how Dewey's description of a $12-million "colossal" racket could be true if Fredericks collected only ten dollars a week from each prostitute and then used some of the money for bail.[32]

Levy, the best of the defense lawyers, argued the weaknesses of the case rather than attacking Dewey. He did not accuse Dewey of suborning perjury, allowing that "Tom Dewey didn't have to do that. Tom Dewey was dealing with a class of people only anxious to find out what lie they could tell. All they needed was a clue, and all they needed was a hint." Once they realized Dewey's target was Luciano, they were happy to vol-unteer information. Levy asserted that Dewey and his staff rehearsed the witnesses to ensure that their testimony would be perfect. Even so, he noted, there were logical inconsistencies in the prosecution's case. On one hand, Luciano was so high up and remote that no one knew him. On the other hand, he supposedly ordered men out of business and gave orders to beat up reluctant madams.[33]

Levy vigorously attacked Dewey's cross-examination of Luciano. He said no prosecutor had a right to convict a man on "insinuations in regard to crimes or attempted crimes years ago" by inflaming jurors so that they asked: "What do we care about this case? We are going to railroad Charles Luciano." Government witnesses were no different from other men in New York: "It was apparent from the newspapers; it was apparent to any intelligent man in the City of New York for weeks that Mr. Dewey's office believed Luciano to be guilty. The high bail referred to, the so-called extradition from Hot Springs; Luciano was the man wanted at all costs, gentlemen. And Cokie Flo jumped in on the band-wagon." Given that fact, Levy said, "It is remarkable that we have not had somebody here from . . . [the] lunatic asylum, because anyone who came by saying anything against Charles Lucania . . . was embraced eagerly and enthusiastically, if not by Mr. Dewey then by some of his very ambitious associates." Levy concluded by saying it was just common sense that Luciano, "living in the royal splendor secretly up in the tower of the Waldorf," would not associate with men in the bonding business. Nor would he be likely to talk with Mildred Balitzer about her husband's pimping.[34]

On Saturday, June 6, 1936, in an irregular and often improper summation lasting nearly six hours, Dewey struck back. He claimed that more than eleven of the thirteen hours of arguments by defense attorneys were "devoted to vilification, abuse and dirt throwing." At times, Dewey said, he wanted to look at the indictment to see if his name was listed. "It has been . . . the most shocking thing I have ever seen. In fact, as I listened to the various summations, I wondered why any man in his right senses—perhaps I wasn't—should give up a perfectly good law practice to live on the meager salary of a prosecutor, just so he can have his character assassinated by criminals and lawyers who, in doing their duty as they see it, do their clients' bidding."[35]

Dewey pointed out there was no way to convict the head of an organization without using his associates, no matter how unsavory the witnesses. He added:

This case has been no pleasure to me or my assistants. If anybody thinks it is a picnic to work for four and a half months of actual work and months in preparation, on a case involving prostitutes, pimps, gangsters, and bookers of women, and to examine them and spend time with them and to persuade them to testify, and to hold their hands and keep them from saying they won't, and for the pitifully small staff of lawyers, seven or eight of them, who have worked on this case continuously with this army of witnesses, to work days and nights and Sundays, they are badly mistaken. . . . If anybody says that is a pleasure he is crazy.

Dewey readily agreed with defense attorneys who claimed he had hidden witnesses, saying such precautions were necessary to keep them from being murdered. As for defense claims that Dewey had not produced all the witnesses he should have, the prosecutor said there was a limit to what his overworked staff could do in a few months. With typical grandiosity, Dewey added: "I could not break the entire underworld. I guess probably we have in this case more underworld testimony than has ever been produced in any twenty cases before in American history. More people have broken that unwritten role, 'Thou shalt not squeal,' because they had to; they were not voluntary."[36]

Dewey then helped fuel the myth that would come to surround Luciano by hinting that the gangster controlled a national crime network. He told the jury that only a man with Luciano's power could summon character witnesses like policemen and district attorneys. Greatly exaggerating Luciano's true importance, Dewey claimed "that the underworld, and the whole underworld, not just New York's underworld, but Philadelphia's underworld, as you will recall; and you can be sure that the whole underworld of this eastern part of the United States, if not the whole United States, was on call for the big boss. And the proof in this case shows it. When there was anybody who could be at all useful, he was produced and put on the witness stand for Luciano." Dewey said, "Of course, we cannot prove Luciano was putting women in houses. Of course, we cannot prove that he was going out sticking men up. He graduated from that."[37]

Dewey described Luciano's testimony about his criminal past as a disgusting display of perjury. In appealing for Luciano's conviction, Dewey strayed far from the evidence. Too much lawlessness existed in the country; too many bosses went free while their underlings went to jail, Dewey declared. "Now I say to you in all seriousness that, so far as I am concerned, unless you are willing to convict the boss, turn them out. Say there cannot be any administration of justice in this country. Say to the world and the public the boss gangsters can go free. It is only the front men who are going to be convicted, and announce it to the world. I say, gentlemen, that you know and I know that we have had convictions of tools and front men for years. You saw what happened in this business." Dewey concluded by demanding "a conviction . . . in the name of the safety of the people of this city."[38]

Defense attorneys, properly, objected to Dewey's impassioned closing. Carlino asked McCook to instruct the jury to disregard Dewey's contention that all the defense attorneys were working for Luciano rather than for their own clients. Levy labeled the "entire summation . . . an inflammatory and prejudicial address" geared toward getting "a conviction by unfair means." Specifically, he asked the judge to disallow Dewey's characterization of his client "as the greatest gangster in America" and his charge that Luciano had close associations with Lepke, Gurrah, and other underworld leaders. McCook agreed and instructed the jury to disregard Dewey's allegations about Luciano's links to other mobsters.[39]

Given the trial's highly charged atmosphere, it would have been difficult for any jury to separate fact from innuendo. It is therefore not surprising that the jury deliberated only six hours before finding all the defendants guilty on all counts. McCook finished his charge to the jury at 7:00 P.M. on Saturday, June 6; the jury brought in its verdict at 5:31 A.M. on Sunday, June 7, 1936. McCook told jurors, "You need have no doubt as to the righteousness of your verdict, I am sure; I have none."[40]

In fact, no one but the defense attorneys questioned the correctness of the jury's verdicts in the halcyon days immediately following the trial. Politicians and civic do-gooders hailed Dewey's victory as a vindication of their own reform efforts. A *Panel* editorial said Luciano's conviction provided "evidence of the foresight and sound judgment of the individual members [of the runaway grand jury] who so courageously obeyed the strong dictates of their convictions." La Guardia, with his long-standing hatred of Italian gangsters, praised Luciano's conviction as "an important step in the elimination of rackets in this city." Politicians, who believed Dewey had convicted Luciano for the wrong crime, recognized the wisdom of keeping quiet. A typical comment came from Lehman's assistant, Charles Poletti, who said Dewey had stretched proper legal boundaries and falsely accused Luciano of heading a prostitution ring. Even court officials, who had reservations about Dewey's plea-bargain arrangements with unreliable witnesses, were impressed by the overall organization it took to convict Luciano.[41]

Trial testimony revealing that female witnesses went to bars and got drunk with police escorts did cause some public concern, but surprisingly little fuss was raised about the more critical issues of the cost or propriety of jailing witnesses for more than three months. Perhaps the nearly twenty thousand dollars paid in witness fees plus the jail and hotel costs seemed small in comparison to the rest of Dewey's expenses and the great success he had achieved.[42] The lack of concern presumably also reflected the public's generally low view of the women; if wealthy businessmen had been jailed the outcry would have been louder.

Even civil libertarians may have been quieted by the fact that Dewey and McCook appeared so solicitous of the women's welfare. Both judge and prosecutor argued that the prostitutes' incarceration offered them the path to a new life through drug treatment and the help of social workers. McCook seemed genuinely to believe in this possibility. On the Monday after the trial ended he began three days of interviews with the witnesses. In retrospect, McCook's paternalistic questions seem naïve, condescending, and misplaced; but they also reflect the degree to which Dewey had convinced everyone, even an experienced trial judge, that the prostitutes were saintly victims instead of hardened streetwalkers.

As McCook repeatedly told the women, he was exhausted after overseeing the lengthy trial. He was talking to them "because my conscience won't discharge me in discharging you, until I have given you a chance." He told one woman, "There is no law which requires me to do what I am doing here. I am doing it because I want you to get the best break in the world." McCook offered them advice, religious wisdom, and the aid of a retinue of social workers from various religious and ethnic organizations. Throughout his talks with the women, the jurist seemed well meaning but often at a loss to understand their problems. As a clergyman's son, McCook apparently believed women became prostitutes because they were suffering from what he called a "moral disease" rather than because of financial necessity or a poor home life. He advised them to see priests, rabbis, and ministers and to get jobs that would keep them walking God's path. In several instances, he advised the women to confess to their parents. He seemed perplexed when they replied that that would be impossible because their mothers were devout Catholics or their fathers would toss them back on the street. When they balked at his advice, he saw it as evidence that personal failings were blocking their salvation. He told one woman she was too strong willed and another that she should get married because after being sexually active she would be unable to avoid future temptations of the flesh.[43]

Seeking common ground, he asked the women about their religious faiths and ethnic backgrounds. To all who claimed Irish descent he expressed pain at seeing someone who shared his love of the "Old Sod" living a degenerate life. He asked one woman if she was Irish but dropped that line of questioning when she said her ancestors were Danish. He found nothing to say to another woman except "You are a Hungarian, nothing but a Hungarian" before consigning her to social workers. He asked one obstreperous witness, "You were brought up by nice people, weren't you?" and seemed surprised when she answered, "I was raised in an orphanage."[44]

Although McCook was sometimes at a loss, most of the women clearly knew what he wanted to hear and were eager to tell him anything that would get them out of jail. Most said they planned new careers—often giving different versions to McCook and the social workers. They vowed to set up needlework or tea shops or to become seamstresses, milliners, waitresses, maids, stenographers, or sales clerks. Most plans met with McCook's approval. He objected to only two professed possibilities: dancing and beautician's work. Both, he argued, attracted tough women. Eager to please him, the budding beautician declared she would become a waitress, and the would-be dancer promised to attend business school. Many expressed a desire to marry. All the women not from New York claimed they would return home to husbands, parents, children, and ailing relatives; those from the city stated they would go to live with relatives in the Bronx and Brooklyn; none said they would stay in Manhattan.[45]

While most women pliantly offered information about intended reformation, a few took a different path. Some admitted they had no plans to go straight, and a handful maintained they had been imprisoned wrongfully. McCook was puzzled by what he regarded as the women's ingratitude. When one said she would not seek spiritual guidance because she wasn't a hypocrite, McCook launched into a lament on his own exhaustion after overseeing the trial and said his conscience dictated that he try to help the woman. He voiced similar complaints to a woman who refused to describe her plans except to say that they included getting out of jail, where she was going crazy.[46]

McCook did not pursue questions of unjust imprisonment. When one woman likened her jail time to being threatened, McCook pointed out that she and her gambler husband were being held as material witnesses for their own protection. She continued to insist that being held in jail as a material witness to events she knew nothing about constituted a threat. This woman had not been called to testify. When McCook asked her if she would like to talk to a social worker about the future, the woman said her only plan was to go stay with her mother. Another woman not called to testify grumbled about being jailed; McCook asked, "Is that is your only complaint?" Several material witnesses were relatives of suspects and defendants, and they claimed to know little about the prostitution racket. One such witness was Nancy Brooks, who said she had already left her husband, another witness, by the time he was arrested and thus had nothing to testify about. She expressed no desire to talk to social workers, saying she just wanted to go home and forget the entire matter. Only once did McCook express sorrow to a witness caught up in the dragnet. Helen Jones, a black maid in one of the whorehouses, had told the truth as soon as she was arrested and was never called before the grand jury. She needed no help getting a job because she already had a new one lined up. McCook told her: "Good-bye. I am sorry that you were detained. You served the state."[47]

Apart from Jones, neither McCook nor Dewey's staff members conceded that any witness had been wrongfully arrested. In keeping with this, they set up three payment schedules based largely on how cooperative the witnesses had been. The material witnesses who fully cooperated received three dollars per day for their jail time; those who told half truths, especially those with children and dependent parents, received a dollar and a half per day; witnesses who continued to insist on their innocence received nothing but their freedom.[48]

After McCook had freed the witnesses, he turned to the next order of business—sentencing. He was as censorious of the defendants as he had been solicitous of the prostitutes. In the sentencing hearing on June 18, 1936, he began by sweeping aside defense objections that the verdict should be overturned because the conspiracy statute was unconstitutional and Dewey's closing had been improper. Then he got down to business. McCook told Luciano he was responsible "in law and morals for every foul and cruel deed . . . performed by the band." Saying there was no sign that Luciano had any remorse or hope for rehabilitation the judge sentenced him to serve a thirty-to-fifty-year sentence. This was the stiffest sentence ever administered in a prostitution case in the state. The judge also gave other defendants lengthy sentences. Calling Pennochio "an habitual criminal," he sentenced him to twenty-five years in prison; and Betillo, whom McCook described "as Luciano's chief and most ruthless aide," received twenty-five to forty years.[49]

The judge told Fredericks he was "an incorrigible criminal. A low and brutal character" and gave him twenty-five years. He also agreed with a probation report calling Wahrman a "depraved character [with] an utter lack of any social responsibility" and sent him to jail for fifteen to thirty years. On a softer note, McCook lectured Liguori that he had "a good family, and enjoyed an opportunity to live a law-abiding life, but chose rather, especially of late, a way which better suited your vain and lazy nature. You are a silly imitator of the racketeers you admire. However, being still young and having no convictions against you, I am affording you, through a comparatively short sentence an opportunity for rehabilitation." He gave him seven and a half to fifteen years. McCook meted out still lighter sentences to Eller, whom he labeled flabby of body and soul but not vicious; to Balitzer, who, he said, "lacks . . . moral sense"; to Weiner, whom he found simply dull; and to Marcus. Eller received four to eight years, Marcus three to six years, and Balitzer and Weiner two to four years each.[50]

Jockeying to get the verdicts overturned began on July 9, 1936, when Luciano's second lawyer, Moses Polakoff, filed an appeal. It would not be heard for another year, but in the interim, Polakoff took other steps. Luciano had been sent to Dannemora Prison in Clinton County, where Polakoff filed a writ of habeas corpus, arguing that trying defendants under the newly passed conspiracy statute, the Dewey Law, violated constitutional prohibitions against ex post facto laws. In August, a Clinton County judge ruled the case did not fall under the provision because when the crimes were committed they violated already existing prostitution statutes; all the Dewey Law did was join them together in one indictment. The court also noted that a writ of habeas corpus was a strange way to appeal a criminal conviction and urged Polakoff to follow a more regular course.[51]

Undaunted, Polakoff pursued another unusual avenue. Luciano continued to claim he did not know any of the four witnesses who had linked him to the prostitution ring. So his lawyer hired two private investigators to check out the stories of Cokie Flo Brown, Mildred Balitzer, Nancy Presser, and Joe Bendix. The results revealed the witnesses' unreliability and Dewey's extreme measures on their behalf. His office had helped two of the women obtain a lucrative magazine contract to share their stories and sent the other woman and a friend to Europe to protect them from threatened retaliation. When their deals went sour, the women began talking to defense attorneys. Bendix, who expected more consideration than he received, was frustrated at being penned up in jail with little hope of early release. He, too, offered to help Luciano.

When the trial ended, MacFadden Publications, publisher of crime magazines, had contacted Dewey about writing his own story of the trial. He turned down the offer and suggested that Cokie Flo Brown and Mildred Balitzer be hired to tell their tale for $50 a week. Before they could begin their journalistic careers, of course, Dewey's staff had to set them free. At the time she began cooperating with Dewey's office Brown had been convicted but not sentenced for soliciting and faced three more trials for running a disorderly house and for drug possession. She remained in jail for a month after the trial; in July Dewey's assistants took her to court, where she pleaded guilty on the outstanding charges and received suspended sentences. Dewey arranged for her to get $1,100 in forfeited bail money, and with that nest egg Brown and Balitzer moved to suburban New Rochelle and began working for MacFadden. Each received about $1,250 for her work. In October, Brown bought a car and the two women moved to Pomona, California, where they bought a gas station.[52]

In her January 26, 1937, statement for the defense, Brown said she first learned about Luciano's trial by reading newspapers in jail, where she was awaiting sentencing and trial on the other charges. Brown knew several of the women being held in the Dewey case, and they told her Dewey had helped get charges dropped against them and might do the same for her. She contacted Dewey's office and was visited by an assistant, who said if she would testify they could help her. "Each day the trial was going on, and each day . . . it seemed to me and everyone else, all the girls there, that the defendants didn't stand a chance. So the more I thought it over, the more I thought that if I gave them a statement, maybe it wouldn't do any harm and I could help myself." Because she was sick from her drug addiction and jail conditions were bad, she felt she could not survive a ten-year sentence. So she told Dewey's assistant she had met Luciano. Although she had never seen him, Brown said it was easy to identify him from newspaper photos. Her false testimony had been bothering her conscience, however, and she said it was time to tell the truth.[53]

Balitzer told a similar story. After she completed a drug cure in jail, she testified, Dewey assistants had told her she could help herself and her husband by telling them how she knew the defendants. When shown a picture of Luciano, Balitzer said the face looked familiar but she could not place it. When told he was head of the racket, she said, "That is ridiculous." Nonetheless, when offered a suspended sentence, she agreed to testify. Balitzer said her husband, who also had agreed to testify for Dewey, had been "double-crossed." Like Brown, she said her guilty conscience, not anger at Dewey's office, motivated her to change her story.[54]

The tale Nancy Presser recounted followed the same line. She said Dewey's assistants told her they wanted Luciano, and if she did not cooperate she would get ten to twenty years for check kiting, prostitution, and drug possession. Presser, who was living with Liguori at the time of her arrest, had seen Luciano from a distance several times but did not know him. When the trial was over, Presser and another witness, Thelma Jordan, continued living in a Washington Square hotel at taxpayer expense. A few weeks later, they were sent to Europe. "Dewey's office," she said, "obtained our passports, and before our departure we were each given $200 in cash." Their passage was paid to Liverpool, where they stayed for five days before moving on to London. When their money ran short, Dewey's office sent them enough to stay for seven more weeks. When they requested still more cash, Dewey's office sent them $100 and ordered them to return home. They arrived in New York on September 19 "dead broke." Dewey then provided them with ten dollars per day and sent them to a charity for further help. Presser stated that she decided to tell the truth about Luciano because her conscience was bothering her, not because the public largess had ended. Her story was bolstered by an affidavit from another witness, Helen Horvath, who had been in jail with Presser. Horvath remembered Presser telling her that Dewey's assistants were pushing her to implicate Luciano; on one occasion she had seen Presser studying a newspaper with Luciano's picture so she could identify him in court.[55]

Perhaps the most credible witness the defense produced to discredit Dewey's case was Muriel Weiss, Joe Bendix's wife. A few days before he was to testify, she said, she visited her husband, who told her he had learned Luciano owned part of a certain restaurant. Bendix said he planned to tell Dewey he had met Luciano there and asked his wife to corroborate his story so he could get a reduced jail term. Although she agreed, Dewey thought she would not make a good witness and never called her to the stand. After the trial ended, she heard from another source that Luciano was not involved in prostitution; when she told Bendix, he "sort of shrugged his shoulders" and said he was only trying to help himself.[56]

In mid-March 1937, Luciano's lawyers asked McCook to grant a new trial based on the recantations. In his May 7 ruling, the judge said the witnesses' new stories were "induced by fear, financial pressure and cravings for drugs, and are poisonously false." McCook also rejected the defendants' other arguments for a new trial; they had asked him to reconsider the ex post facto ban, claimed that one juror had shown bias, alleged that the special jury had been unfair, and called Dewey's conduct inflammatory. McCook responded that conspiracy laws had been on the federal books for a long time and created no new crimes and that the reasons for a special jury were clear under state law. While he agreed that one juror had known about the case beforehand, he said that was no reason to unseat him. Finally, McCook defended Dewey's conduct. Conceding that a few of Dewey's remarks were impassioned, McCook declared, "the guilt of these defendants was made out so convincingly and established so clearly that it is impossible to argue that anything that the prosecutor said or did could have had any influence upon the jury's verdict." Sounding more like a prosecutor than a judge, McCook added that the defense lawyers had demeaned themselves by cross-examining witnesses about "entirely irrelevant matters and inquiry into the most nauseating and revolting minute details of their prostitution activities." Moreover, defense attorneys had spent too much time "in attacking the honesty and integrity of the prosecutor and his staff." Given those circumstances, McCook argued that Dewey "was entitled to some leeway in his answering the accusations made against him . . . and to some freedom in portraying the evidence."[57]

McCook's rulings were predictable. He had always been predisposed to Dewey and was unlikely to decide that the prosecutor had committed grave errors. In retrospect, and even at the time, it was apparent to other observers that the appellate case was far from airtight. Dewey recognized this difficulty and assigned the appeal to the best legal mind on his staff, Stanley Fuld, a future chief justice of New York's highest court. Looking back, Fuld said: "It was a very hard case to sustain. There were a number of errors committed. There was some error in summation, some error in the admission of evidence. It was a novel case. It was the first time that a long sentence had been given. Then, too, there was a recantation of evidence. Everything piled up to make it not too strong a case to argue, though the guilt seemed to us very, very clear, but Dewey argued the appeal for an hour or so, and he argued it very, very forcefully." Dewey, then and later, recognized the close call; when someone asked for his autograph after the Luciano argument he referred him to Fuld, the man "who wrote the brief."[58]

Because it was his first and perhaps most controversial case, the Luciano conviction would haunt Dewey for the rest of his prosecutorial and political career. Although early critics of his handling of the trial could be silenced, in later years Dewey's political ambitions raised questions about his fairness. Dewey himself never doubted his handling of the case. When two key witnesses, Peter Balitzer and Joe Weintraub, used the consideration they got for testifying to return to the prostitution business, some of his assistants were upset. Dewey, however, was not bothered by it.[59]

His major concern was the fact that some people looked upon his first blockbuster as a prostitution case rather than a devastating blow to the underworld. He delivered a typical Dewey lament in a 1937 speech: "Most of the people still think we were prosecuting whores, I don't know why. . . . But what we were doing of course was getting a mob of gunmen and dope peddlers who had taken over the industry of prostitution. . . . I haven't got the answer to prostitution and if anybody has, he is an awful lot smarter than I am." Despite public confusion about Dewey's accomplishments in the Luciano case, it established his reputation as the country's leading racket buster. That renown gave him the freedom to pick future cases for prosecution that had the greatest chance of conviction. Before Luciano, he had been forced to take tips from all sources; now he could snub those he deemed beneath him.[60] Dewey had very little time to ponder the Luciano verdict, however, for he was quickly caught up in the twin juggernauts of more important cases and the launching of his political career.

≈ ≈ ≈ ≈

CHAPTER EIGHT

Fighting Labor Rackets

*F*OR MONTHS public attention was riveted on the glitzy Luciano case, while behind the scenes Dewey's staff worked on investigations of far greater substance. Letters to his office confirmed that although many citizens worried about prostitution, labor racketeering affected all residents of the city. Honest workers and businessmen suffered from its violence, and consumers paid higher prices for goods that carried hidden surcharges to offset payoffs to racketeers. Labor racketeering was nothing new; it had existed long before Dewey and would continue long after his term as special prosecutor. But like so much crime in that era, labor racketeering was increasing as tolerance for it decreased. Yet, unlike organized crime, which all good citizens could agree was a sinister force, labor racketeering was a more controversial and complex problem.[1]

The 1930s was an era of political and economic transition, and nowhere was this more apparent than in the changing American labor movement. Seemingly all society's confusion about labor's growing demands for political legitimacy and the continuing debate about how to right the nation's economic woes were reflected in the criminal justice system. While some citizens continued to inundate Dewey with letters against prostitutes, others issued a plethora of complaints about alleged labor racketeering. Complainants sought a variety of remedies for a variety of wrongs. Businessmen who had taken advantage of the weakened state of unionism in the 1920s wanted continued supremacy; some defined any attempt at labor organizing as racketeering and sought Dewey's help in stamping out legitimate labor activities. Their pleas were often overshadowed by realistic concerns about gangsters infiltrating unions and harassing businessmen. Ultimately, this ambiguity enhanced Dewey's political career. He appealed to bona fide unions as a crusader against racketeers, while winning over Republicans who interpreted his prosecutions as moves against labor itself.

Criminals had begun infiltrating the labor movement almost as soon as workers began militant organizing efforts in the 1880s and employers responded by hiring strong-arm men to break up picket lines. In some strikes, companies hired police or private agencies such as the Pinkertons; in New York City, gangs that were already doing the bidding of politicians were recruited by management. Initially, unions fought back with their brawniest members. But even these proved no match for professional gangsters, and unions began hiring their own toughs. Until the 1920s such arrangements were temporary; like those hired during elections, thugs worked only for the duration of the strike. The onset of Prohibition, however, brought wealthier gangsters who parlayed temporary positions into more permanent strongholds. The prosperous 1920s spawned increased competition among businesses and a general weakening of the labor movement. Gangsters were able to exploit the resulting chaos in industrial relations through several kinds of rackets. In some industries they created so-called trade organizations; businessmen unwilling to join were threatened until they agreed to pay fees guaranteeing freedom from union trouble. To keep such illicit bargains, the gangs violently took over legitimate unions, using intimidation tactics ranging from ordinary beatings to dynamite, stink bombs, and arson.

Not surprisingly, one of the chief architects of this transformation was Arnold Rothstein. He played a major role in the famous twenty-eight-week strike of the International Ladies Garment Workers Union (ILGWU) that began July 1, 1926. The employers hired Legs Diamond, and the union hired Little Augie, a Brooklyn mobster. Neither side knew that both men were working for Arnold Rothstein, who planned to use the principles that guided his other criminal enterprises to infiltrate and organize the garment industry.[2]

Although Rothstein died before consolidating his control, two protégés of his henchmen Little Augie—Louis "Lepke" Buchalter and Jacob "Gurrah" Shapiro—carried out his program. Both earned their monikers growing up in the slums of Manhattan's Lower East Side. Buchalter's nickname was a variation on his Jewish mother's pet name for him, Lepkele; Gurrah won his nickname for his inability to say "Get out of the way" in Yiddish. Both men first ran afoul of the law in 1915. Gurrah began his career as a petty thief, was arrested twice that year for malicious mischief, and was sent to a reformatory for burglary. Lepke's similarly checkered past included three jail terms. When the pair became partners in 1917 their careers took off. In Dewey's words, they became such "big shots" they were able to elude the law. Dewey described Gurrah as "one of the first to realize that crime today must be organized—and that the big shot must stay removed from the actual sluggings and bombings. Teamed with Lepke, he gathered around him a band of assorted gangsters."[3]

Lepke and Gurrah's rise paralleled Luciano's ascent through the Masseria family. According to Dewey, the two began as "free-lance sluggers who sold their services in industrial disputes to the highest bidder. They began to emerge from obscurity as ranking members of the Little Augie mob in the late 1920s." When further advancement was blocked, they killed Little Augie with the help of another gang member. Lepke and Gurrah then turned on their accomplice, killing him, weighting his body with concrete, and tossing it into the East River.[4] By the 1930s Lepke and Gurrah had risen to the top of New York's industrial rackets.

According to Mafia mythmakers, Lepke and Gurrah were only small-time operators until Lucky Luciano took them under his wing. With his help and financial backing, they supposedly worked out a blueprint for taking over New York's garment district. In reality, Lepke and Gurrah were powers in their own right long before they met Luciano. The three men were equal business partners rather than members of a hierarchical crime pyramid. In exchange for backing Lepke and Gurrah's racketeering operations, Luciano received a return on his investments and gained a market for his bootleg liquor in the garment district.[5]

Luciano's money gave Lepke and Gurrah another tool for taking over the smaller garment makers—loan sharking. Clothing was a high-risk industry in the 1920s. As styles changed, manufacturers needed ready capital to invest in new materials. Smaller companies often had trouble obtaining bank loans to finance the changes and turned to mobsters for funds. Unable to keep up with exorbitant interest rates, some owners found themselves in business with Lepke and Gurrah. Prohibition provided the profits for this kind of expansion and gave gangsters a foothold in industries from which they otherwise would have been blocked by legitimate unions such as the ILGWU. The mobsters solved the problem of union opposition by taking control of trucking, the lifeblood of New York's main industries.

Canny gangsters like Rothstein, Luciano, Gurrah, and Lepke recognized the value of the trucking business and, then as now, how comparatively easy it was to infiltrate. Because many teamsters were independent and self-employed, they were susceptible to pressure; the solitary nature of their work left drivers more vulnerable to intimidation than workers in shops. In the garment industries during the 1920s and 1930s, clothing was not produced in one plant. Unfinished goods and finished products were shuttled between manufacturers and subcontractors; by blocking transportation, racketeers could bring the whole industry to a halt. They used this leverage to form the Truckman's Association, forcing truckers to join for a fee and raising the price of clothing by several cents. The costs were passed along to consumers, and the spoils were divided between truckers and gangsters.

Although Lepke and Gurrah focused on the garment industry, their control of the truckers put them atop a diffuse but vast labor racketeering empire. Like criminals in other areas of organized crime in the harried days after Prohibition, these two gangsters cooperated to share the spoils and eliminate unnecessary competition and violence. Racketeers controlling other facets of illegal enterprise in the garment and transportation industries paid them allegiance, and virtually every business that relied on trucking came under the gangsters' purview. By the mid-1930s authorities estimated that Lepke and Gurrah were earning more than $2 million annually. According to Dewey, Gurrah "became a familiar figure in nightclubs, at hockey games and at the race track. His clothes were costly and his habits expensive." The less flamboyant Lepke lived as a rich businessman "in a luxurious apartment overlooking Central Park. He traveled about town in a high-powered motorcar driven by a chauffeur and he patronized night clubs and race tracks."[6]

The gangsters' lavish life-styles came at the cost of the average consumer and the health of New York industry. Although costs varied from business to business, each year enterprises and consumers paid thousands of dollars in tribute to racketeers and their allies. Dewey estimated that racketeering cost the nation $1 billion annually. Although law enforcement officials were the first to recognize the high cost of crime, reform politicians quickly picked up on the issue as a rallying point. Taking advantage of popular concern about the depression, reform rhetoric centered on the luxurious life-styles of criminals. Industry also recognized the increasingly high cost of doing business in New York City and began moving south. This geographic shift was also attributable to pressure for higher wages from New York's legitimate labor movement, and it is impossible to sort out how many companies left because of racketeering and how many sought lower production costs. It is clear, however, that panic over high wages drove many businesses into the arms of gangsters who promised to keep down labor costs. The Depression thus put a new spin on the old story of New York labor relations in which racketeers worked for both sides.[7]

Because it served an institutional function in the chaos of Depression economics and labor instability, racketeering posed unique problems for law enforcement. Many legitimate interests were involved. The fact that businessmen often paid tribute to gangsters to thwart organized labor irked reformers. William Jay Schieffelen, president of the Citizens' Union, blamed "unmitigated profit seeking" as the reason so many members of the Chamber of Commerce paid tribute to crooked politicians and gangsters. Dewey too found businessmen's cooperation with the underworld an affront and a frustrating stumbling block to his efforts. He advocated the use of grand juries in part because they could compel reluctant businessmen to testify about racketeers.[8]

By the early 1930s law enforcement officials recognized that labor racketeering had become a national menace. During the late 1920s bootleggers had reinvested some of their profits in legitimate enterprises such as labor unions, a process that speeded up with the end of Prohibition. Although racketeering was a national problem, reformers recognized it could be fought most effectively at the local level.[9] Unfortunately in most localities, and especially in New York, labor racketeering presented almost insurmountable obstacles for reform by existing institutions. Before Dewey's investigation, New York County district attorneys and La

Guardia had found their battles against labor racketeers frustrating and ineffective.

When he took office in 1930, District Attorney Crain had promised to make racketeering one of his primary targets. Recognizing that rackets existed largely because many businessmen and other New Yorkers acceded to them, he saw enlisting popular support as the only way to combat the problem. To do so, he formed a Committee of Public Safety comprising prominent citizens and tried to rally public support with radio addresses and press releases. He mailed questionnaires to businessmen to gain a better understanding of the racketeers' methods.[10]

The ultimate failure of Crain's efforts was confirmed by Roosevelt's appointment of Seabury to investigate Crain's office. Seabury concluded that Crain's attempt to combat racketeers had been largely ineffectual; the citizens' committee did little and businesses failed to cooperate. Crain had pursued approximately thirty racketeering investigations, including one into price-fixing at the Fulton Fish Market controlled by Joseph "Socks" Lanza and another in the garment district, where Little Augie held sway. Seabury concluded that despite a few victories, Crain and his assistants accomplished little because of their incompetence, naïveté, and impossibly heavy workloads. In the end, all the district attorney's war accomplished, according to Seabury, was to raise public alarm without offering any solution or concrete results. Although Seabury criticized Crain's handling of specific cases, his report was largely a testament to the institutional problems posed by racketeering. The reformer conceded that racket investigations "were burdens presenting extraordinary difficulties" and had to be handled outside the regular channels of an overworked office pursuing approximately eighteen thousand cases annually.[11]

The complexity of the problem was demonstrated again when La Guardia took over as mayor and announced his goal of running racketeers out of the city. As a congressman La Guardia had become the hero of labor by writing and then struggling for eight years to pass the Norris–La Guardia Act of 1932. The measure prohibited yellow-dog contracts, which kept workers from joining unions, and banned federal court injunctions against legitimate strikes. As mayor, La Guardia recognized the threat to legitimate organizing efforts posed by gangsters and appointed William Fellowes Morgan commissioner of markets, in part to fight labor racketeers. Although Morgan appeared to be the perfect choice—he had brought Socks Lanza's activities to Crain's attention—he had as little success tackling racketeering as Crain. Dewey assistant Sol Gelb later remembered Morgan was "a well-intentioned man. That's all I can say about him. He talked about rackets, but I think he was powerless to do anything about them, but even if he had power—and I don't know how much power he had—I considered him nothing more than a well-intentioned man."[12]

Just as Seabury had lambasted Crain, so Dewey and his staff discounted the effectiveness of their predecessors, including Morgan. Stanley Fuld remembered that "We felt that we couldn't rely too much on what had been done before. What attempts there had been to get into the investigation of rackets had failed."[13] Such criticisms, however, stemmed from a desire to make their own efforts look more impressive and failed to acknowledge how many more advantages they enjoyed. Dewey's large budget, limited mission, and large staff, including accountants to pore over union books, gave him tools Crain and Morgan would have envied.

Despite these advantages, Dewey's staff did not face an easy task. In the highly charged labor atmosphere of the 1930s, experienced union leaders had too often seen the law twisted to thwart strikes. Their main concern was that Dewey's investigation would undermine public faith in unions and set a dangerous precedent for fighting legitimate labor efforts. In the hard-fought battle for the Norris–La Guardia Act, unions had won the right to strike; but Dewey's investigation, they believed, would open a new avenue by which employers could attack union organizing efforts merely by arguing that they were attempts at racketeering. As the secretary of a utility union said, "While on the face of it, this investigation might appear perfectly in order, this investigation if permitted to continue . . . may [allow] an authorized body to enter any labor organization and demand its records on the pretext of uncovering labor racketeering. Such procedure can only lead to an unwarranted exposure of the records of union membership to the employer, which in turn will serve as an attack against organized labor."[14]

Unions were especially mistrustful of Dewey. As a Republican, he did not share the pro-labor credentials of Democratic prosecutors. When his name came up for the special prosecutor's job, he received the backing of many antiunion Republicans. Initially, labor leaders viewed Dewey as an ambitious Republican hoping to make political hay at their expense. In the early days of his probe, his actions confirmed their worries; as his staff tracked down leads, the investigation's most publicized activity was subpoenaing union records. Because Dewey refused to divulge the purpose of his activities, union leaders often assumed the worst. Their fears seemed realized when Dewey broke his silence to issue a vituperative attack on Local 3 of the International Brotherhood of Electrical Workers (IBEW).

His fight with the union became public on January 14, 1937, when he subpoenaed its records and issued a press release accusing the local of corrupting New York's construction industries. Dewey contended that violence had driven many contractors out of the area and cost New York City $2 million in overcharges. In addition, he said, the union's racketeering activities had led to the murder of one of its members in 1933. The local's leaders fought back. They called a rally attended by five thousand people on January 30, 1937, at the St. Nicholas Palace on West 66th Street. The business manager told the rally that "If there were crimes and racketeering, they were due to unemployment, poverty and low wages." The local's president charged that Dewey spent 70 percent of his time investigating labor unions and was "rapidly becoming a labor baiter."[15]

Dewey's attack on the electrical workers alarmed other union leaders, who saw his statements as the opening salvo in a war against labor. They responded by coming to the IBEW's defense and firing off letters to La Guardia and Lehman. A bricklayers' local called Dewey's investigation into rackets "a vicious attack against organized labor . . . designed not to aid the labor movement, but to destroy it." A bakery union charged that Dewey's attack on the electrical workers was an "attempt to discredit Labor Organizations in the eyes of our Citizens" by portraying unions as agencies of racketeering. Echoing this concern, an official of the upholstery union said, "Mr. Dewey seems to have a mania without scruples for newspaper publicity. . . . We object to Mr. Dewey trying cases in newspaper paragraphs before any proper investigation is made or indictments obtained. We believe that the principle of American Justice is that a defendant is considered innocent until found guilty. Mr. Dewey first hangs them through press publicity and without facts or foundation prejudices the case before it gets into the courts."[16] A few historians have argued that the unions complaining to La Guardia and Lehman were in fact controlled by racketeers. But most of the letters seem to have resulted from an orchestrated effort by the American Federation of Labor (AFL) to ensure that Dewey stuck to his stated goals of fighting racketeers, not legitimate labor organizing.

From the outset, Dewey attempted to calm labor's fears by drawing a distinction between legitimate union organizing efforts and racketeering. In his first radio speech in July 1935, he said: "No intelligent man, whether he be employer or employee, can fail to support enthusiastically the cause of organized labor. Neither business nor labor can prosper unless business is fair to organized labor and labor, by collective bargaining, can enforce its demands for decent living conditions and a fair wage." But, he added, "It would indeed be a calamity if a few gangs of thugs, masquerading as labor union delegates, should discredit the cause of organized labor in this country." Eventually Dewey won support from William Green of the American Federation of Labor and George Meany, then president of the New York State Federation of Labor.[17]

Even if he had started with the support of labor, Dewey and his men would have faced the same problems as their predecessors in trying to crack labor racketeering. Foremost among them was the difficulty of eliciting testimony from victims of shakedowns. One Dewey assistant remembered that "witnesses would have done anything to avoid testifying." He added that it was "hard" to get testimony about Luciano, but "it was murder" to get witnesses against Lepke and Gurrah. While few people knew of Luciano before Dewey made his a household name, by the early 1930s Lepke and Gurrah were "almost a legend." Businessmen lived in fear of receiving a visit from henchmen who claimed to work for "L & G." According to Dewey, mere mention of "the boys" was a "message of terror" that left victims abjectly cooperative. Several victims said they would prefer jail terms to testifying against the racketeers. One man insisted that the $400 weekly payoffs shown on his books went to a mistress; only after much questioning did he admit he had no mistress and was paying the money to Lepke and Gurrah to stop stink bombs. Further complicating the investigation was the complexity of the duo's empire. Rumors linked them to many New York businesses, and Dewey's men spent fruitless hours checking out false leads.[18]

Despite Dewey's best efforts, Gurrah and Lepke always escaped his grasp. He indicted them for running rackets in the bakery and garment industries, but his cases were overshadowed by prosecutions in federal and other state jurisdictions. Nevertheless, Dewey outshone his contemporaries in the public's perception of him as the man who broke the back of labor racketeering in New York City. The stage for his success was set with his first labor racketeering case against the restaurant and waiters' union in 1937. Although it was not his most important labor case, or even the most difficult, it cemented his reputation. The public's interest in Dewey's success had been primed by the Luciano prosecutions and was heightened by several other factors. First, there was the built-in appeal of a case involving New York's most popular eateries, an appeal Dewey capitalized on by calling such prominent witnesses as restaurant owner and boxer Jack Dempsey. In addition, the case clearly showed the degree, the means, and the ease with which racketeers had been able to take over an entire industry and become respected and politically influential labor leaders.

Compared to other rackets, the restaurant case proved easy to prosecute. Witnesses came forward willingly. It was already common knowledge that Dutch Schultz had taken over the restaurant and cafeteria workers' union through a henchman, Jules Martin. The New York attorney general had conducted a short-lived investigation into the charges. Moreover, stubborn waiters who refused to cave in to the mobsters had hired their own lawyer and tried, unsuccessfully, to press their cause through the press and New York County's lower courts. Thus, when waiter Benny Gottesman approached Dewey as a last resort in August 1935, Dewey could not claim to be breaking new ground or uncovering previously hidden scandal. Nonetheless, the case offered him the chance to prove he could achieve breakthroughs that eluded other law enforcement officials.

Gottesman's evidence described how the gang led by Dutch Schultz had infiltrated the two unions during the summer of 1932. The cafeteria workers' and restaurant workers' unions each had a handful of members who believed they could make more money by aligning with Schultz than with the legitimate organizing efforts of the American Federation of Labor. The gangsters agreed to help the dishonest cadres gain control of their locals. When they lost the first election, Schultz's men stole and burned the ballot box. At the next election, goons with guns showed up to ensure that voting went their way. Once the corrupt leadership was in place, the new union leaders set up picket lines and made impossibly high demands on targeted restaurants. The gangsters then offered to help the businessmen, saying they could settle the strike for payoffs as high as $1,000; a graduated scale of payoffs was arranged in accordance with the size of the restaurant. For an additional sum, racketeers agreed to eliminate union threats altogether. The workers never saw the money, which was split between the crooked union leaders and their gangland backers. The gang increased its profits by creating the Metropolitan Restaurant and Cafeteria Association in late 1933, urging restaurants and cafeterias to join for $250 plus $5 a week. Reluctant businessmen were coerced by threats of strikes, stink bombs, and beatings. The intimidation tactics worked; by mid-1935 the association had more than three hundred members.[19]

Several businessmen and honest union members took evidence of the racket to court. Soon after the shakedowns began, a restaurant owner filed charges against a union leader, but a magistrate dismissed the case. In early 1933, another restaurant owner filed charges with the district attorney's office, but that case also was ignored. Later that year, Benny Gottesman complained to the president of the international union, went to the newspapers, and hired his own lawyers. He was later joined by other honest union members in an appeal to the district attorney. As a result of their complaints, most of the gang members except Dutch Schultz were arrested in the summer of 1933. Yet, in spite of complainants' attempts to publicize the case, when it came to trial five months later in the Court of Special Sessions it drew little press attention and ended in acquittals for all defendants. Emboldened by the legal victory, the racketeers accused complaining union members of being Communists and expelled them. With their critics swept out of the way, the racketeers consolidated their positions in the unions. As Dewey noted years later, "A great industry by now had final notice that there was only one thing to do and that was pay up, shut up and keep quiet for good. Restaurant after restaurant, cafeteria after cafeteria, and finally large chains themselves, fell before it with never a complaint. There was just a haggling over price, and extortions ranging from $500 to $50,000 were demanded and paid. The racket association was set up in fancy offices and the whole organization was in full swing."[20] The two unions meanwhile became stronger, and the president of the cafeteria workers became vice president of the international and a political force in New York City and Albany. He later served on the National Recovery Administration Board. Soon after Dewey's charges against him were announced in October 1936, he committed suicide.

Even with Gottesman's help and the evidence from earlier cases, putting together the restaurant racketeering prosecution took time and effort. The first order of business was protecting Gottesman. As Dewey recalled later, "We had to put police in his house and for five long months, Benny Gottesman didn't work. And he lived—God knows how he lived. For five months he begged and he borrowed. For five months he gave up the right to earn a living. . . . He went out of New York at a time when I thought it was necessary to send him away for a whole month and he submitted without a single complaint."[21]

Even with Gottesman's testimony as the linchpin, Dewey's staff had to come up with corroborating evidence. In gathering this information, Dewey tested the laborious methods his staff would use to prosecute all later labor-racketeering cases. He subpoenaed the financial records of the restaurant association, the union, and victimized restaurants and cafeterias. Accountants pored over the books seeking discrepancies that would indicate payoffs. He called reluctant businessmen before the grand jury and questioned them about their books. Fearful of retribution, owners often lied about the purpose of the payments, and Dewey was forced to hold grand jury sessions at night to protect witnesses. One frightened victim was interviewed in a cruising taxicab so he could not be followed. Others refused to testify because they had become collaborators. As Dewey said, "They were dummies it is true, but they lent their names, their prestige and their respectability to the operation of a criminal enterprise. They were in fact victims of extortion but in some respects they were equally guilty with those who were convicted."[22]

For every witness willing to testify, Dewey's men interviewed dozens in private, grilling some several times, and threatening others with contempt proceedings. Ultimately, it took four lawyers, three accountants, and ten police detectives eighteen months to gather enough evidence to win indictments in the case. Dewey and other New York City reformers were convinced that earlier cases had failed because of corruption and political links. Considering that it took Dewey's staff eighteen months to investigate the charges, an equally likely explanation is that handling such a full-scale probe was beyond the capacity of the ordinary machinery of justice.[23]

The indictment handed up on October 21, 1936, named fourteen defendants, including two lawyers, Abraham Cohen and Harry Vogelstein. The four organizers of the ring were dead: Dutch Schultz; his henchman Jules Martin, who was gunned down in March 1935; and two alleged crooked union officials, Abe Borson and Harry S. Koenig, who had also been shot. Dewey said the four had formed the union racket in 1932, and then, as a sideline, organized the Metropolitan Cafeteria Owners Service Company (later the Metropolitan Restaurant and Cafeteria Association) to collect payoffs from restaurant owners. In addition, the indictment charged the racketeers with embezzling one-third of the union dues as well as $120,000 from the Metropolitan, $75,000 from Local 6, and $45,000 from Local 302.

When Dewey announced the indictment, he titillated the New York press by hinting that the defendants had been involved in even more sinister activities. He resurrected the specter of Schultz and implied that the ringleaders had been involved in the murders of the original crooked union officials. Dewey revealed that ex-heavyweight champion Jack Dempsey, who owned a restaurant at Eighth Avenue and 50th Street, had appeared before the grand jury to describe how he had paid to join the restaurant association and had served as toastmaster at one of its dinners. Eager to calm labor's fears, Dewey said honest labor unions were "betrayed and robbed [by men who] tried to ruin organized labor" and predicted the case would wrest "the freedom of labor from their clutches." The indictment named but did not charge J. Richard "Dixie" Davis, who was undergoing disbarment proceedings for his representation of Schultz. Dewey's comments attracted the hyperbole that characterized all press coverage of his investigations. Even the normally subdued *New York Times* wrote in a page one story, "Striking with the precision and force that characterized his assault on the vice and loan shark rings, Special Prosecutor Thomas E. Dewey smashed yesterday at a restaurant racket that had been taking $2,000,000 a year from owners."[24]

The following day, Dewey's staff conducted a raid on a bakery union. The new case gave Dewey the chance to mention Lepke and Gurrah, who, he claimed, were behind a flour trucking racket. At the same time, he brought out new information on the restaurant investigation, revealing that when he had indicted Dutch Schultz for tax evasion years earlier, the gangster had turned over the café racket to Jules Martin and Samuel Krantz. When Martin refused to pay over his profits, Schultz had him gunned down in Troy, New York, in March 1935. Dewey also named two of the five defendants still at large in the restaurant case—Krantz and Louis Beitcher, who had worked as the gang's collector. Krantz, he said, had gone by many aliases and had been judged incorrigible by the New York courts in 1915. Beitcher also used several aliases and had been arrested in Pennsylvania in 1932 for procuring and in the Bronx in 1935 for carrying a weapon.[25]

Dewey continued to fuel public interest in the case for the next two weeks. At a bond hearing on October 23, he implied that four of the leading defendants had been involved in four murders, not just the two mentioned several days earlier. He claimed the ring was involved in the killings of Dutch Schultz and his assistant, Martin, as well as those of the crooked union leaders Boorson and Koenig. Despite Dewey's statements, Justice John V. McAvoy reduced bail for Abraham Cohen, the racket's ringleader, and for three other defendants—Max Pincus, John Williams, and Irving Epstein. The following day, the *New York Times* said the restaurant indictments reflected Dewey's goal "to get the racketeers who prey on legitimate businessmen" and were based on thousands of witness interviews. Another story on the same day alleged that while Dewey's fight against Luciano demonstrated his great abilities, it had been an easier case than the restaurant probe. *Times* reporter Russell Owen asserted that the "quiet and meticulous way in which [Dewey] puts together his cases is the first concentrated effort to rid Manhattan of this form of extortion." On October 31, the *Times* published a list of the 110 victimized restaurants, including such well-known spots as Jack Demp-sey's, Lindy's, the Hollywood, and the Brass Rail. The occasion for the story was an expanded indictment. The first charges had accused the defendants of embezzlement and conspiracy; the superseding indictment added a charge that the thirteen men had extorted $150,000 from cafés. Dewey never explained the discrepancy between that amount and the $2 million originally alleged.[26]

The restaurant case came to trial on January 18, 1937, with nine de-fendants. The roster included one gangster, Louis Beitcher; two lawyers, Abe Cohen and Harry Vogelstein; the head of the Metropolitan Restau-rant Association, Philip Grossel; and five union leaders, Paul Coulcher, a Russian immigrant, and Aladar Retek, an Austrian immigrant, who both helped organize Local 16, and Irving Epstein, Charles Baum, and John Williams from Local 302. Four others linked to the racket were either dead or fugitives: union leader Max Pincus had committed suicide after being named in the indictment; and gangsters Samuel Furstenberg, Samuel Krantz, and William Kramer had gone into hiding. The most prominent gangster of the original group, Louis Beitcher, surprised the other defendants on the eve of the trial by pleading guilty and agreeing to testify against them. Defense attorneys demanded that the prospective jurors, who witnessed the plea, should be released "on the ground that Mr. Dewey had no right to subject them to dramatics." When Judge McCook disagreed, defense lawyers asked McCook to step down because he favored the prosecution. Dewey characterized the charge as "ridicu-lous" while wearing what the newspaper called "a faint smile at the cor-ners of his mouth," and McCook refused to recuse himself. When jury selection began, Dewey further aroused press attention by mentioning Tammany Hall boss Jimmy Hines and by arranging to seat boxer Jack Dempsey at the back of the courtroom. Dewey explained that Hines's name would surface during the trial and that jurors who knew him could not serve on the panel. Dempsey, he said, was his first witness, although he sent him home until after jury selection was completed.[27]

Picking the jury proved a laborious, four-day task. Louis Waldman, a Socialist and well-known labor lawyer representing Charles Baum, maintained that the trial was an attempt to undermine labor organizing. His tactic from the outset was to find jurors sympathetic to unions—no mean task considering the prosperous background of most blue ribbon jurors. By the end of the first day of jury selection, only one of the twelve men questioned had expressed sympathy for labor; John M. Heaton of West 16th Street said he had never dealt with a union but believed labor had the right to strike and establish picket lines. Dewey objected to the defense's lengthy questioning on this issue, saying labor's right to strike was not an issue in the case: "This indictment charges extortion; there is no union on trial here. There are on trial five men who are leaders in two unions. The men, and not the unions, are on trial." After four days in which eighty-two jurors were questioned, eleven had been selected. Of those questioned, only four had held union posts, a fact the *New York Times* found unsurprising because blue ribbon panels were "traditionally composed of men of business success." One of the four was dismissed because he characterized Dewey's activities as antiunion. Jury selection was a major concern for the defense, as it had been in the Luciano trial. Lawyers contended the defendants would suffer from the jury's unrepresentative composition. John F. Finnerty, a Washington, D.C., lawyer hired by Retek, argued that the defense's twenty peremptory challenges were insufficient to protect all the men and therefore violated the Fourteenth Amendment. Neither McCook nor New York's appellate courts found the complaint justified.[28]

The ten-week trial opened on January 24, 1937, with the introduction of the prosecution's first exhibit—a four-by-five-foot chart depicting the racket and displaying Dutch Schultz's name at the top. The exhibit, hung behind McCook, provided a way to keep names straight; according to one newspaper account, it served "as a continuous reference for the jurors who cannot escape seeing the big white rectangle as they look at the witness box." In his opening, Dewey assistant William Herlands said the racket had three parts. The first was the strong-arm crew that initially included Dutch Schultz and Jules Martin; after their deaths, it was composed of Krantz and his assistant, Louis Beitcher. After others had contacted restaurant owners, the enforcers would collect the shakedown cash or use stink bombs and violence against recalcitrant restaurateurs. The racket's second division included union officers, who called strikes and made outrageous demands on owners. When the effects of these tactics had almost driven restaurants out of business and owners were ready to reconsider payoffs, union leaders would dispatch the strong-arm team to work out an arrangement. The tribute demanded ranged from $2,000 to $17,000, depending on the labor services provided: no contract, a contract with a fifty-cent or one-dollar increase, or a closed shop. The third part of the operation was the Metropolitan Association, an employers' group organized by Martin at the behest of Schultz. Lawyers Harry Vogelstein and Abraham Cohen wrote the organizational papers, while Philip Grossel served as nominal head of the association. A restaurant paid $250 to join the association, and $5 in weekly membership fees. In addition to supplying money, the association gave the racket a legitimate front.[29]

One week into the trial, the *New York Times* ran an article reflecting the degree to which Dewey received accolades even before proving himself. In the opinion of writer Russell Owen, Dewey's methods were so advanced that the trial was won already; he predicted the racketeering case would have far-reaching consequences. "The scrappy young man with the black mustache who has been putting away racketeers regularly since he was appointed to the job by Governor Lehman in July 1935, has a way of making an airtight case before he starts trial. . . . His record of convictions is almost one hundred percent perfect." Owen cited Beitcher's guilty plea as "merely another of the dramatic incidents in Mr. Dewey's career since he started on an endless task." Owen did not question the ethics of having the man who was second in charge of the ring testify against his underlings; nor did he point out that the initial claim of a $2-million racket had been drastically downscaled. Instead, he argued that the $300,000 spent on the Dewey investigation was worth the cost because the crackdown could ultimately save the $100,000,000 prosecutors estimated was paid by businesses and victims annually. Dewey, said Owen, had triumphed despite unremitting difficulties but faced an uncertain future as a public servant: "How long he can afford to continue in his present investigation is problematical, for he is working for much less than he could earn in private practice."[30]

From the outset, defense attorneys were outmatched. In their opening remarks to the jury, they argued that the wrong people were on trial. They declared the unions legitimate and said the real culprits were the restaurant owners, whose niggardly management had thrown the industry into chaos. Waldman said the restaurant business was notorious for long hours, low wages, and the "small side rackets by which the already overworked and impoverished waiter was still further imposed upon." Such side "rackets" included forcing waiters to buy their uniforms from specified shops. Lawyers charged that it was the restaurant owners who, by dealing with bootleggers during Prohibition, had brought thugs into the industry. Proof of this, according to Waldman, was the life-style of his client Charles Baum. If Baum had been part of a $2-million restaurant racket, Waldman asked, why was he living on $45 a week, why was his wife forced to work to help support him, why were the couple and their grandson living in one or two furnished rooms instead of an elegant apartment?[31]

It is not clear how sympathetic jurors might have been under the best of circumstances, but Dewey gave them no chance to ponder such questions. He called as the first prosecution witness artist Gerhard Schutes of Elkhart, Indiana, who had designed the restaurant association plaque. During a meeting about the emblem, Schutes said, Coulcher, Retek, Baum, Williams, and Goldstein conferred with a pajama-clad Martin, who was lying in bed at a Fifth Avenue hotel. Martin was pleased when Jack Dempsey's restaurant had joined the group because it proved their racket "was going to town."[32] As was always true during trials, Dewey was cocky when things went his way but irate when they did not. He lost his temper with the second witness—a hapless electrician and distant relative of Jules Martin—who became nervous and recanted his testimony on the stand. The *New York Times* reported that Dewey's "furious attack" on his own witness prompted defense attorneys to shout objections to his "browbeating tactics." It was, the newspaper noted, the "liveliest scene so far produced at trial." McCook restored order by overruling defense objections with "unperturbable calm."[33]

Dewey's success with other witnesses bolstered his case and provided ample copy for reporters looking for ways to capture the color of New York's seamier side. The girlfriend of Jules Martin and Krantz, "Edith Doe," fit the bill. Her testimony provided details of meetings between the defendants, but newspaper accounts seemed more enthralled with her personal attributes. She "applied an English accent to the jargon of Broadway" and would have been pretty had her sad eyes and drooping mouth not given her face an "unchangeably dolorous" look. While providing details about Doe's appearance and clothes, the story passed over the fact that she had been under house arrest since October 20. More substantive testimony came from members of Local 1. One waiter, Samuel Spiegel, identified Beitcher as the mob messenger sent in to take over the local in the fall of 1933. When Spiegel resisted the deal, Beitcher told him it was useless to fight because the gang controlled politicians and city officials, and anyway the fifty-cent increase in union dues paid to the crooked leaders was insignificant. Nonetheless, Spiegel had refused to pay and had taken the case to District Attorney Dodge, who conducted an investigation and indicted several men for extortion.[34]

Benny Gottesman, the former local secretary who had approached Dewey, described in more detail how Martin interfered with union activities in 1933. During a strike at a Broadway restaurant in January, Martin showed up and told the pickets to go home. When Gottesman said that was a decision to be made by local members, Martin threw a card in his face, and said: "Don't think this is a joke. I'm coming for the Dutchman. Jimmy Hines is behind this move. Here's his card. Call him up. Call up the police if you want to." Gottesman answered that he would not call the police or the Tammany Hall boss. Martin then asked him about the union's membership; when told the local had two thousand members, Martin responded, "What does 2,000 men mean when the Dutchman could send men down with machine guns?" Martin returned twice more that day with goons; walking up to one leader, he shoved a gun in his ribs and said, "Now listen, Pop, I'm giving you five minutes to take that picket line off, and if you don't I'm going to walk you out." The president of the union's joint board witnessed the threats and called off the strike. During subsequent meetings Martin told Gottesman to "wise up" as Coulcher had done; he claimed he had given Coulcher great power and could do the same for Gottesman. If anyone complained about the arrangement, Martin said, he had "ways of cooling them off." When Gottesman said it would be impossible to get away with a payoff scheme in his local, Martin said he had a good lawyer, Dixie Davis, and a good accountant, "who could cover your books so you could take them to any authorities and they couldn't find anything." If he had any trouble, Martin said, Jimmy Hines could easily fix a case. When Gottesman still re-

fused to go along, he was threatened repeatedly. The *New York Times'*
blow-by-blow account reported that Gottesman's "story was delivered
in a high-pitched and tense voice. His narrative teemed with idiomatic
expressions delivered so breathlessly that sometimes whole sentences became jumbled and his meaning confused, as if the terror of that year,
during which he had a weapon poked in his ribs more than once, had
not yet died away."[35]

The waiters' stories were followed by grisly testimony from restaurant owners who described how they had been coerced into joining the
Metropolitan Restaurant Association. Samuel Klaye, who owned a bar
and grill at Seventh Avenue and West 48th Street, said that in 1934 he
had been forced to join and sign a statement denying he had been coerced. Klaye said he decided to pay Pincus and Beitcher $3,500 to avoid
paying $18,200 in payroll increases. Louis Rubin, who owned a chain of
doughnut shops, said he paid $5,000 to Beitcher and $10,000 to the restaurant association to end stink bomb attacks and picketing by Local
302. Max Rosoff, who owned a restaurant on West 43rd Street, told how
picketing by Local 16 ended after he paid $3,500. Rosoff, one of the own-
ers who admitted lying to the grand jury, said he had changed his story
after being confronted by bookkeeping entries he could not explain. Another restaurant owner described just how costly noncompliance could
be. Joseph Rosenbloom owned a restaurant at Broadway and West 72nd
Street; he paid Beitcher $1,500 in 1933 but balked at paying another
$5,000 the following summer. Beitcher, he claimed, returned four times
and threatened trouble. Subsequently, on a Saturday night when the restaurant was filled with customers, an unpleasant smell permeated the
building. The patrons left without paying their bills, and Rosenbloom
had to pay an exterminator $75 to get rid of the stench. Guaranteeing
himself headlines, Dewey called a "Who's Who" of New York restaurateurs, including Leo Lindeman, the husband of singer Anne Miller and
owner of Lindy's, and the owners of the Brass Rail.[36] The testimony demonstrated how difficult it was for restaurant owners to withstand pres-
sures from the gang. Dewey's case also made it clear that the unions
themselves were victims. One restaurant owner, whose children were
threatened with kidnapping if he did not cooperate, said Vogelstein told
him, "Those pickets are only poor saps. A good talker gives them a nice

pep talk and those pickets walk up and down, but they don't get anything out of it."[37]

Dewey tied the various threads of his case together with testimony from Beitcher, who had served as the number-two man in the ring. Beitcher substantiated the victims' stories with tales of how he had collected more than $100,000 for each of the four years he worked for the ring. He linked all but one of the accused to the scheme, provoking an outburst by defendant Aladar Retek, who leapt out of his chair shouting, "You're a contemptible liar. I can't stand this lying." According to the newspaper account, "Retek's lips worked hysterically, tears flowed down his face and he made an effort to advance upon the witness." After Retek was subdued by police and his lawyer, Beitcher continued his testimony. As the *New York Times* noted, "The accusation had no effect on Beitcher. He leaned forward in the witness chair, looked at Retek, bared his teeth for a moment and went on with his catalogue of extortion in an unruffled voice." He proved an excellent prosecution witness. Not only did he name other defendants, he also remained calm under pressure and stymied defense attorneys' questions about inconsistencies in his testimony by claiming frequent memory lapses.[38]

Initial press releases about the case had billed the ring as a $2-million-a-year racket, but the evidence presented to the jury fell far short of that mark. Throughout the trial, figures of thousands of dollars were bandied about, and Beitcher claimed to have collected $100,000 per year. At the end of the government's case, however, Dewey assistant William Herlands asked McCook to dismiss twenty of the indictment's forty-nine counts because the restaurants' managers would not be called. The charges dropped included one accusing the ring of extorting $250 from Jack Dempsey's restaurant; others charged defendants with extorting $71,795 and attempting to extort another $1,500.[39]

The defense case failed to garner the same press attention or gather the same momentum as Dewey's had. Whereas most of the articles recounting Dewey's evidence appeared on the front page, many stories about the defense were on the inside, partly because the defense was less sensational. Dewey showed how rank-and-file union members had been victimized by Jules Martin and the gang; defense lawyers tried to convince jurors that the five union leaders had also been threatened and forced to pay tribute. Typical was defendant Irving Epstein, who took the stand in his own defense. The thirty-four-year-old Russian immigrant had but three years of schooling and worked in delicatessens and lunchrooms on the Lower East Side. He had joined Local 302 early in his career and become its business agent in 1930, when it was given jurisdiction over Manhattan. Epstein testified that three men walked into the union offices on 125th Street in the spring of 1933 and said, "You're Epstein. We came to take over the union." When Epstein asked what was going on, he said one of the men told him, "If you will stand in our way, imagine how you would look without ears. . . . We come from the Dutchman's mob; we'll be back."[40]

Epstein claimed that he unsuccessfully sought help from leaders of the American Federation of Labor in Buffalo and Washington but finally decided to tell the Schultz lieutenants he would neither stand in their way nor help them. They told him he should resign without giving a reason; later one of the racketeers told him it would be "unhealthy" for him to stay in New York. Epstein said he decided to stay after receiving first a telegram, then a letter in Yiddish from Max Pincus saying the union had reached an agreement to pay the hoodlums $2,500. His story was supported by a telegram, a letter, and the minute books of the local. The payoffs did not stem the reign of terror, however, and Epstein testified he had to leave town at least twice more after crossing the gangsters. On one occasion, he said, Martin had punched him, called him a vulgar name, and told him to resign, adding, "do it fast or you won't live that long."[41]

Epstein provided a version of Abe Borson's activities different from the prosecution's. In his early press releases, Dewey had portrayed Borson as a crooked union leader who helped organize the racket, then was gunned down after falling out with the gangsters. But Epstein said Borson was shot and killed in 1933 because he had tried to stop the racketeers' infiltration of the union. He averred that Borson had accompanied him and Pincus on a trip to Buffalo to get AFL help against the hoodlums. Epstein claimed that word of Borson's shooting kept him out of New York until Pincus told him Jules Martin was dead. Pincus could not corroborate Epstein's story; he had committed suicide on the eve of the trial. Another Local 302 officer, William Mesevich, did describe how several members of the executive board broke into tears at an April 1933 meeting when they realized Schultz would either take over their union or wreck it. He verified that he, Epstein, Borson, and Pincus had sought help from state union leaders, who advised them to take their complaints to the district attorney.[42]

As was true with all Dewey defendants, the press delighted in comparing their personal mannerisms with those of the so-called average New Yorker. For example, the *Times* noted that even though Epstein was a foreigner, his "speech was almost free of idiom." Dewey attacked Epstein's story on cross-examination, asking Epstein how, on his $4,200 annual salary, he had been able to make deposits in his savings account ranging from $38 to $900. At first, Epstein said he could not remember; then he said some of the deposits were repayments of loans to friends and the $900 was Pincus's gambling winnings, given to him for safekeeping. Dewey tried to discredit Epstein's testimony by showing that he had deposited more than $11,000 in thirteen months, but the defense showed that much of that money represented recirculated loans to friends. In the end, Dewey conceded there had been a net increase of only $1,735 in Epstein's finances—still a suspicious amount considering his salary.[43]

Dewey's cross-examination of Epstein reflected the prosecutor's eye for detail and his dogged trial tactics. Yet Epstein's four days on the stand also raised more serious questions about how far Dewey would stretch legal niceties to his advantage. A key element of the defense case rested on the argument that union leaders had been forced to cooperate against their will. To that end, they sought to use Abe Borson's shooting on Armistice Day 1933 to prove how far the gang would go to intimidate labor leaders. They had unsuccessfully subpoenaed the murder records from the police department but learned, in a court recess during Epstein's testimony, that Dewey had had the records all along. In what newspapers called a "flare up," Epstein's attorney, David Goldstein, accused Dewey of "tampering with and intercepting evidence." In typical fashion, Dewey became indignant at being accused of tampering and argued that it was the district attorney's job to "protect confidential records of the police department." The disputed records, he said, had been in court for the entire trial; he would have turned them over had any defense attorney asked for them. McCook reacted to the high-handed tactics without rebuking Dewey but said the prosecutor should tell him if similar situations arose in the future. The following day, however, McCook put a serious dent in the defense case by ruling that evidence of Borson's death should be excluded. Dewey had convinced the judge that the killing was unrelated to the labor trial because three other men already had been tried and convicted. No one raised the point that Dewey himself had tied Borson's murder to the rackets case in his October press releases.[44]

To bolster its contention that the union officials were victims rather than perpetrators, the defense argued that the restaurant owners and not the unions were to blame for racketeering in the industry. In his opening statement, Louis Waldman, Charles Baum's lawyer, said he hoped to show that when the unions became very successful at winning concessions for their members, restaurant owners became concerned and called in the racketeers to subdue unionizing efforts. Once Schultz gained a foothold, Waldman contended, he began to terrorize union officials and extort money from them. To prove this point, defense attorneys called a number of waiters to testify about their deplorable working conditions before joining the union. Marius Amato, a waiter at a Broadway restaurant and nightclub, said that after he joined Local 16 in February 1933 his pay doubled to six dollars a week and his typical workday went from fourteen to ten hours. In addition, after joining the union he had to buy a new uniform only once each year rather than four or five times a year—a considerable savings with outfits costing between forty and fifty dollars. Amato also described how the union had reined in his boss, whom he likened to Simon Legree; before the union a waiter who arrived five minutes late to work would be sent home without pay for the rest of the day. Amato said he was fired simply because the boss said "he did not like my face after I had been there eight years." The union arranged his reinstatement and also saw to it that he began receiving sick pay, death benefits, and doctors' services.[45]

McCook hampered defense efforts by curtailing testimony about how unionizing had improved working conditions. He limited testimony to waiters working in places mentioned by the prosecution and excluded those from restaurants named in the original indictment but later dropped. Waldman protested the decision saying it would seriously hamper his case.[46] Several days later, McCook cut off all testimony about improved conditions, ruling favorably on Dewey's motion, which argued that working conditions were irrelevant to the case. Relationships between employers and unions, the prosecutor said, were merely a backdrop to the only important question: Had union leaders conspired with the gangsters to use picket lines and threats to extort money from restaurant owners?[47]

Defense attorneys turned to bolstering their case with the testimony of their own clients, all of whom claimed they had been dragged into the scheme by threats and violence. Philip Grossel, portrayed by prosecutors as the mob member delegated to oversee the restaurant association, testified that he believed the organization was legitimate. He had been hired by a friend, Sam Furstenberg, and believed Jules Martin to be a legitimate businessman. Grossel said he first learned the truth in November 1934 when Furstenberg walked into the office, announced "I'm through," cleared out his desk, and left. Furstenberg, a disbarred lawyer, was still a fugitive when the trial took place. A few days after Furstenberg walked out, Grossel said, Martin telephoned and told him, "I want you to know that I'm running the place. You will pay me a certain amount of money or your members will suffer the consequences." When Grossel said he would resign, Martin threatened his family: "Your wife just gave birth to a baby, didn't she? You'd like to see that baby again? You just do as you're told, or your body will be found in the river and something will happen to the rest of your family." Grossel said there was elation at the association when they heard Martin had been killed, but the joy was short-lived; ten days later Krantz announced he was taking over.[48]

Retek, an Austrian World War I veteran, testified that Martin had forced him and Coulcher to cooperate in the takeover of Local 16. Under pressure, Retek said, he appointed three employees of Martin's gang to tally the votes in a union election; Coulcher was elected secretary, Retek business agent, and Baum president of the local. Coulcher then took the stand. Like Retek, he was foreign-born and poorly educated. He grew up in Russia and had been exiled to Siberia for taking part in the abortive revolution of 1905. When his father died, he quit school, coming to the United States in 1911 and becoming active in the labor movement the following year. In 1925 he organized Local 16 and was its chief figure until

Martin took over the union in 1933. Coulcher claimed he had no choice but to cooperate with Martin after the gangster said he was backed by Dutch Schultz and powerful politicians. Nonetheless, Coulcher initially tried other options; he reported the threat to the New York City police commissioner and the president of the international union. When they provided no help, he said, the local paid Martin $3,810 between March and August of 1933 for what they listed in their books as his "organizational experience."[49]

Dewey's cross-examination of Coulcher provided some of the most heated exchanges in the trial. Coulcher called Dewey's case against him nothing but "rotten vengeance" and at one point yelled, "You were looking to brutalize me, to crucify me! You were not interested in what is going on in the restaurant and cafeteria industry; you were looking to lynch me." Several times McCook warned Dewey about "speechifying" in response. When Coulcher said he had told Dewey assistant William Herlands he wanted to speak to Dewey personally, Dewey sneered, "And did Mr. Herlands tell you that I don't talk to gangsters?"[50]

Before testimony ended, one of the defendants, Charles Baum, was dismissed from the case because he was ill. The only other defendants who did not take the stand in their own defense were the two lawyers—Vogelstein and Cohen. Cohen believed he could help his cause by presenting his own closing arguments, but when he attempted to tell his side Dewey objected that his closing was more like testimony than argument. McCook agreed. Other defense attorneys made more conventional pleas to the jury. John Finnerty, the Washington attorney representing Retek, described Dewey "as a hard working and zealous prosecutor who did not know much about labor conditions." Had he known more, Finnerty argued, Dewey never would have charged union leaders who "had been as much the victims of extortion and gang violence as had the restaurant keepers." Other defense attorneys echoed that argument. The various defense attorneys spent eighteen hours arguing their cases to the jury. Only one vituperatively attacked Dewey. David Goldstein, who represented Epstein, said Dewey's unfair tactics had been proven by his handling of a witness. Learning that this witness had been subpoenaed by the defense, Goldstein said, Dewey sent for him. As a result of the prosecutor's interference the witness changed his testimony on the stand.

Goldstein told the jury, "If I had done that, I would not have been permitted to finish this case. I would have been indicted and tried for obstructing justice. If that's what the people have to resort to, then I say amend the indictment and put me in it. My God, are those the means they must resort to, to send these men to jail?"[51]

In his three-hour closing statement, Herlands ridiculed the defense arguments. He lambasted the two attorneys on trial, saying crooked lawyers who sold their knowledge to racketeers were worse than the dumb gangsters who hired them. Herlands also said it was ridiculous to believe that restaurant owners hired gangsters and were willing to go out of business just to get rid of unions. He described the racket as a cancer that would have continued growing had it not been for Dewey's investigation. He also advised jurors that they had an obligation going beyond the restaurant case. "This is the first time that a full industrial racket has been presented in a single case. If there is anything that is important to the community today, it is a warning that rackets can be prosecuted and broken. If we cannot get convictions in this case, there never again will be the opportunity to try a whole industrial racket at one time as we have tried to present here."[52]

The jurors took Herlands' argument to heart; they spent only three and a half hours rereading the 153-page indictment and poring over the testimony of the more than a hundred witnesses who appeared during the ten-week trial. They found all the defendants guilty on all twenty charges. McCook had made the jurors' job much easier when he told them to disregard much of the defense case. No evidence had been presented, he said, that justified the union leaders' cooperation with the gangsters; the jury should not, therefore, consider any of the testimony about duress. The judge also undercut defense arguments that the extortion profits went to the gangsters, not the union members. It did not matter who got the money, he said; what mattered was whether it was extorted in the first place.[53]

According to the *New York Times*, when foreman John Heaton, an oil salesman, read the jury's verdict he prompted "one of the most dramatic scenes in the Supreme Court in recent years." The newspaper duly noted each defendant's reaction. Cohen leaned on his arms at the table with his "eyes showing fright." Coulcher "winced as if his face had been slapped." Retek's "head began bobbing like the head of a toy on the end of a spring [as] a small smile spread over his features." Williams "licked his lips and the lines on his seamed face deepened." Epstein "gulped hard. It seemed he had been hoping up to the last moment." Williams muttered and when the sheriff grabbed him he swore and screamed as he was led from the courtroom. Dewey, on the other hand, was over-joyed; he told reporters that "this would eventually become one of the most important trials in the history of criminal prosecution in the coun-try." The newspaper noted: "Thus ended a ten-week trial that will form a basis for larger and more spectacular prosecutions by Mr. Dewey in the future."[54]

The restaurant racket convictions were heralded in many quarters. The *Times* account was typical: it labeled the case a "spectacular" victory and praised the thirty-five-year-old Dewey as the boy wonder from Owosso, Michigan, who had "distinguished himself in Manhattan by applying the mass-production methods of his native state's automobile industry to the mass destruction of rackets." The newspaper adopted Dewey's claim that the restaurant case represented the first time an entire industrial racket had been crushed and predicted he would score similar victories in pending cases in the garment, poultry, bakery, and bricklay-ing industries.[55]

McCook signaled his own belief in the case's extraordinary impor-tance by meting out harsh sentences. On April 8, 1937, he said: "In rela-tively recent years, and especially within the past decade the industrial racket has emerged as a grave menace to the larger communities throughout this country." The judge criticized the defendants and their attorneys for wrapping themselves "in the mantle of labor" and accusing Dewey of trying to "injure the cause of unionism." The claim of victim-ization was "shallow," he said, because the evidence clearly indicated that the defendants had subjected hundreds of businessmen "to a verita-ble reign of terror" while betraying their own membership. He described the defendants as cowards; if they had been manly enough they would have pled guilty and saved the state the cost and time of trying them. His sentences were stiff, considering that most of the defendants were first-time offenders. Calling Coulcher the most "treacherous of all," McCook sentenced him to fifteen to twenty years. Cohen, Epstein, and Grossel each received ten to fifteen years; Retek and Williams got seven and a half to fifteen years; and Vogelstein got five to ten.[56]

Dewey scored many victories against labor racketeering, but both he and McCook always counted the restaurant case among their greatest legal achievements. In a speech six months later, Dewey said his eighteen months of "intensive and grueling investigation" had succeeded where other agencies of law had failed. Since his victory, he claimed, members of the victimized unions had held honest elections for the first time in four years. They "have adopted and re-established new and model constitutions of labor democracy. They have elected their own officials, in many cases the men who led the long and hopeless fight. The disrepute which once attached to their picket lines has vanished; the workers have become real trade unionists and not mere paper members without rights. Contracts have become a living reality and decent working conditions have been actually procured." Dewey said union membership had grown from sixty-nine hundred to twenty-one thousand in the six months since the trial. Through honest bargaining, the unions had procured wage increases of $2.3 million.[57]

While Dewey claimed his efforts had put a permanent dent in New York labor racketeering, McCook and others were more realistic. In a speech to the U.S. Conference of Mayors in November 1937, McCook outlined his role in the Dewey investigation and said that, of all Dewey's cases, the restaurant probe had been the most complex and difficult because of reluctant witnesses. All cities with populations of more than a hundred thousand had racketeering; this, he conceded, was nothing new. What had changed was the larger scale of the crimes and "the perfection of organization, the number of people involved, the skill and power of leaders, terror displayed by victims and the incredible sums of money at stake." These developments made the current fight against racketeering imperative. The judge attributed much of Dewey's success against organized crime to grand juries and their power to hold witnesses who refused to testify in contempt of court. Some of his friends, McCook said, had made light of the special probe, dismissing racketeering as a recurring fact of urban life. McCook conceded that organized crime could not be eradicated; but, he asked, "Do you fail to cut your hair because it grows out again?" He declared himself optimistic about the determination of the American people who, once aroused, would vigorously defend themselves against organized crime.[58]

Taking the long view, McCook was more prescient than Dewey. Labor racketeering did not disappear in the 1930s despite Dewey's best efforts. An accurate description of the problem was offered by Herbert Brownell, a Dewey associate who became U.S. attorney general in the Eisenhower administration. Brownell's prosecution of Jimmy Hoffa in the 1950s led him to ponder union corruption, and he concluded: "It's a never-ending problem. There will always be employers that will try to bribe labor union leaders, and labor union leaders that will try to get sweetheart contracts. It's human nature, I guess, to expect that sort of thing." What had changed, according to Brownell, was that the fight against racketeering had become a routine aspect of law enforcement. Even so, he said, labor racketeering went in cycles: "if you have a strong prosecution program, it slows down for a while—a weak prosecution program, it speeds up again."[59]

By drawing attention to labor racketeering, Dewey drove it further underground so that it become less blatant in New York City during the late 1930s. Yet another factor in union activities was the New Deal legislation that brought greater stability and peace to labor negotiations. Passage in 1933 of the National Industrial Recovery Act, which established the National Recovery Administration, signaled a growing acceptance of labor's right to negotiate. In industries where labor was recognized, peace increasingly replaced violence. One indication of this was the acceptance of industry-wide collective bargaining agreements like the one adopted by New York City garment workers. As Dewey assistant Murray Gurfein said, "These agreements united labor and management in a process which raised wages and by the same method, prices. If basically all labor costs were equal, disastrous price competition . . . was virtually eliminated. Thus, after the lean years of the late twenties and early thirties, industry as a whole prospered." The result of this relative peace was that labor racketeering shifted to the periphery. Whereas Lepke and Gurrah had been able to infiltrate whole industries, as time wore on their successors were reduced to dealing principally with smaller businesses that fought unionization.[60]

The ramifications of this change for law enforcement were apparent to contemporaries. Benjamin Stolberg, a prominent labor journalist of the era, noted that Dewey and his Brooklyn counterpart, William O'Dwyer, could not have made inroads against industrial racketeers until the late 1930s when "industrial developments had sufficiently undermined the position of the gangster in the economic setup. For, fantastic as it may sound, the gangster of the twenties and early thirties was able to enter and then to entrench himself in certain industries because he offered a stabilizing force in the chaos which resulted from the murderous competition among the manufacturers and the impotence of the labor unions. The NRA [and the NLRA], which forced some degree of organization upon both management and labor, cut the ground from under the feet of the industrial gangster."[61]

The restaurant racket case may not have been as seminal in legal annals as Dewey claimed, but it did provide him with the credentials he needed to become an important political candidate in New York. A few union leaders and Tammany Hall politicians always saw Dewey as a foe of labor, but his handling of the labor case deflected some of the criticism. Throughout the investigation and trial, he characterized the case as not only a blow against racketeers but also a victory for legitimate labor organizing. Pointing out that labor faced two foes—greedy businessmen and racketeers—he publicly disdained them both. Thus, Dewey was able to establish his credentials as a friend of unions, a political necessity, given their growing power in the 1930s. At the same time, Dewey's prosecution appealed to Republicans and conservatives who still believed racketeering was behind most labor unrest. In a very real sense, the restaurant case provided the springboard from which Dewey successfully launched his first successful political campaign in mid-1937.

≈ ≈ ≈

CHAPTER NINE

Reform Politics

$\mathcal{A}$LTHOUGH DEWEY had scored spectacular courtroom victories and La Guardia had brought a semblance of order to city government, reformers in the 1930s were still dissatisfied. Whereas earlier do-gooders had assumed Tammany and its corruption would eventually return, La Guardia and other Fusionists believed they could permanently improve the city's politics. Fusion reform movements were as much a part of the city's political fabric as the Republican party and the corruption of Tammany. The wisest 1930s Fusionists realized that their nonpartisan organization would eventually collapse, just as earlier coalitions had done. Therefore, they centered their efforts on institutional changes that would outlast their temporary affiliation. Although their basic politics may have differed, Fusion reformers shared a vision of efficient city management and incorruptible law enforcement. They believed their efforts could spell the death of the Tammany Tiger and pave the way for long-lasting good government. To that end, reformers passed a new city charter to replace the outdated one, which had been drafted in 1897, when the five boroughs were merged into New York City. In 1937 they overcame political and personality clashes to keep La Guardia as mayor and elect Dewey as district attorney and bolstered both men's positions by promoting changes in the state constitution. The reformers' actions mortally wounded Tammany. With the Democratic machine in its death throes, the one issue uniting the coalition disappeared. That fact, combined with Dewey's insatiable political appetite, drove a wedge between Fusion forces. Dewey's first successful run for political office came in 1937, when he was elected as district attorney. The following year he unsuccessfully opposed Lehman in the gubernatorial race. Within three more years he was running for the presidential nomination. Promoting or thwarting Dewey's political ambitions replaced fighting Tammany as the lightning rod of New York politics.

To expand public support of Dewey's efforts, the special prosecutor and La Guardia supported creation of a citizens' crime commission. The idea of involving citizens in law enforcement machinery was not new. Decades earlier, New Yorkers led by Charles Parkhurst had investigated vice. In the mid-1920s, both Franklin Roosevelt and Al Smith joined the National Crime Commission, which publicized problems with crime and the legal system. Al Smith appointed a New York State Crime Commission in 1927. In Chicago citizens created the first city commission in 1919. Other cities followed suit, including Baltimore, Cleveland, and Philadelphia. The Manhattan grand jurors' association had been pushing for a similar organization in New York City since the early 1930s. A 1931 article in *The Panel* said, "experience in all countries has proved that betterments in government or judicial institutions . . . are merely temporary unless groups of private citizens see to it that the ground is held." The article argued that if New York had created a crime commission, the wrongdoing that led to the Seabury investigation would not have occurred. Initially, the jurors' association found little support for its ideas. Tammany clearly opposed establishing a commission that would be manned by its critics. Many lawyers and judges, including Seabury, were willing to use public outrage to their advantage but did not want to share control with lay people. Others, who saw the National Crime Commission and the 1927 New York State Crime Commission as ineffective, had little faith in citizens' groups.[1]

By late 1936, the Association of Grand Jurors of New York County found a more receptive audience for its idea. The previous year, Lehman had made public concern a cornerstone of his crime conference; and Dewey continually stressed the need for citizens, especially victimized businessmen, to cooperate with his investigation. His desires dovetailed with those of the grand jury association's June 30, 1936, report, which was issued by the second special grand jury. Expressing shock at many businessmen's refusals to testify, the grand jurors predicted that cooperation would be more forthcoming if the city's most prominent citizens served as role models. They argued that a committee composed of "persons of high standing [could] crystallize civic moral support in the world of law enforcement."[2]

La Guardia, who was always looking for ways to appear tough on crime, enthusiastically endorsed the proposal. Earlier in the summer, he had drawn criticism by authorizing police to conduct sweeping raids of whorehouses by using wiretaps. Among the brothels targeted was one run by the city's high-class madam Polly Adler. Publication of her clients' names prompted one newspaper to complain that the mayor's crusade had made Adler's activities seem as venal as those of the Lindbergh kidnapper. The *New York Daily News* argued that La Guardia's puritanical streak ran against "the customs, ideals and prejudices of the voters." By contrast, supporting a citizens' crime commission was far less controversial. So La Guardia backed Dewey's proposal to create a group headed by Harry F. Guggenheim, a member of one of New York's wealthiest families, the former ambassador to Cuba, and the future publisher of *Newsday*. Guggenheim proved an ideal head for the commission because he offered to raise $200,000 in start-up funds from private sources. During the second week of August, Dewey and La Guardia hammered out details and issued press releases announcing formation of the group. Its vice presidents included George Medalie and Lee Thompson Smith, president of the grand jury association. Other officers were Artemus L. Gates, president of the New York Trust Company; Raymond Moley, a Columbia Law professor, a former Roosevelt "Brain Truster," and the author of two books about crime; C. C. Burlingham, a lawyer and architect of the Fusion movement; and many prominent bankers and businessmen.[3] The committee set up offices on Broadway and hired the former journalist William P. Beazell as its executive secretary.

In publicity statements, Guggenheim said creation of the committee proved New York was "emerging from that apathetic state of mind in which we were engulfed by World War weariness." He told one interviewer, "We are neither a group of vigilantes nor of reformers; nor are we a group dealing in theories and abstractions. We shall not be a political scalp-hunting body." Instead, he said, the group would function as the "eyes of the city" by coordinating efforts between area law enforcement agencies. Guggenheim's vision for the crime commission closely mirrored Dewey's hopes in sponsoring it. Dewey said profits from gambling and vice lined gangsters' pockets and in the process created a law enforcement crisis. The problem was exacerbated by the scattered efforts of the five local district attorneys' offices, the racket bureau of the attorney general in New York County, two U.S. attorneys' offices, and various police agencies. Together they employed more than eighteen thousand people and spent more than $3.5 million annually. Even though there were clearly enough law enforcement agencies to do the job, Dewey said, the lack of cooperation among them created "a labyrinth of procedure and overlapping and conflicting jurisdictions which would almost seem to have been specially designed for the comfort of criminals." He believed the solution was a new, permanent outside organization. Whereas police commissioners and U.S. and district attorneys changed with each election, a citizens' committee would function on a continuing basis. He maintained that "No racket can develop and exist if its every act is recorded, studied and ultimately exposed as part of a complete picture. . . . A day to day record of the thousands of cases which are constantly going in and out of the courts, the police stations and the prosecutors' offices, kept in one place and studied by experts will provide the first intelligent effort to handle this problem this City has ever made. In my judgment it could prove to be the solution of the problem of organized crime."[4]

Despite some early successes, however, the committee never fulfilled La Guardia's and Dewey's heady expectations. It accomplished the most during its early years when public concern with crime peaked. In December 1937, the commission issued its first report, outlining how it had helped witnesses' families and generated nine thousand file cards to track cases from indictment to discharge. Its best-publicized finding was that the number of sex crimes in the city, excluding rape and prostitution, had increased from 1,251 in 1936 to 1,891 in 1937, a fact for which it offered no explanation except to say that New York, like the rest of the nation, was undergoing a "wave of sex offenses." It argued that the city needed a new method of dealing with such crimes, because only one in five perpetrators was punished. In July 1938, the commission published its second report, "Twelve Months of Crime in New York City," which contained crime statistics. In the following years, enthusiasm for the project waned, and by 1940 the commission was struggling for public donations.

Guggenheim wrote La Guardia that the committee needed $150,000 to continue its efforts. The mayor praised the group and said its dissolution "would deprive us of the knowledge that is the real basis of power to deal intelligently and effectively with crime." But aside from sending a check for $25 and his hopes that the committee would get the needed money, the mayor did nothing. The following January, with the citizens' group facing extinction, both Dewey and La Guardia offered their support: Dewey provided a statement urging businessmen to fund the project, and La Guardia mailed solicitation letters.[5]

Many people undoubtedly supported the group in hopes it would fight crime in the city but lost interest in it as they realized it offered no panaceas. By the 1940s, World War II was dominating public concern and eclipsing crime. Guggenheim's group had another flaw; it was increasingly perceived as a vehicle for Dewey's political aspirations rather than a genuine civic organization. Spruille Braden, who headed a New York anticrime commission in the 1950s, learned from the city's experience with the Guggenheim Committee that his own efforts would have to be strictly apolitical. Braden said Guggenheim had admitted his group "was formed with the exclusive purpose of booming the political fortunes of Dewey." His review of the earlier committee's records convinced Braden it had "just dilly-dallied around and made motions and put out announcements and got nowhere."[6]

Nevertheless, the 1936 launching of the Citizens' Crime Committee seemed a sign reformers were gaining the upper hand against the forces of evil in New York City. Combined with La Guardia's successes at trimming the budget, that perception provided a heady year for Fusionists. Their optimism was channeled into a more difficult goal that had long eluded reformers—creation of a new city charter. New York City's constitution, hastily drawn in 1897 when the five boroughs were merged into one city, was an unwieldy 600-page document of 1,620 sections.[7] It never received unanimous support, and dissatisfaction with it grew along with the city's size and complexity. The original charter gave executive control of city government to the mayor and legislative power to the city council, known as the Board of Aldermen. In the 1890s, reformers and Republicans pushed for the charter and consolidation for different reasons. Reformers believed it would create nonpartisan, good government, while state Republican boss Thomas Platt hoped to bolster his party's power at Tammany's expense. No charter could have accomplished both of these contradictory tasks, and the result was a flawed document that paved the way for Tammany hegemony.

Unhappy with what they had wrought, reformers and Republicans pushed for, and achieved, a new charter as early as 1901. They hoped to curtail Democratic control by cutting back on the broad mayoral powers granted by the original charter. They accomplished these goals by creating the Board of Estimate, which had both executive and legislative powers and passed on most key bills affecting the city's management. The composition of the new board—the mayor, the president of the Board of Aldermen, the city comptroller, and the five borough presidents—was intended to dilute the mayor's power while giving borough officials and political leaders a stronger voice. The result was what Wallace S. Sayre and Herbert Kaufman call "a system of 'open' politics, the absence of a single dominant ruling elite, a pattern of competition and bargaining from which no group is for long alienated or excluded."[8]

Although the system ensured that many groups could be heard, it did not guarantee them power. The result was continuous instability. Democrats did not have complete control, but the existence of their powerful borough machines made it difficult for other groups to gain a foothold. This factor, in addition to the lackluster nature of reform candidates, explains why previous Fusion efforts had been short-lived. Another source of discontent with the 1901 charter was the fact that it had been drafted in Albany. Because the city's charter was technically state law, changes had to be approved in the state capital. In 1923 this problem was addressed by passage of the Home Rule Act, an amendment to the state constitution giving New York City voters power to approve their own charter. A committee led by the prominent lawyer Henry De-Forest Baldwin drafted the legislation, which he predicted would leave the city's governmental structure intact while streamlining its management.[9]

Because the 1923 legislation did not address the basic flaws in municipal government the charter continued to come under attack. As one writer noted, the document "was a hodgepodge of some sixteen hundred sections and just as many amendments. Some of its provisions contradicted others. It was so out of date that it included a law stating that 'horses, cows, calves, swine and pigs, sheep and goats may not be kept in lodging houses.' " La Guardia called it "a horse-car charter in an airplane age." Critics were outraged by the charter's more serious faults, including the undemocratic means by which members of the Board of Aldermen were elected. Moreover, because the charter had not kept pace with the city's population growth, there was no standardization of voting districts. In one Manhattan district it took 6,000 votes to elect an alderman; in another, it took 30,000. An alderman in one Queens district represented 232,000 voters, while a member from Manhattan had only 69,000 constituents. The result of this electoral pattern was that Democrats normally controlled between 85 and 95 percent of the aldermen's seats.[10]

Charter reform became an even more controversial topic in the wake of the Seabury investigation. Seabury himself had urged replacement of the city's electoral system with proportional representation to ensure participation by minority parties. In 1932 even former Governor Al Smith spoke at the state legislature in favor of a plan to pattern city government after the federal system—with two legislative houses, an elected mayor, and elimination of many county and borough offices. The result, he argued, would streamline the city's management while cutting costs. Tammany successfully fought off the attack. Mayor John P. O'Brien responded to critics by appointing a charter commission but told members their purpose was to write a report recommending against changes. When that report was issued in January 1933, it provided more fodder for La Guardia's mayoral campaign.[11]

In promising a new charter, La Guardia argued that Tammany efforts to prevent change were blatant attempts to maintain a lock on city politics. He appealed to Depression era concerns about money by claiming that charter reform would eliminate hundreds of needless patronage jobs that cost the city $2.3 million a year. Under pressure from La Guardia and Lehman, the legislature created a charter commission, with Al Smith as chairman and Seabury as vice chairman. Soon after its first meeting in 1935, both men resigned. Seabury objected to the fact that the majority of commission members were Tammany hacks, and Smith agreed: "The people I couldn't get along with were the stowaways who were put on board with monkey wrenches to throw into the machinery and scuttle the ship." La Guardia argued that even if the commission had good intentions, it lacked credibility and "the only thing to do is to begin again." The mayor, Smith, Seabury, and Lehman renewed their pressure, and the legislature appointed a smaller, nine-member committee. When both Smith and Seabury declined to serve, New York Bar Association President Thomas Thacher, a Dewey mentor, was appointed chairman.[12]

The small group worked well together. In addition to Thacher, who did a good job of easing potential differences, the committee included city comptroller Joseph McGoldrick, Judge Joseph Proskauer, and law professors Charles Evans Hughes, Jr., and Genevieve Earle, a civic leader who later served on the City Council. During their twice-weekly meetings at the bar association, the group hammered out a compromise package, proposing needed changes but not going as far as some reformers would have liked. For example, the charter retained the city's division into five boroughs, each with some degree of autonomy. Yet it curbed borough power by centralizing maintenance, highway, and planning jobs. The committee discussed creating a city manager but rejected the idea in deference to New York's long history of strong mayors. To ease the burden on La Guardia, however, the committee created the position of deputy mayor.[13]

From the outset the commission members shared two goals. First, they wanted to strengthen La Guardia's ability to abolish Tammany patronage jobs. The means to do this was their second goal: replacement of the Board of Aldermen with a smaller, more efficient city council. When La Guardia took office, New York City's personnel picture was a confusing patchwork. As the city's mayor, he controlled employees in centralized departments but lacked jurisdiction over another 834 workers employed by the boroughs. La Guardia argued that he needed control over all city employees. According to attorney Reuben Lazarus, many of those holding jobs in county sheriff offices could barely read but were paid "fat salaries for doing little or no work [while they] relaxed in the rays of political sunshine. There, untroubled by Civil Service requirements or any qualifications other than a letter from a district leader, the boys luxuriated." Lazarus drafted an amendment to the state constitution that would eliminate "that beautiful Shangrila of politics," and in 1935 voters approved the measure, giving city officials the right to abolish most county offices except judicial and prosecutorial jobs. Ultimately, however, power to eliminate jobs depended on the willingness of the Board of Aldermen to approve such decisions. Because Tammany still controlled sixty-two of the sixty-five votes on the board, La Guardia's efforts were unsuccessful.[14]

Undermining the board's power thus became a primary goal of the charter commission. The aldermen had few supporters outside of Tammany. During the nineteenth century the board's peopling by political hacks had earned it the nicknames "Boodle Board" and "Forty Thieves." Critics in the 1930s saw no reason to change their opinion. Under normal circumstances the board acted as a haven for incompetents and a rubber stamp for decisions made by the mayor and the more powerful Board of Estimate. The Board of Aldermen rose to prominence only when its Democratic members could fight an opposition party mayor. Before the mid-1930s, the board usually had a Democratic membership of more than 85 percent. The charter commission abolished the board and replaced it with a twenty-five-member city council but was divided about how to elect council members. Reformers urged adoption of proportional representation to ensure inclusion of minority parties. The commission, unable to reach a consensus, left the matter up to voters in a separate bill that appeared on the same ballot as the proposed charter revision.[15]

The commission finished its proposal in the spring of 1936, then lobbied hard for it in thirteen public and thirty-seven private hearings. Ultimately, the new charter won praise from all New York's major civic groups and most reform-minded politicians. Even such skeptics as La Guardia and Seabury, who believed it did not go far enough in eliminating machine politics, backed it. Nevertheless, the reform sparked bitter opposition. Some city workers were legitimately concerned that centralization would mean lost jobs. The bitterest opposition came from Tammany, which recognized it would lose power under the charter. Using so-called taxpayer groups as fronts, Tammany instigated a series of lawsuits claiming that the new charter was unconstitutional. Reformers were not surprised at Tammany's complaints. As the *New York Times* editorialized, "A charter which failed to meet with the determined opposition of Tammany Hall would hardly be worth drafting."[16]

Critics faulted the timing of the charter vote because it coincided with the presidential campaign of 1936. Admitting that voters might feel inundated by two major campaigns, Earle said the charter commissioners decided to go ahead with the vote because they "wanted to have it presented at a time when there would be the greatest number of people voting." They also wanted to avoid waiting until the following year's election, when it would become enmeshed in the mayoral campaign. Nevertheless, politics did play a role in passing the charter. A combination of Tammany stupidity and La Guardia's astuteness balanced the scales for charter reform. Rather than offering its own plan or acknowledging that some changes were needed, Tammany's lackluster leaders dug in, waging a bitter campaign in which they looked like grasping dinosaurs. Such tactics had prevailed against earlier charter reformers, but La Guardia was a cannier opponent. Reuben Lazarus said the "many meetings held by 'do-gooders' to promote the charter . . . merely muddied the issue." He attributed the large favorable turnout to La Guardia's decision to put a bill promoting changed working conditions for city firefighters on the same ballot. As Lazarus said, "every fireman and his friends and all their friends worked diligently; and all those dragged to the polls, having been told, 'Don't make any changes. Vote yes on every proposition, so that you do not make a mistake about the three-platoon system.' "[17]

For whatever reason, the charter was approved by 927,336 to 583,044 votes, with only Richmond County voting against it. The proportional voting measure ensuring minority parties seats on the new city council was passed by an even larger margin. The effect was immediate; in the first election after the charter was adopted, Democrats captured only thirteen of the twenty-six council seats. The new charter also established a commission to reorganize the previously haphazard city laws into a new legal code. The adoptions of the charter and code were among the greatest achievements of La Guardia's first term as mayor. Together they ensured the reduction of Tammany Hall's control over New York City politics. It was only fitting that La Guardia would be the first to reap their benefits. The new charter went into effect on January 1, 1938, the day he began his second term as mayor.[18]

La Guardia's ability to implement the charter depended on his election to a second term in 1937. He won in 1933 only because two Democratic candidates had split the ticket. History also worked against him; New Yorkers never had elected a Fusion mayor to a second term. As political observer Paul Windels sagely noted, Fusion movements tended to be short-lived because interest in good government was cyclical. "When we get good government, that interest fades. Then we get bad government, we get a bit hysterical about it and everybody gets mad, and then they want to do something. It's just as sporadic as that."[19] La Guardia provided good government during his first term, and most Fusionists realized they needed to give him another four years to root out gangsters and Tammany corruption. Given his often abrasive personality and the lack of a permanent party structure, his reelection in 1937 necessitated rebuilding the Fusion coalition.

These efforts were undoubtedly made easier by continued divisions in the city's Democratic and Republican parties. The Democrats were weaker and more divided than they had been in 1933. Tammany—technically the Democratic machine of New York County alone—historically had been synonymous with the citywide Democratic party because of Manhattan's domination of the other boroughs. That situation was changing in the 1930s. As the number of Democrats in the Bronx, Brooklyn, and Queens grew, they developed strong factions with their own interests and leaders. At least three of these leaders—Edward Flynn of the Bronx, Frank Kelly of Brooklyn, and James Farley—wisely sided with Roosevelt rather than Tammany. From Washington, Roosevelt proved to be a formidable foe. Although he never publicly broke with Tammany, he worked with Flynn and Farley behind the scenes to break the Hall. He never forgave Tammany for opposing his nomination in 1932 and recognized La Guardia as a useful tool for revenge. By channeling federal money for the Works Progress Administration through the mayor's office rather than through Tammany, Roosevelt undercut the party's traditional source of strength—the ability to offer jobs and distribute favors.[20]

In what would prove an even more devastating move, FDR privately backed creation of the American Labor party. In addition to weakening Tammany, this support dealt a powerful blow to the Socialist party. In 1936, Socialists split into two ineffectual camps; those on the left stayed with Norman Thomas and kept the old name, while more conservative members created the Social Democratic Federation. Still others, such as David Dubinsky, president of the International Ladies Garment Workers Union, left the party completely. Once a devout Socialist, Dubinsky became a leading supporter of Roosevelt and the New Deal. He decided that union members, who disliked both Tammany and the antiunion Republicans, needed an independent party. Dubinsky's goals meshed with those of the president, who backed the third party despite objections from Flynn and Farley. He argued that hundreds of thousands of New Yorkers supported New Deal legislation but were unwilling to join the Democratic party. The challenge, FDR said, would be "molding them into a party." Flynn, Farley, and Dubinsky enlisted the aid of labor leaders like Sidney Hillman, Fusion architects like Adolph A. Berle, and intellectuals like Dorothy Thompson.[21]

Roosevelt's machinations deeply divided Tammany. Members who believed fighting with Lehman and Roosevelt had undercut their power and led to La Guardia's election voted to oust leader John Curry in 1934. The fact that Curry was unseated by a majority of only one vote indicates the rift within Tammany. Even a capable leader would have had trouble mending the divisions, but Curry's successor, James Dooling, was particularly unfit for the task. One Tammany stalwart described Dooling as "a nice boy with practically no ability." Among his other failings, Dooling blocked a plan to reapportion voting districts in the state; his action denied Democrats a majority in the Senate and a probable majority in the Assembly. The situation was further complicated by the fact that Dooling became ill in 1936 and retreated to Miami, Florida, to recuperate. Dooling appointed a triumvirate to control Tammany in his absence, which created further strife. In January 1937 the party called a meeting to replace Dooling in preparation for the mayoral election. The *New York Times* correctly predicted that none of the aspirants would get the post because the party was too fractured to line up behind one candidate. Pressure continued mounting throughout February. Dooling remained in Florida, while Fusion forces and the American Labor party began organizing efforts for La Guardia. Finally, in March, the Hall chose Christopher D. Sullivan, a former member of Dooling's triumvirate, as acting leader despite the objections of Tammany's most powerful boss, Jimmy

Hines. Without Hines's backing, Sullivan was in a weakened position. His goal to control New York City was also blocked by Flynn, who was by then the Democratic national committeeman from New York.[22]

While Tammany members were arguing about a new leader, they chose their candidates. Their first choice for mayor was the aging U.S. senator, Royal S. Copeland, who publicly declined the nomination. Political pundits interpreted Copeland's refusal as a sign that Flynn and Farley would not support his candidacy. Tammany finally chose New York Supreme Court Justice Jeremiah T. Mahoney for the mayor's job and Harold Hastings, an eighteen-year veteran of the district attorney's office, to replace Dodge as New York County district attorney.[23] Ironically, the Democratic split provided disgruntled Republicans with a mayoral candidate. Aggravated by support for La Guardia and Roosevelt within their own ranks, conservative Republicans chose Democratic Senator Copeland as their candidate. The party's old guard had never trusted La Guardia but it supported him in 1933 as the lesser of two evils. During his four-year term, La Guardia continued to alienate large numbers of Republicans with his costly social welfare policies. Even moderate Republicans were angered by his open support of Roosevelt over Alf Landon in the 1936 presidential election. The result was a deepening split within the city's Republican party. In 1935, Kenneth Simpson replaced Chase Mellon as New York County chairman; city party leader Samuel Koenig had wanted Mellon out because of his alliance with reformers. Simpson too was allied with the party's new guard, but Koenig supported him as a compromise candidate. Eager to demonstrate his independence and strengthen the party, Simpson balked at letting either the Fusion Committee or Seabury dictate the party's candidates for the 1937 election. The problem was aggravated by the fact that La Guardia and Simpson were both temperamental and disliked each other. As Walter Mack remembered, "Get them in a room together, and they both start bubbling over and not listening to each other, and end up pounding the desk. Nobody would get anywhere. They both needed handling."[24]

Facing Democratic opposition and uncertain Republican support, La Guardia relied heavily on his Fusion backers to create order out of chaos. A masterful political manipulator with a strong personality, La Guardia played factions against one another. While railing against politicians, he made deals with all of them. At the same time, the mayor's flamboyant personality and political balancing act were also his greatest liabilities. When it came time to choose a ticket for 1937, some Fusionists, offended that La Guardia had violated the nonpartisan spirit of Fusion by endorsing Roosevelt the previous fall, wanted him replaced. Others said that even though he had brought needed reforms to the city, his tactics were dictatorial. They called him "a little sawed-off Napoleon," "the Miniature II Duce," or "the sawed-off Mussolini." Still others argued that Fusion had devolved into a personality cult of La Guardia rather than a fight against Tammany and a drive for good government.[25]

Nonetheless, most Fusion leaders still saw La Guardia as the logical and strongest candidate for mayor. Fusion had never been more than a loose coalition of reform groups; its only structure came when members rallied around a specific candidate or issue. The last such occasion had been the charter drive; thus, it was fitting to announce plans to reelect La Guardia at the testimonial dinner for the charter commission in January 1937. The mayor explained that while he would accept backing from the Republican and American Labor parties, he would continue Fusion's nonpartisan philosophy of municipal government. In keeping with that declaration, the New York Times speculated that the architects of La Guardia's candidacy in 1933—Charles Burlingham and Samuel Seabury—would remain his chief advisors. Knowledgeable observers never questioned whether La Guardia would be the Fusion candidate. It was acknowledged in the press that even Roosevelt supported La Guardia, although he could not alienate Tammany or Flynn by endorsing him openly. In February, Fusionists vowed to fight Tammany to the finish and opened campaign headquarters throughout the city.[26]

Even with the support of independent Democrats and the American Labor party, Fusion leaders realized they still needed Republican support. Simpson and other Republican leaders also recognized they would have to cooperate with Fusion in order to win; if they did not, they would be accused of cooperating with Tammany. On the other hand, going with La Guardia would split the party and rankle many members. Just how deeply the resentment against La Guardia ran was demonstrated by a brawl that broke out in an Upper West Side Republican clubhouse. After more than an hour of squabbling and by a thirty-to-ten vote, the Republican Club of the Ninth Assembly District voted to endorse the mayor. When losers accused Republican leader Arnold Ross of using steamroller tactics to win, a lawyer accused the sergeant at arms of being a bum. In the ensuing ruckus, the sergeant at arms responded by punching both his accuser and Ross. The fight was broken up by other members of the club but not in time to keep the thirty women in the room from becoming "agitated by the disorder." Increasingly, reaching a compromise became the goal of both sides, and more and more the compromise centered on running Dewey for district attorney of New York County. When Simpson mentioned Dewey's name in early March he said it did not make sense to nominate a Republican candidate who supported the New Deal and Governor Lehman; but he agreed to analyze the situation in New York City carefully before making a decision. Simpson said that as the major problem confronting the city was racketeering, running Dewey with La Guardia would make "a well-balanced ticket."[27]

The idea of running with Dewey rankled the mayor, who perceived him as a strong political rival; he also resented Simpson's maneuvering. Problems between Simpson and the mayor continued into July 1937, when La Guardia refused to run as a Republican. The mayor said he wanted to keep his independent label, in part because he resented Simpson's trying to pick his slate, which included Joseph McGoldrick for comptroller, Newbold Morris for president of City Council, and Dewey for district attorney. Because their prestige was at stake, both La Guardia and Simpson resisted compromise on Dewey's candidacy. But ultimately, it was Dewey's egotism that seriously threatened the Fusion coalition during the summer of 1937.

Trouble began when Berle, a Fusion leader who functioned as La Guardia's unofficial campaign manager, interviewed Dewey about the nomination. As Berle said, "Dewey's vanity, always disagreeable was working overtime." The special prosecutor laid down outlandish conditions for his candidacy, including public requests by Lehman and Roosevelt that he run; a guarantee of a $300,000 campaign fund; a three-day public clamor for his nomination; the right to campaign independently; and assurance that without him La Guardia would lose the election. His demands offended La Guardia, Berle, and many idealistic Fusionists, including Seabury, who said later that Dewey was already eyeing the presidency.[28]

Throughout late July and early August, Republicans and Fusionists searched for a compromise. On July 27, 1937, a group of Fusion backers met with Seabury. The group included such Dewey allies as Charles Evans Hughes, Jr., Charles Tuttle, George Medalie, and Maurice Davison, head of the citizens' group that first suggested Dewey's candidacy in February. After tedious negotiations, La Guardia accepted the slate including McGoldrick and Morris on July 30, agreeing that the Republican party could choose the district attorney candidate as long as the nominee was "responsible and acceptable." Still, squabbling continued as Fusionists resisted Dewey. The Fusion party backed Irving Ben Cooper, while the Nonpartisan Citizens' group and Seabury backed William C. Chanler, a former city solicitor. Simpson and the Republicans continued pushing for Dewey. On August 5, Thomas Thacher, president of the New York bar, met with Simpson and Seabury, but his peacemaking efforts failed. Ultimately, the Republicans prevailed. Seabury and the Fusionists realized they needed the Republicans to win; they were not willing to risk their movement to stop Dewey.[29]

Dewey officially accepted the nomination and agreed to run five minutes before the filing deadline on August 15. He had won several of his demands, although the Fusionists never asked La Guardia to say that Dewey's candidacy was essential to his own reelection. They correctly argued that such a statement would hinder the mayor's ability to run his office. La Guardia did agree not to criticize the Republican party publicly, and Dewey did receive three days of clamoring for his nomination, generous campaign funds, and the right to run an independent campaign. Although publicly the Fusionists and Dewey campaigned well together, behind the scenes bickering continued. As Stanley M. Isaacs, who ran on the Fusion ticket for Manhattan borough president, recalled, "I've never campaigned with a more selfish individual in my life than Tom Dewey. He insisted that in all his headquarters that there should be no pictures of any other candidate except himself—which is not very sound municipal campaigning." On his side, Dewey viewed La Guardia as an "explosive" egotist. As he later recalled, La Guardia "was unpredictable. He could be both the most gracious, kindly and attractive man you ever met in your life and the cruelest. He could be utterly irresponsible in his statements and indulge in demagoguery of the most unbelievable character, but at the same time he tried to get good people in public office, and he expected the highest standards of integrity and proper administration."[30]

Despite their differences, the two proved to be a formidable combination. Dewey's reputation as a racket buster had made him a public hero. His cool demeanor offset La Guardia's temperamentalism, while La Guardia's buoyant personality balanced Dewey's aloofness. As one Dewey assistant remembered, "La Guardia very shrewdly exploited Dewey as being on his team and together they lent each other strength. In other words, La Guardia's warmth, humanity and public spirit which appealed to everybody, was transferred to Dewey because he was running with La Guardia, and Dewey's integrity and merciless fight against crime was assimilated to La Guardia so that they were a great team together." The two were hailed in the New York press. The *New York Daily News*, for example, announced that, "With smash crime as the battle cry, the forces of Mayor La Guardia and Thomas E. Dewey launched a vigorous campaign in the Republican city primary yesterday." Publicly, at least, the two candidates complimented each other graciously. Dewey acknowledged that without help from La Guardia, his investigation could not have succeeded. La Guardia said, "No real rats were eliminated from New York County until Tom Dewey was appointed as a special prosecutor. . . . We have scientists and biologists who will attend to the rats, but I am interested in the political and the social rats, and that is why we want to elect Tom Dewey district attorney of New York County."[31]

The first order of business after announcement of Dewey's candidacy was fighting off Royal Copeland's candidacy for mayor. Had Copeland won the September 16 Republican primary, the resulting split would have paved the way for a Tammany victory. Fear of such a split became the overriding early-campaign theme, as typified by a handbill headed "Mark Your Ballot as Shown Here to Keep Tammany Out of City Hall and Racketeers Out of New York." The pamphlet advised Republican voters to concentrate on city rather than New Deal issues and cannily avoided discussing La Guardia directly. Instead, it focused on his running mates and advised that a vote against Copeland would "lead to the continuance of the present able, honest Fusion City Administration" and election of Dewey, Morris, and other Republicans to the City Council, Board of Estimate, Assembly, and upcoming constitutional convention. Those successes, the pamphlet said, would "be the first step in the permanent rehabilitation of the Republican Party in this city and will point the way to a permanent anti-Tammany organization here, with which more effectively to fight for Republican principles in years to come. It will also insure the efficient functioning of the new City Charter." By contrast, a vote for Copeland could "lead to dismemberment of the party as a constructive force for good local government [and] a surrender of the party to Tammany Hall."[32]

After La Guardia defeated Copeland, the Fusionists turned their attention to fighting Tammany. Perhaps the best indication of the Hall's continued anemic leadership was its lackluster and often contradictory campaign. Tammany's mayoral candidate, Jeremiah T. Mahoney, continually accused La Guardia of being a "Red" whose pro-labor sympathies were driving industry from the city. It was true that La Guardia had received an endorsement from the Communist party, although he tried to disown this dubious honor by announcing that Communists "will get no aid or succor from me." Yet Mahoney continued to attack La Guardia as if communism were the only issue in the campaign. As Dewey said years later, Mahoney "waged the worst campaign I ever saw. He didn't talk about anything but Communism." Mahoney's perceived rebuff of labor, one of the party's traditional bases of support, alienated some union leaders. For example, one called Mahoney's antilabor, antiprogressive rhetoric stupid and chastised U.S. Senator Robert Wagner for appearing at a Mahoney rally.[33]

The campaign Harold Hastings ran against Dewey was little better. Hastings, a lawyer with thirty years' experience, was even more nondescript than Mahoney. As Dewey said, "Harold was quite a respectable, pleasant fellow. There was nothing wrong with him. He just never did anything, and that's just exactly the kind of district attorney that Tammany Hall wants, a fellow who likes his job, his car, his salary and will be duly grateful to the organization for remembering him so well." Hastings tried to offset Dewey's reputation as a hard-hitting crime buster by portraying himself as a kind man who stressed the gentle side of the law. In one speech, he discussed the importance of helping teens avoid crime by providing them with playgrounds.[34]

Other Tammany stalwarts portrayed Dewey as a dangerous demagogue who exaggerated his own accomplishments and twisted the legal system to serve his ruthless ambition. Samuel Untermyer, who had represented District Attorney Crain in the Seabury investigation, said Dewey's claim that crime had gone unpunished for twenty years was ridiculous. Untermyer, a special prosecutor in 1923, said his investigation yielded $700,000 in fines, 666 indictments, and 416 convictions, even though he had worked frugally by using volunteers from the bar association. By contrast, Untermyer said, Dewey's probe spent more than $1 million to convict 71 defendants. Untermyer's own successes, he argued, showed it "does not require any such sensational plays for the gallery or judicial strong arm methods, or the flagrant, reckless violations of constitutional rights as I charge against Mr. Dewey, in order to break up racketeering." Untermeyer asserted that Dewey's unfairness was shown by his routine requests for excessive bail. He also called the prosecutor's claim that he had driven Gurrah and Lepke from New York sheer hyperbole because the two crooks had been convicted of antitrust violations in federal court.[35]

Perhaps the most scathing commentary against Dewey came from District Attorney Dodge, who obviously relished attacking the man who had upstaged him:

Ballyhoo has never appealed to me. As I see it, the duty of a district attorney is to prosecute without the blowing of trumpets. A special prosecutor, with about a million dollars at his disposal, with the pick of the police department at his hand, with a specially constructed office to prevent leaks, with every newspaper publishing, in advance of the arrest of prospective defendants, details of the crime and thereby inflaming public opinion against the accused—that type of prosecutor is not justified in proclaiming that the county in which he has officiated for the past two and a half years is an unfit place to live. This special prosecutor has had cooperation and assistance such as no district attorney within the memory of man has ever had. Yet, on the eve of an election, after two and a half years of activity as a special prosecutor, he states that the county of New York is reeking with corruption.[36]

Tammany's critiques of Dewey's prosecutions contained a kernel of truth, but they gained little credence in the heated campaign. The Democrats' only substantive attack focused on Dewey's alleged antiunion bias. Hastings claimed Dewey's comments and prosecutions had smeared the entire labor movement. He contended that many labor leaders distrusted Dewey, but were afraid to criticize him for fear their unions would become his next targets. Although Dewey claimed to be a friend of labor, Hastings advised unionists to see where he got his campaign contributions. Dewey's financial backers, he said, included the Rockefellers and the corporate lawyers who led the bar association.[37]

Democratic characterizations of Dewey's contributors were unfair. Although he received endorsements from most leaders of the New York bar, many of these men, such as Burlingham and Seabury, were not corporate lawyers. Others, such as Charles S. Whitman—known as New York's last crusading district attorney because of his efforts during the Progressive Era—supported Dewey because he was independent of Tammany. Dewey also garnered many labor endorsements, such as that of the pressmen's unions, which said the special prosecutor had "established himself as a fearless, impartial and brilliant prosecutor by his work in investigating racketeering in our city." Running with La Guardia also offset any antiunion sentiment Dewey may have engendered.[38]

In contrast to Tammany's fumbling for campaign issues, Dewey and La Guardia found a surefire message in lambasting crime and political corruption. Their campaign literature was filled with hyperbole, especially about Dewey. A Yiddish-language pamphlet claimed that the mere mention of Dewey's name "calls forth a fear and a terror in the underworld" because he had been "the most energetic and most competent prosecutor that New York has ever had." Material targeted for educated audiences argued that Dewey had convicted most of the defendants he prosecuted, that the district attorney's office should not be a "political plum," and that Dewey had "proved that Modern Prosecuting Methods can cope with Modern Criminal Methods." Most of Dewey's pamphlets

incorporated rhetoric describing gangsters as big shots who enjoyed privileges paid for by ordinary New Yorkers. One brochure, "The Challenge
of Crime," estimated that New York's annual crime costs totalled $15
billion, more than the national budget. Two years without crime in New
York, it said, would pay the national debt. Dewey's campaign staff was
successful at blanketing New York with leaflets and pictures; his face
appeared in every busy section of Manhattan. His picture also cropped
up in some unexpected quarters, such as the front of a church bulletin.
His visibility was heightened even further with production of a campaign
film, *Smashing Crime with Dewey*, which contained dramatic reenact-
ments of racket shakedowns, a talk by Dewey, and campaign endorsements by Seabury and other civic leaders. Five sound trucks projected
the film on street corners nightly between October 19, 1937, and Election
Day.[39]

Dewey proved to be a tireless speech maker and spoke to several
groups daily. But his most electrifying addresses were five radio talks
delivered during October. The first came two days after a Dewey witness,
Max Rubin, was shot in the back. Rubin, a hireling of labor racketeers
Lepke and Gurrah, had agreed to testify about their involvement in the
flour-trucking industry. He was the first Dewey witness to be harmed
since the special investigation began, but Dewey accepted no responsibility for the event because Rubin had refused police protection. Dewey
interpreted the shooting as "the frightened act of a desperate criminal
underworld. The racketeers have flung down their challenge. Tonight I
accept that challenge." Dewey said his success in prosecuting racketeers
had struck fear into the hearts of the city's gangsters, who were hiding
and hoping that the fight against organized crime would dissipate. He
characterized Lepke and Gurrah as the most notorious of New York's
fugitives, describing how they had used murder and violence in their rise
from petty street punks to wealthy crooks. He invoked the by-now-famil-
iar descriptions of their extravagant life-styles and asserted that they and
other criminals hoped he would not be elected, so they could "be safe
under the same system under which they grew fat and remained safe for
many years." Dewey urged voters to keep this from happening. If elected,
he vowed to break the underworld's hold on New York during his four-
year term.[40]

Dewey found an equally dramatic opening for his second radio address by offering a $5,000 reward for the capture of J. Richard "Dixie" Davis. Davis, a disbarred New York lawyer, had been the brains for Dutch Schultz and had taken over his gambling interests when the racketeer was murdered in 1935. He would become a key figure in Dewey's prosecution of Tammany leader Jimmy Hines. The following week's speech had the familiar tone and dramatic appeal of a bedtime story. "Tonight I am going to talk about the poultry racket and about a man who worked his way up from bouncer in a dance hall to czar of a fifty million dollar industry, and levied a tax on every man and woman in New York. This bouncer was no ham-fisted Bowery bruiser. He was a slim, slick-haired fellow who cowed the nosy with a cold eye or crippling, unexpected blow. His liking for barbershops and liberal use of sweet-smelling oils and tonics won him the nickname 'Tootsie.' " Dewey said Arthur Herbert, a truck driver by day and a bouncer by night, nursed a secret "ambition to be a Big-shot and to make the big money that comes easy and quick outside the law. He succeeded, and for more than ten years he was immune to the state's laws in the County of New York." Dewey explained how the twenty-four-year-old Herbert used canniness and force to take over the chicken drivers' union.[41]

He consolidated his control by appointing convicts to union offices, then engineering his election as president for life. Next, he took over the chicken slaughterers' union, then the poultry merchants. He levied a one-cent tribute on each of the fifty million live chickens sold in the city every year. Those who tried to intervene with Herbert's takeover met violent reprisals: trucks and chicken coops were burned; one person had his house bombed; and another had paving stones dropped on his truck as he drove under a bridge. The federal government prosecuted Herbert for violating antitrust laws, a misdemeanor that put him back on the streets in short order. Prison had little effect on Herbert; once out, he quickly "regained his healthy coat of tan, sitting in his regular, reserved seat in the stands behind third base at the Polo Grounds and the Yankee Stadium. His pockets bulged with money and he was a willing bettor. His voice ran with the old authority as he called his challenge, 'Lay you five hundred. Lay you a grand.' " As usual, Dewey laid great stress on the gangster's lavish life-style. "His apartment on West 86th Street was

richly furnished with the guidance of an interior decorator. He frequented night clubs, hockey games and race tracks. He was no easy
spender. When Ziggie, one of his underworld friends, sailed off for Europe, Tootsie tenderly sent him a sixteen dollar basket of flowers paid for
with union funds."[42]

Herbert was one of Dewey's great success stories. Before Dewey's
appointment as special prosecutor, Herbert enjoyed freedom from local
law enforcement. Dewey changed that by indicting him. During his trial
in the summer of 1937, Herbert pleaded guilty to charges of grand larceny
and, before going to prison, repaid $25,000 that he had stolen from the
union. According to Dewey, "The downfall of Tootsie Herbert was another heavy blow to the underworld of this city. To see pretty-boy Tootsie stand up and plead guilty was to see another public enemy removed.
The back of the underworld has been broken in these two years. For the
first time in twenty years the challenge of the underworld has been answered in New York County. With your help on Election Day, the
strange immunity of big shot gangsters in this county will be ended for
good."[43]

Perhaps the most dramatic of Dewey's radio addresses came the following week, when he identified a politician with close ties to racketeers.
He had hinted at the connection two weeks earlier but waited to announce the name until libel lawyers gave the go-ahead. He began this
fourth speech with typical bombast: "Tonight I am going to talk about
the alliance between Crime and Politics in the County of New York. I
am going to tell you about a politician, a political ally of thieves, pickpockets, thugs, dope peddlers and big-shot racketeers. Albert Marinelli,
county clerk of New York, powerful leader of half the second assembly
district, dominates the whole. He attained power by staying in the dark
and keeping his mouth shut. Tonight we turn on the spotlight." Dewey
described how Marinelli's name had been used by racketeers to frighten
their victims. One hapless owner of a small trucking business, William
Brown, refused to pay gangsters Jimmy Doyle and Dominick Didato,
even though they claimed to be protected by Marinelli. Goons beat
Brown and his brother with axe handles and poured emery powder into
the crankshaft of his best truck. The scare tactics caused Brown's wife to
suffer a nervous breakdown. When Brown took his problems to the po-

lice in May 1933, Marinelli connived to get the case dismissed on a technicality.[44]

Marinelli numbered Lucky Luciano among his friends. The two attended the 1932 Democratic National Convention together and shared a suite at the Drake Hotel. Three years later at a political fund-raiser for Marinelli, the guest list included Benny Spiller, a loan shark; Jesse Jacobs, a crooked bail bondsman; and "Little Davie" Betillo, a triggerman for Al Capone who had become Luciano's chief assistant. All three were convicted with Luciano in the prostitution case. Marinelli also befriended Socks Lanza, who controlled the Fulton Fish Market until he was indicted by federal authorities. On a typical day, Dewey said, Marinelli could be found in the basement of Manhattan's Criminal Courts Building conducting business with "bondsmen, lawyers, and hangers on."[45]

As he had with his other targets, Dewey described Marinelli's ascent from his humble beginnings in Little Italy to a life of luxury. "Al Marinelli is one of the most powerful politicians in New York. This shadowy figure gives no interviews to the press. His history is shrouded in mystery. No one even knows just how he rose to power." Marinelli gained control of one Manhattan assembly district in 1931; by 1935, with the help of gangsters, he had spread his power to other districts. Much of his political control depended on using intimidation at the polls. Dewey explained how, in the 1933 election, 4,534 votes were fraudulently added to the Tammany candidates in Marinelli's district and 3,535 were stolen from the opposition. Dewey told Marinelli supporters that they might "be interested to know that he has a luxurious estate surrounded by an iron fence . . . on Long Island. From his several motor cars, he chooses to drive back and forth in a Lincoln limousine; and his Japanese butler, Togo, serves him well." Dewey concluded by listing eight members of Marinelli's county committee who had criminal records for offenses like dope dealing, counterfeiting, extortion, carrying a gun, horse thieving, assault, and impersonating a policeman. Several of his associates had avoided convictions for murder and assault. Dewey denied that his attack on Marinelli was political: "There can be no difference of opinion on the questions involved. Gorillas, thieves, pickpockets, and dope peddlers in the political structure are not the subject of argument. There is nothing political about human decency."[46]

As the election came down to the wire, Tammany faced more problems. The Democrats wanted and needed the support of Roosevelt and Lehman to win the city election, but they were unsuccessful in getting either endorsement. Roosevelt initially tried to appease Tammany by remaining publicly neutral. But on the Saturday before election day, Roosevelt sent La Guardia a special delivery letter endorsing his candidacy. Supporters Paul Windels and Roy Howard thought the letter would make it look as if Roosevelt controlled La Guardia, and the mayor decided not to release it. In spite of Tammany's desperate resort to election fraud, La Guardia and Dewey won handily. La Guardia netted 1,344,630 votes, compared to Mahoney's 890,000. The American Labor party provided him with more than 482,000 votes. In New York County, Dewey scored a victory larger than La Guardia's; the mayor won by 94,000 votes while Dewey carried the county by 106,000. A deputy police commissioner sent Tammany the skin of a tiger he had shot in India to signify the end of the party's hegemony.[47]

Dewey hoped to begin his new job with an honest clerk of courts. He received help from the Citizens' Union in ousting Marinelli. In mid-November, the group urged his discharge on the grounds that he had never answered Dewey's charges. On November 25, Marinelli issued a general denial, saying he liked his job but not well enough to be slandered. As public criticism continued, Lehman asked Dewey for specific charges. After using the grand jury to question three hundred Marinelli associates, Dewey sent the governor a five-page report detailing his accusations. Marinelli resigned on December 4 and was replaced by Andrew B. Keating, the editor of the *New York Law Journal.*[48]

Dewey faced other new challenges as district attorney. As a special prosecutor, he had a huge reservoir of good will, seemingly unlimited resources, and a select caseload. In going from "special" to "regular" Dewey gained a larger staff but less freedom to choose his cases. His first task was to clear the office of Tammany holdovers. He fired forty of the office's sixty-five process servers after determining that many did little work. One man's sole responsibility was carrying the district attorney's hat and taking off his coat; another did nothing but stamp mail. Dewey estimated that, on average, most served one subpoena a day rather than the eight they should have delivered.[49]

Dewey brought over the twenty lawyers from the special prosecutor's office and rehired only two of Dodge's sixty-four assistants. The Democratic lawyers included John McDonald—a war veteran with so much experience that "he could try certain types of minor cases blindfolded, and could dispose of more cases in one day than a battery of assistants could in a week"—and Felix Benvenga—who handled appeals and was well regarded in New York's higher courts. Dewey admirers always claimed that he kept the office free of partisanship, but eleven of his first appointments went to Republicans and two to members of the American Labor party. Nonetheless, he demonstrated his independence from party leaders by appointing only a handful of men suggested by Simpson.[50]

By reducing salaries, Dewey was able to expand the number of his assistants from sixty-four to seventy-two. He also continued his practice of hiring "dollar-a-year" men willing to work essentially as volunteers. As he had in earlier positions, Dewey surrounded himself with younger men willing to work for lower pay. The New York Times reported in December 1937 that Dewey's staff was the youngest in years; the average age was thirty-two, whereas in Dodge's office it had been forty-four. Although the youthful staff was enthusiastic, it created a rocky start for the office. As Harris Steinberg recalled, Dewey's staff consisted of "a bunch of young fellows who didn't know their asses from first base." Steinberg, who had worked for Dewey when he was a special prosecutor, pointed out that the young assistants had little time to learn the district attorney's job, a situation that created even more chaos. What saved them in the early days was "the good will, the public respect for the office, and even the respect and fear of those Tammany judges over there [who] smoothed it over until everybody got a little experience." Dewey agreed, admitting that his inexperienced staff had squeaked through with the patience of judges and the cooperation of grand jurors.[51]

Dewey's hiring practices ran afoul of state civil service requirements. As special prosecutor, the commissioners gave him ninety-seven exemptions because they believed the jobs would be temporary. When he wanted to make these jobs permanent, the commission balked. During a January 1938 hearing, Dewey asked for continued exemption from normal requirements. His needs, he said, were unique because he was trying to extend his racket-busting techniques to the regular machinery of government and needed specially trained accountants and investigators. For example, he had an Italian investigator and eventually might "need a good Greek or a hunchback or a man of one special type." He also wanted to extend his staff from four to forty highly qualified legal researchers in order to "start stretching the criminal law back to where it belongs [by] . . . searching cases in the U.S. and England for authority so that we can proceed on a wider front." As a federal prosecutor he had also found that stenographers hired under civil service requirements were less willing to work long hours. Eventually, Dewey said, he wanted to bring some of his staff into the civil service. In the meantime, however, he was "not much concerned about form" because he had a mandate from the people to continue his racket fight. With the help of pressure from Governor Lehman, Dewey won his exemptions.[52]

Once his staff eased into new responsibilities, the district attorney's office began running smoothly. With the money saved by cutting back on process servers and hiring young lawyers, Dewey created two new departments. The first was an accounting bureau to investigate fraud. In previous years, white-collar cases in Manhattan had been handled primarily by federal prosecutors; at the state level, district attorneys who brought indictments had no accountants to prepare the cases for trial and usually had to abandon them. Dewey's second addition was a racket bureau consisting of ten lawyers led by Murray Gurfein. In essence, this office continued the long-range investigations of the special prosecutor's office.[53]

As he set up his office in 1938, Dewey watched events in Albany, where legislators were discussing two measures that could have undermined his prosecutorial efforts. The first would have eliminated the blue ribbon juries that had been so instrumental to his previous successes. Defense attorneys in all Dewey's cases had argued against the special juries, claiming they were biased against defendants. Dewey and other prosecutors had prevailed against those arguments by saying that special panels were more knowledgeable and experienced and so better able to judge complex cases than ordinary juries. The controversy was reopened on January 15, 1938, when the state judicial council decreed the juries unfair. In its fourth annual report to the legislature, the council reported on its study of special jury trials held between June 1, 1932, and June 30,

1937. The study showed that the percentage of convictions, 78 percent, was much higher than in cases before regular juries. The report also noted that of 383 defendants tried during those years, only 5 had asked for a special jury; prosecutors had requested the rest. The preponderance of special jury cases had been in New York County, where there had been only 84 acquittals, compared to 299 convictions. The report concluded that "every petit jury should be uniformly high caliber and capable of giving a fair trial in all cases. To attain this goal the ordinary jury, as now provided, may be in need of improvement. It is, however, unjust and should be unnecessary to select special juries in specific cases."[54]

On February 5, after the state Senate voted to abolish the blue ribbon panels, the matter was taken up in the assembly. Critics said prosecutors kept special jury lists as a way to ensure that special juries would become "prosecuting juries." Such lists excluded anyone who had previously served on a hung jury or one that voted for acquittal. Lawyer Samuel Leibowitz said the panels were un-American because they barred blacks and Italians. Louis Waldman, a lead defense lawyer in the restaurant rackets case and a member of the executive committee of the American Labor party, described most special panel members as "smug, satisfied members of the richer classes" who had no sympathy for poor defendants. Dewey, unable to attend the hearings, sent a letter denying that most special jurors were wealthy. The juries included anyone who could "divorce himself from opinions and impressions formed outside the courtroom and is free from prejudice against capital punishment, circumstantial evidence, certain types of crime, certain kinds of defense, and a defendant who fails to take the witness stand and testify in his own behalf." Ultimately, Dewey and his law-and-order supporters prevailed; New York's blue ribbon juries were not struck down as unconstitutional until the early 1960s.[55]

A second measure that would have hampered Dewey's efforts was aimed at limiting wiretaps. The proposal, which was pushed by labor groups whose leaders argued that law enforcement officials abused wiretaps, became a major source of controversy at the fractious 1938 state constitutional convention. The convention's composition reflected the state's splintered politics: ninety-two Republicans and seventy-five Democrats were elected to the convention, which began in April. Democrats were divided between those who favored Roosevelt's New Deal policies and those who opposed them. Anti–New Dealers looked to Al Smith for guidance; he was chosen honorary president of the convention despite the Republican majority. Every measure that came up in the convention fell prey to partisan politics; the proposal to limit wiretapping was no exception.

The American Labor party enlisted Supreme Court Justice and former Lehman aid Charles Poletti to speak for the proposal. The party also joined with the American Civil Liberties Union to argue that wiretaps and the evidence gleaned from them should be held to the standards followed by the federal courts. To ensure this, they argued, the legislature should require police agencies to obtain court orders and then exclude evidence obtained illegally. Lehman backed this measure, saying that espionage and wiretapping were among the "most vicious weapons that a dictatorship invokes against individual rights of its citizens." He called wiretapping a "vehicle of great oppression [which had] caused people to be afraid of discussing their most intimate personal problems."[56]

Partly because it was supported by the Democrats and American Labor party, Republicans rejected the suggestion to exclude illegally obtained evidence. One leading critic of the bill was Dewey, who claimed it would shackle law enforcement. He argued that the proposal "in theory would enlarge the rights of the people, but in practice would subject them to the depredations of organized crime." Dewey's cases had relied heavily on wiretaps to gather evidence, but he had always offered corroborating evidence in court. Excluding such evidence would protect only the guilty: "No innocent citizen, no law abiding person can benefit by the suppression of evidence, however obtained." Dewey added that just because federal law enforcement agencies were bound by such rules was no reason to shackle local officials. After all, he explained, the state had control over the most dangerous crimes, such as murder, arson, robbery, and assault. In certain kinds of cases, wiretaps were essential. He added that he knew of no case in which the police had overstepped their bounds or in which a case had been prosecuted without other overwhelming evidence. Proponents of wiretapping limits, Dewey concluded, could not cite a single example where an innocent man had been convicted, whereas he could cite hundreds of cases that would have been lost without secretly recorded conversations.[57]

LaGuardia and McCook also opposed the proposal, arguing that the abuses of wiretapping were meager compared to the havoc that would result from hampering law enforcement. "Let us not," McCook urged, "defeat our ends; let us not by enacting a constitutional prohibition directed at relatively unimportant abuses, tie the hand that holds the sword of justice; let us rather leave to the blindfolded goddess in this respect the power and the freedom to use that sword as and when she must." As the debate raged through June, Republicans claimed wiretapping abuses could be avoided merely by amending the state constitution to criticize illegal searches. Civil libertarians and labor leaders such as George Meany argued that an exclusionary rule was needed to give the amendment teeth. Ultimately, the Republicans prevailed, after adopting Dewey's suggested wiretapping law that omitted the exclusionary rule but set stiff standards for judicial approval of wiretaps.[58]

The primary reason for the politicized atmosphere of the constitutional convention was the pending gubernatorial race. Both parties were already vying for public favor before they had chosen their candidates. Medalie and other leading Republicans had been grooming Dewey for the governor's chair, and in 1938 they saw their chance. Medalie, Newbold Morris, and Edwin F. Jaeckle, the new party boss in Buffalo, orchestrated his nomination. The timing seemed perfect. Dewey had become a national hero; two movies based on Dewey's career—*Smashing the Rackets* and *Racket Buster*—had come out that year. Letters arrived at the district attorney's office addressed only to "Racket Buster, New York" or "Thomas E. Dewey, Enemy of Corruption." One father wrote Dewey saying that his ten-year-old daughter, upset about rainy weather, had threatened to sue God. When he told her she could never win such a lawsuit, she replied; "I could if Dewey was my lawyer." Dewey thrived on his fame. After a five-day vacation in the Blue Ridge Mountains of Virginia, he complained that he had been approached by only one autograph seeker.[59]

Basking in national attention and local adoration, Dewey and his advisors thought they saw a clear path to the governor's chair. Republican support for his candidacy began in April when the Young Republicans boosted him for the governorship. Dewey accepted the nomination at the Republican State Convention in Saratoga on September 29, 1938. With a typical lack of modesty, he asserted that some Republicans had advised him not to run for office because he was the only one able enough to fight crime as district attorney. This was not true, Dewey said; he had already accomplished his primary goal by "saving the district attorney's office from political allies of the underworld." Besides, he argued, he would be better poised to fight organized crime from Albany because its tentacles reached across county lines.[60]

Dewey accepted the nomination in part because Lehman had announced he would not seek reelection. The governor planned to campaign for the Senate seat vacated by the death of Royal Copeland earlier in the year. The Democrats wanted to run Attorney General John Bennett for governor but had abandoned the idea when the Republicans nominated Dewey. Roosevelt and Farley convinced Lehman he was the only candidate capable of defeating Dewey, and he decided to postpone his congressional ambitions. Lehman took pride in having continued the progressive leadership of Smith and Roosevelt and feared Dewey would undo their achievements if elected.[61]

With Lehman back in the race, Dewey found himself in an unwinnable contest. Many who had supported him for district attorney felt betrayed by his decision to seek higher office after less than a year. Such labor groups as the American Labor party, the American Federation of Labor, and the CIO had backed Dewey for district attorney, but they had no intention of supporting him against their progressive, honest, and hardworking governor. New York City's major newspapers also urged Dewey not to run. La Guardia, who disliked Lehman personally but feared Dewey as a political rival, remained neutral. Of the major non-Republicans in the Fusion coalition, only Seabury endorsed Dewey. As head of the Nonpartisan Citizens' Committee for Dewey for Governor, Seabury argued that Dewey would bring fresh enthusiasm to the job. Lehman, by contrast, had clearly lost interest, as shown by his stated desire not to run for reelection.[62]

Lehman's accomplished record and extensive administrative experience left Dewey with few viable campaign issues. As *New York Times* reporter Warren Moscow said, Dewey was reduced to running a campaign that "paid no attention to the actual specific issues. It was a campaign of half-truths and appeals to prejudice." Dewey set the tone for the campaign when, in his acceptance of the Republican nomination, he alleged that "without meaning to be so, any Democratic governor is, perforce, the good-will advertising, the front man, the window dressing for what is in part, at least a thoroughly corrupt machine. The objectives of respectable governors have been dangled as bait before the people by an organization whose sole basic purpose was politics for profit." Dewey's first official campaign release picked up this theme with a "scathing exposé and . . . denunciation of the 'tragic failure' of the Democratic State Administration."[63]

Dewey's criticism sparked similar vitriolic responses from Lehman, who accused him of trying "to achieve through vilification, disrespect and false innuendo what he knew he could not achieve through legitimate means." The governor harped on Dewey's lack of experience, his reliance on political handlers, and his desire to leave the district attorney's office early in his term. In response to Dewey's bragging about his successes as a crime buster, Lehman pointed out that he had appointed Dewey to office and had passed the most comprehensive anticrime package in New York's history. As the election neared, Lehman told voters they were faced with only one issue: Did they want to elect a prosecutor or a governor as the state's chief executive? Despite the hollowness of Dewey's charges against Lehman, he might have won the election had it not been for the anti-Semitism of his running mate, Frederick Bontecou. Bontecou's comments directed at Lehman played well in upstate New York but created a backlash in New York City and ultimately cost votes. Even so, Dewey lost by only 64,000 votes—an incredibly small margin considering that Lehman had won the 1936 election by more than half a million votes.[64]

Although he lost, Dewey's campaign rejuvenated the lagging fortunes of the state Republican party and heightened his national prominence. Republicans won control of the state Senate for the first time in six years and recognized Dewey as their new leader. One typical letter came from a federal judge in Malone, New York, who assured Dewey that although he had lost the governorship, he had "won a great victory." Political observers across the nation agreed that the New York gubernatorial race was the most important contest of 1938 and offered various interpretations of Dewey's fortunes. It was a good year for Republicans nationally as voters expressed their displeasure with the implementation of the New Deal and Roosevelt's attempt to pack the U.S. Supreme Court. Given Lehman's close identification with Roosevelt, the fall in his vote margin was not unexpected. Yet, many commentators argued, Dewey's victory went beyond the Republican landslide. A survey of three hundred editorials from around the country revealed that only forty-five said the election had hurt Dewey; another forty-five argued that the election had helped him; and the rest saw him as a major factor in national politics. Although many writers believed Dewey too inexperienced for the governor's job, most agreed he would be unbeatable in the next gubernatorial race. Some even correctly predicted that the 1940 Republican presidential nomination would come down to a race between Dewey and Senator Robert Taft of Ohio.[65] For reformers in New York City, Dewey's loss proved a victory of another sort. It meant he would remain in the district attorney's job long enough to provide the symbolic death blow to Tammany by successfully prosecuting boss Jimmy Hines.

CHAPTER TEN

≈ ≈ ≈

Jimmy Hines and the End of Old Tammany

S UCCESSFUL prosecution of James J. Hines represented the pinnacle of success for both New York City's reform movement and Dewey's prosecutorial career. Throughout the 1930s reformers led by La Guardia and Dewey had argued that there was a dangerous nexus between gangsters and politicians. No one disputed that criminals and Tammany Hall leaders had been partners since the beginning of the nineteenth century; but the relationship, according to reformers, had grown more menacing. In the past, politicians had used criminals merely as minions, calling them out at election time, then pushing them into the background. Reformers believed that the old system had broken down during prohibition, when wealthier gangsters came to control politicians, not vice versa.[1] It seemed inevitable that the reform cycle that began with Rothstein's murder would culminate with the prosecution of the Tammany boss most suspected of betraying the public trust, Jimmy Hines.

Even as an assistant U.S. attorney, Dewey had targeted the blacksmith-turned-politician. Still, it took the paroxysm of reform during the Seabury probe, five years of Fusion government, and Dewey's special investigatory techniques to make catching Hines feasible. Even then, the canny boss proved an elusive quarry, in part because Dewey's political ambitions marred his judgment. It is fitting that the case against the Tammany politician proved to be the most politicized of Dewey's prosecutions, figuring prominently in his campaigns for district attorney and governor. His overzealousness resulted in one mistrial and almost led to another.

It is perhaps symbolic that Hines was born in New York City in 1876, only a month after Boss Tweed was extradited from Spain to begin serving a prison sentence for plundering the city's coffers.[2] Hines grew up in Harlem; at fifteen, he began working as a blacksmith with his father. In 1912, he sold the family business and became a contractor and insurance salesman. He compensated for a lack of business acumen by taking an active role in Democratic city politics. From 1913 to 1915 he served as clerk to the Board of Aldermen and was very successful at gathering supporters. On his return from World War I, he was greeted by more than two thousand well-wishers at a party at the Monongahela Club in the Eleventh Assembly District in Harlem. Hines's political fortunes continued to grow, and by 1919 he was sparring with Charles Murphy about control of Tammany Hall. During one fractious meeting in September 1921, Hines called the aging political boss a "millstone around the neck of the Democratic Party." After Murphy's death in 1924, Hines was the logical successor, but other Tammany sachems thought elevating Hines to the leadership position would dishonor Murphy's memory. When Hines sought nomination as New York County sheriff the following year, the Hall gave the nod to another candidate.

By November 1929, however, Hines's position as a Tammany leader and political fixer was secure. He relished being the power broker behind the scenes and never again sought to be nominal head of the machine. Former police commissioner Richard Enright claimed that Hines regularly influenced the appointment of New York City judges. Enright cited one instance in which Hines arranged for appointment of a friend's inexperienced son to the city court, passing over older and much more capable candidates. The same month, the *New York Times* reported that a milk racketeer, Larry Fay, was seeking Hines's help in overturning a license suspension stemming from his company's falsification of pasteurization labels. Two months later, federal agents raided a drug ring controlled by Arnold Rothstein and found Hines's telephone number. During the Seabury investigations, a police informer said that Hines arranged for the dismissal of cases investigated by the vice squad. In 1932 a member of the electrical workers' union testified that his local had paid protection money to Hines.[3]

Honest civil servants who crossed Hines faced a vindictive and powerful foe. Traditionally, policemen who raided protected vice rackets were transferred to undesirable beats; one popular dumping ground was Canarsie, the terminus for the city's sewer system. Samuel J. Battle, the first black patrolman in Manhattan and later the city's first black police commissioner, was transferred to Canarsie for nearly three years after he raided a protected spot in the 1920s. Although Battle's fight was not with Hines, the latter continued his predecessors' practice of demanding the punishment of honest policemen. Parole officer David Dressler was one person who felt Hines's wrath. Listening to his colleagues talk about Hines, Dressler concluded that he "seemed to be the most powerful man in town." He recalled that parole officers were always fearful when a case involved someone from Hines's district. Dressler's first run-in with the politician came after the arrest of a numbers racketeer. When another gangster came in to discuss the case, Dressler refused to talk about it. The man then said: "See this hat? [It] cost $15. Can you afford $15 hats? Goddamn right you can't! You play it smart, and you can afford $15 hats." Dressler told the visitor he did not wear hats and suggested he see the commissioner in charge of the office. "I don't bodder wit' commissioners! I'll see Jimmy Hines," the gangster answered. Later that day, Hines called and demanded release of the racketeer. When Dressler refused, Hines contacted his boss, who ordered the man freed. Dressler had him picked up a second time on different charges. His boss lost the reports and again released the man. The charade ended when the racketeer was arrested for murder and hanged himself in the jail while awaiting trial.[4]

Given the publicity surrounding Hines's activities, it was not surprising that he became a target of law enforcement agencies. In 1932, Medalie and Dewey tried to link Hines to José Miro, head of the numbers racket in Harlem. During the investigation, evidence showed that Miro had paid $196 for twelve shirts delivered to Hines. Dewey and Medalie offered Miro whatever he wanted if he would testify against the Tammany boss, but the gambler refused. He reportedly told his lawyer: "Christ, my life wouldn't be worth a nickel. . . . I'll go to the pen." Dewey prosecuted Miro on tax evasion charges, and he was sentenced to prison. Hines remained unscathed, and Dewey and Medalie became even more determined to catch him. In August 1933, when he was no longer U.S. attorney, Medalie publicly offered to tell a grand jury the names of six politicians who helped racketeers. All had been investigated by his office but none had been indicted. Jimmy Hines headed the list. In the 1933 mayoral election, both La Guardia and Recovery party candidate Joseph McKee picked up the refrain of Hines's corruption.[5]

Rumors about Hines were nothing new. Throughout the 1930s he lived in a high style reminiscent of Boss Tweed. In addition to receiving silk shirts from gangsters, Hines played the stock market and frequented hotels with Lucky Luciano. Nominally, he earned his living by managing turf clubs and horse breeders' associations, jobs that paid at most $3,300 a year. Yet Hines spent considerably more than that; for example, in 1929, when his income was allegedly $3,300, he opened an investment account worth $4,000. In 1931, when he supposedly earned the same amount, Hines paid a bookmaker $8,395. He sometimes took part in lucrative transactions without putting up any money himself. In 1930 he persuaded a friend to purchase $114,750 of stock in the New York Giants franchise and put it in Mrs. Hines's name. His sons attended Harvard and Yale, and he set one of them up in the furniture business to bid on government contracts.[6]

Hines's skill at grasping for dollars was not always matched by a keen political sense. In the early 1930s he made three fatal mistakes. In 1932 he and Curry shortsightedly backed Al Smith over Roosevelt for president. In the process, they not only ensured that the future president would deny them patronage, they also alienated Herbert Lehman. The rift could have been smoothed over, but Hines refused to compromise. Once, when Lehman backed longtime Democrat Jonah Goldstein for the judiciary, Hines, miffed that he had not been consulted, blocked the nomination. Hines also thwarted La Guardia's bid for reelection to Congress in 1932. La Guardia, realizing the election would be a Democratic landslide, hoped to capitalize on his Progressive and pro-labor record by garnering support from both parties. Labor leaders such as William Green and John L. Lewis appealed to Hines to go along with the plan, and Brooklyn boss John McCooey was willing to support the arrangement. McCooey told La Guardia, "I'd like to see you made Ambassador to Australia; but failing that, I'll try to send you back to Washington. Anywhere so long as you're kept out of New York City." Hines refused the deal, thereby laying the groundwork for La Guardia's contribution to the destruction of the Democratic machine.[7]

Hines's position as Tammany's power broker and his highly visible life-style made him a perfect target for the 1935 runaway grand jury. The earlier panel, which issued its report in December 1934, described the lenient treatment certain gambling cases received in special sessions court. Despite the fact that many of the defendants had prior convictions, all received only suspended sentences or small fines. The grand jury was stymied in its attempts to learn who was fixing the cases and suggested that a second jury be assigned to pursue the matter. As the "runaway" grand jury examined the situation, it became public knowledge that the target was Dutch Schultz, who had taken over small numbers operations like those of José Miro and consolidated them into a lucrative syndicate. Always lurking behind the scenes was Schultz's Tammany connection, Jimmy Hines.[8]

Not surprisingly, when Dewey was appointed special prosecutor his main targets were Schultz and Hines. He had inherited transcripts of 1933 wiretapped conversations in which Schultz and his lawyer, J. Richard "Dixie" Davis, discussed pending cases before "Jim's judges." Dewey arranged for new taps on Davis's phone and assigned investigators to sift through court records, looking for evidence of Hines's efforts for Schultz. The Dutchman's assassination in October 1935 deprived Dewey of his main gangland target and delayed his prosecution of Hines for nearly three years.[9]

In keeping with the tactics used so successfully against Luciano, Dewey launched another spectacular raid against the heirs to Schultz's numbers ring. On January 7, 1937, McCook issued arrest warrants for seventy participants in the Harlem racket, and a special squad of police was dispatched to begin the arrests that evening. The raids netted many potential witnesses but not the ring's leaders. Davis, racket manager George Weinberg, and bankers Alexander Pompez and Joe "Spasm" Ison eluded Dewey's clutches. Nonetheless, by July Dewey's staff had gathered enough evidence to present an indictment.[10]

The charges described how Schultz and his henchmen had begun consolidating New York's independent numbers runners in 1931. The spoils were well worth their efforts. According to Dewey, the Harlem numbers games generated an estimated $35,000 a day. Schultz's takeover of the gambling rackets paralleled his efforts in the restaurant industry; independent operators who refused to join the ring were threatened. The twelve men charged with running the syndicate until January 1937 included Davis, manager Weinberg, his brother, "Bo" Weinberg, the ring's treasurer, "Big Harry" Schoenhaus, Martin "Moe" Weintraub, Ison, and Pompez.[11]

In the weeks following the indictment, public attention was riveted on attempts to arrest the principal defendants. Pursuit of Pompez took on an international flavor. The former cigar maker from Key West, Florida, had formerly lived in Paris, Barcelona, Canada, and Spain. Dewey's office wrote authorities from Hot Springs, Arkansas, to Memphis, Philadelphia, and New Orleans before finally locating Pompez in Mexico. Dewey enlisted the aid of the U.S. State Department to get Pompez extradited to New York in the fall of 1937. As one of the first bankers dragged into Schultz's ring, he would be a key prosecution witness.

Pompez's arrest was dramatic, but Dewey devoted more hyperbole to the capture of Davis. Dewey's investigation of the gambling rackets coincided with his run for the district attorney's office. In one of his most memorable speeches during the campaign—the October 10, 1937, radio address—he offered a $5,000 reward for Davis's capture. Acknowledging that such tactics were more typical of the "Old Wild West" than modern New York City, Dewey said the extraordinary measure was necessary for a man he likened to Jesse James and Billy the Kid. Dewey said Davis, a disbarred New York lawyer, had been the brains behind Dutch Schultz. Together they had run "one of the most menacing and murderous mobs which ever rode roughshod over a great city while politically picked prosecutors slept soundly on their jobs." After Schultz was gunned down, Davis took over the racket, which, Dewey alleged, raked in more than $860,000 in a five-week period.[12]

Dewey described Davis as an unlikely gang leader. He came from a small town in upstate New York, worked his way through law school, and then was employed at a prestigious law firm. Davis was ambitious, however, and wanted to get to the top "the easy way." Within three years of his admission to the bar in 1927, Davis joined Schultz and began helping him organize New York's disparate gambling underworld into one orderly racket. "They decided that with Dutch Schultz's muscles and Dixie Davis' brains, the golden stream of profits from this game should no longer go to the little bankers, but to the mobsters, to be used to help muscle in on still bigger business." The takeover involved murders, which Dewey admitted he could not detail, and tremendous profits. As he did with all gangsters, Dewey harped on Davis's luxurious life-style and fondness for nightlife. Davis's office occupied the entire floor of a skyscraper on West Broadway and cost $13,000 annually. Davis had three apartments—one each on West End Avenue and Park Avenue and a penthouse on East 92nd Street. His wardrobe included sixteen $165-dollar suits, $190-overcoats, and $8-shirts, which he wore to New York's finest night clubs. He also enjoyed links to New York politicians. According to the prosecutor, Davis's hold on the city was broken only after Dewey's appointment, when he went on the lam.[13]

It took several months, but a tipster finally came forward to claim Dewey's reward for the capture of Davis. Early in February 1938, a man approached Dewey assistant Paul Lockwood and said he would write down Davis's address after he was given the money in small bills. While the city controller gathered the reward, Dewey dispatched detectives to Philadelphia; they found Davis in bed with his girlfriend, Hope Dare, a red-haired rodeo rider and bit-part Broadway actress. The detectives snared an unexpected prize when they discovered defendant George Weinberg in the same apartment. It was Davis who was the most important witness, because he could provide the strongest evidence linking Hines to Schultz. The politician's name was conspicuously missing from the early indictments because Dewey's office had only piecemeal evidence against him. After his extradition to New York, Davis expected Hines to intervene on his behalf by arranging for reduction of his $300,000 bond. When nothing happened, Davis believed Hines had betrayed him and he offered to talk.[14]

With Davis's testimony in hand, Dewey could finally move against Hines. Ultimately, the case proved easier to put together than Dewey's earlier prosecutions. Without Schultz's backing, Hines posed much less of a threat to potential witnesses than other Dewey defendants. As Sol Gelb said, "Where the defendant was a politician—nobody is afraid of a politician. Once he's in trouble everybody curses him anyhow. The underworld wasn't much concerned about Hines. They didn't care about his conviction. They considered him a leech anyhow."[15] A superseding indictment issued in May 1938 named Hines as the lead defendant. According to the charges, he had joined Schultz's ring in the spring of 1932. Consolidating Harlem's disparate numbers operations into one organization had made gambling more visible and meant that police raids could be more costly. Schultz and his henchmen met with Hines to discuss how best to intimidate and bribe policemen and judges. Initially, Schultz agreed to pay Hines $1,000 for his help, then $500 to $1,000 a week; after Schultz's death, he received between $250 and $500 each week until October 1936.

Hines's influence was evident in at least three cases. In two raids, the police had arrested employees working out of the ring's headquarters on Lenox Avenue. On another occasion, police arrested one of the ring's leaders, Lou "Lulu" Rosenkranz, in possession of betting slips. In all three cases, evidence of guilt was overwhelming. Nevertheless, after Hines intervened, all three cases were dismissed by magistrates. In other situations, Hines used the well-worn technique of having troublesome honest cops transferred.[16]

The pretrial wrangling apparent in all Dewey's cases was even more bitter in the Hines case, partly because of the personalities involved. Dewey had decided to try the case himself, and, as usual, he was pugnacious. Hines's attorney was Lloyd Paul Stryker, a one-time nominee for a federal judgeship and a self-professed lover of civil liberties. Stryker had written books on Andrew Johnson and John Erskine, a Scottish law commentator. As one Dewey assistant remembered, "He was like a powder [pouter] pigeon. He had a good strong physique, a big strong chest, a crew hair cut, a ruddy face, and he looked like a tough, strong man and spoke that way. He was accustomed to dominating the courtroom because of his physical vitality and his reputation." The two lawyers' egos clashed from the start. Dewey exaggerated his nettlesome courtroom mannerisms, such as interrupting the proceedings by taking ceremoniously long drinks of water. His habits irritated Stryker, who developed an obvious loathing for the prosecutor. The friction began during a pretrial hearing on July 27, 1938, when Stryker asked the clerk of courts if Dewey had advised him to strike from the rolls jurors who had voted for acquit-

234 FIGHTING ORGANIZED CRIME

tals in previous cases. Clerk Archibald R. Watson admitted that he had discussed jury qualifications with Dewey and had removed names based on information supplied by the special prosecutor; he denied, however, the removals had anything to do with jurors' previous verdicts. Dewey called Stryker's question "a slimy insinuation." Stryker said he resented Dewey's comments and added, "I think the time should come when counsel should not be impugned, simply because this man happens to be a public officer. He is the lawyer of the other side of the case, and that is all." Not to be outdone, Dewey said, "And may I point out that this counsel has the brass nerve to impugn my integrity in this courtroom, and now he puts on the mantle of virtue." Judge Ferdinand Pecora ended the bickering by telling both lawyers that "indulgence in personalities" would not influence his decisions.[17]

Exacerbating the acrimony was the obvious importance of the Hines prosecution to Dewey's political career. The case came to fruition eight months into his term as district attorney and just as he began planning his run for the governor's seat. A week before pretrial hearings began, the *New York Times* speculated that Dewey needed to win the Hines case to get the nomination. As usual, Dewey refused to comment on his candidacy without a groundswell of public clamoring. His coyness displeased Stryker, who said Dewey should deny the rumors if he did not intend to run, so that the Hines case "would cease to be a political football." In the meantime, he commented, the prosecution was "a potential springboard from which [Dewey] . . . hopes to elevate himself to higher office."[18]

Stryker and the other defense lawyers complained about Dewey's plans to try the case in Manhattan before a special jury. They argued that the trial should have been moved from New York County, where Dewey's grandstanding had made its details common knowledge. In arguing for a change of venue at least a hundred miles away, defense attorneys noted that Dewey had blamed Tammany leaders for the city's crime throughout his well-publicized campaign for district attorney. When Hines was indicted, "every newspaper in this city, without exception, carried news items, editorials, special articles and cartoons, which unequivocally assume" his guilt. The attorneys produced affidavits from residents of Hines's district, all of whom said they had read about the case and had concluded he was guilty. Defense Attorney Joseph Shalleck argued that newspaper publicity had created the assumption that anyone indicted by Dewey "is automatically guilty or he would not be indicted." In the Hines case that was particularly true because media accounts had described the case as the "coup" or "grand slam [that] represents the culmination of several years of effort on the part of the prosecutor to stamp out racketeering in this city."[19]

Hines's attorneys used the argument made by all defense attorneys in Dewey cases: there was no reason for a special jury. Drawing on the debate about special juries that had taken place in the legislature earlier that year, Stryker echoed the opinion of the state judicial council that blue ribbon panels were unfairly biased toward prosecutors. He also maintained that there was no reason for a special jury in the Hines trial because it did not meet the primary condition stipulated in state law, which was that a case be unusually important or intricate. Dewey assistant Charles Grimes stated that he had proven the case would be intricate, but Stryker responded, "If this case is too intricate for an ordinary jury to determine, then there is something the matter with our whole jury system." Stryker said he had tried hundreds of civil cases involving much more "abstruse, difficult and complicated questions of medical science" that made the relatively easy questions involved in the Hines case look like "child's play."[20]

Stryker rejected Grimes's claim that the case was very important and quoted a June 9 newspaper article in which Grimes had said, "This is just another lawsuit as far as we are concerned. The defendant Hines is just another defendant." Judge Pecora commented that no case that charged judicial-influence peddling could be considered unimportant, but Stryker pointed out that if Dewey had evidence Hines had bribed a judge, he would have charged him with it. Instead, he had merely indicted the politician for participating in a gambling ring. Pecora disagreed with Stryker's contention that special juries were pro-prosecution. But the defense lawyer said if they were not, why did Dewey rely on them for all his important cases? Listing the normal jury requirements in New York state, Stryker scolded: "So now it is not sufficient to try this man before American citizens between the ages of 21 and 70. It is not sufficient to try this defendant before American citizens possessed only of $250, or a wife or a husband of such a person. That is not enough. It is not sufficient that they be intelligent and not possessed of any infirmities as provided for in the judiciary law. That is not sufficient. That won't do to try Mr. Hines before, because, you see, they want a winning, convicting blue ribbon jury." In the end, Pecora agreed with the prosecution's argument that it was up to the legislature, not Stryker, to determine the validity of blue ribbon juries. The judge also ruled that the case was important enough to merit a special panel because it involved questions of judicial propriety.[21]

Although Pecora's pretrial rulings favored the prosecution, the judge never trusted Dewey as McCook had. Pecora's background, his own success as a prosecutor, and his political ambitions made him much more independent minded. Unlike the patrician, even-tempered McCook, Pecora "was a prima dona in his own right" and, like Stryker, he bitterly resented Dewey's attempts to upstage him. A native of Sicily, Pecora was a liberal with a street fighter's mentality. Whereas McCook was a devout Republican, Pecora was a Democrat and former leader of New York's Progressive party. He had served twelve years as an assistant district attorney, had led a U.S. Senate investigation into corruption on Wall Street, and had been a member of the Securities and Exchange Commission. In 1933 he ran for district attorney against William Copeland Dodge on the Recovery party ticket. In early 1936, Lehman assigned him to the special investigation after Dewey successfully lobbied for a second grand jury because his staff was turning up more information than could be handled by one panel and McCook.[22]

According to one account, Dewey was leery of Pecora's appointment from the outset because of the judge's Democratic affiliation and political ambitions. But initially the two men were on good terms. Pecora had held Dewey's coat when he was sworn in as district attorney on December 31, 1937. In fact, if Dewey was fearful, it was more likely because he recognized Pecora as a strong, independent judge who would hold him to a strict code of legal behavior. The trial opened with press hoopla on August 16, 1936. Reporters from across the nation attended, and newspapers such as the *New York Mirror* ran headlines describing the trial as "the Battle of the Century." The newspapers and the crowds flocking around the courthouse recognized that the implications of the trial went beyond the issues of Dutch Schultz's moribund racket to the very heart of New York City's traditional politics.[23]

Although the case was nominally about Jimmy Hines's involvement with gambling kingpins, both sides realized that Tammany Hall was itself on trial. In that sense, the Hines case may have been the most ambiguous of Dewey's famous prosecutions. Few people had any sympathy for racketeers like Luciano or Dutch Schultz, but Hines, crooked though he may have been, represented a political system that still had many adherents. As police commissioner Samuel Battle said, Hines was a Robin Hood figure who stole from the crooks to provide services to the poor. When Battle was a detective in Hines's political district, he recalled, "There were many times when poor people were being dispossessed for lack of rent, many times when poor people didn't have coal or fuel, that I went to Jimmy Hines, and Jimmy Hines would call the city marshal and say: 'Come and see me, don't dispossess those people.' He did so many things from the humanitarian standpoint for those people. . . . Of course, we know he had to get the money from somewhere."[24]

Judge Samuel Rosenman described how Hines and other political leaders provided necessary social services in the desperate poverty that predated the New Deal. He said politicians of both parties would be at their district clubhouses every night to meet with needy constituents. "Packages of food would very frequently be sent to hungry families of the district, or buckets of coal to keep apartments warm—that kind of activity was the normal day-to-day job of the district leader. All of those things have now gone by the board, and it's very difficult for a district leader these days to obtain the same kind of popularity among the residents of the district that he could in those days before government had taken over." Rosenman allowed that such activities were costly and that, in time, Hines "fell into bad company to pay for them. He became very powerful in the city, and racketeers and gangsters who wanted favors from the city, and protection, soon began to teach him how to make soft money."[25]

Later in his life, Dewey said he realized that Tammany had helped the poor and the immigrants, but he still believed that the costs paid for corruption outweighed the benefit of the social services. To Dewey and many other reformers who came from New York's professional and wealthier classes, the case against Hines was clearcut. Dewey had come to New York with "an inborn conviction that Tammany Hall was the epitome of corruption and oppression of the poor," and he was always mystified by its influence; he could not understand how anyone could support "such a foul government." Even those more innately sympathetic to the poor, such as La Guardia, argued that the New Deal had ushered in welfare systems that obviated the need for Tammany's traditional role. Yet, as Frances Perkins noted, the nation's welfare and political systems were still in flux during the 1930s. What she said about the Seabury investigation applied as well to Dewey's prosecution of Hines: "There was a stiff upper lip, hard-boiled, exact, rigid rule of conduct being applied." Perkins approved of reform efforts, but she also recognized that many people did not hold her standards. Like Seabury, Dewey never "felt badly at having to condemn these quite good men who were kind, generous and helped out an awful lot of people out of sheer good will, but had done a number of other crooked things."[26]

Hines's popularity was shown by the many loyal followers who mobbed the courthouse as the trial began. Parole officer David Dressler, who worked across the street from the courthouse, was amazed at the scene. He remembered, "I was fascinated by the fact that the public sympathy—if you could judge by those people in Foley Square, if they represented a random sample—their sympathies were all with Hines. When he appeared, they would applaud, and they'd cry, 'Jimmy Good Luck to you, Jimmy!' When one of Dewey's men appeared, they quieted down. Then when Dewey showed up, they actually hissed him." Publicly, Hines seemed to take the case in stride. On the opening day of trial, in a clear reference to Dewey, he noted that "young men are always cruel."[27]

Dewey steered clear of any ambivalence about Hines's activities. His goal was to paint the politician with the same broad brush as the racketeers, thereby denying him sympathy. To prove the extent to which Hines and Tammany had corrupted justice, Dewey went beyond demonstrating his ties to Schultz; he dredged up the whole question of the 1935 investigation. In essence, Dewey was proving that the runaway grand jury had been right about the "big shots" behind the rackets. He picked up on the 1935 grand jury's belief that those beholden to Hines included former District Attorney Dodge. In so doing, Dewey went beyond the scope of the indictment and seriously jeopardized his case. Dewey always was convinced that Dodge was crooked and not merely incompetent or ineffectual. Lehman regarded the former district attorney, more accurately, as an honest but weak man who "let his lackluster subordinates run the office." Lehman's assessment was probably correct, because despite great efforts, Dewey's office was never able to gather enough evidence to indict Dodge. Perhaps out of frustration, Dewey attempted to use the Hines trial to prove Dodge's corruption. He told the jury that Hines had picked Dodge as district attorney because "he's stupid, respectable, and my man." Dodge had not stood for reelection, and dragging his name into the case complicated it needlessly. Still, Dewey might have prevailed had he been trying the case before McCook. But Pecora had a stronger sense of fair play.[28]

From the outset, Dewey faced an uphill battle against Stryker and Pecora. The defense attorney criticized the prosecutor's every move, and Pecora often upheld his objections. Dewey, unused to rebukes, sulked and complained. At one point, he accused Pecora of treating him like "an interloper in the courtroom." On August 23, Dewey objected to the defense attorneys' calling of sidebar conferences, saying that members of his office knew the criminal law well enough to proceed without interruption. Pecora replied that he would call conferences regardless of objections from either side. When Dewey complained that Pecora chastised him more than he did Stryker, Pecora denied favoritism. He did admit to calling "the district attorney's attention, perhaps at times forcibly, to certain acts, certain statements, certain conduct that I thought were improper and should not have been indulged in in the presence of the jury." For example, Pecora admonished Dewey for interrupting the testimony of one of his own witnesses by asking him to step out of the witness chair and plead guilty. "That was wholly improper," Pecora stated, "and should not have been done, and I would rebuke anybody for doing a thing like that." Dewey continued to argue with the judge about his alleged unfairness; Pecora insisted he wanted to be fair to both sides and would afford the defendants all their rights under the law. To Dewey's complaint that Pecora's remarks were "sharp," the judge answered: "The District Attorney occupies no higher status on this trial than does counsel for the defendant so far as the court is concerned. The district attorney is the attorney for one party to a litigation, which is this criminal trial or action, and as such has no greater rights than counsel for the defendant. That is true and should be true in every criminal defense."[29]

The bickering continued when Dewey called the former manager of the Schultz operations, George Weinberg. Weinberg described how he delivered money to Hines at his Central Park West apartment, prompting Hines to yell out, "You know you lie." Stryker later showed that Schultz did not move to the apartment until several weeks after Weinberg claimed to have visited him there. Weinberg's description of how Schultz arranged for cases to be dismissed and police transfers to aid the racket drew numerous objections from Stryker and moved Pecora to restate many of Dewey's questions so they would be "proper." Dewey was so angered by Stryker's interruptions and Pecora's corrections that he told the judge, "May I suggest, Your Honor, that you permit me to examine the witness." The continual squabbling drew as much press attention as the evidence. Dewey was typically cocky. On August 10, 1938, he wrote his mother: "Don't be disturbed about the press reports of conflict in the court room. It is highly necessary to cool off my noisy opponent once in a while, and both interchanges have been highly profitable. I don't believe I can educate him into conducting himself like a lawyer, but I do think I can teach him that some things will do him more harm than good. If I can do that, the [Hines] trial will move more rapidly."[30]

During his month-long presentation, Dewey called more than fifty witnesses, including Tammany boss John Curry, who testified against his chief rival for control of the Hall. Pecora later recalled that "Curry was obviously ill at ease and perspiring profusely" as he described Hines's many requests for transfers of honest police and for the nomination of Dodge as district attorney. When Curry finished, Hines stood up and, "in a voice that trembled with emotion but which was otherwise firm, he said, pointing his finger at Curry as Curry was leaving the stand, 'John, you lie, and you know that you lie.' " The highlight of Dewey's case was Dixie Davis, who described how Hines persuaded Dodge to stymie the 1935 grand jury investigation. On September 7, Dewey closed his case and Stryker moved for dismissal of the charges, claiming Dewey had not adequately proven the existence of a conspiracy. Pecora refused the motion after Dewey's staff persuaded him with a twenty-six-page brief to the contrary.[31]

Stryker began the case for the defense by criticizing Dewey's key witnesses, calling Dixie Davis a crook and Weinberg a rattlesnake. His first witness was Lyon Boston, the Dodge staff member assigned to the 1935 grand jury investigation. Dewey had maintained that Dodge assigned Boston to the complex inquiry because he was the least experienced member of his staff. Boston, whose father was president of the American Bar Association, testified that he had been assigned to the probe because he was one of the two Republicans in the district attorney's office. He defended his handling of the case and his failure to pursue leads about Hines's wrongdoing. The only direct evidence about Hines, Boston said, came from a reluctant newspaper reporter. Although others named the politician, their testimony was based on rumors and Boston judged it "equally incompetent." On cross-examination Dewey pressed Boston by reading from grand jury minutes, which indicated that one of those "unreliable" witnesses was Commissioner of Markets William Fellowes Morgan. When Boston claimed he could not remember Morgan's testimony, Dewey reminded him that Morgan had testified about Hines's connection to poultry racketeer Tootsie Herbert. Stryker objected and asked for a mistrial on the grounds that Dewey had prejudiced the jury by raising evidence of another crime. Dewey defended himself, claiming that Stryker had opened the line of questioning by instructing Boston: "Just tell the entire story of the March grand jury." Pecora angrily disagreed and said he would consider the mistrial motion over the weekend.[32]

During the weekend Dewey assistant Stanley Fuld delivered a twenty-page brief to Pecora's home on Riverside Drive. After considering it and hearing arguments from both sides on Monday morning, Pecora declared a mistrial on Monday, September 13. He announced his decision in a "two-hour lecture about law and justice." "This court feels that a very serious and fatally prejudicial error was caused to this defendant by the asking of that question. This court feels that no amount of instruction, regardless of how so ever carefully phrased, and regardless of the amount of earnestness with which the court could convey its instructions to the jury, could guarantee that this jury, composed as I believe it to be of men of intelligence, would literally follow that instruction."[33]

Hines was cheered by his supporters outside the courtroom, while Dewey and his men were booed. The district attorney took his first major defeat sullenly. He could not understand Pecora's ruling. He had mentioned collateral crimes in the Luciano prosecution numerous times without problems. Dewey, ever convinced of his own rectitude, jumped to the conclusion that Pecora's decision "was not all according to Hoyle" and that he may have been "reached" by someone in the Democratic party. Years later, the defeat still smarted. He saw Pecora's comments during the trial as a "strictly political" attempt to thwart his gubernatorial ambitions. "We were supported by the law, but Pecora for his own reasons granted a mistrial, and some of his New Deal friends on law school faculties sustained his action in law review articles."[34]

In fact, most trial lawyers and even members of Dewey's staff recognized he had erred. In later years, Pecora said he was "surprised" when Dewey asked his question because it revealed a weak understanding of evidentiary rules. As the judge noted, "A good working knowledge of the law of evidence is the hallmark of a good trial lawyer." In addition, Pecora also commented that Dewey's "tendency to be too histrionic" showed he was a better administrator than a trial lawyer. Fuld, who described Pecora as a "very careful judge," thought he had gone too far in declaring a mistrial but admitted that the issue "was an open one in law journals of the times." Another Dewey assistant, Sol Gelb, also believed Pecora's ruling wrong, but he remembered that he had warned Dewey about "going a little too far into collateral matters. . . . The red light shone for me, apparently it didn't shine for Dewey." Publicly too the case raised questions about Dewey's legal skills. Columnist Drew Pearson said the mistrial proved that Dewey was nothing more than an arrogant and "slipshod" lawyer. Another Dewey assistant, Harris Steinberg, described Dewey as a competent but not a great trial lawyer and pointed out that he didn't have a great deal of experience. Dewey "wasn't essentially a trial lawyer," Steinberg said. "He was a prosecutor, an administrator, the head of an office."[35]

Dewey worried that the Hines mistrial might hurt his gubernatorial chances. Several hours after Pecora's ruling he met with Medalie, Kenneth Simpson, and his other political advisors to assess the damage. They spent several hours trying to predict the effect of the mistrial on the public perception of Dewey. Gelb recalled that there was a lot of discussion about whether Dewey "should show the public that he was on the job" by indicting someone in the next day or two. Finally, the politicians decided to follow Gelb's suggestion that Dewey issue a statement saying, "Make no mistake about it, Hines will be brought to justice." His statement the next day received front-page coverage, and Dewey's supporters took it as a sign that even abject defeat could not dishearten their hero. As one commentator noted, "If ever a man stood face to face with catastrophe, Dewey did on that day. The prosecution's case against Hines had been completely disclosed to the defense, and now—mistrial. The wiseacres predicted that Hines would never face trial again. Dewey would call the thing off. Many of his friends thought that would be the wiser course, but Dewey faced his dejected assistants in his office and said 'let's get busy boys. We're going to start all over.' "[36]

Dewey was able to retain public esteem in part because many members of the press and public, failing to appreciate the legalities underlying Pecora's ruling, believed Pecora had released a clearly guilty man on a mere legal technicality. The New York Times wrote that Pecora, by declaring a mistrial, had "made useless for all present purposes a great mass of evidence, which was carefully and painstakingly adduced. He has imposed on the community the expense of a new trial. He had made it necessary for the people to begin the case anew, searching in the first instance for a jury which will not be prejudiced, now that so much evidence and so detailed an account of all the court disputes have been spread upon the record, fully published and widely read. Justice Pecora has made a profound mistake of judgment."[37]

In response to the stinging editorial Pecora called a press conference to defend his action. He also met with Lehman, who regretted the situation but could do nothing. Taking advantage of public outrage, on September 15 Dewey discussed various options, including asking Lehman to assign the case to a different judge or having it moved to the regular state Supreme Court docket. On September 21, Pecora agreed to transfer the case to a general sessions court but retained the right to sentence the government witnesses. In his decision, Pecora said, he had "always con-curred in the wisdom of the custom, long prevalent . . . that the retrial of a case be held before a Justice other than the one who presided over the original trial—regardless of whether the retrial be necessitated by a mistrial or a reversal of justice."[38]

Pecora's declaration of a mistrial benefited Dewey in two ways. First, it paved the way for a stronger case and surer conviction the second time around. As Dewey assistant Harris Steinberg recalled, the jurors in the first trial were not impressive; moreover, because the judge was hostile, the jury may well have acquitted Hines. Second, the ruling helped rather than hindered Dewey's gubernatorial aspirations. According to Dewey Republicans viewed the Hines mistrial as a rallying call against Demo-cratic corruption and the decision created "unusual unity between the older and newer elements of the Republican Party."[39]

Dewey received the party's nomination in late September and spent the next six weeks campaigning against Lehman. He tried to capitalize on the Hines mistrial by arguing that it indicated a Democratic conspir-acy, but Lehman successfully countered allegations that he was tied to Tammany by pointing to his record. After Dewey lost the election, he settled back into the district attorney's job and prepared for the second trial. He immersed himself in the case to such an extent that he missed the opportunity to meet Anthony Eden, the future prime minister of England. Eden and his wife were visiting city councilman Joseph Clark Baldwin and asked to meet Dewey. As Baldwin recalled it, "Tom said that he was too busy with the Hines case but if the Foreign Minister of Great Britain would come down to his office, he'd be happy to give him a few moments. He said that he would send a motorcycle escort for him. . . . I explained to him that a man of Mr. Eden's importance couldn't quite accept that kind of an invitation and that furthermore he had his own motorcycle escort."[40]

The Hines retrial began on January 23, 1939, before General Sessions Judge Charles C. Nott, Jr., an experienced trial judge who had served as an assistant district attorney to the legendary William Travers Jerome. Nott "had ice water in his veins and was a very fine lawyer." Thus, he kept a much tighter rein on the high-spirited lawyers for both sides than Pecora had. Dewey's staff was much better prepared for the retrial because they had already been through "a dress rehearsal." The extra preparation paid off when one of Dewey's key witnesses committed suicide during the first week of trial. On January 29, while George Weinberg was being protected by police in a rented house in White Plains, he took a gun a guard had left in a closet, went into the bathroom, and shot himself. Dixie Davis said Weinberg worried that he would become a gangland target when Dewey left office. News of Weinberg's death was kept from the jury until it was time for his testimony; then Nott calmly told the jury about Weinberg's suicide. Dewey's staff introduced Weinberg's evidence by reading his testimony from the first trial into the record.[41]

Weinberg's death was not the only dramatic episode in the retrial. Mrs. Dutch Schultz took the stand to describe how her husband had introduced her to Hines, then told her to forget she had ever met him. But the highlight of the prosecution's case came when former District Attorney Dodge was called to describe his dealings with Hines. He had known Hines for twenty years and regarded him as a parent figure; they often played golf together and visited each other's homes. Dodge admitted that Hines had contributed to his campaign in 1933, but the district attorney denied any quid pro quo. Dodge said he never believed Hines was dishonest, or that the Tammany boss interfered with his investigations. Dodge explained that he had appointed Boston to the 1935 grand jury investigation because he was not affiliated with the Democratic party; his lack of experience had nothing to do with the decision. Dewey's sniping at Dodge nearly cost him the second trial. He questioned Dodge about his campaign contributions, trying to show that much of the money had come from illicit sources. When he referred to Dodge's "gangster contributors," Stryker moved for a mistrial. Dewey and Stryker argued so bitterly that Nott finally threatened to hold both of them in contempt of court.[42]

Dewey was so concerned about the weakness of his case that he resorted to a "psychological" strategy to keep Hines from testifying in his own behalf. On February 22, the day of the politician's scheduled testimony, Dewey staffers brought a large file cabinet into the courtroom; it presumably held enough evidence to attack any statement Hines made. Dewey also prepared to call Hines's mistress, who had been "kept under wraps . . . ready to blast apart what remained of Jimmy's reputation as a

God-fearing family man." Hines declined to testify, and Dewey prepared his final arguments for the jury.[43]

Stryker's emotional closing attacked the credibility of Dewey's witnesses. He also questioned Dewey's ethics for impugning other witnesses, such as Dodge, without indicting them. The district attorney replied that he had no evidence to indict Dodge or the magistrates who did favors for Hines. He explained that there was nothing to show that the legal officers set out to help gangsters; they did not know "they were doing anything more than a favor for a politician to whom they were beholden." Dewey insinuated there was something sinister about the fact that Dodge had turned to Hines for money instead of one of the thirty-four other Democratic district leaders in New York County. "Why Hines, unless . . . Hines picked Dodge. Hines financed his campaign. Hines asked for no other candidates that year on the county ticket. He was interested in only one on the city-wide ticket. No county office, no judicial office, just DA. Why just DA? . . . Well, if you were Dutch Schultz, trying to figure out how to keep your power, to be safe, what would you do?"[44]

Nott's instructions to the jury lasted only forty-five minutes, and the jurors took less than a day to convict Hines. When their decision was announced, "Stryker wept. Hines said he felt as if he'd just been kicked in the belly. . . . Dewey declared the verdict a victory for decency." On March 23, 1939, Nott sentenced Hines to four to eight years in the penitentiary. If any of the witnesses against him were threatened, he warned, Hines would get the maximum term. Meanwhile Judge Pecora, who retained power to sentence the government witnesses, gave Davis one year and the bankers Pompez and Ison suspended sentences. Stryker withdrew from the case, and Hines appointed a new attorney who persuaded Supreme Court Justice Peter J. Schmuck to release him pending his appeal. Hines, ever popular in his home district, was greeted by cheers from supporters at the Monongahela Club.[45]

The Hines appeal raised and settled a key issue in New York criminal law. It was the first time the appellate courts had considered the culpability of a "fixer." Dewey had indicted Hines for taking part in a racket because it was easier than trying to prove he had corrupted the justice system through Dodge and several magistrates. Pecora had objected to the charges, saying that Dewey was taking a backdoor method, but the New York high courts upheld Dewey's approach. In *People* v. *Hines*, the Court of Appeals held "that a person who fixed, or attempted to fix arrests and prosecutions—who obtained for his confederates a freedom from arrest and a virtual immunity from conviction—was a principal in the crimes with which his associates had been charged, and that he could be prosecuted."[46]

The Hines case cemented Dewey's reputation as a crime buster and won him plaudits from across the nation. A typical letter of praise came from William C. Clohan of Martinsburg, West Virginia: "As one of thousands of young 'red-blooded Americans' who believe in the American principles and for everything that is right and just, I read with a great deal of joy and satisfaction, that you again had triumphed after a hard fought battle. . . . Millions of Americans who have been watching with a great and keen interest your fight against heavy odds for the better things of life, are pulling for you 100%. This victory instilled in me and many millions of others, faith and hope that you with divine guidance are the one to lead this great country of Our's . . . back to a period of Normalcy, Common Sense and Reconstruction."[47]

Pecora recognized that the Hines case had taken on symbolic value far beyond its individual merit. After the first trial, Pecora received letters and news clippings about his ruling from across the country, and even from England. The case "seemed to epitomize, or to culminate, a great moral and political crusade. . . . As a matter of fact, there is no Democratic organization called Tammany Hall. It's an idiomatic term, and particularly west of the Hudson River, it has connotations of fraud and corruption to an almost supernal degree." After Hines, the only famous New York crooks of the 1930s who eluded prosecution were labor racketeers Lepke and Gurrah. They remained fugitives until the mid-1940s. With his prosecutor's job seemingly done, Dewey turned his attention to his party's 1940 presidential nomination. Recognizing how close he had come to losing the Hines trial, Dewey never again tried another case himself. As he told Republican party chairman Kenneth Simpson, losing a case might "jeopardize his reputation."[48]

$$\approx\ \approx\ \approx\ \approx$$

Conclusion

ITH THE CONVICTION of Hines, reformers had achieved their ultimate goal of crippling the Tammany Tiger. The political machine that had ruled New York since the early nineteenth century lay in symbolic ruins. Of course, reformers could not claim all the glory; political machines in cities across the nation were waning, their strength and raison d'être undermined by demographic shifts and expanding social services. Still, the evolution from old to new did not come easily. In fact, the whole 1930s reform decade in New York County serves as an example of just how much energy went into this wrenching transformation. *Rising crime rates, racketeers,* and *political corruption* became catchwords by which contemporaries labeled deeper institutional changes they did not fully comprehend.

The reform efforts of the 1930s did not eradicate crime in New York County. But assessing just how effective the efforts were is problematic. Crime statistics are notoriously unreliable, and in New York County the methods of keeping them varied from year to year, making comparisons impossible.[1] Further complicating any discussion of crime, then or now, is the difficulty of defining the term. La Guardia's first police chief saw crime largely in terms of communist disruption and worker unrest. The mayor, a supporter of the labor movement, believed greater evils lay in racketeering. A mugging victim and the cop on the beat were more concerned with street crime. Dewey, of course, focused on racketeering, which he defined as "the business of intimidation for the purpose of regularly extorting money."[2] Defining terms precisely is a task for scholars, but for the public crime is usually a confusing nexus that does not distinguish among social unrest, teenage delinquency, street violence, and gangsters. Thus, when Governor Al Smith took a stand against corruption in New York City's magistrates' courts, he received accolades for fighting gambling and bootlegging. And, despite Dewey's well-publicized mission as a special prosecutor investigating organized crime, he was inundated with tips about streetwalkers and juvenile delinquents.

This confusion about the definition of crime helped create a constant reservoir of fear that could be tapped by politicians appealing with equal success to foes of public corruption, widows worried about street muggings, and businessmen concerned about labor racketeering. At the same time, such political expediency made meaningful change difficult, because reformers rarely worked from a clear definition or agenda. Politicians took credit for cleaning up crime as a general problem by citing specific examples and narrow areas of improvement; and without clearly stated goals, voters were unable to measure the accuracy of their self-congratulatory claims.

The politicians of New York successfully played on these shifting and contradictory notions of crime. La Guardia attacked vice mongers, labor racketeers, business executives, and Tammany hacks with equal vigor. Lehman took an equally comprehensive approach to the problem. Those attending his crime conference discussed every possible aspect of law enforcement, from prayer in school to murder. Dewey benefited politically from his labor racketeering prosecutions, which many Republicans took to be a drive against union organizing.

Although measuring crime and evaluating the success of anticrime measures is difficult, discerning anxieties about crime is not. The literature and cinema of the 1930s clearly show a nation in the throes of one of its periodic cycles of concern with crime; contemporaries sincerely believed that the number and severity of crimes were increasing. The 1930s was not unique in this regard. It would be impossible to show that the gangsters of the 1930s attracted more attention than the gunslingers of the Old West or the drug dealers of the 1990s. The common theme among these disparate crime waves is the perception that the judicial system has been overwhelmed by a changing, increasing, or misunderstood criminal menace. A study of law enforcement in the Indian Territory during the 1890s shows an area overwhelmed by population growth and complex demographic shifts, while its courts and sheriffs were underfunded and understaffed.³ In New York County during the 1920s and 1930s, the organization of crime created new problems for similarly outmoded legal machinery geared to less-sophisticated criminal enterprises.

Politicians argued that crime had increased so much and grown so sinister that only extraordinary and expensive methods could be used to eradicate it. To some extent, this theory was justified. Crime had changed. Rothstein and his followers organized the city's small, ethnic gangs into large-scale operations modeled after corporations. Historians have argued that this transformation took place during Prohibition, but it began much earlier. If anything, the huge profits raked in during Prohibition only speeded up a process already under way. This was apparent in New York City, where Arnold Rothstein began bankrolling other criminals in the 1910s. Schultz, Luciano, Lepke, and Gurrah adopted Rothstein's methods and became the banes of law enforcement. Plagued by insufficient budgets and old-fashioned methods, New York's police and prosecutors were ill equipped to fight organized crime. They occasionally arrested lower-level members of these syndicates but were unable to pierce the middle and upper echelons.

Since the 1920s legal reformers had theorized about how organized crime should be fought. Inspired partly by the rise of sociology and its sister field, criminology, reformers believed crime could be fought on a more scientific basis; close study of its causes would point the way to eradication. Although not all judges and prosecutors joined in this cheery prediction, most seemed tinged with a new hope that the modernization of investigative methods and prosecutions could make significant inroads. In New York, legal experts pushed for a "crime bureau" modeled after J. Edgar Hoover's recently created Federal Bureau of Investigation; it would rely on "scientific" methods of fingerprinting, wiretapping, and statistics generation. Leading members of the criminal bar pushed for the type of costly, complex prosecutions U.S. Justice Department lawyers had used effectively against Al Capone.⁴

Persuading New Yorkers to underwrite such expensive changes at the state level was never easy. Reformers during the 1920s had not recognized the extent to which public support was needed to modernize the legal system. Only when astute politicians such as La Guardia, Lehman, and

Dewey adopted well-publicized anticrime agendas did reform go forward. Recognizing that galvanizing public support would help fight crime while furthering his political career, La Guardia made "tin horn gangsters" a major campaign theme. Lehman convened a meeting of experts to raise public awareness about crime, and Dewey expostulated on the political influence of sinister racketeers. All three men fanned the belief that New York was in the midst of a crime wave and, through their competing interests, helped bring New York's criminal justice machinery up to date.

To find the origins of the 1930s crime wave, it is necessary to dig through the mythology of the Dewey probe to its political roots. Dewey's supporters and biographers argued that New York's concern with crime began with the independent actions of New York County's special grand jury, which rebelled against a clearly dishonest Tammany district attorney. Then, Dewey was chosen as special prosecutor because his fame as a U.S. attorney made him the logical choice of grand jurors and leaders of the New York bar. In fact, New York City's anxieties about crime during the 1930s stemmed back to events that predated even the Seabury investigations of several years earlier. Nor was District Attorney Dodge as corrupt as his critics claimed. Like his predecessor, Thomas C. T. Crain, Dodge was no visionary. Both Tammany prosecutors were senior members of the bar who conducted business in a traditional fashion. They misunderstood the serious problems posed by organized crime, and they overestimated their ability to fight it without new methods. Yet, even if Crain or Dodge had had the desire to experiment with the new techniques advocated by legal reformers, they lacked the wherewithal to do so. Both district attorneys were hampered by straitened budgets, civil service hiring requirements, and the burdens of combating ordinary day-to-day street crime. Perhaps the best evidence that the two were ineffectual rather than dishonest is the fact that neither was indicted.

Closer inspection also reveals flaws in the myth of the independent runaway grand jury. In 1935 two major factors came together to bring about the grand jury's action. First was the revival of the Association of the Grand Jurors of New York County. Recognizing a threat in the growing criticism of the panels, jurors banded together in the mid-1920s to save their beloved institution. They argued that although grand juries were no longer needed to carry out their original purpose of reviewing indictments, they could still help prosecutors control crime. Federal prosecutors recognized the potential of the grand juries and used them in complex investigations. Grand jurors believed they could play a similar role at the state level and seized on their disagreement with Dodge to prove their contention. Earlier, obstreperous grand jurors were held in check by Tammany, but the Seabury investigation and La Guardia's election had begun to paint the machine as a toothless tiger.

The association's goals dovetailed with those of the Republican leaders promoting Dewey's career. Yet, Dewey, a young and relatively inexperienced trial lawyer, was not the logical choice for the special prosecutor's post. Such positions normally went to senior members of the bar such as Thomas Thacher, Charles Evans Hughes, Jr., and former U.S. attorneys George Medalie and Charles Tuttle. At Medalie's urging, the Republicans turned down Lehman's request that one of them become the special prosecutor; they astutely maneuvered the Democratic governor into launching Dewey's career. Yet, despite his inexperience, Dewey brought many skills to the special prosecutor's job. He was a hardworking, determined, and able administrator. His experience in the federal courts and his alliance with Medalie provided him with a blueprint of how to fight organized crime successfully.

He also benefited tremendously from working in a supportive environment other prosecutors would have envied. His ability to rely heavily on blue ribbon jury panels helped him choose jurors already predisposed to his cases. Critics recognized the favoritism inherent in the special jury concept, but it was not abolished as discriminatory to defendants until the 1960s. Dewey's huge budget and the independent office space he rented with it put him in a position to provide confidentiality to his witnesses. Lehman's intervention in obtaining exemptions from civil service hiring requirements meant he could employ an exceptional staff. The governor also appointed Judge Philip McCook, whose sympathetic rulings provided Dewey and his staff with a favorable judicial forum. Lastly, while all prosecutors have some degree of discretion in choosing their cases, Dewey enjoyed unusual freedom to pick only sure winners.

These advantages, combined with some of his questionable techniques, reflect the elasticity of the legal system at times of perceived crisis.

Few of his contemporaries questioned Dewey's decision to arrest hundreds of material witnesses in the Luciano case and hold them without charges until they provided the testimony he needed. In the restaurant rackets case, Dewey withheld crucial evidence from the defense and heightened public awareness by exaggerating the amounts of money involved in the racket. His handling of the Hines case was often inept. Despite these failings, few people criticized Dewey in the heated anticrime atmosphere of the 1930s. Both Dewey and La Guardia defended questionable methods by accusing critics of coddling crooks. Even Lehman, a man more attuned to civil liberties, employed harsh rhetoric about those who questioned whether a war on crime was necessary.

A prime reason that Seabury, La Guardia, Lehman, and Dewey seized on crime as a political issue was their hatred of the links traditional politicians formed with New York's underworld. Politicians and criminals had long been bedfellows in New York City, where both Democratic Tammany and the Republicans relied on thugs to harass voters and fix elections. For most of its history, however, Tammany held the upper hand, using the gangsters only as minions and sources of bag money. Critics claimed that Prohibition had tipped the power balance the other way and that well-heeled gangsters were openly buying and controlling Tammany politicians. To the extent that such a shift did take place, it was probably attributable more to the crumbling power of Tammany leadership than to any great changes in criminal influence. Still, this view took hold in the 1930s, and opposition politicians exploited it.

Splits in both the Democratic and Republican parties strengthened the appeal of the crime issue. Tammany's weakening hold over New York politics had been accelerated by the growth of progressive Democratic leaders like FDR and his handpicked successor, Lehman. This division between the old and new guard was mirrored in the Republican party, which was undergoing its own modernization efforts. Enlightened leaders such as George Medalie recognized the trend and encouraged the efforts of the Young Republicans and Dewey. Reformers were able to step into the temporary gap created while the political parties were struggling to regain unity. Disenchanted Republicans and Democrats rallied around reform efforts, creating the Fusion movement that led to La Guardia's election. To a large extent, criticism of Tammany by Seabury,

Lehman, Dewey, and La Guardia translated into a hatred of Tammany's links to the underworld.

Of course, there was nothing new about politicians' capitalizing on crime and political corruption. In 1876 Samuel Tilden had come close to capturing the White House, at least partly on his reputation as the man who brought down Boss Tweed. Theodore Roosevelt successfully parlayed his anticorruption credentials into the New York governorship and, later, the presidency.[5] Seabury, La Guardia, Lehman, and Dewey recognized the advantages of this approach. Samuel Seabury attended the 1932 Democratic National Convention hoping to be chosen as a dark horse candidate for the presidency. La Guardia made crime fighting a cornerstone of his mayoral campaigns. Lehman launched his anticrime crusade and sponsored his crime conference to counter Dewey's growing political capital. Dewey's friends viewed his appointment as special prosecutor as the first step in a triple play that would lead through Albany to the White House. Perhaps with greater success than any other local prosecutor in American history, Dewey was able to manipulate the system to further his own career. Within less than a year of winning election as district attorney, Dewey was running, albeit unsuccessfully for governor, solely on his reputation as a racket buster. Only two years later, he made an abortive bid for the Republican presidential nomination.

Dewey's early runs for political office on such limited experience are testaments to his naïveté and arrogance. Combined with his two later unsuccessful bids for the presidency, they also illustrate the limits of prosecutorial politics. Even though he received accolades as a prosecutor and later as governor of New York, many people viewed Dewey's administrative experience and credentials as limited. Moreover, his arrogance, suspicion, and reformer's smugness were not necessarily the traits of a successful national politician.

Whatever the political motives of the crime fighters, it would be a mistake to ignore the real reforms achieved in New York's legal system during the 1920s and 1930s. Public concern provided the legal system with funding and elasticity. Both state and federal law enforcement responded to the modernization of crime by advocating new techniques—wiretapping, conspiracy laws, more efficient extradition—and old ideas such as limiting Fifth Amendment privileges, instituting gun control, and revitalizing the grand jury system. Many of these proposals became reality in New York through Lehman's legislative crime package, which paved the way for uniformity and efficiency in many aspects of state law enforcement. Their value became apparent in Dewey's investigations. He employed grand jury secrecy and wiretaps to gather valuable evidence. With the use of joinder indictments, he was able to prosecute complex criminal enterprises and high-level gangsters. Dewey showed how federal strike-force techniques, especially the use of teams of accountants and lawyers, could be used to map rackets and track political payoffs.

Lehman, Dewey, and La Guardia also demonstrated that government could be run more effectively and cheaply without machine politics. They shared an optimistic belief that "no goal was out of reach" and government could work.[6] Their concrete actions created an admirable legacy. Lehman eliminated huge budget deficits while sponsoring social legislation that made New York the state laboratory for the New Deal. La Guardia expanded social services to right the city's economic woes and oversaw implementation of a modern city charter and legal code. Dewey suggested new laws, streamlined indictments, and rejuvenated the grand jury system. Together, they weakened Tammany Hall and stripped away its worst excesses.

Yet, despite their triumphs, the crime-fighting politicians of the 1930s had their flaws. In great part, their selfishness and ambition made them more successful than their predecessors. There is no doubt Roosevelt, Seabury, Lehman, La Guardia, and Dewey sincerely believed change was needed; but their vision of reform was not the do-goodism of traditional civic groups. With the exception of Lehman, what set them apart was a conceited sense of their own destinies. Their self-righteousness fueled ruthless ambition in which questions of fairness were often lost. As newspaperman Arthur Krock said, "Men in a hurry—no matter whether their objective is good or not—cut corners. They will disregard laws and customs that society puts upon itself to assure justice. They are so confident in their own causes that they will say, 'You can trust me with doing that, but don't trust him,' so they would do things they didn't believe anybody else should be allowed to do." Nevertheless, their zeal proved more effective than the sterile reform of previous decades. Or, as one contemporary aptly argued, "cupidity can be not only a more efficient, but a more compelling civic force than stupid and timorous honesty in government."[7]

Afterword

*T*HE CATACLYSMIC EVENTS of World War II pushed crime and other domestic concerns from the forefront of national attention. In part, the more relaxed public attitude about crime reflected declining crime rates as the draft depleted the ranks of men in their late teens and twenties who habitually cause most crimes.[1] But even if crime had continued at previous levels, politicians would have turned their attention to the world stage. New York's most ambitious leaders—Lehman, La Guardia, and Dewey—lusted after larger roles in the nation's fight against foreign evil. Even the city's most notorious gangsters, including Lucky Luciano, helped defeat fascism.

Lehman, who in 1938 had agreed to run for governor again only reluctantly, was even more eager to leave Albany in 1942. Roosevelt quickly tapped him to manage American refugee relief efforts as director of the Office of Foreign Relief and Rehabilitation, which soon merged with the United Nations Relief and Rehabilitation Administration established in 1943. In keeping with his philanthropic character, Lehman refused the job's $15,000 annual salary and paid all his own expenses. In a few years he grew tired of the international bickering entailed in running far-flung relief efforts and quit to lay the groundwork for a senatorial campaign. In 1946, after completing his third term as mayor of New York City, Fiorello La Guardia took over Lehman's job at the U.N.

La Guardia's last years in the mayor's office disappointed his supporters. Trouble began near the end of his second term, when La Guardia appointed his disgraced predecessor, Jimmy Walker, to a $20,000-a-year job adjudicating labor disputes in the women's garment industry. After resigning the mayor's job in 1932, Walker had attempted to flee his creditors by moving to England, marrying his girlfriend, Betty Compton, and living off her money. When Walker's creditors sued him in the London courts, the couple returned to New York, where they eventually settled at Northport, Long Island, adopted two children, and raised chickens and Irish terriers. He remained a popular figure, and his Democratic supporters lobbied La Guardia to find him a more lucrative job. As chair of the National Cloak and Suit Industry, Walker oversaw the work of thirty-five thousand employees and two thousand employers in New York City's women's garment business. When his four-year appointment in the garment industry ended, he pursued his favorite hobby, music, by becoming a record company executive. He was president of Majestic Records Company when he died of a brain clot on November 18, 1946, at the age of sixty-five.[2]

Seabury blamed Roosevelt for inducing La Guardia to appoint Walker and "forget his obligations as the reform, nonpartisan mayor of New York City." Despite their disagreements, however, La Guardia and Seabury joined forces one last time in the 1941 mayoral race. Seabury and the other Fusionists realized that La Guardia was the only independent candidate who could win the election. His narrowest victory margin, only 132,000 votes, signaled New Yorkers' waning interest in reform. The election was also Seabury's last major action for New York reform politics, although he did not die until May 7, 1958.[3]

In part, La Guardia's weaknesses during his last years as mayor can be attributed to his growing frustration at not being able to play a larger role on the world stage. One reason he appointed Jimmy Walker to the garment job was to curry favor with Roosevelt. The mayor hoped the president would put aside Democratic politics to name him secretary of war. When Roosevelt awarded that post to Henry L. Stimson, La Guardia sought appointment as a general. The Little Flower had been a major during World War I and achieved distinction as a pilot-bombardier on the Italian-Austrian front. Stimson, arguing that La Guardia could serve a much more useful role on the domestic front, appointed him director of the nation's civil defense efforts.

La Guardia's thwarted ambitions colored both his tenure as mayor and his health. He left city government in 1945 "looking older than his

62 years," according to his biographer Arthur Mann. His international relief experience took an even greater toll; by 1947 he had slipped back into the Jeremiah role he had played in his 1929 mayoral campaign against Jimmy Walker. In his last public appearance, in 1947, La Guardia intoned gloomily, "My generation has failed miserably . . . it requires more courage to keep the peace than to go to war." He died a few months later, on September 20, of pancreatic cancer.[4]

When La Guardia declined to run again in 1945, the mayoral race took a strange twist. Longtime Democrat Jonah Goldstein ran as a Republican. Goldstein had played a small role in New York's cycle of reform when Mayor Walker appointed him to investigate corruption in the magistrates' courts in an unsuccessful attempt to forestall the Seabury investigations. Goldstein was handily beaten by William O'Dwyer, a former Brooklyn judge who had risen to brigadier general in the Army Air Corps during World War II. O'Dwyer had also served for six years as Brooklyn's district attorney and had convicted labor racketeer Lepke of hiring hitmen in an operation the media dubbed "Murder, Inc." The gangster was sentenced to death and went to the electric chair in March 1944. O'Dwyer was a dismal failure as mayor, however, and gladly gave up the office in 1949 to become ambassador to Mexico. He was replaced by another lackluster mayor, Vincent R. Impellitteri. In 1950, Impellitteri won a three-way race that pitted him against Republican Edward Corsi and Judge Ferdinand Pecora, who ran as a Democrat and Liberal. Pecora, of course, had gained fame for declaring a mistrial in the first Hines case.[5]

New York City's tumultuous mayoral politics stood in stark contrast to the stability that marked the Manhattan district attorney's office. When Dewey left in 1941, he chose a list of four assistants who would make good replacements. As the only Democrat, Frank Hogan was the most logical candidate. Forward-looking Tammany bosses, tired of being battered by reformers, decided Hogan would make them look good. After meeting with Tammany Hall General Sessions Court Judge John Mullen, Dewey agreed to arrange Fusion and Republican backing for Hogan if the Democrats would support him. He easily won the November 1941 election. Ironically, the man who would serve as New York County's district attorney for more than thirty years began his political career working for Jimmy Hines. He quit the Hall after becoming disenchanted with Hines's crooked dealings and, as a Dewey assistant, helped develop the case against the Tammany boss. Hogan was district attorney when Hines was paroled on September 9, 1944, and was still Manhattan's chief legal official when Hines died thirteen years later. Earning the nickname "Mr. Integrity," Hogan ran eight times with multiparty backing and served as district attorney an unprecedented nine terms before dying in his sleep in 1974. He institutionalized and improved upon many of Dewey's reforms; in the process, he made the New York County district attorney's office a model for the nation.[6]

Although Roosevelt and Lehman feared Dewey would reverse the trend of their reforms, he proved to be a progressive and able administrator during his twelve years as governor of New York. Among other improvements, he supervised the reapportionment of congressional and state legislative districts, increased state aid to education, established the state's first commission to eliminate religious and racial discrimination, and liberalized the unemployment insurance laws. His stellar judicial appointments included George Medalie, who died in 1946 after Dewey had elevated him to the New York Court of Appeals.[7]

Dewey's efforts in New York politics were always overshadowed by his thwarted ambitions to become president. In 1940, he sought the Republican presidential nomination on the basis of his limited experience as Manhattan's district attorney. When the nomination went to Robert Taft, party leaders began cultivating Dewey for 1944. With World War II still raging, it was no surprise when Dewey lost the election to Roosevelt, but 1948 was different. Every leading journalist and political commentator in the nation predicted a Dewey victory. When Harry S. Truman scored the stunning upset, Dewey joined the small but select group of sure winners who ended up losing. The other two were also New Yorkers: Samuel Tilden, who achieved fame for prosecuting Boss Tweed; and Charles Evans Hughes, a heavyweight of the New York bar, former U.S. chief justice, and governor of New York. One of the few people not surprised by the election result was Alice Roosevelt Longworth, who said, "We should have known he couldn't win. A soufflé never rises twice.[8]

In his last years as governor, Dewey's otherwise unblemished record was marred by two controversies. The first centered on the 1950 gubernatorial race. Lieutenant Governor Robert Hanley announced plans to run when it appeared that Dewey would not seek a third term. When Dewey decided to run again, he and other Republican leaders persuaded Hanley to campaign for a U.S. Senate seat against Lehman. Hanley agreed to run only after Dewey and other party leaders promised to pay off his debts and guarantee him a state job if he lost the tough election. When the trade-off came to light in October 1950, Dewey and Hanley denied the blatant deal making, but their stories were belied by a letter Dewey had written to Hanley, which fell into the hands of the Democrats. *New York Post* columnist Max Lerner said Dewey's excuses were "reminiscent of the delightfully involved explanations the Tammany boys under Jimmy Walker used to have about their little tin boxes. And what an irony it is that a man like Dewey, whose whole career has been built on care and canniness and cunning—should now have taken such a whopper."[9] Dewey was reelected by a large margin despite the controversy, which later became the subject of a U.S. Senate subcommittee investigation.

A second major controversy revolved around Dewey's decision to commute Lucky Luciano's sentence so that he could be released from prison and deported to Italy on February 2, 1946. Political critics claimed Dewey released the gangster after Luciano gave large campaign contributions to the Republican party. In reality, Luciano had helped the American war effort by recruiting gangster associates in New York and Sicily to gather information for naval intelligence. Early in the war, U.S. officials became concerned about the large number of German U-boats sinking ships off the Atlantic Coast. They reasoned that the submarines could remain close to shore only if they were receiving supplies from the coast. To obtain information about suspected saboteurs, his Washington superiors ordered Naval Commander Charles R. Haffendon to enlist the help of Joseph "Socks" Lanza, the gangster who controlled New York's docks. Haffendon contacted Murray Gurfein, who still worked in the district attorney's office, and Luciano's lawyer, Moses Polakoff, to obtain Lanza's aid. With the approval of Judge McCook, they arranged meetings between Lanza and Luciano; the latter gave the go-ahead to the deal and also tried to use his Sicilian contacts to provide information for the Allied landing in Italy. In exchange, Luciano was promised he would be freed and deported after the war.

Initially, Luciano's parole provoked little controversy. He was one of seven foreign-born criminals Dewey paroled for deportation on January 3, 1946. The press release announcing the commutations was routine. Luciano's designation as Public Enemy Number One was gone; he was referred to only as leader of a prostitution syndicate with a former conviction of drugs possession; he was forty-eight years old, had a satisfactory prison record, and had helped the armed services. The state parole board approved all seven commutations. In the early 1950s, however, Dewey's action took on a sinister aura amid a new wave of public hysteria about organized crime generated by the U.S. Senate investigation named for its chair, Estes Kefauver, a Democrat from Tennessee.[10]

Facing public pressure, both the navy and the former head of wartime intelligence, William Donovan, denied they had recruited gangsters like Luciano, Lanza, Joe Adonis, and Meyer Lansky, who had all provided help to the federal government during the war. Naval officials refused to let Haffenden tell the Kefauver committee the truth about the New York operations, and he died a broken and disgraced man in December 1952. Dewey claimed to be "indisposed" and refused to appear at the Kefauver hearings. Tabloid journalists criticized Dewey's failure to testify; one claimed that Dewey had risen to national fame by framing Luciano on perjured testimony, commuted Luciano's long sentence because he feared exposure, then spent taxpayers' money on a cover-up.[11]

Questions about Dewey's actions in the Luciano case provoked such controversy because the Kefauver hearings fueled the myth that a well-organized, secretive Italian crime syndicate, the Mafia, controlled vice in the United States. According to this rewriting of history, Luciano had fathered modern organized crime by uniting disparate vice operations and running the various enterprises along business principles. His deportation only added to his mystique. Harry Anslinger, U.S. commissioner of narcotics, made much of this theory, arguing that Luciano remained czar of a vast drug empire that provided most of the heroin flowing into the United States. The rumors continued until Luciano's death from a heart attack on January 26, 1962, in Naples. His family retrieved the body and interred him in the family vault at St. John's Cemetery in Queens.

As Luciano's reputation waxed, Dewey left the public limelight and began a lucrative law practice, continuing to play an important role in

Republican party politics. Perhaps his most noteworthy action as the party's elder statesman was persuading Eisenhower to choose Richard Nixon as his running mate. Later, in 1968, Nixon offered to nominate Dewey as chief justice of the Supreme Court, but Dewey declined because of his age. He remained a frequent visitor to the Nixon White House until his death from a heart attack at age sixty-eight in March 1971.[13]

Unlike Dewey, Lehman completed his life in public service with an unblemished record. In a state served by some of the nation's most skilled and charismatic politicians, Lehman set a record by winning eight statewide elections. His first and only loss came in 1946, when he ran for the U.S. Senate against Irving M. Ives, who had been a major opponent of his crime package in the 1936 legislature. In the scandalous 1950 Senate race, Lehman ran again, this time handily defeating Robert Hanley. He continued to push for progressive legislation and made headlines as an outspoken critic of Senator Joseph McCarthy's high-handed red-baiting tactics during the Cold War. Lehman recognized that fighting the junior senator from Wisconsin was not popular at the time, but declared that "My conscience will be easier, though I realize my political prospects may be more difficult."[14]

In 1956 Lehman refused to run again; at age 78, he said, he was too old. He did help found the New York Committee for Democratic Voters that year and influenced New York Mayor Robert Wagner to declare war on the New York County Democratic bosses led by Carmine DeSapio. The anti-boss movement peaked in the 1961 election, which sent DeSapio into political no-man's-land and resulted in a big Wagner victory. Two years later, when Lehman died from a heart attack at age eighty-five, the *New York Times* called him "a towering figure in the liberal political movement in the United States and a noted philanthropist."

≈ ≈ ≈

Notes

PROLOGUE

1. Damon Runyon, *Guys and Dolls,* in *The Damon Runyon Omnibus,* 78, 141, 149.
   F. Scott Fitzgerald, *The Great Gatsby,* 69–74, 134–35, 166–67, 171–73.
2. Eliot Asinof, *Eight Men Out: The Black Sox and the 1919 World Series,* 12–15,
   45–47, 132–36, 147–48; David Quentin Voight, *American Baseball II: From the
   Commissioners to Continental Expansion,* 124–26, 131–33; Leo Katcher, *The Big
   Bankroll: The Life and Times of Arnold Rothstein,* 144. Voight's is the most
   coherent and plausible description of the 1919 fix, but Katcher and Asinof
   dispute his interpretation.
3. Myron J. Smith, Jr., lists articles and books about the scandal in *Baseball: A
   Comprehensive Bibliography,* 76–79.
4. Herbert Asbury, *The Gangs of New York: An Informal History of the Underworld;* Katcher, *Big Bankroll,* 230, 232; Craig Thompson and Allen Raymond,
   Gang Rule in New York: The Story of a Lawless Era.
5. Benjamin Stolberg, *Tailor's Progress: The Story of a Famous Union and the Men
   Who Made It Great,* 139; for information on the testimonial dinner, see Katcher, *Big Bankroll,* 12. Clarke, *The Age of Rothstein,* 15, 19–20, 135.
6. Katcher, *Big Bankroll,* 232–35.
7. Stolberg, *Tailor's Progress,* 253, and, for Rothstein's role in the garment strike,
   138–41. Katcher, *Big Bankroll,* 284–86, puts a somewhat different spin on the
   story.
8. Harry J. Anslinger and William F. Tompkins, *The Traffic in Narcotics,* 263–64.
   For more information about the federal war against narcotics, see ibid., chap.
   5; for details about drugs in New York City during the 1920s, see ibid., 193–99;
   and Katcher, *Big Bankroll,* 283–84. Congress passed the first act regulating
   narcotics in 1909 and put teeth in the law in 1914 by enacting the Harrison
   Narcotic Law, which levied a tax on producers, importers, and sellers of opium
   and coca leaves. Enforcement of the Harrison Act began in earnest in the early
   1920s after the Supreme Court ruled it constitutional.

9. Katcher, *Big Bankroll*, 23–29, 74, 292.

10. *The Reminiscences of Ferdinand Pecora* (1962), 557–61, Oral History Collection, Columbia University (hereafter COH).

11. Katcher, *Big Bankroll*, 1, 318–19, 336–44.

12. Pecora, COH, 559–81.

13. Ibid., 582.

14. *The Reminiscences of Frances Perkins*, Part 3 (1951–55), 3:450, COH; *The Reminiscences of Reuben Lazarus* (1949–51), 123, 127, COH.

15. Perkins, COH, 3:411, 421–22; Ernest Cuneo, *Life with Fiorello*, 2.

16. *The Reminiscences of William H. Allen* (1949–50), 451, COH; Arthur Mann, *La Guardia: A Fighter Against His Times 1882–1993*, 270–78; Lawrence Elliott, *Little Flower: The Life and Times of Fiorello La Guardia*, 162–63; William Manners, *Patience and Fortitude: Fiorello La Guardia*, 42, 90–92; Bella Rodman with Philip Sterling, *Fiorello La Guardia*, 78–79.

   The Reminiscences of Paul Windels (1949–50), 76–78, COH; *The Reminiscences of Mrs. Walter Bunzl* (1949), 86–87, COH. La Guardia received only 368,000 votes to Walker's 865,000, while Socialist candidate Norman Thomas picked up 175,000.

17. Katcher, *Big Bankroll*, ix; for details of La Guardia's congressional career and analysis of his relationship to contemporary political movements, see Mann, *La Guardia*, 281–313, 320–26, 223–230.

CHAPTER ONE

1. *The Reminiscences of George W. Alger*, Part 2 (1952), 2:286, *The Reminiscences of Jeremiah T. Mahoney* (1949), 124; *The Reminiscences of David Dressler* (1960–61), 133–33a—all in COH. In New York, trial courts and lower appellate courts collectively are called the Supreme Court. The state's highest appellate court is known as the court of appeals.

2. Report of the Municipal Court Commission, 25 February 1923 (hereafter Court Report); Public Papers of Governor Al Smith, New York State Archives, Albany (hereafter Smith Papers), 2, 9, 11, 15, 19, 23–24. The Democrats controlled the first, fourth, and sixth, while the Republicans controlled the fifth and ninth wards.

3. Court Report, 3–4, 27.

4. New York's attempts to outlaw liquor were contained in two laws passed by the 1921 legislature: Chapter 156 added a new section to the penal code, and Chapter 157 was a civil statute allowing recovery of money damages from liquor sellers whose customers injured third parties, Laws of New York, vols. I–III, 144th sess. (1921): 513–22.

   "A rapidly growing cancer" quote from *The Reminiscences of Charles Tuttle* (1961–64), 178, COH; Louis A. Cuvillier to Al Smith, 26 April 1923, Smith

Papers. This incident took on a comic tone when Enright filed a $100,000 slander suit against Cuvillier and Cuvillier responded by filing Assembly Bill No. PR. 2368 calling for a legislative investigation. He also asked Smith to appoint a state attorney to represent him, but Smith declined to get involved in the matter, urging him to contact the attorney general himself. Cuvillier to New York State Attorney General Carl Sherman, 2 June 1923, Smith Papers.

5. Additional Grand Jury, 1922, New York County; presentment filed with Judge Francis X. Mancuso of the Court of General Sessions of the Peace in and for New York County, 21 December 1922, Smith Papers.

6. Tuttle, *Reminiscences,* COH, 178, 186. Repeal of Mullen-Gage Bill, Laws of New York, vol. I–II, 146th sess. (1923), chap. 871, 1690. La Guardia's actions were denounced by state officials in Albany, who vowed to arrest anyone making beer in New York. La Guardia staged another well-publicized show in New York City and asked to be arrested, but a policeman refused, saying: "Oh, that's a job for a Prohibition agent" (Elliott, *Little Flower,* 153–54). Discussions about Prohibition in New York politics are found in Richard O'Connor, *The First Hurrah: A Biography of Alfred E. Smith,* 141–43, and Paula Eldot, *Governor Al Smith: The Politician as Reformer,* 343–77.

7. Mahoney, *Reminiscences,* COH, 124; *The Reminiscences of Edward Flynn* (1950), 11, COH.

8. Perkins, *Reminiscences,* COH, 2:299–301. Many historians have argued that women's suffrage made little difference because women followed their husbands' lead at the polls. Perkins rejects this notion, citing the creation of new political organizations formed by women, such as the citizens' committee supporting Al Smith. Other women, such as Belle Moskowitz, who had long been active in politics, played a larger role when they got the vote. See Elisabeth Israels Perry, *Belle Moskowitz: Feminine Politics and the Exercise of Power in the Age of Alfred E. Smith.*

9. Flynn, *Reminiscences,* COH, 6; *The Reminiscences of Arthur Krock* (1950), 3, COH; *The Reminiscences of Herbert H. Lehman* (1957–59), 222, COH; Perkins, *Reminiscences,* COH, 1:97, 2:84. For a more complete discussion of Murphy's views, see John Allswang, *Bosses, Machines and Urban Voters,* 75–78.

10. Olvany quoted in Herbert Mitgang, *The Man Who Rode the Tiger: The Life and Times of Judge Samuel Seabury,* 163; Perkins, *Reminiscences,* COH, 2:292–93. Smith's first choice for boss was Murphy's idealistic son-in-law, James Foley, a surrogate's court judge. Foley did replace Murphy but resigned after a day on the job. Perkins said he withdrew because he foresaw the infighting and corruption that would tear Tammany apart. James J. Farley said Foley quit because his wife objected. *The Reminiscences of James J. Farley* (1957–58), 48, COH.

11. Mitgang, *Seabury,* 163–64; Perkins, COH, 2:356–57.

12. Perkins, COH 2:363–66.

13. Ibid., 358–60.

14. O'Connor, *First Hurrah*, 143–66; *The Reminiscences of Samuel Rosenman* (1959–60), 87, COH; Lehman, *Reminiscences*, COH, 221; Farley, *Reminiscences*, COH, 50.

15. Farley said Roosevelt tried to work with Tammany but its leaders, particularly Curry, rebuffed his efforts. Farley, *Reminiscences*, COH, 50–51. For the complex relationships between national Democratic politicians and Tammany, see Perkins, *Reminiscences*, COH, 1:426.

16. For details of the testimonial dinner, see Mitgang, *Seabury*, 167; and Richard Norton Smith, *Thomas E. Dewey and His Times*, 109.

17. Mitgang, *Seabury*, 160–61.

18. *The Reminiscences of Joseph Clark Baldwin* (1949–50), 12, COH; Mitgang, *Seabury*, 170, 203, 218.

19. Mitgang, *Seabury*, 16, 152–53, 171.

20. Ibid., 115–16, 144, 153.

21. Perkins, *Reminiscences*, COH, 3:433–34.

22. *The Reminiscences of Jonah Goldstein* (1964–66), 60–73, 443–49, COH.

23. Perkins, *Reminiscences*, COH, 3:430–31; Mahoney, *Reminiscences*, COH, 126–27; In the Matter of the Investigation, under Commission issued by the Governor of the State of New York, of Charges Made Against Hon. Thos. C. T. Crain, District Attorney of New York County: Report and Opinion of Samuel Seabury (hereafter Crain Report), in Papers of Franklin D. Roosevelt, New York State Archives, Albany (hereafter FDR Papers). Roosevelt, disgusted with the revelations, pardoned at least six women who had been falsely convicted. Mitgang, *Seabury*, 180–85.

24. Mitgang, *Seabury*, 189–93; Karen Berger Morello, *The Invisible Bar: The Woman Lawyer in America: 1638 to the Present*, 227–30.

25. Mitgang, *Seabury*, 199–200.

26. Petition and Roosevelt quote in Crain, Thomas C. T. file, FDR Papers (hereafter Crain Letters); Perkins, *Reminiscences*, COH, 3:429.

27. James E. Cleary to Roosevelt, 9 March 1931, Crain Letters; Crain Report, 5.

28. Pecora, *Reminiscences*, COH, 492–598; Marie Rooney of New York City to Roosevelt, 17 April 1931, Crain Letters; Dalton to Roosevelt, 21 March 1931, ibid.; Chisling to Roosevelt, 24 March 1931, ibid.

29. Rutgers Club Resolution in President Abraham L. Smolens to Roosevelt, March 1931, Crain Letters; Herbert A. Hughes, vice president, Donald W. Brown Real Estate, New York City, to Roosevelt, 28 March 1931, ibid.

30. Revised Summary of Argument of Mr. Samuel Untermyer, with Extracts from

Brief of Messrs. Untermyer and Hartman (hereafter Revised Summary), FDR Papers; Untermyer to Roosevelt, 2 September 1931, Crain Letters.
31. Crain Report, 29–31, 33–34; Revised Summary, 35.
32. Crain Report, 9–26.
33. Ibid., 82, 6–7.
34. Ibid., 83.
35. Quoted in Mitgang, *Seabury*, 215.
36. *The Reminiscences of Genevieve Earle* (1949–50), 18, COH; *The Reminiscences of Herbert Brownell* (1967), 1, COH; Bunzl, *Reminiscences*, COH, 87, 92–93. The Citizens' Union was formed in 1898 to report on legislative records. Perhaps its most famous candidate was Teddy Roosevelt, whom it backed as an Independent in his 1898 gubernatorial bid.
37. *The Reminiscences of William Jay Schieffelin* (1949), 35–36, COH.
38. Mitgang, *Seabury*, 220, 227, 248. Mitgang offers an extensive description of the investigation of minor city officials (216–44) and of Walker (245–65).
39. *New York Times* quoted in ibid., 263; ibid. 269.
40. Goldstein, *Reminiscences*, COH, 455–56, 470.
41. Allen, *Reminiscences*, COH, 456, 459–61.
42. Mahoney, *Reminiscences*, COH, 126.
43. Roosevelt quoted in Mitgang, *Seabury*, 263–64; Perkins, *Reminiscences*, COH, 3:439–40.
44. Wilbur Cross, editor, *Yale Review*, to Moley, 5 February 1932, enclosed in Raymond Moley to Samuel Rosenman, 7 February 1932, FDR Papers.
45. Mahoney, *Reminiscences*, COH, 126; Perkins, *Reminiscences*, COH, 3:435–38; Flynn, *Reminiscences*, COH, 14.
46. *The Reminiscences of George Harrison Combs, Jr.* (1949–51), 63–64, COH; Mitgang, *Seabury*, 278–80.
47. Flynn, *Reminiscences*, COH, 14–15; Perkins, *Reminiscences*, COH, 3:438–48.
48. Perkins, *Reminiscences*, COH, 3:434–35.
49. Lazarus, *Reminiscences*, COH, 154; Mitgang, *Seabury*, 282–99.
50. Lehman, *Reminiscences*, COH, 210; Powell Hickman, "Profiles: The Governor," *The New Yorker*, 2 May 1936, 25; Combs, *Reminiscences*, COH, 128–29; *The Reminiscences of Morris Strauss* (1951), 361, COH.
51. Herbert Lehman, *Liberalism: A Personal Journey: A Survey and Prospect of American Liberalism*, 9–10.
52. Oscar Handlin, *Al Smith and His America*, 168; Lehman, *Reminiscences*, COH, 299–303, 306–7.

CHAPTER TWO

1. Many articles in *The Panel* addressed this question, e.g.: "Grand Jury Charge April Term by Judge Collins," 2:4 (April 1925): 2; "Judge Cornelius Collins of

Ct. of General Sessions in Recent Public Address," 4:1 (January 1926): 6; T. McGill, "Grand Juries and Crime Waves," 4.4 (April 1926): 6; "Judge Mulqueen Charge to the Grand Jury," 3:2 (March 1925): 4; Charles C. Nott, Jr., "Improving the Criminal Law," 3:3 (October 1925): 1; "Judge Talley on Crime," 4:6 (June 1926): 4; "Editorial," 5:6 (June 1927): 4; "The Cause and the Cure," 3:3 (October 1925): 6.

2. "Compulsory Registration," *The Panel* 3:3 (October 1925): 4; Judge John F. McIntyre, "On Crimes of Violence," ibid. 3:4 (November 1925): 1; Justice Isaac M. Kapper, "Disarm the Gunman," ibid. 4:4 (April 1926): 4; Judge Francis X. Mancuso, "Suggestions to Check Crime," ibid. 4:6 (June 1926): 1. For a description of similar proposals in another era, see Mary M. Stolberg, "The Evolution of Frontier Justice: The Case of Judge Isaac Parker," *Prologue* 20:1 (Spring 1988): 18–20; on reformers' views on the need for uniform state crime laws and improved extradition (not enacted in New York until the Dewey years), see Michael H. Cahill, "The Need for Uniform Crime Laws," *The Panel* 7:5 (September–October 1929):3.

3. Material on the cost of crime compiled by Max E. Halpern, in Thomas E. Dewey Papers, Rush Rhees Library, University of Rochester (hereafter Dewey Papers). For details of the reformed laws, see the following articles from *The Panel:* "Thumbs Down on Thuggery," 3:2 (September 1925): 3; "The State Crime Commission," 5:1 (January 1927): 3–4; "Practical Results of the Baumes Law After Seven Months," 5:2 (February 1927): 3–4; "Senator Baumes Introduces Bill to Make Grand Jury More Efficient," 5:4 (March 1927): 1–3; "The Latest Baumes Law," 5:5 (May 1927): 2; "Editorial," 5:9 (November–December 1927): 2.

In 1929 President Herbert Hoover appointed former U.S. Attorney General George W. Wickersham to head the National Commission on Law Observance and Law Enforcement. The panel, better known as the Wickersham Committee, issued its report in 1931. Although it did detail crime costs, the report is best known for its criticism of federal enforcement of Prohibition. For information about organized crime commissions in Philadelphia and Chicago, see Thomas Meryweather, "The Philadelphia Criminal Justice Association," and E. J. Davis, "What Ails Chicago," both in *The Panel* 9:2 (March–April 1931): 18, 24; Mark Haller, "Police Reform in Chicago: 1905–1935," *American Behavioral Scientist* 12 (May–August 1970): 649–66, and "Urban Crime and Criminal Justice: The Chicago Case," *Journal of American History* 57 (December 1970): 619–35.

4. Bunzl, *Reminiscences*, COH, 84–85; Lazarus, *Reminiscences*, COH, 158–61; Combs, *Reminiscences*, COH, 71–73.

5. Allen, *Reminiscences,* COH, 474; the Republican party was divided equally between conservative leaders and a new guard epitomized by Dewey. Description
of McKee's role in August Heckscher with Phyllis Robinson, *When La Guardia
Was Mayor: New York's Legendary Years,* 28, 159; *The Reminiscences of Newbold
Morris* (1950), COH, 23; Manners, *Patience and Fortitude,* 145. Mitgang, *Seabury,* 313–20, describes Seabury's role. See also Goldstein, *Reminiscences,* COH,
106; *The Reminiscences of Charles C. Burlingham,* 33–34, COH; Windels, *Reminiscences,* appendix, 1, COH; and Mann, *La Guardia,* 53.

6. James Farley later persuaded Straus to run as the Recovery party's nominee
for president of the Board of Aldermen. When the ticket lost, Roosevelt appointed him head of the National Recovery Administration in New York. *The
Reminiscences of Nathan Straus, Jr.* (1950), 75–76, COH, and *The Reminiscences
of Walter Mack, Jr.* (1950), 45–46, COH. La Guardia's last day in Congress was
4 March 1933. For an analysis of the election, see Mann, *La Guardia,* 150; Rodman, *Fiorello,* 90; Elliott, *Little Flower,* 180–83; and Manners, *Patience and Fortitude,* 135, 143–44.

7. Manners, *Patience and Fortitude,* 148; Seabury quoted in Mitgang, *Seabury,*
320; Windels, *Reminiscences,* COH, 79–80.

8. Morris, *Reminiscences,* COH, 21–22; Burlingham, *Reminiscences,* COH, 33; *The
Reminiscences of Samuel Koenig* (1950), 45, COH. La Guardia's congressional
efforts in Elliott, *Fiorello,* 174–80, 184–87; and Lazarus, *Reminiscences,* COH,
218.

9. Manners, *Patience and Fortitude,* 151–52; and Windels, *Reminiscences,* COH,
79–80, addendum 2.

10. For details of the 1922 campaign, see Elliott, *Little Flower,* 125–28, 137–39. "In
any three-sided . . . ," in Combs, *Reminiscences,* COH, 79; "I don't know," in
The Reminiscences of Stanley Isaacs (1949–50), 73, COH; Manners, *Patience and
Fortitude,* 142, 155; Straus, *Reminiscences,* COH, 78–81; Windels, *Reminiscences,*
COH, 17. La Guardia, realizing Lehman's popularity with the voters, urged
Seabury to leave the governor alone. Mitgang, *Seabury,* 321–22.

11. After losing the mayoral race, McKee left politics. Other details in Flynn, *Remi-
niscences,* COH, 19; and Windels, *Reminiscences,* COH, 78. Fusionists in New
York were not the only ones to trumpet the costs of crime; see also Davis,
"What Ails Chicago?" 24.

12. Rodman, *Fiorello,* 147; Manners, *Patience and Fortitude,* 161, 165; Elliott, *Little
Flower,* 205; Heckscher, *When La Guardia Was Mayor,* 16.

13. Rodman, *Fiorello,* 151; Dressler, *Reminiscences,* COH, 46–48. At his request,
parole officers provided La Guardia with a list of possible appointees to head
the Municipal Parole Commission. In characteristic fashion, he ignored the

suggestions and named Lou Gehrig. Despite parole officers' reservations, the baseball star succeeded in the job because of his industry and ability to motivate others.

14. Heckscher, *When La Guardia Was Mayor*, 39–40. For details of La Guardia's other actions in office, see Rodman, *Fiorello*, 158–60, 169–70; Manners, *Patience and Fortitude*, 161; and Heckscher, *When La Guardia Was Mayor*, 16–18.

15. The battle against unemployment was a constant concern of La Guardia's until World War II. In 1934 the situation was particularly precarious because of the inadequacy of existing services and the city's financial plight. For more details, see Heckscher, *When La Guardia Was Mayor*, 37–42, 60–66, 79–81.

16. Ibid., 104, 106–7; Isaacs, *Reminiscences*, COH, 79; Manners, *Patience and Fortitude*, 188.

17. Heckscher, *When La Guardia Was Mayor*, 109–10.

18. *New York Times*, 29 December 1933; radio broadcast on station WOR, 10 December 1933, in District Attorney's Files, James J. Hines Case (hereafter Hines Files), box 2321, file William Copeland Dodge, City of New York, Department of Records and Information Services, Municipal Archives (hereafter New York City Archives).

19. Samuel Seabury speech to Yale University, 21 November 1933, and Dodge speech to Government Club, 4 December 1933, both in Hines Files.

20. Speech at Government Club, 4 December 1933; *New York Times*, 5 February 1921, carried a story about Dodge's letter to Governor Miller; Dodge's comments about Al Smith were made on 1 March 1935 and reported in the *New York Times*, 30 April 1933; all three clippings are in Hines Files.

21. *New York Times*, 25 February 1934 and 6 August 1934, ibid.

22. In its presentment filed 17 December 1934, the grand jury cited testimony of attorney Harry Vogelstein. Quotes from that report are in the presentment issued by the regular February grand jury and filed 17 December 1934, before J. Corrigan, Dewey Papers. For more general discussions of that jury's work, see two articles by Robert R. Wilkes in *The Panel*: "1934 Grand Jury Presentments Expose Flagrant Conditions in New York County," 13:1 (January–February 1935): 1, 9; and "A History Making Grand Jury," 13:2 (September–October 1935):1.

23. Copy of sermon included in document dated 30 January 1935, Microfilm Roll 70, Governor Lehman's Correspondence, the Herbert H. Lehman Collection, Columbia University (hereafter Lehman Papers).

24. La Guardia's meetings as listed in his daily appointment register and Valentine's memo in press release 11 March 1935, in Fiorello La Guardia Papers, New York City Archives (hereafter La Guardia Papers); comments by Egbert and

Valentine about gambling locations in Egbert to Police Inspectors Archibald H. McNeil and John J. Martino, 27 February 1935, Lehman Papers; analysis of Valentine's answer to Mayor La Guardia in reference to letter of 27 February 1935, from the Society for the Prevention of Crime to Inspector of the 5th and 6th Divisions of the Police Department, undated, ibid.; comments on accompanying documents, undated, ibid.

25. *New York World-Telegram,* 28 February 1935, 1 March 1935, 4 March 1935, and 6 March 1935, and *New York Times,* 1 March 1935—clippings in Hines Files.

26. Lehman, *Reminiscences,* COH, 636, names two of the other groups criticizing Dodge as the Citizens' Union and the City Affairs Committee headed by John Haynes Holmes. Dodge's day-by-day comments in the *New York World-Telegram* and "History of the Dewey Investigation," Dewey Papers.

27. "H. Phillips Chronology, 1931–41" (hereafter Phillips chronology), 13:6, Dewey Papers.

28. March 1935 Grand Jury Notes, Lehman Papers; Paul Lockwood interview about Boston, Dewey Papers.

29. Almirall to Smith, 15 October 1919; Swann to Smith, 10 October 1919, 23 October 1919, and 21 November 1919; Smith to Swann, 25 November 1919; Smith to Grand Jury, 21 December 1919; Swann to Grand Jury, 13 December 1919; I. F. Flatts to Smith, 8 December 1919; Governor's Press Release, 16 December 1919—all in Smith Papers.

30. *New York World,* 27 January 1920; Tom O'Donnell to Smith, 25 June 1920, Smith Papers; Pecora, *Reminiscences,* COH, 190, 266–67.

31. For the history of the grand jury, see Richard D. Younger, *The People's Panel: The Grand Jury in the United States;* Albert Lieck, "Abolition of the Grand Jury in England," *Journal of Criminal Law and Criminology* 25 (November– December 1934): 623–25, and W. J. Heyting, "Abolition of Grand Juries in England," *American Bar Association Journal* 19 (November 1933): 648–49.

32. Editorial, "Get Better or Get Out!" 4:4 (April 1926): 5; Alex Konta, "Gentlemen of the Grand Jury, Know Yourselves," 7:5 (September–October 1929): 11; "Criticism of the Jury System," 5:8 (October 1927): 2; "Food for Thought," 2:4 (April 1925): 1—all in *The Panel.*

Manhattan was the only county in New York with a special jury commission; in other parts of the state these duties were handled by the board of supervisors. For specifics on requirements, see "Qualifications for Jury Service," *The Panel* 5:7 (September 1927): 1. A more complete description of how the process worked is in "Memo on Selection of Grand Jurors," La Guardia Papers. Rockefeller's role in the association is in "Its History and Development," *The Panel* 4:9 (November 1926): 1, 3.

33. Quotes from "How Say You Gentlemen?" *The Panel* 4:5 (May 1926): 7. Other suggestions in *Panel* articles cited in note 32 and H. F. J. Porter, "Is the Grand Jury What It Should Be?" 4:7 (September 1926): 7–8, ibid.

34. Bruce Smith, "Uniform Crime Statistics and Their Importance," 9:1 (January–February 1931): 3; "Fingerprints," 5:6 (June 1927): 3; "Uniform State Crime Laws and the Governors' Conference," 7:5 (September–October 1929): 1–2, "New State Central Bureau," 6:3 (May 1928): 4; Herbert H. Lehman, "Extradition from an Executive Viewpoint," 8:2 (March–April 1930): 7; Philip J. Goodhart, "The Indiscriminate Sale of Revolvers," 2:2 (February 1925): 3; "Address on Perjury by Frank E. Carstarphen," 5:9 (November–December 1927): 7; Robert Appleton, Address, "Feigned Omissions of Fence," 6:3 (March 1928): 3; "Receipts 5, 931.78," 5:2 (February 1927): 1, 3; and "Stiffer Rules of Legal Practice," 5:5 (May 1927): 4—all ibid.

35. Editorial, ibid. 2:2 (February 1925): 8.

36. A. M. Kidd, "Why Grand Jury's Power Is a Menace to Organized Crime," 12:3 (September–October 1934): 32–34; William Feather, "Foreman Tells Why Criminals Fear Action by Grand Jury," 12:2 (March–April 1934): 17; Robert Appleton, "Grand Juries Beginning to Act on Their Own Motion," 11:3 (November–December 1933): 23—all ibid.

37. Unanimously Approved by the March 1935 Grand Jury and Read in Court on May 7, 1935, Lehman Papers.

38. Phillips chronology.

39. Executive Committee of March 1935 Grand Jury to Lehman, 15 June 1935; March 1935 Grand Jury Notes, Lehman Papers; transcript of grand jury proceedings, 10 June 1935, Hines Files.

40. Hughes manuscript, 10:118, 101–2, Dewey Papers; Abraham Tolleris to Lehman, 17 June 1935, and C. A. Rogers to Lehman, 19 June 1935, Lehman Papers.

41. Lehman, *Reminiscences,* COH, 631, 635, 644.

42. Lehman to Dodge, 24 June 1935, Lehman Papers.

43. Dodge to Lehman, 26 June 1935; Dodge to Lehman, 27 June 1935; part of press release from four men, undated and untitled; press release copy of telegram from Lehman to Hughes, Medalie, Thacher, and Tuttle, 27 June 1935; press statement covering conference held at Governor Lehman's apartment, 29 June 1935—all ibid.

44. Telegram, Robert Appleton, president, Association of Grand Jurors of New York County, to Lehman, 28 June 1935. The executive committee of the bar association began pushing for Dewey in mid-June; see Clarence J. Shearn, president, Association of the Bar of the City of New York, to Lehman, 17 June 1935, Lehman Papers. Newspaper support is described in Hughes manuscript, Dewey Papers.

Lehman, *Reminiscences,* COH, 640–43. Some historians, including Dewey's biographer Richard Norton Smith, have argued that Lehman claimed to be worried only about Dewey's inexperience, when in reality the governor was terrified of the young lawyer's political acumen. Smith, *Thomas E. Dewey,* 149. This is an anachronistic reading of the facts based on Dewey's later success. Dewey was successful, for a young lawyer, but Lehman certainly had more to fear politically from such Republican heavyweights as Medalie, Hughes, and Tuttle.

45. *The Reminiscences of Charles Poletti* (1978), 167–69, COH.

CHAPTER THREE

1. *The Reminiscences of Thomas E. Dewey* (1966), 34, 37–42, COH.
2. Smith, *Thomas E. Dewey,* 68–86.
3. James F. Dealy interview, 2, Dewey Papers; Harlan Phillips interview with Dewey 27 March 1958 (hereafter Phillips interview), 224–25, ibid.; Smith, *Thomas E. Dewey,* 91–92, 101–2.
4. Smith, *Thomas E. Dewey,* 111; Radio talk for Monday night, during 1932 Medalie Senate campaign, Dewey Papers; George Z. Medalie biography, 2, Dewey Papers; Hughes manuscript, 36, Dewey Papers.
5. William B. Herlands interview, 6–8, 11, Dewey Papers (hereafter Herlands interview).
6. Herlands interview, 21; Phillips interview, 27 March 1958 226; Smith, *Thomas E. Dewey,* 92–93; *The Reminiscences of Francis R. Stoddard* (1949), COH, 97; Dewey to Clarence H. Fay, 5 September 1928, Dewey Papers; Samuel H. Hofstadter to Dewey, 8 November 1928, ibid.; Dewey to Thomas J. Lewis, 19 November 1928, ibid.
7. Information about Young Republican leadership and the club's purpose in Committee Reports Nominations and Certificate of Incorporation of New York Young Republican Club, Inc., in *New York Young Republican* 4 (January 1929). See also letter (probably from Dewey) to Ellwood Colahan, 8 February 1928, Dewey Papers.
8. "Drunken Sailors" by Dewey, undated; William Hayes to Dewey, 11 February 1927; Hayes to Dewey, 15 February 1927; memo from David Barnett to members, City Affairs Committee, 28 February 1927; An Open Letter to the Civic, Business, and Patriotic Organizations of the City of New York from Young Republican Club, 3 August 1927—all in Dewey Papers.
9. Dewey to "Dear Speaker," 23 October 1930; A. O. Dawson to Dewey, 20 June 1929; David Peck to Dewey, 24 March 1930; Dewey to Koenig, 4 November 1930, Draft of Resolution—all in Dewey Papers.
10. J. Edward Lumbard to Hon. H. Edmund Machold, state Republican chairman, 4 May 1929; Dewey to Lumbard, 8 May 1929—both ibid.

11. Dewey to Medalie, 2 March 1931, ibid.; Dewey to Medalie, 6 March 1931, ibid.; on Buckner, see *The Reminiscences of David Peck* (1978), 54–56, COH; Herlands interview, 22.

12. A duplicate of Dewey's tax return for 1930 shows his salary as $5,700; miscellaneous fees, mostly from sales of bonds and real estate, brought his income to $10,103.11: Dewey Papers; Assistant Attorney General Charles Grissom to Dewey, 31 March 1931, appointing him effective 1 April 1931, ibid. For Dewey's version of events, see Phillips interview, 27 March 1958, 227–28; Smith, *Thomas E. Dewey*, 112–13.

13. Phillips interview, 27 March 1958, 234–35; Cuneo, *Life with Fiorello*, 156; Herlands interview, 5–6.

14. Herlands interview, 33–35.

15. Ibid., 41–43.

16. Ibid., 36–38.

17. Ibid., 29–33, 39–40; Phillips interview, 15 April 1958, 302.

18. Haller, "Police Reform" and "Urban Crime," in *The Panel*.

19. Phillips interview, 27 March 1958, 233; ibid., 15 April 1958, 300; details of trial in Smith, *Thomas E. Dewey*, 131–40.

20. Mack, *Reminiscences*, COH, 21–39.

21. Ibid., 40.

22. Herbert Brownell interview, 51–52, 78–81, Dewey Papers; for an example of campaign material approved by Dewey, see 15 October 1931 memo, ibid.

23. The new party chairman, Chase Mellon, proved even less effective than Koenig. He was ultimately replaced by Ken Simpson, who, Dewey said, "represented the reform and vigorous leadership in a minority party in a big democratic city." Dewey became disenchanted with Simpson in later years, calling him an unstable alcoholic. Phillips interview, 27 March 1958, 209–10; for details of the Medalie campaign, see Dewey Papers.

24. U.S. Attorney General Homer S. Cummings wrote to Franklin Delano Roosevelt on 21 November 1933 that Medalie was retiring and suggested appointing Conboy as a lawyer of equal stature. "President's Secretary File," Papers of Franklin Delano Roosevelt, FDR Presidential Library, Hyde Park, New York (hereafter FDR Papers).

Phillips interview, 28 April 1958, 309; Keyes Winter to Dewey, 18 January 1933; Dewey to Winter, 19 January 1933, Dewey Papers. For other evidence of Dewey's rising fortunes in the party, see Dewey to W. Kingsland Macy, chairman Republican State Committee, 15 November 1932; and Dewey to Melvin C. Eaton, chairman Republican County committee, 20 December 1932. The letterhead of Charles S. Whitman to Dewey, 12 January 1933, indicates that

Medalie was on the mayoral committee; Dewey accepted the job in Dewey to Whitman, 17 January 1933; on Dewey's assistance to La Guardia, see Paul Blanshard to Dewey, 20 October 1933. All the above correspondence is in the Dewey Papers.

25. William Gilligan to Association of the Bar, 16 April 1931, ibid. The same file contains copies of other letters recommending Dewey and Dewey's acceptance letter, 12 May 1931. Information about Medalie's investigation of Vitale is from Herlands interview, 17–18.

26. Kenneth Dayton, chairman, Committee on Courts of Limited Jurisdiction, to La Guardia, 5 December 1933; and Bar Association, La Guardia 1933–1935—both in La Guardia Papers.

27. Certificate of Incorporation, New York Young Republican Club, Medalie quotation, and a list of Medalie's speeches—all in Dewey Papers.

28. Medalie, president, Jewish Board of Guardians, to La Guardia, 28 December 1933, and Mayor's Daily Appointments, La Guardia Papers; Herlands interview, 45. Medalie assistants working for La Guardia included Herlands, Edmund I. Palmieri, and Alvin McKinley Sylvester.

    Medalie to Lehman, 2 July 1935, Lehman Papers, outlines his work on the bar committee. Medalie's *Panel* articles included "Interstate Exchange of Witnesses in Criminal Cases," 7:2 (March 1929): 3; "Grand Jury Investigations," 7:1 (January–February 1929): 6–7; "A Symposium on the Subject of Material Witnesses," 8:1 (January–February 1930): 1–3; "Grand Jury's Value Presentments—Fraudulent Bankrupts," 9:2 (March–April 1931): 16–17, 23; and "Fighting Stock Market Racketeers in the Federal Courts," 9:3 (May–June 1931): 28–29.

29. Thacher to Dewey, 15 June 1934; To the Executive Committee of the Association of the Bar of the City of New York and In the Matter of the Application of the Association of the Bar of the City of New York for Removal from Office of Harold L. Kunstler, Justice of the Municipal Court of the City of New York, Dewey attorney for the petitioner—both in Dewey Papers.

30. Dewey to Thacher, 12 July 1934, and Charles H. Strong to Dewey, 23 July 1934, ibid.

31. Dewey to Thacher, 19 February 1935; transcript, Comments by Thomas E. Dewey, Chairman, Committee on Criminal Courts Law and Procedure of the Association of the Bar of the City of New York; press release, 25 February 1935—all ibid.

32. Bennett to Thacher, 4 February 1935; American Bar Association to members of the Committees on Criminal Law, Police and Prosecution, and Criminal Procedure, 12 December 1934—both ibid.

33. "Effective Prosecution: A Method of Crime Prevention," address by George Medalie at the Attorney General's Conference on Crime, 11 December 1934, Lehman Papers.

34. Phillips interview, 28 April 1958, 326; Charles H. Strong to George W. Alger, 11 April 1935, Dewey Papers.

35. Dewey to E. J. Davis, Better Government Association of Chicago, 21 May 1935, ibid. Dewey wrote the letter at the request of Robert Appleton, president of the Grand Jurors Association, in response to an April 8 letter he received concerning proposals to do away with the grand jury system in Illinois.

36. Telegram, Appleton to Lehman, 28 June 1935, supporting Dewey's appointment, and Medalie to Lehman, 2 July 1935, Lehman Papers; Report, Nominating Committee of the Young Republican Club, 30 December 1926, and Certificate of Incorporation, New York Young Republican Club, Inc., Dewey Papers.

37. "A Well Wisher" to Lehman, 1 June 1935, Lehman Papers. Quotations from Dewey's friends in Dewey Papers: Glenn Munn to Dewey, July 5, 1935; and F. Julian Kleeman to Dewey, 17 July 1935. For other, similar letters, see Eugene Bigelow to Dewey, 19 July 1935; Joseph S. Blume to Dewey, 2 July 1935; P. Hodges Combier to Dewey, 5 July 1935; Harry G. Herman to Dewey, 2 July 1935—all ibid. Information about Medalie's efforts for Dewey in *The Reminiscences of Warren Moscow* (1951), 17, COH.

38. Phillips interview, 28 April 1958, 327–28.

CHAPTER FOUR

1. Press releases, 28 June 1935, 2 July 1935, and 5 July 1935, Lehman Papers; Phillips interview, 28 April 1958, 330 describes easing of civil service requirements.

2. Dewey's meetings with Washington officials ended up being largely for show; none of them provided any help for his investigation; see Phillips interview, 8 May 1958, 363, 369–70; Egbert to Dewey, 2 July 1935; Dewey to Thomas Cooke to Dewey, 11 July 1934; John Haynes Holmes to Dewey, 19 July 1935—all in Dewey Papers.

   For Dewey's contacts with the media, see Marty J. Berg, editor, *Police Gazette*, to Dewey, 31 July 1935; Arthur Brisbane, a Hearst columnist, to Dewey, 31 July 1935; Joseph Early, editor, *Brooklyn Times-Union*, to Dewey, 5 July 1935 and 19 July 1935; and Arthur Hays Sulzberger to Dewey, 16 July 1935—all ibid.

3. Mann, *La Guardia*, 47, 116. See also Phillips interview, 8 May 1958, 361–63, Dewey Papers; and, in La Guardia Papers, Phillip J. McCook to La Guardia, 18 December 1933; McCook to La Guardia, 18 October 1938; McCook to La Guardia, 13 December 1934; and La Guardia to McCook, 5 February 1935. McCook was listed as director of the Young Republicans on the club's Certificate of Incorporation.

4. In La Guardia Papers, see "Dewey Investigation," broadcast by Dr. Fleisher, WNYC, 15 July 1935; Dodge to La Guardia, 19 October 1934; and Dewey to Dodge, 15 July 1935. See also Manners, *Patience and Fortitude,* 19.
5. To ensure more secrecy, Dewey posted detectives in the lobby to watch for gangsters. Untitled manuscript, 3, 16–17, Dewey Papers.
6. *New York World-Telegram,* 25 July 1935, *Klein* v. *Frank Taylor,* Comptroller of the City of New York and decision by Judge J. Lauer, Dewey Papers; Heckscher, *When La Guardia Was Mayor,* 111; and Smith, *Thomas E. Dewey,* 157–58.
7. Emmanuel L. Robbins interview, 7, 14, Dewey Papers (hereafter Robbins interview); Frank A. Neary to Dewey, 23 May 1935, ibid.; details about applications in untitled, undated manuscript, ibid. Dressler, *Reminiscences,* COH, 53, 144; Phillips interview, 28 April 1958, 311; Smith, *Thomas E. Dewey,* 154; Mitgang, *Seabury,* 173–74.
8. Jerold S. Auerbach, *Unequal Justice: Lawyers and Social Change in Modern America,* 159; he discusses these trends in chapter 6.
9. Robbins interview, 13; Harris B. Steinberg interview, 1, 22–23, 74, Dewey Papers (hereafter Steinberg interview); Morello, *Invisible Bar,* 150.
10. Robbins interview, 3–4; Smith, *Thomas E. Dewey,* 157.
11. Radio address, July 30, 1935, over WABC, WOR, and WMCA, Dewey Papers.
12. Ibid.
13. Ibid.
14. Ibid.
15. Steinberg interview, 12–13; Robbins interview, 10; unmarked manuscript—all ibid.
16. Dewey to Poletti, 18 December 1935, Lehman Papers; Herlands interview, 56; Robbins interview, 16, 22; Paul Lockwood interview, 108, Dewey Papers (hereafter Lockwood interview).
17. Miro quoted in Joseph Panuch interview, 36; Sol Gelb interview, 7; Confidential memorandum re: Albert Marinelli, 30 September 1937; Medalie speech and newspaper clippings—all in Dewey Papers.
18. Stanley Fuld interview, Dewey Papers (hereafter Fuld interview), 6–7; and Charles Breitel interview, pp. 25, 36–37, ibid.
19. Fuld interview, 8–9; Lockwood interview, 108; *The Reminiscences of Stanley Fuld* (1977), 17–18, COH.
20. For information about utilization of the police, see Robbins interview, 24, 34; and Herlands interview, 53–55.
21. Steinberg interview, 13.
22. Dewey to La Guardia, 20 April 1936, La Guardia Papers; information about Tossone case in History of Dewey Investigation, Dewey Papers; Smith, *Thomas E. Dewey,* 162.

23. Martin A. Gosch and Richard Hammer, *The Last Testament of Lucky Luciano,* 177–82.
24. Ibid., 187; Smith, *Thomas E. Dewey,* 168–69, 172–73.
25. The Special Sessions Court retained the less formal rules of procedures it had used since colonial times. This dual system was abolished in 1967 and replaced by the Criminal Court of the City of New York. On methods employed in the usury cases, see Steinberg interview, 15, 19–20, 38.
26. Phillips interview, 8 May 1958, 380.
27. *New York Mirror,* 30 October 1935, clipping file, Dewey Papers; *New York Times* quoted in Smith, *Thomas E. Dewey,* 177–78.
28. Third chapter, third draft, 13:4, 30, Dewey Papers; Phillips interview, 8 May 1958, 380.
29. Grand Jury Report to the Honorable Phillip J. McCook, 26 December 1935, La Guardia Papers; press release, 27 December 1935, Lehman Papers.

CHAPTER FIVE

1. Smith Address, 1 March 1926, Smith Papers; 115-page report, ibid.
2. Richard Robertson to *Brooklyn Eagle,* with copy to Smith, 9 August 1925; open letter to Adolph Lewisohn (unattributed), 23 March 1926; W. J. Maroney to Smith, 14 August 1925—all ibid.
3. Attorney Cecile Scheur to Smith, 12 December 1927; John P. Lindsay to George P. Graves, assistant and secretary to Smith, 11 April 1927; Alexander Fischandler, principal of New York Board of Education, to Smith, 23 December 1927; Herman A. Metz to Smith, 18 September 1925—all ibid.
4. Until then Roosevelt had paid Howe's expenses himself. Kenneth S. Davis, *FDR: The New York Years, 1928–1933,* 33.
5. For a sample of these letters in the Smith Papers, see A. N. Eshman, president of the National Council of Better Citizenship, Estill Springs, Tennessee, 6 August 1925; Mrs. N. I. Potter, Chippewa Falls, Wisconsin, 10 August 1925; W. A. Hall, Farmersville, Texas, 30 July 1925; and Elbridge W. Cain, Edgewater, Colorado, 31 July 1925. Eugene F. Moore, Dorchester, Massachusetts, refers to Smith's presidential ambitions and his work with the national group. August (n.d.), 1926.

   Also in the Smith Papers, see Message on Crime and Its Prevention to the Legislature, 1 March 1926. Smith's appointees were David S. Taylor, managing editor of the *Buffalo Courier;* Thomas S. Rice, editorial writer, *Brooklyn Eagle;* Col. George F. Chandler, a surgeon who helped organize the state police; William Lewis Butcher, superintendent, Brace Memorial Newsboys Home; and Jane Hoey, head, Welfare Council of Greater New York. Press release, 18 May 1926, and Commission to Investigate Defects in the Law and its Administration, both in Smith Papers; see also Chapter 460, *Laws of New York.*

6. W. J. Maroney to Smith, 14 August 1925, Smith Papers.

7. William G. Bell, Austin, Texas, to Smith, 31 January 1927, ibid.

8. Julius Hallheimer, "Justice by Formula: Who Is an Habitual Criminal and What Is a Felony," *Century Magazine* 17:2 (December 1928): 232–33.

9. De Silver Drew to Smith, 8 December 1927, and Ben Marinoff to Smith, 14 December 1926, Smith Papers; Banton quoted in Hallheimer, "Justice by Formula," 233–34; address by Raymond Moley, 30 September 1935, Lehman Papers.

10. For information about the national conference, see *The Reminiscences of Gordon Dean* (1954), 82–84, COH; and Mary M. Stolberg, "Policing the Twilight Zone: Nationalization of Crime Fighting in the New Deal," *Journal of Policy History* (Fall 1995).

11. Telegram J. Edgar Hoover to Lehman, 14 September 1935, Lehman Papers; Lehman to Chief Justice Charles Evans Hughes, 7 September 1935, ibid.; Richard C. Patterson, Jr., president, NBC, to Lehman, 10 September 1935, ibid.; unsigned and undated memo for the governor, with two-page list of media invitations, ibid.; Phillips interview, 28 April 1958, 331–32.

12. Anna Kross to Lehman, 28 August 1935; Robert Daru to Poletti, 5 August 1935; Robert Appleton to Poletti, 26 July 1935—all in Lehman Papers. Both men were eventually invited.

13. Phelps Phelps to Lehman, 24 September 1935; Charles Burdick to Lehman, 10 September 1935; Logan Billingsley to Lehman, 30 September 1935; Joseph Proskauer to Lehman, 30 September 1935; Jonah Goldstein to Lehman, 30 July 1935—all in Lehman Papers.

14. Lehman's opening address at Governor's Conference, "Crime, the Criminal, and Society," 30 September 1935, Albany, ibid.

15. State of New York, *Proceedings of the Governor's Conference on Crime, the Criminal and Society,* September 30 to October 3, 1935 (hereafter *Governor's Crime Conference*), ibid.

16. *Governor's Crime Conference.*

17. A copy of the editorial was enclosed in Fry Kehaya, president, National Herald, Inc., to Lehman, 30 September 1935, Lehman Papers. See also James Keeshen, Oklahoma City, to Lehman, 16 October 1935, and Guy M. Gray, Greenfield, Massachusetts, to Lehman, 1 October 1935. These and many similar letters are in the Lehman Papers.

18. Mrs. Dora Lamon to Lehman, 28 October 1935, ibid.; Jefferson Seligman to Lehman, 3 October 1935, ibid.

19. Michael Nox to Lehman, 30 September 1935, ibid.; *Rochester Democrat and Chronicle,* 28 November 1935; Sarah Shimkin, Williamsburg, to Lehman, 2 October 1935, Lehman Papers; Richard C. Berresford to Charles Poletti, 25 Octo-

ber 1935, ibid.; Richard Hartshorner, chairman, Interstate Commission on Crime, to Lehman, 18 December 1935, ibid.; and Edith B. Drellich to Poletti, 17 October 1935, ibid. Announcement of Lehman's appointments to the committee in press release, 22 October 1935, ibid.

20. Address by Raymond Moley, 30 September 1935, ibid.

21. Mayor's Daily Appointments, 3148; 11, La Guardia Papers; Phillips interview, 8 May 1958, 383, Dewey Papers.

22. Heckscher, *When La Guardia Was Mayor,* 111–12.

23. Ibid.

24. *People of New York* v. *Sam Pieri,* 269 NY 315, 327; press release, 8 January 1936—both in La Guardia Papers.

25. This push for legislation was mirrored at the federal level and resulted in such new laws as the Fugitive Felon Statue, which made it illegal to cross state lines after committing a felony; a law making the robbery of a national bank a federal offense; kidnapping statutes; and weapons regulations aimed at curbing machine guns, sawed-off shotguns, and silencers. See Dean, *Reminiscences,* COH, 50–52; and M. Stolberg, "Policing the Twilight Zone."

26. Lehman's specific recommendations are in "Special Message of the Governor to the Legislature: Recommendations for the Improvement of Criminal Law Enforcement," and *Governor's Crime Conference.*

27. *Governor's Crime Conference.*

28. Robert Appleton, "New York Legislature of 1934 Proves that Stronger Criminal Law Must be Made Major Political Issue," *The Panel* 12:2 (March–April 1934): 13, 20. Appleton's resignation is chronicled in ibid. 14:3 (March 1936): 4, and "First Banquet in Association's History Proves Big Success," ibid. 14:2 (May–June 1936): 5. For earlier legislative proposals, see "Judge Nott Boldly Recommends Seven Criminal Law Changes," ibid. 9:5 (November–December 1931): 49; and Appleton, "Working Program for Improving Criminal Law and Procedure Offered by Association of Grand Jurors and the Panel," ibid. 12:1 (January–February 1934): 1–2.

29. Appleton, "Working Program," 1–2; Jim Wallace to La Guardia, undated memo, La Guardia Papers.

30. John McKim Minton, "Eliminate 'Third Degree' By Compelling Accused to Explain or Stand Convicted," *The Panel* 10:2 (March–April 1932): 15; John J. Bennett, Jr., "Attorney General of New York Urges Criminal Law Reform," ibid. 10:4 (September–October 1932): 45–46. Dewey speech, "Public Opinion and Law Enforcement," 25 January 1936, Dewey Papers.

31. Powell Hickman, "Profiles: The Governor II," *The New Yorker,* 9 May 1936, 26. During his second term, Lehman declared he would not run again so that he could devote more time to his family's business. He changed his plans after

receiving a personal appeal from Roosevelt, who said their work to make New York exemplary in social legislation would fail if Lehman quit. Roosevelt to Lehman, 29 June 1936, Lehman Papers.

32. ACLU Bulletin, no. 702, 14 February 1936, 2; Charles Poletti to Roger Baldwin, 22 February 1936, Lehman Papers, pointed out that only four of the six bills were introduced by the governor. Those calling for universal fingerprinting and permitting magistrates to hold lawyers in contempt were not sponsored by Lehman.

33. West Bronx Workers Club to Lehman, 18 February 1936; Herman S. Farber, Secretary, Local 1102 Retail Dry Goods Clerks' Union, to Lehman, 18 February 1936, Lehman Papers.

34. Robert B. Marshal to Lehman, 15 March 1936. For a sampling of other letters, see David J. Roberts to Lehman, February (n.d.) 1936; Robert Scott to Lehman, 24 February 1936, and Members of the Port Washington Gun Club to Lehman, 19 February 1936—all ibid.

35. Lehman's comments on the legislative wrangle from speeches he gave 23 February 1936 and 26 March 1936; see Governor's Speeches 1936, ibid. For another perspective on the legislative fight, see Brownell interview, Dewey Papers.

36. Thomas S. Rice, "Association's Program before New York Legislature of 1933," *The Panel*, 10:5 (November–December 1932): 55; John H. Barker, New York City, to Lehman, 13 February 1936, Lehman Papers; William P. Lawler to Lehman, 13 February 1936, ibid.

37. "Address of Governor Herbert H. Lehman on "The Fight Against Crime," broadcast, 23 February 1936, Governor's Speeches 1936, ibid. (hereafter Fight Against Crime speech); Hickman, "Profiles," 26; Lee Smith to Charles Poletti, 20 April 1936, ibid. Letters from other supportive groups in ibid.

38. Fight Against Crime speech; Lehman endorsement of Dewey's proposal, 5 March 1936, Governor's Speeches 1936, ibid. For a complete list of bills approved and not approved, see Anti-Crime Program, Special Subject Files, Campaign Materials, 1936, ibid.; Poletti, *Reminiscences*, COH, 150, describes Lehman's pleasure; Phillips interview, 4 April 1958, 264.

CHAPTER SIX

1. Martin A. Gosch and Richard Hammer, *The Last Testament of Lucky Luciano*, 3–4.

2. Robert Lacey, *Little Man: Meyer Lansky and the Gangster Life*, 34, 42, 61.

3. Herbert Asbury, *The Gangs of New York: An Informal History of the Underworld*, 238. Asbury describes other gangs in Manhattan during the nineteenth century, estimates their numbers, and discusses their links to politicians and businessmen. Craig Thompson and Allen Raymond, *Gang Rule in New York:*

The Story of a Lawless Era, 3, describe the ethnic makeup of gangs in the pre-Prohibition era.

4. Thompson, and Raymond, *Gang Rule*, 4.

5. Lacey, *Little Man*, 49–50. According to Sol Gelb, the worst effect of Prohibition was making criminals socially acceptable. Gelb interview, 75, Dewey Papers.

6. For a description of the effect of Prohibition profits on the underworld, see Tuttle, *Reminiscences*, COH, 178.

7. Alan Block, *East Side–West Side: Organizing Crime in New York, 1930–1950*, 1.

8. Ibid., 256.

9. Gelb interview, 6, 10.

10. Cuneo, *Life with Fiorello*, 82; Lacey, *Little Man*, 92.

11. Smith, *Thomas E. Dewey*, 183.

12. Biographical information about Carter from an unmarked manuscript in the Dewey Papers and *New York Times*, 29 December 1937, 8.

13. Adler quoted in Mitgang, *Seabury*, 187–88; Dewey's Response to Luciano's Motion for a New Trial (hereafter Dewey's Response), Luciano case files, New York County District Attorney's Office, New York City Archives (hereafter Luciano Files).

14. Smith, *Thomas E. Dewey*, 181. Smith argues that Gurfein and Carter worked together in the early stages, but memos of the district attorney's office in the Luciano case show that initially she worked alone—a reflection of Dewey's belief that this would be a blind alley. See memo, Wayne Merrick to William B. Herlands, 16 October 1935, Luciano Files. Herlands passed the memo on to Carter with the following note: "In view of the fact that you will be practically the only assistant working on this record, the attached papers should be included in your files."

15. Unsigned 3-page letter to Dewey, 7 July 1935; A Sucker to Dewey, 28 September 1935—both in Luciano Files. The case files contain hundreds of these letters, some addressed to the police, La Guardia, or Lehman and forwarded to Dewey.

16. George Worthington H. Carter, 25 September 1935. He went on to serve with the Federal Alcohol Administration in Washington. See also William H. Baldwin to William B. Herlands, 20 September 1935; Worthington to Herlands, 3 October 1935; K. D. Metcalf, chief of reference, New York Public Library, to Carter, 22 October 1935—all in Luciano Files.

17. Carter memo (n.d.), Luciano Files, indicates probable houses of prostitution as of January 1936 based on wiretaps; Dewey's Response, 4; Smith, *Thomas E. Dewey*, 181.

18. Smith, *Thomas E. Dewey*, 185–86; memoranda 2:380b and 380c, Luciano Files.

19. Fuld interview, 35, Dewey Papers; Smith, *Thomas E. Dewey*, 185–87; Breitel interview, 49–53, Dewey Papers.

20. Breitel interview, Dewey Papers, 49–53; claims of employment, Trial Transcript, 677, Luciano Files (hereafter Transcript); Dewey's Response, 6–13.
21. Smith, *Thomas E. Dewey*, 188.
22. Breitel interview, 51–53; Betty Anderson to Mrs. William Polin, 10 February 1936; Cleo Gold to Mable Hogue, 8 February 1936; Marion Pollarine to Michael Pollarine (n.d.); Celia Newman to her daughter (no name), 8 February 1936; Helen Williams to Billie Howard (n.d.); Attorney Joseph I. Erenstoft to Celia Newman, received 8 February 1936—all in Luciano Files.
23. The district attorney's files provide evidence for an alternative interpretation that Luciano was an early target. They contain hundreds of surveillance reports revealing that the New York police already were watching Luciano and his favorite haunts in the fall of 1935. It is unclear whether the surveillance was conducted as part of the Dewey investigation or became part of the case files later. Luciano Files; see Smith's alternative view in *Thomas E. Dewey*, 188–89.
24. Transcript, 680; Dewey's Response, 16–17.
25. Dewey's Response, 4–11, 16.
26. Gosch and Hammer, *Last Testament*, 193–94.
27. Affidavit by Dewey, 4 April 1936, Luciano Files.
28. For more on the New York legislation and its effect on the trial in appellate arguments, see Fuld interview and Moses Polakoff, Transcript, 115, 124–26, 132–33. The thirteen different versions of the indictments are in the Luciano Files.
29. For an outline of the syndicate see Transcript, 54–56; and for Dewey's description of the violent defendants, see Dewey's Response, 18.
30. Dewey's Response, 19.
31. Transcript, 679–81.
32. Ibid., 4, 12–14, 20.
33. In one instance, Dewey's investigators arrived at the home of a juror the same day he received his notice for jury duty. They questioned the man about his job, marital status, and the length of time he had lived at one address. Dewey said such investigations were routine; what made this one unusual was that the detectives had spoken with the subject of their investigation; in most cases they talked with third parties. Ibid., 160, 178, 180–83.
34. Ibid., 49, 53–54.
35. For the flap between Levy and Dewey, see ibid., 168 and 144, 150, 294, 502, 605, 607.
36. For jurors expressing unconstitutional views, see 326, 348, 363, 499–501; for mentions of previous jury service, see 207, 326, 412; for prejudgments of cases, see 73, 90, 524–26; for views of prostitutes, see 407, 506—all ibid.
37. The question of the number of challenges arose when defense attorneys unsuccessfully tried to strike a retired bank executive who was seated as the twelfth

juror, 621; the juror denied having made the "hell" quote under Dewey's questioning, 113; investigation of jurors, 160, 163, 183; shame to convict, 292; bail excessive, 493; truth of witnesses, 151, 309, 552—all ibid.

38. Ibid., 107–9, 120, 131, 135, 224, 228, 235, 264, 300, 377–78, 435, 438, 453–56, 475, 546, 612–13; for sequestration and court schedule, see 636–38, ibid.

CHAPTER SEVEN

1. Trial Transcript, 650–51, Luciano Files, N.Y. County District Attorney's Office, New York City Archives (hereafter Transcript).

2. Ibid., 658–60, 664, 677–83, 686–89.

3. Ibid., 660–61, 696–97, 700–704.

4. Ibid., Murray, opening statement, 739–41; Carlino opening statement, 709–17.

5. Ibid., Siegel opening statement, 735–37; see also comments by Samuel Siegel representing James Fredericks, ibid., 726–30.

6. Mitgang, *Seabury*, 174; Transcript, Levy opening statement, 720–24.

7. Transcript, 750, 846, 967–68, 1081–88, 1288, 1302, 1517, 1914, 2009, 2046, 2057, 2084, 2223, 4654, 4713, 4718.

8. Ibid., 753–79.

9. Ibid., 1301–16, 1324–25, 1348, 1439–41.

10. Kelly's testimony, ibid., 2915, 2925–26, 2940. Rose Cohen said she met with Dewey's staff four times in February, and finally told the truth in March after being questioned five times for two to three hours each. Ibid., 791–94. For details of other threats and promises, see ibid., 802–3, 875, 1101, 1564, 2034.

11. Ryan testimony, ibid., 884–89; Dewey described his "outing" policy, 1114; see also ibid., 796, 1099–1100, 2135.

12. Green testimony, ibid., 1566–77, 1587, 1594, 1601, 1681; Tach testimony, ibid., 2163–71, 2197.

13. Weiner testimony, ibid., 1122, 1129, 1145, 1157, 1171–77; Marcus's testimony, ibid., 1691–97, 1703–16, 1723–29, 1851.

14. Leonard testimony, 1914, 1918, 1921; Caputo testimony, 2252–55, 2340, 2409; Weintraub testimony, 4455, 4532–36; William Peluso said Fredericks also complained to him about the mob taking over but did not mention Luciano, 2499, 2507–8—all ibid.

15. Peter Balitzer testimony, ibid., 2588–89, 2607–9, 2667–70.

16. Mildred Balitzer testimony, ibid., 4906–11, 4919–30, 4936, 4960, 4965–71, 4977, 4999, 5113–18a, 5161, 5174–75.

17. Brown testimony, ibid., 3273–89, 3298–3302, 3313–14, 3316–19, 3331–33, 3349, 3358, 3364–66, 3392–93, 3397–3406.

18. Presser testimony, ibid., 3954–71, 3992–97, 4003–6, 4191, 4209–10, 4216–17, 4287–4301, 4635, 4639–40.

19. Bendix testimony, ibid., 2981–82, 2991, 2995–96.

20. Ibid., 3003–17, 3022–24, 3034–49, 3056–61, 3069–76, 3088–97, 3155.

21. Ibid., 2469, 2458.

22. Ibid., 3618–20, 3633, 4329–42, 4359–60, 4364, 4367, 4369, 4409, 4425–26, 4885.

23. Franco testimony, ibid., 5885, 5878, 5880, 5889–90, 5939, 5946; Heidy testimony, ibid., 6318, 6328–31, 6336–39.

24. Siegel testimony, ibid., 6277–80.

25. Anna Liguori testimony, ibid., 5526–32.

26. Policeman's testimony, ibid., 5573–75; Panger testimony, ibid., 5621–24, 5630–35.

27. Defense witnesses on Luciano as gambler, ibid., 5578, 5599, 5609, 5672–77, 5687–91, 5737, 5757–58, 5807, 5809, 5870, 6188.

28. Liguori testimony, ibid., 5348, 5375–86, 5435, 5447–50, 5471–76.

29. Luciano testimony, ibid., 5985–91, 5999, 6002–6, 6018, 6025, 6042, 6049, 6057, 6060, 6063–67, 6108–9, 6138–48, 6172–82.

30. Barra statements, ibid., 6365–67; Paley statements, ibid., 6406.

31. Carlino quotes, ibid., 6443–49, 6467.

32. Siegel quotes, ibid., 6525–26, 6533–35, 6555.

33. Levy statements, ibid., 6623–28, 6646.

34. Ibid., 6684, 6705.

35. Dewey quote, ibid., 6742–43, 6747–49.

36. Ibid., 6747–48, 6772.

37. Ibid., 6766, 6773, 6876.

38. Ibid., 6867, 6871–72, 6881–83.

39. Ibid., 6884–6901.

40. McCook statement, ibid., 7061.

41. Probation officer David Dressler, however, said too many higher-ups got off while "smaller potatoes" were convicted; see Dressler, *Reminiscences,* COH, 59; see also "The Dewey Investigations," *The Panel* 14:2 (May–June 1936): 2; press release, 8 June 1936, La Guardia Papers; Manners, *Patience and Fortitude,* 196; Poletti, *Reminiscences,* COH, 332, 476. Benjamin Stolberg claims Luciano was convicted for the wrong crime in "Thomas E. Dewey, Self-Made Myth," *American Mercury* 1:198 (June 1940): 146.

42. See Investigation by the Justice Who Presided at the Recent Trial of Luciano and Others [McCook] with a View to Investigating the Circumstances of Preparation for, and Conduct of Trials, with Particular Reference to the Material Witnesses and Their Treatment, and in Preparation for Their Discharge, Transcript (hereafter McCook interviews), 355, Luciano Files. The $20,000 figure is a rough estimate based on witness fees listed in Luciano Files. It is unclear whether the costs of shopping, movies, and restaurants were included in these

totals. The jail costs were not. None of the available court records indicate the total costs involved in the case.

43. McCook interviews, 40, 43, 46–48, 57–58, 231.

44. Ibid., 18, 92–93, 302.

45. Citations to these kinds of comments are too numerous to list; for examples, see ibid., 5, 8–9, 13, 31, 35–36, 43, 81–82, 88, 247–50, 252, 254, 256–58, 265; for references to the dancer and the beautician, see 66–68, 73, 252.

46. Ibid., 43, 57–58, 96.

47. Ibid., 116, 271–73, 276, 345–46.

48. Ibid., 438–43.

49. Transcript, sentencing hearing, 18 June 1936, 7077–84.

50. Ibid., 7085–97.

51. Trial Appeal (hereafter Appeal), Respondent's Brief, Luciano Files.

52. Appeal, Brown and Balitzer affidavits.

53. Ibid., Brown affidavit, 1–6, 12–13.

54. Ibid., Balitzer affidavit, 2–6, 9–13.

55. Ibid., Presser affidavit, 2–11; Horvath testimony, 9–11.

56. Ibid., Weiss affidavit, 2–8.

57. Ibid., McCook denial of motion for new trial, 7 May 1937, 7–8, 37–38, 55–56, 61, 70, 73–75, 78, 149–54, 157.

58. Fuld interview, 31, Dewey Papers; Gelb interview, 19–20, ibid. Gelb also recognized the weaknesses and attributed them to Dewey's youth and relative inexperience.

59. Gelb interview, 65–66.

60. Speech to chapel stewards of the Printers' Unions, 22 October 1937, Dewey Papers; Dewey to La Guardia, 20 April 1936, La Guardia Papers.

CHAPTER EIGHT

1. Hundreds of letters about prostitution generated by the Luciano case publicity are in the Luciano Files.

2. For a detailed description of the strike, see Benjamin Stolberg, *Tailor's Progress, The Story of a Famous Union and the Men Who Made It,* 135–41.

3. Radio speech, 3 October 1937, Dewey Papers.

4. Ibid.

5. Martin A. Gosch and Richard Hammer, *The Last Testament of Lucky Luciano,* 39, exaggerate the degree to which Luciano controlled Lepke. For more realistic perspectives, see Gelb interview, Dewey Papers, 6; and Robert Lacey, *Little Man: Meyer Lansky and the Gangster Life,* 89–90.

6. *The Reminiscences of Solomon A. Klein* (1962) 72–73, COH; B. Stolberg, *Tailor's Progress,* 253–55; Dewey, radio speech, 3 October 1937, Dewey Papers.

7. Dewey to E. J. Davis, 21 May 1935, Dewey Papers; Klein, *Reminiscences,* COH, 75–76.
8. Schieffelen, *Reminiscences,* COH, 37–38; Dewey to E. J. Davis, 21 May 1935, Dewey Papers.
9. Samuel Seabury held this opinion; see Crain Report, 10.
10. Ibid., 10–11.
11. Ibid., 9–26.
12. Lawrence Elliott, *Little Flower: The Life and Times of Fiorello La Guardia,* 179; Bella Rodman, *Fiorello La Guardia,* 128–29; Gelb interview, 37, Dewey Papers.
13. Fuld interview, 7, Dewey Papers.
14. J. J. Schubert, Utility Workers Local Number B752, to La Guardia, 22 February 1937, La Guardia Papers.
15. "New Dewey Drive Begins on Racket in Electrical Jobs," *New York Times,* 14 January 1937, 1, 3; and "Dewey Is Attacked at Labor Rally," ibid., 30 January 1937, 7.
16. President Jacob Mirsky, Bricklayers, Masons and Plasterers International Union of America, Local 37, to La Guardia, 17 February 1937; J. Meyerowitz, secretary, Bakery and Confectionery Workers International Union of America, Local 79, to La Guardia, 17 February 1937; James A. Weaver, secretary-treasurer, United Upholsterers' Union of New York, Local 44, to La Guardia, 2 March 1937. These letters and others in the La Guardia Papers.
17. Dewey radio address, 30 July 1935, and undated manuscript, Dewey Papers.
18. Gelb interview, 8, 37; Dewey radio speeches, 3 October 1937 and 15 October 1937—all ibid.
19. Dewey, speech to Citizens' Committee on the Control of Crime in New York, 11 May 1937, ibid.
20. Dewey, speech at banquet in honor of Benny Gottesman, 26 October 1937, ibid.
21. Ibid.
22. Dewey address, Governor's Conference on Crime, 2 October 1935, ibid.; "Café Union Heads Linked to Schultz," *New York Times,* 24 January 1937, 16.
23. Dewey, speech to Citizens' Committee on the Control of Crime, 11 May 1937; and extemporaneous talk to unidentified union group, 8 October 1937—both Dewey Papers.
24. "Nine Seized as Dewey Strikes at $2,000,000 Café Racket," *New York Times,* 21 October 1936, 1.
25. "New Dewey Drive Revealed by Raid in Bakery Racket," ibid., 22 October 1936, 1–2.
26. "Bail Cut for Four Men in Restaurant Racket," 24 October 1936, 5; "Restaurant Racket," 25 October 1936, 2E; Russell Owen, "Drive on Rackets Was Long

Planned," E7; "13 Names in Racket that Shook Down Cafeterias for $150,000," 1, 20—all ibid.

27. "Number Two Man in Café Racket Confesses as Trial Opens," ibid., 19 January 1937, 1, 2.

28. "Café Racket Trial Made 'Labor' Case," 20 January 1937, 4; "Wiretapping Hines Given in Café Case," 22 January 1937, 12; "Café Jury Picked; Defendants Jailed," 23 January 1937, 1, 5—all ibid.

29. "Café Union Heads Linked to Schultz," ibid., 24 January 1937, 1, 16.

30. Russell Owen, "City's Racket Tribute Is Reduced by Dewey," ibid., 24 January 1937, 10E.

31. "Café Racket Onus Is Put on Owners," ibid., 26 January 1937, 44L.

32. "Slain Schultz Aide Linked to Café Men," ibid., 27 January 1937, 1.

33. "Hesitant Witness Assailed by Dewey," ibid., 28 January 1937, 3.

34. "Racketeer Opened Union, Girl Swears," ibid., 29 January 1937, 1, 8.

35. "Hines Name Linked to Café Gangsters," ibid., 30 January 1937, 1, 7.

36. "7th Avenue Café paid $3,500 Shakedown to Schultz Gang," 2 February 1937, 1; "Two Rackets Linked by Victim at Trial," 3 February 1937, 1, 24; " 'Shakedown' Strike Used as a Weapon in the Café Racket," 4 February 1937, 1, 22; "Racket Chief Uses Club Owner's Name," 7 February 1937, 1–2—all ibid.

37. "$100,000 Café Shut by Racket Bombs, Owner Testifies," ibid., 6 February 1937, 1, 36.

38. "Racket Collector Implicates Union," ibid., 16 February 1937, 2.

39. "Dewey Rests Case in Trial of Racket," ibid., 19 February 1937, 1,10.

40. "Café Defendants at Odds on Stories," 20 February 1937, 34; "A.F.L. Leaders Left Union to Gang," 21 February 1937, 17—both ibid.

41. "A.F.L. Leaders Left Union to Gang," 21 February 1937, 17; "Café Union Chief Tells of Threats," 23 February 1937, 1, 28—both ibid.

42. "A.F.L. Leaders Left Union to Gang," 21 February 1937, 17; "Café Union Chief Tells of Threats," 23 February 1937, 1, 28; and "Blind Man Accuses a Dewey Witness," 27 February 1937, 1–2—all ibid.

43. "Union Chief Banked $11,534 in 13 Months," 24 February 1937, 18; "Café Union Leader Explains Deposits," 25 February 1937, 3; "Café Union Slaying Laid to Employers," February 26 1937, 3; on Borson's murder, see "Nine Seized as Dewey Strikes at $2,000,000 Café Racket," 21 October 1936, 1, and "Bail Cut for Four Men in Restaurant Racket," 24 October 1936, 5—all ibid.

44. "Union Chief Banked $11,534 in 13 Months," 24 February 1937, 18; "Café Union Leader Explains Deposits," 25 February 1937, 3; "Café Union Slaying Laid to Employers," 26 February 1937, 3—all ibid.

45. "Union Is Praised at Racket Trial," ibid., 28 February 1937, 26.

46. Ibid.

47. "Defense Is Curbed in the Café Trial," ibid., 4 March 1937, 8.

48. "Schultz Aide Got $21,000 by Threat," 6 March 1937, 34; "Tribute Put at 90% in the Café Racket," 7 March 1937, 38—both ibid.

49. "Martin's Waiters Tallied Union Vote," 11 March 1937, 48; "Waiters Paid Gang, Leader Testifies," 12 March 1937, 3; "Union Man Admits Paying Café Thugs," 13 March 1937, 5—all ibid.

50. "Outburst at Trial by Café Union Chief," ibid., 17 March 1937, 19.

51. "Rackets Defendant III, Wins Mistrial Despite Protests and Attacks on Dewey," 14 March 1937, 1; "Café Racket Trial Nearing Its Close," 19 March 1937, 48; "Café Case Lawyer Makes Own Plea," 23 March 1937, 2; "Café Racket Jury to Get Case Today," 24 March 1937, 52—all ibid.

52. "Racket Lawyers Scored at Trial," ibid., 25 March 1937, 52.

53. "Seven in Café Racket Guilty; Dewey Scores a Victory in Industrial Gang War," ibid., 26 March 1937, 1–2.

54. Ibid.

55. "Racket's Last Ride," ibid., 28 March 1937, 2E.

56. "Café Racketeers Get 5 to 20 Years; Scored by Judge," ibid., 8 April 1937, 10.

57. Radio speech to American Labor Party broadcast, 30 September 1937; speech at Yorkville Casino, 14 October 1937; speech at Fifth Assembly District South Republican Club, 15 October 1937—all in Dewey Papers.

58. McCook address, U.S. Conference of Mayors, 16 November 1937, ibid.

59. Brownell, *Reminiscences* (1967), 322–23, COH.

60. Gurfein, August draft, Dewey Papers.

61. B. Stolberg, *Tailor's Progress*, 255.

CHAPTER NINE

1. "Greater New York Needs Criminal Justice Association," *The Panel* 9:2 (March–April 1931): 14; and Richard H. Chamberlain, "Alameda County Forms Model Anti-Racket Council," ibid. 11:3 (November–December 1933): 26. For failure of the National Crime Commission, see *The Reminiscences of Frederick Trubee Davison* (1955), 90–92, COH; and W. J. Maroney to Al Smith, 14 August 1925, Smith Papers. Maroney said the group learned little and fanned xenophobia. For the New York Crime Commission, see Smith's Message on Crime, 1 March 1926, and press release, 18 May 1926, ibid.

2. Lehman's and Dewey's comments, *Governor's Crime Conference*, 25, 30–31, 119; "Second Racket Grand Jury Recommends a Citizens' Committee," *The Panel* 14:3 (November–December 1936): 7.

3. August Heckscher, *When La Guardia Was Mayor: New York's Legendary Years*, 135–36; Dewey to Stanley Howe, executive secretary to La Guardia, 10 August 1936, La Guardia Papers; W. P. Beazell, "Crime Control Committee of Citizens," *The Panel* 14:3 (November–December 1936): 1, 11.

4. Beazell, "Crime Control Committee," 1, 11; press release with copy of Dewey Speech to Citizens' Committee on the Control of Crime in New York, 11 May 1937, Dewey Papers.

5. Citizens' Committee on the Control of Crime in New York, report, 31 December 1937, "Twelve Months of Crime in New York City," 1 July 1938; La Guardia to Guggenheim, 8 May 1940; press release, Citizens' Committee, 22 January 1941; L. O. Head, president, Railway Express Agency, to La Guardia, 23 January 1941; Charles G. Small, American Ice Co., to La Guardia, 23 January 1941—all in La Guardia Papers.

6. *The Reminiscences of Spruille Braden* (1956), 1960, COH.

7. Wallace S. Sayre and Herbert Kaufman, *Governing New York City: Politics in the Metropolis,* 14.

8. Ibid., 14–17.

9. Baldwin to Al Smith, 10 March 1923, Smith Papers; Baldwin to Smith, enclosing copy of report by Charter Commission, 5 March 1923, ibid.

10. Rodman, *Fiorello La Guardia,* 172; and Sayre and Kaufman, *Governing New York City,* 617.

11. Emily Smith Warner with Hawthorne Daniels, *The Happy Warrior: A Biography of My Father Alfred E. Smith,* 272; Sayre and Kaufman, *Governing New York City,* 94, 114–16.

12. La Guardia swore in the charter commission on 22 January 1935, La Guardia Papers; Warner, *Happy Warrior,* 272; Mitgang, *Seabury,* 346; Earle, *Reminiscences,* COH, 23. For another interpretation, see *The Reminiscences of Leonard Wallstein* (1948–49), 97–101, COH.

13. Earle, *Reminiscences,* COH, 22–26, 28–31.

14. Rodman, *Fiorello La Guardia,* 173; Lazarus, *Reminiscences,* COH, 196.

15. Earle, *Reminiscences,* COH, 29–30; Sayre and Kaufman, *Governing New York,* 616–20.

16. "Out in the Open," *New York Times,* 30 October 1936, 22; Earle, *Reminiscences,* COH, 33–34, 36, 38; Mitgang, *Seabury,* 347.

17. Earle, *Reminiscences,* COH, 36, 38; Lazarus, *Reminiscences,* COH, 196, 218–20; and Windels, *Reminiscences,* COH, 105. Windels also attributes the charter's passage to the fact it was linked with more popular bills.

18. "Charter Wins," *New York Times,* 4 November 1936, 1, 4; and Earle, *Reminiscences,* COH, 29–30. According to Sayre and Kaufman, *Governing New York City,* 620, the Democrats quickly regained a majority, and the diversity of that first election was not repeated. Proportional representation was abolished in favor of district voting in 1947. See Mitgang, *Seabury,* 347; and Windels, *Reminiscences,* COH, 107.

19. Windels, *Reminiscences,* COH, appendix, 13–14.

20. Lazarus reveals that New Deal money normally went through political channels; see his *Reminiscences,* 193–94.
21. B. Stolberg, *Tailor's Progress,* 192; Flynn, *Reminiscences* (1950), COH, 21; *The Reminiscences of Ben Davidson* (1977–78), 78–79, COH.
22. Mahoney, *Reminiscences* (1949), COH, 143–44; Farley, *Reminiscences* (1957–58), COH, 269, 271, 273; "Tammany to Act on Leader Today," *New York Times,* 12 January 1937, 1; "Dooling Remains at Tammany Helm," ibid., 13 January 1937, 1; "Tammany to Seek an Acting Leader for Fall Contest," ibid., 8 March 1937, 1; and "Temporary Chief," ibid., 9 March 1937, 27.
23. "Mayoralty Moves," *New York Times,* 21 February 1937, 2E.
24. Baldwin, *Reminiscences* (1949–50), COH, 18; Rodman, *Fiorello La Guardia,* 185; Phillips chronology, 96; Isaacs, *Reminiscences* (1949–50), COH, 81–82; Mack, *Reminiscences* (1950), COH, 52–54.
25. "Handicapping Fusion," *New York Times,* 30 October 1936, 22; Combs, *Reminiscences* (1949–51), 132–33; Allen, *Reminiscences* (1949–50), COH, 3:443, 473–4.
26. "Backers of Mayor Draft Campaign," 11 January 1937, 8; "City Campaign Waits on Democratic Move," 21 February 1937, 10E; "Fusionists Push Campaign Plans," 23 February 1937, 28—all in *New York Times.*
27. "Fists Fly as Club Endorses Mayor," *New York Times,* 2 March 1937, 1; "Campaign to Draft La Guardia Begins," ibid., 1 February 1937, 1, "Republican Revolt on Mayor Grows," ibid., 9 March 1937, 1; Phillips interview, 8 May 1958, 388.
28. Mitgang, *Seabury,* 348; Berle quoted in Manners, *Patience and Fortitude,* 237–38.
29. Phillips chronology, 96–98.
30. Isaacs, *Reminiscences,* COH, 89; Phillips interview, 27 March 1958, 213.
31. Steinberg interview, 46–47; *New York Daily News,* 15 August 1937, 4; Dewey speech to Republican Women's Luncheon, 13 September 1937, Dewey Papers; and La Guardia endorsement, ibid.
32. Republican handbill for 1937 primary election, 16 September, Dewey Papers.
33. Manners, *Patience and Fortitude,* 238; Phillips interview, 8 May 1958, 401, 403; press release of letter from Alex Rose, state executive secretary, American Labor party, to Senator Robert Wagner, 17 October 1937, Dewey Papers.
34. Phillips interview, 8 May 1958, 403; and Harold Hastings, radio speech, 5 October 1937—both in Dewey Papers.
35. Samuel Untermyer speaking for Tammany candidate Hastings, 24 October 1937, ibid.
36. William Copeland Dodge radio speech for Hastings, 29 October 1937, ibid.
37. Hastings speech to labor rally at Cooper Union, 18 October 1937; and Hastings radio address, 30 October 1937—both ibid.

38. Charles S. Whitman for Dewey, October (n.d.) 1937; press release, 5 October 1937; "Support Dewey," New York Printing Pressmen's Union, No. 51—all in ibid. Files 3 and 7 contain numerous additional endorsements.
39. "Throwaway in Yiddish"; "A Primer on the DA and Organized Crime"; "The Challenge of Crime"; "Crime Is Run by Big Shots"; "District Attorney Thomas E. Dewey," draft; Gelb interview, 44; Bulletin of Metropolitan Church Life, 7 October 1937; press release on film, 19 October 1937—all ibid.
40. Radio speech, 3 October 1937, ibid. Rubin lived to testify in the flour trucking case. For speeches Dewey gave at various political rallies and civic meetings, see campaign files, ibid.
41. Radio speeches, 10 October 1937 and 17 October 1937, ibid.
42. Radio speech, 17 October 1937, ibid.
43. Ibid.
44. Memo, Eugene O'Brien to Merrick, re: Al Marinelli, 16 April 1936; radio speech, 24 October 1937—both ibid.
45. Radio speech, 24 October 1937, ibid.
46. Ibid.
47. Windels, *Reminiscences*, COH, 89–90; Flynn, *Reminiscences*, COH, 20–21; election results in Manners, *Patience and Fortitude*, 237, 240, and Phillips interview, 8 May 1958, 395.
48. Phillips chronology, 103–4.
49. Ibid.
50. Steinberg interview, 53; and Phillips interview, 8 May 1958, 417.
51. "Dewey Appoints 14, Average Age Is 32," *New York Times*, 29 December 1937, 8; Steinberg interview, 54; Dewey, "Grand Jury the Bulwark of Justice," *The Panel* 19:1 (May 1941): 3.
52. Civil Service Commission, hearing on the matter of filling positions in the Office of the District Attorney of New York County, 19 January 1938, Lehman Papers.
53. Dewey, "Grand Jury the Bulwark of Justice," 3.
54. Quoted in Phillips chronology, 107.
55. Ibid., 105–6.
56. Ibid., 111–19.
57. Speech to State Association of District Attorneys, Cooperstown, 11 June 1938, Dewey Papers.
58. Phillips chronology, 117–19, 124–25. For more on the politics of the constitutional convention and the amendments passed, see Warner, *Happy Warrior*, 290–93.
59. Harlan Phillips Drafts, chap. 4, first draft, 606, 658, Dewey Papers; Smith, *Thomas E. Dewey*, 250.

60. Phillips interview, 8 May 1958, 453; and speech at Saratoga, 29 September 1938, Dewey Papers.

61. Lehman, *Reminiscences,* COH, 653; Phillips Drafts, chap. 4, first draft, 607, Dewey Papers.

62. The *New York Daily News, World-Telegram, New York Post,* and *Daily Mirror* supported Lehman; see Phillips Drafts, chap. 4, first draft, 615–16, 622, 645; and press release, 2 November 1938—both in Dewey Papers.

63. Moscow, *Reminiscences,* COH, 17–19; speech at Saratoga, 29 September 1938, Dewey Papers; press release, 3 October 1938, Dewey Papers.

64. Addresses by Governor Herbert H. Lehman, 24 October 1938, 31 October 1938, 3 November 1938, Lehman Papers; Moscow, *Reminiscences,* COH, 19.

65. U.S. District Judge Frederick Bryant, Malone, N.Y., to Dewey, 10 November 1938, Dewey Papers; memoranda on editorial reaction to election and on post-election comment on Dewey, both dated December 1938, ibid.

CHAPTER TEN

1. For a succinct example of this argument, see Leo Katcher, *The Big Bankroll: The Life and Times of Arnold Rothstein,* 256–57.

2. For a description of Tweed's flight and return, see Leo Hershkowitz, *Tweed's New York: Another Look,* 280–96.

3. Hines Case documents, Hines Files; memorandum to Mr. Grimes, 12 September 1938 with summary of newspaper articles about Hines, ibid.

4. *The Reminiscences of Samuel J. Battle* (1960), 36–37, Columbia Oral History (COH); Dressler, *Reminiscences,* COH, 65–66, 69–71.

5. Panuch interview, 36, Dewey Papers; timetable of Medalie speeches, Dewey Papers.

6. Hines Files.

7. Goldstein, *Reminiscences,* COH, 211; Cuneo, *Life with Fiorello,* 147–49.

8. Presentment issued by regular February grand jury, filed 17 December 1934, Dewey Papers; outline of newspaper coverage of 1935 grand jury investigation, ibid.

9. Gelb interview, 12.

10. Smith, *Thomas E. Dewey,* 215.

11. Copy of indictment; and Sol Gelb to Frederick Moran, 24 March 1943—both in Hines Files.

12. Dewey radio speech, 10 October 1937, Dewey Papers.

13. Ibid.

14. Smith, *Thomas E. Dewey,* 173, 248–49; Gelb interview, 13.

15. Gelb interview, 37.

16. Copy of indictment; and Sol Gelb to Frederick Moran, 24 March 1943—both in Hines Files.

17. Steinberg, interview, 62–63; transcript of minutes in a hearing before Ferdinand Pecora, 27 July 1938, 138, 141–44, Hines Files.

18. Transcript of minutes of a hearing before Ferdinand Pecora, 27 July 1938, 114, Hines Files.

19. Joseph Shalleck, memorandum in opposition to demurrer and motions to change the place of trial, granting a separate trial, and for a bill of particulars, 4–5; Shalleck, brief in support of defendants' motion to change venue, for a severance of the trial, and for a bill of particulars—both ibid.

20. Transcript of minutes of a hearing before Ferdinand Pecora, 27 July 1938, 74–76, 78–79, ibid.

21. Ibid., 107, 117–19, 122.

22. Steinberg interview, 63; *The Reminiscences of Martin C. Ansorge* (1949), COH 21; Fuld, *Reminiscences,* COH, 24.

23. For information about Pecora and Dewey, and the opening day of the trial, see Smith, *Thomas E. Dewey,* 208, 242, 255.

24. Battle, *Reminiscences,* COH, 47–48.

25. Rosenman, *Reminiscences,* COH, 31.

26. Phillips Drafts, chap. 1, copies of second draft, 1, 52–53, Dewey Papers; Perkins, *Reminiscences,* COH, 3:437–38.

27. Dressler, *Reminiscences,* COH, 144; Phillips chronology, 143.

28. Phillips interview, 15 April, 301. Lehman, *Reminiscences,* COH, 644. For information on Dewey's investigation of Dodge, see files William Copeland Dodge, Dodge, and Dodge, William Copeland, Policy, Hines Files.

29. Phillips chronology, 144–47.

30. Smith, *Thomas E. Dewey,* 256–59 letter to his mother in Phillips Drafts, 669, Dewey Papers.

31. Pecora, *Reminiscences,* COH, 1048–49; Smith, *Thomas E. Dewey,* 261.

32. Lockwood interview, 95; Phillips Drafts, chap. 4, first draft, 572, Dewey Papers; Phillips chronology, 152; John M. Maguire, "The Hines Mistrial," *The Bar Bulletin,* no. 140 (October 1936).

33. Phillips Drafts, chap. 4, first draft, 573, Dewey Papers; Phillips chronology, 153.

34. Fuld interview, 62–63; Phillips interview, 27 May 1958, 444–45, 449.

35. Pecora, *Reminiscences,* COH, 934–35; Fuld interview, 55; Gelb interview, 18; Steinberg interview, 60; Pearson quoted in Smith, *Thomas E. Dewey,* 262.

36. Gelb interview, 26–27; Fulton Oursler, radio speech, 20 October 1942, Dewey Papers.

37. *New York Times* quoted in Phillips chronology, 153–54.

38. Fuld interview, 59; Phillips chronology, 156; Pecora's opinion, 19 September 1938, Hines Files.

39. Phillips Drafts, chap. 4, first draft, 606, Dewey Papers. Steinberg interview, 65.
40. Baldwin, *Reminiscences,* COH, 67.
41. Fuld interview, 61, 64; Steinberg interview, 65; recommendation in respect of defendant George Weinberg, deceased, Hines Files; Phillips Drafts, chap. 4, first draft, 676–68, Dewey Papers.
42. Phillips Drafts, chap. 4, first draft, 692–95, Dewey Papers; Smith, *Thomas E. Dewey,* 283–84.
43. Smith, *Thomas E. Dewey,* 284.
44. Phillips Drafts, chap. 4, first draft, 700, 704–5, Dewey Papers.
45. Fuld interview, 64; Smith, *Thomas E. Dewey,* 285; Gelb to Frederick Moran, Chairman of Board of Parole, Sing Sing, 24 March 1943; Hines Files; Phillips Drafts, chap. 4, first draft, 709, Dewey Papers.
46. *People* v. *Hines,* 284 NY 93, cited in Phillips Drafts, chap. 4, first draft, 709–10, Dewey Papers.
47. Clohan to Dewey, 6 March 1939, Dewey Papers.
48. Pecora, *Reminiscences,* COH, 1092; Simpson and Manhattan Borough President Stanley M. Isaacs were both put off by Dewey's decision; they believed "that no man holding public office had a right to let his conduct be dictated by that particular attitude." Isaacs, *Reminiscences,* COH, 184.

CONCLUSION

1. Statistics for New York arrests and court clearance rates are found in early issues of *The Panel.* For a discussion of the larger issues involved, see Roger Lane, "Urbanization and Criminal Violence in the 19th Century: Massachusetts as a Test Case," *Journal of Social History* 2 (1968): 468–83.
2. Dewey radio address, 30 July 1935, Dewey Papers.
3. M. Stolberg, "Evolution of Frontier Justice."
4. For a description of national and federal criminal legal reform efforts during the 1920s and 1930s, see M. Stolberg, "Policing the Twilight Zone."
5. I am not arguing that Tilden's and Roosevelt's careers were based solely on crime fighting. In fact, the depth and variety of their experiences contrast sharply with Dewey's narrow career. For details about Tilden, see Alexander Clarence Flick, *Samuel Jones Tilden: A Study in Political Sagacity,* 192–241; for information about Roosevelt, see *The Autobiography of Lincoln Steffens,* 247–65, and William Harbaugh, *The Life and Times of Theodore Roosevelt,* 69–92.
6. Elliott, *Little Flower,* 229, makes this claim for La Guardia; it also applies to the others.
7. Krock, *Reminiscences* (1950), COH, 47–48; George Hamilton Combs, *Reminiscences* (1949–51), COH, 133.

AFTERWORD

1. "Citizens' Committee Reports Sharp Decrease in Crime," *The Panel* 22:1 (January 1940): 10.
2. "Ex-Mayor Walker Succumbs at 65 to Clot on Brain," *New York Times,* 19 November 1946, 1; Mitgang, *Seabury,* 354.
3. Mitgang, *Seabury,* 355–56.
4. Arthur Mann wrote the entry for La Guardia in the *Dictionary of American Biography,* 466.
5. Sayre and Kaufman, *Governing New York City,* 696–97.
6. For information about Hogan's office staff, see "Advice to Grand Jurors in Present World Crisis," *The Panel* 20:1 (March 1942): 3; "Jimmy Hines Dead; Ex-Tammany Chief," *New York Times,* 26 March 1957, 1; Barry Cunningham with Mike Pearl, *Mr. District Attorney,* 3, 12, 33.
7. "Judge G. Z. Medalie Dies in Albany at 62," *New York Times,* 5 March 1946, 27.
8. "Thomas E. Dewey Is Dead at 68," ibid., 17 March 1971, 1.
9. Max Lerner, "Payoff Blues," *New York Post,* 18 October 1950, 48; also in "The Story of the Dewey Double Deal," 1950 Senate [c237–21], Lehman Papers.
10. Press release 3 January 1946, Dewey Papers.
11. Charles Poletti, *Reminiscences* (1948), COH, 477, takes the view that Dewey received payoffs from Luciano; the full story of the Luciano deal found in the Dewey Papers; "Up and At 'Em Dewey," *Louisville Times,* undated clipping, ibid.; Joachim Joesten, "A Devastating Exposé Dewey, Luciano and I," *Behind the Scene,* 1 (January 1956), ibid.
12. Mary M. Stolberg, entry for Luciano, *Oxford Dictionary of American Biography.*
13. "Thomas E. Dewey Is Dead at 68," 1.
14. "Herbert Lehman, 85, Dies: Ex-Governor and Senator," *New York Times,* 6 December 1963, 1.

Bibliography

Archival Sources

Albany, New York
   New York State Archives
      Franklin Delano Roosevelt's Governor's Papers
      Al Smith's Governor's Papers

Hyde Park, New York
   FDR Presidential Library
      The Papers of Franklin Delano Roosevelt

New York, New York
   Columbia University
      Columbia Oral History Project
         Alger, George W.
         Allen, Dr. William Harvey
         Ansorge, Martin C.
         Baldwin, Joseph Clark
         Battle, Samuel J.
         Braden, Spruille
         Brownell, Herbert
         Bunzl, Mrs. Walter
         Burlingham, Charles Culp
         Combs, George Hamilton, Jr.
         Davidson, Ben
         Davison, Frederick Trubee
         Dean, Gordon
         Dewey, Thomas E.
         Dressler, David

Earle, Genevieve B.
Farley, James A.
Flynn, Edward J.
Fuld, Stanley H.
Goldstein, Jonah J.
Isaacs, Stanley M.
Klein, Solomon A.
Koenig, Samuel S.
Krock, Arthur
Lazarus, Reuben
Lehman, Herbert H.
Lumbard, Joseph Edward, Jr.
Mack, Walter S., Jr.
Mahoney, Jeremiah T.
Moscow, Warren
Peck, David W.
Pecora, Ferdinand
Perkins, Frances
Poletti, Charles
Rosenman, Samuel I.
Saxe, Martin
Schieffelin, William Jay
Stoddard, Francis R.
Straus, Nathan
Strauss, Morris
Tuttle, Charles H.
Wallstein, Leonard M.
Wardwell, Allen
Windels, Paul
The Herbert H. Lehman Papers

New York City Records Administration
The Fiorella La Guardia Papers
New York County District Attorney's Files
New York State v. *Charles Lucianio et al.*
New York State v. *James J. Hines*

Rochester, New York
The University of Rochester
Thomas E. Dewey Papers

Unpublished Material

Finch, Edward R. "Hands in Your Pockets: A Survey of the Background and Work of the New York County Rackets Bureau," Senior thesis, Princeton University, 1948.

Published Sources

PUBLIC DOCUMENTS

State of New York: *Proceedings of the Governor's Conference on Crime, the Criminal and Society, September 30 to October 3, 1935.* Albany, N.Y.
The Laws of New York, 1921–1938.

NEWSPAPERS AND MAGAZINES

New York Times (1920–1971).
The Panel, 1–23 (1924–1945).

BOOKS

Allsop, Kenneth. *The Bootleggers and Their Era.* Garden City, N.Y.: Doubleday, 1961.
Allswang, John. *Bosses, Machines and Urban Voters.* Baltimore: Johns Hopkins University Press, 1986.
Asbury, Herbert. *The Gangs of New York: An Informal History of the Underworld.* New York: Alfred A. Knopf, 1927.
Anslinger, H. J., and William F. Tompkins. *The Traffic in Narcotics.* New York: Funk & Wagnall's, 1953.
Asinof, Eliot. *Eight Men Out: The Black Sox and the 1919 World Series.* New York: Holt, Rinehart and Winston, 1963.
Auerbach, Jerold S. *Unequal Justice: Lawyers and Social Change in Modern America.* London: Oxford University Press, 1976.
Bergreen, Lawrence. *Capone: The Man and the Era.* New York: Simon & Schuster, 1994.
Beyer, Barry K. *Thomas E. Dewey, 1937–1947: A Study in Political Leadership.* New York: Garland, 1979.
Block, Alan. *East Side–West Side: Organizing Crime in New York, 1930–1950.* Cardiff, Wales: University College Cardiff Press, 1980.
Clark, Norman H. *Deliver Us From Evil: An Interpretation of American Prohibition.* New York: W. W. Norton, 1976.
Clarke, Donald Henderson. *In the Reign of Rothstein.* New York: Vanguard Press, 1929.

Cummings, Homer, and Carl McFarland. *Federal Justice: Chapters in the History of Justice and the Federal Executive.* New York: Macmillan, 1937.

Cuneo, Ernest. *Life with Fiorello.* New York: Macmillan, 1955.

Cunningham, Barry, with Mike Pearl. *Mr. District Attorney: The Story of Frank S. Hogan and the Manhattan DA's Office.* New York: Mason and Charter, 1977.

Davis, Kenneth S. *FDR: The New York Years, 1928–1933.* New York: Random House, 1985.

Eldot, Paula. *Governor Alfred E. Smith: The Politician as Reformer.* New York: Garland, 1983.

Elliott, Lawrence. *Little Flower: The Life and Times of Fiorello La Guardia.* New York: William Morrow, 1983.

Fitzgerald, F. Scott. *The Great Gatsby.* New York: Charles Scribner's Sons, 1925.

Flick, Alexander Clarence. *Samuel Jones Tilden: A Study in Political Sagacity.* Reprint, Westport, Conn.: Greenwood Press, 1973.

Friedman, Lawrence M. *Crime and Punishment in American History.* New York: Basic Books, 1993.

Garrett, Charles. *The La Guardia Years, Machine and Reform Politics in New York City.* New Brunswick, N.J.: Rutgers University Press, 1961.

Gentry, Curt. *J. Edgar Hoover: The Man and the Secrets.* New York: W. W. Norton, 1991.

Gosch, Martin A., and Richard Hammer. *The Last Testament of Lucky Luciano.* Boston: Little, Brown, 1974.

Handlin, Oscar. *Al Smith and His America.* Boston: Little, Brown, 1958.

Hapgood, Norman, and Henry Moskowitz. *Up from the City Streets: Alfred E. Smith.* New York: Harcourt, Brace, 1927.

Harbaugh, William. *The Life and Times of Theodore Roosevelt.* London: Oxford University Press, 1975.

Heckscher, August, with Phyllis Robinson. *When La Guardia Was Mayor: New York's Legendary Years.* New York: W. W. Norton, 1978.

Herskowitz, Leo. *Tweed's New York: Another Look.* New York: Anchor Books, 1978.

Hughes, Rupert. *The Story of Thomas E. Dewey, Attorney for the People.* New York: Grosset & Dunlap, 1944.

Katcher, Leo. *The Big Bankroll: The Life and Times of Arnold Rothstein.* New York: Harper & Brothers, 1958.

Kessner, Thomas. *Fiorello H. La Guardia and the Making of Modern New York.* New York: McGraw-Hill, 1989.

Lacey, Robert. *Little Man: Meyer Lansky and the Gangster Life.* Boston: Little, Brown, 1991.

Lehman, Herbert H. *Liberalism: A Personal Journey.* New York: Astoria Press, 1958.

Mann, Arthur. *La Guardia: A Fighter Against His Times, 1882–1933.* Philadelphia: J. B. Lippincott, 1959.

Manners, William. *Patience and Fortitude: Fiorello La Guardia.* New York: Harcourt Brace Jovanovich, 1976.

Messick, Hank. *John Edgar Hoover: An Inquiry into the Life and Times of John Edgar Hoover, and His Relationship to the Continuing Partnership of Crime, Business and Politics.* New York: David McKay, 1972.

Mitgang, Herbert. *The Man Who Rode the Tiger: The Life of Judge Samuel Seabury and the Story of the Greatest Investigation of City Corruption in This Century.* New York: Viking Press, 1970.

Morello, Karen Berger. *The Invisible Bar: The Woman Lawyer in America, 1638 to the Present.* Boston: Beacon Press, 1986.

Nevins, Allan. *Herbert H. Lehman and His Era.* New York: Charles Scribner's Sons, 1963.

O'Connor, Richard. *The First Hurrah: A Biography of Alfred E. Smith.* New York: G. P. Putnam's Sons, 1970.

Pasley, Fred D. *Al Capone: The Biography of a Self-Made Man.* Reprint, Freeport, N.Y.: Books for Libraries Press, 1971.

Perry, Elisabeth Israel. *Belle Moscowitz: Feminine Politics and the Exercise of Power in the Age of Alfred E. Smith.* New York: Oxford University Press, 1987.

Powers, Richard Gid. *Secrecy and Power: The Life of J. Edgar Hoover.* New York: Free Press, 1987.

Rodman, Bella, with Philip Sterling. *Fiorello La Guardia.* New York: Hill and Wang, 1962.

Runyon, Damon. *Guys and Dolls.* In *The Damon Runyon Omnibus.* Garden City, N.Y.: Sun Dial Press, 1944.

Sayre, Wallace S., and Herbert Kaufman. *Governing New York City: Politics in the Metropolis.* New York: Russell Sage Foundation, 1960.

Schwartz, Jordan A. *Liberal: Adolf A. Berle and the Vision of an American Era.* New York: Free Press, 1987.

Smith, Myron J., Jr. *Baseball: A Comprehensive Bibliography.* Jefferson, N.C.: McFarland & Co., 1986.

Smith, Richard N. *Thomas E. Dewey and His Times.* New York: Simon and Schuster, 1982.

Steffens, Lincoln. *The Autobiography of Lincoln Steffens.* New York: The Literary Guild, 1931.

Stolberg, Benjamin. *Tailor's Progress: The Story of a Famous Union and the Men Who Made It.* New York: Doubleday, Doran, 1944.

Theoharis, Athan G., and John Stuart Cox. *The Boss: J. Edgar Hoover and the Great American Inquisition.* Philadelphia: Temple University Press, 1988.

Thompson, Craig, and Allen Raymond. *Gang Rule in New York: The Story of a Lawless Era*. New York: Dial Press, 1940.

Voight, David Quentin. *American Baseball, Volume II: From the Commissioners to Continental Expansion*. Reprint, University Park. Pennsylvania State University Press, 1983.

Waldman, Louis. *Labor Lawyer*. New York: E. P. Dutton, 1945.

Warner, Emily Smith, with Hawthorne Daniels. *The Happy Warrior: A Biography of My Father Alfred E. Smith*. Garden City, N.Y.: Doubleday, 1956.

Younger, Richard D. *The People's Panel: The Grand Jury in the United States*. Providence, R.I.: Brown University Press, 1963.

ARTICLES

Bellush, Jewel. "Roosevelt's Good Right Arm: Lieutenant Governor Herbert Lehman." *New York History* 41:4 (October 1960): 423–43.

Brainin, Joseph. "Herbert Henry Lehman." *Opinion: A Journal of Jewish Life and Letters* 22:6 (September–October 1952): 16–18.

Cook, Fred J., and Gene Gleason. "The Shame of New York." *The Nation* 189:14 (31 October 1959): 261–321.

Chalmers, Leonard. "The Crucial Test of La Guardia's First Hundred Days: The Emergency Economy Bill." *New-York Historical Society Quarterly* 57:3 (July 1973): 237–53.

Curtiss, Willis David, Jr. "Evidence: Mistrial: Questions of District Attorney." *Cornell Law Quarterly* 24 (1938–39): 122–26.

Duram, James C. "The Labor Union Journals and the Constitutional Issues of the New Deal: The Case for Court Restriction." *Labor History* 15:2 (Spring 1974): 216–38.

Friedman, Milton. "Herbert Lehman 'Conscience of the Senate.'" *The Sentinal* 194:6 (30 August 1956): 6, 10.

Haller, Mark. "Police Reform in Chicago: 1905–1935." *American Behavioral Scientist* 12 (May–August 1970): 649–66.

Haller, Mark. "Urban Crime and Criminal Justice: The Chicago Case." *Journal of American History* 57:3 (December 1970): 619–35.

Hallheimer, Julius. "Justice by Formula: Who is an Habitual Criminal and What is a Felony." *Century Magazine* 117:2 (December 1928): 232–40.

Heyting, W. J. "Abolition of Grand Juries in England." *American Bar Association Journal* 19 (November 1933): 648–49.

Hickman, Powell. "Profiles: The Governor." *The New Yorker* (May 2, 9): 21–26; 25–30.

Hurwood, David. "Grass-Roots Politics in Manhattan." *Atlantic* 206:4 (October 1960): 65–70.

Ingalls, Robert P. "New York and the Minimum-Wage Movement, 1933–1937." *Labor History* 15:2 (Spring 1974): 179–98.

Kay, James. "Evidence—Admissibility." *Journal of Criminal Law and Criminology* 29 (1938–39): 293–95.

Lane, Roger. "Urbanization and Criminal Violence in the 19th Century: Massachusetts as a Test Case." *American Law and the Constitutional Order: Historical Perspectives,* ed. Lawrence M. Friedman and Harry N. Scheiber (Cambridge: Harvard University Press, 1978). Reprinted from *Journal of Social History* 2 (1968): 486–93.

"Legislation: Legal Implications of Labor Racketeering." *Columbia Law Review* 37 (1937): 994–1102.

Lieck, Albert. "Abolition of the Grand Jury in England." *Journal of Criminal Law and Criminology* 25 (November–December 1934): 623–25.

"Recent Statutes." *Columbia Law Review* 37 (1937): 1028–31.

Regensberg, S. "An Interview with Herbert Lehman Who Is Celebrating His 80th Birthday Today." *Jewish Daily Forward* (28 March 1958). Trans. from Yiddish.

Stolberg, Benjamin. "Thomas E. Dewey, Self-Made Myth." *American Mercury* 50:198 (June 1940): 135–47.

Stolberg, Mary M. "The Evolution of Frontier Justice: The Case of Judge Isaac Parker." *Prologue* 20:1 (Spring 1988): 7–23.

———. "Policing the Twilight Zone: Federalizing Law Enforcement in the New Deal." *The Journal of Policy History* 13:2 (Fall 1995).

"Streamlining the Indictment." *Harvard Law Review* 53 (1939–40): 122.

Waite, John Barker. "Criminal Law and Procedure." *Michigan Law Review* 37 (1938–39): 113–15.

Wechsler, Herbert. "A Caveat on Crime Control." *Journal of Criminal Law and Criminology* 27 (1937): 629–37.

Woolfe, S. J. "Lehman Outlines His Social Philosophy." *New York Times Magazine* (9 August 1936): 5, 23.

Index